Modern Data Protection
Ensuring Recoverability of All Modern Workloads

W. Curtis Preston

Beijing · Boston · Farnham · Sebastopol · Tokyo

Modern Data Protection

by W. Curtis Preston

Published by O'Reilly Media, Inc., 1005 Gravenstein Highway North, Sebastopol, CA 95472.

O'Reilly books may be purchased for educational, business, or sales promotional use. Online editions are also available for most titles (*http://oreilly.com*). For more information, contact our corporate/institutional sales department: 800-998-9938 or *corporate@oreilly.com*.

Acquisitions Editor: Mary Preap	**Indexer:** Potomac Indexing, LLC
Development Editor: Melissa Potter	**Interior Designer:** David Futato
Production Editor: Kristen Brown	**Cover Designer:** Karen Montgomery
Copyeditor: nSight Editorial Services, Inc.	**Illustrator:** Kate Dullea
Proofreader: Piper Editorial Consulting, LLC	

May 2021:   First Edition

Revision History for the First Edition

2021-04-29:   First Release

See *http://oreilly.com/catalog/errata.csp?isbn=0636920469216* for release details.

978-1-492-09405-0

[LSI]

Table of Contents

Foreword. xiii

Preface. xv

1. Risks to Your Data: Why We Back Up. 1
   Human Disasters   2
      Accidents   3
      Bad Code   4
      Malicious Attacks   5
      Terrorism   6
      Electronic Attacks   6
      Ransomware   7
      Internal Threats   8
   Mechanical or System Failure   12
      Power Disruptions   12
      There Is No Cloud   13
      System Failure   13
   Natural Disasters   14
      Floods   15
      Fires   15
      Earthquakes   16
      Hurricanes, Typhoons, and Cyclones   16
      Tornadoes   17
      Sinkholes   17
   Takeaways   18

2. Gathering and Determining Service Levels. **19**

What Does Your Organization Do? 20

Build Yourself a Framework 20

Document Templates 21

Review/Advisory Boards 22

Collecting Requirements 23

What Are RPO and RTO? 23

Find the Subject Matter Experts 23

Solicit Requirements 25

Review Requirements 26

Design and Build Your System 28

Draw up Multiple Designs 29

Review the Designs 30

Select and Build the System 30

Document and Implement the New System 31

Defining Operational Responsibility 31

Operations Review and Documentation 32

Documentation Is Good 32

Runbooks 33

Implement the New System 33

Takeaways 34

3. Backup and Archive Are Very Different. **37**

Before We Get Started 37

What Is Backup? 38

"Copy" 39

"Stored Separately from the Original" 40

"For the Purposes of Restoring" 40

What Is a Restore? 40

How Does a Restore Work? 41

The 3-2-1 Rule 42

What Is an Archive? 47

To Serve as a Reference 48

Stored with Additional Metadata 48

What Is a Retrieve? 49

Protecting Backup and Archive Data 50

Encryption 50

Air Gaps 51

Immutability 55

Takeaways 57

4. Backup and Recovery Basics..................................... 59

    Recovery Testing   59

    Backup Levels   60

        Traditional Full Backup   60

        Traditional Incremental Backup   61

        Do Backup Levels Matter?   67

    Metrics   68

        Recovery Metrics   69

        Capacity Metrics   72

        Backup Window   74

        Backup and Recovery Success and Failure   75

        Retention   75

        Using Metrics   76

    Backup and Archive Myths   77

    Item- Versus Image-Level Backups   82

        Item-Level Backup   82

        Image-Level Backups   83

        File-Level Recovery from an Image-Level Backup   84

        Combining Image- and File-Level Backups   84

    Backup Selection Methods   85

        Selective Inclusion Versus Selective Exclusion   85

        Tag-Based and Folder-Based Inclusion   86

    Takeaways   87

5. Using Disk and Deduplication for Data Protection.............................. 89

    Deduplication   90

        What Can Dedupe Do?   90

        How Dedupe Works   93

        Target Deduplication   96

        Source Deduplication   99

        Target Versus Source Deduplication   99

        Hybrid Dedupe   100

        Selecting the Right Dedupe for You   101

    Using Disk in Your Backup System   102

        Disk Caching   102

        Disk-to-Disk-to-Tape (D2D2T)   104

        Disk-to-Disk-to-Disk (D2D2D)   104

        Direct-to-Cloud (D2C)   106

        Disk-to-Disk-to-Cloud (D2D2C)   106

    Recovery Concepts   107

Image Recovery   107
File-Level Recovery   108
Instant Recovery   111
Choosing a Recovery Type   113
Takeaways   113

6. Traditional Data Sources. 115
Physical Servers   116
   Standard Backup   116
   Bare-Metal Backup   116
   Backing Up NAS   117
Virtual Servers   119
   VM-Level Backups   120
   What Is VSS?   121
   Specialized Backups for Hypervisors   122
Desktops and Laptops   126
   Laptops as a Cache   127
   Normal Desktop and Laptop Usage   127
   Desktop and Laptop Backup Options   128
Mobile Devices   130
   Cloud Sync   131
   Physical Sync   131
   Mobile Device Backup   131
   Mobile Device Management (MDM)   131
Takeaways   132

7. Protecting Databases. 133
Database Delivery Models   133
   Traditional Database Software   134
   Platform-as-a-Service   135
   Serverless Databases   136
Database Models   137
Consistency Models   139
   Traditional Databases Running in Your Datacenter   140
   PaaS and Serverless Databases   141
Traditional Database Terminology   142
   Instance   143
   Database   143
   Table   143
   Index   143
   Row   144

Attribute   144
Data File   144
Tablespace   144
Partition   144
Master File   145
Transaction   145
Transaction Log   145
Backing Up Traditionally Delivered Databases   146
Cold Backup   147
Split Replica   147
Hot Backup Mode   147
Snap and Sweep   147
Dump and Sweep   148
Stream-to-Backup Product   149
Transaction Log Backup   149
Master File   150
Backing Up PaaS and Serverless Databases   150
Dump and Sweep   151
Integrated Backup-as-a-Service   151
Recovering Traditional Databases   155
Recovering Modern Databases   156
Takeaways   157

8. Modern Data Sources. 159
The Public Cloud   159
Infrastructure-as-a-Service (IaaS)   160
Platform-as-a-Service (PaaS)   165
Serverless Services   166
Software-as-a-Service (SaaS)   166
You Need to Protect the Cloud   172
Hybrid Cloud Configurations   177
NFS/SMB Gateway   177
The Cloud in a Box   178
Docker and Kubernetes   179
How Containers Break Backups   180
Dockerfiles   181
Docker Images   181
Kubernetes etcd   182
Persistent Volumes   182
Databases   183
Kubernetes: A New Path   184

The Internet of Things (IoT)   185
Making Backup Decisions   186
  Criticality to the Organization   186
  Consider the Source   187
Takeaways   188

9. Backup and Recovery Software Methods. **189**
Is Everything Backup?   189
Backup Methods Supporting a Traditional Restore   190
  Multiplexing   191
  Traditional Full and Incremental Backups   191
  File-Level Incremental Forever   192
  Block-Level Incremental Forever   193
  Source Deduplication   194
Methods Supporting Instant Recovery   196
  Replication   196
  Continuous Data Protection (CDP)   198
  Snapshots   200
  Near-Continuous Data Protection (Near-CDP)   202
  Copy Data Management   204
  Other Software with Instant Recovery   205
Leveraging Backups for More   206
Deciding on a Backup Method   208
  Does What You Have Meet Your Needs?   208
  Advantages and Disadvantages of Different Approaches   209
  Complete Solution   210
Takeaways   211

10. Archive Software Methods. **213**
A Deeper Dive into Archive   213
Retrieval Versus Restore   214
Types of Archive Systems   215
  Traditional Batch Archive   215
  Real-Time Archive   216
  HSM-Style Archive   217
Deciding on an Archive System   218
  Do You Need One?   219
  Requirements   220
Takeaways   223

11. Disaster Recovery Methods. 225

Disaster Recovery Becomes Paramount   225
Ransomware Changed Everything   226
An Overview of Disaster Recovery   228
What Is in a DR Plan?   229
   A Box of Tapes Isn't a DR Plan   231
   A Replicated Dedupe Appliance Isn't Much Better   232
   It's All About the RTA   232
Building a Recovery Site   233
   Roll Your Own DR Site   233
   Recovery-Site-as-a-Service   234
   The Public Cloud Was Born for DR   235
Keeping the DR Site Up to Date   236
   Cold, Hot, and Warm Sites   236
   Choosing Hot, Warm, or Cold   237
   Recovery Mechanisms   237
Software or Service   245
   Commercial DR Software   245
   DR-as-a-Service   246
   All-in-One or Best of Breed?   248
Choosing a Plan   249
Creating a DR Runbook   250
   Runbook Goals   250
   Overview   252
   Technology Inventory   253
   Contact Information   253
   Procedures   254
   Exception Processing with Escalation   256
Takeaways   256

12. Data Protection Targets. 257

Tape Drives   257
   What Tape Is Good At   258
   What Tape Is Bad At   262
   How Did This Happen?   265
   Tape Drive Technologies   266
Optical Media   267
Individual Disk Drives   268
Standard Disk Arrays   269
Object Storage   270

Target Deduplication Appliances   272
  Virtual Tape Libraries   272
  NAS Appliances   273
Public Cloud Storage   274
Choosing and Using a Backup Target   275
  Optimize the Performance of What You Have   275
  Select a More Appropriate Device   278
Takeaways   283

13. Commercial Data Protection Challenges. **285**
A Brief History of Backup   285
Challenges with Commercial Backup Solutions   287
  Size the Backup System   288
  Maintain Backup Server OS   292
  Maintain Backup Software   293
  Manage Multiple Vendors   294
  Separate System for DR   295
  Separate System for E-Discovery   295
  Tape-Related Challenges   296
  Disk-Related Challenges   298
  Large Up-Front Capital Purchases   299
  Overprovisioning Is Required   300
  Difficult to Scale   300
Difficulty of Changing Backup Products   301
  Let Them Expire   301
  Use a Service   301
  Restore and Backup   302
Takeaways   302

14. Traditional Data Protection Solutions. **303**
Not Naming Names   304
Traditional Backup Solutions   304
  Advantages of Traditional Backup   305
  Challenges with Traditional Backup   306
  Analysis   307
Target Deduplication Backup Appliances   309
  Advantages of Target Dedupe   310
  Challenges with Target Dedupe   311
  Analysis   313
Takeaways   314

15. Modern Data Protection Solutions. **315**

Virtualization-Centric Solutions 316

Advantages of Virtualization-Centric Solutions 317

Challenges of Virtualization-Centric Backup 318

Analysis 319

Hyper-Converged Backup Appliances 320

Advantages of Hyper-Converged Backup Appliances 321

Challenges with HCBAs 323

Analysis 324

Data-Protection-as-a-Service (DPaaS) 325

Advantages of DPaaS 328

Challenges of DPaaS 329

Analysis 331

Fully Managed Service Providers 332

Advantages of Using an MSP 333

Challenges of Using an MSP 333

Analysis 334

Adapting to the Market 334

Traditional Backup Appliances 334

Subscription Pricing 335

Responding to the Cloud 335

Takeaways 337

16. Replacing or Upgrading Your Backup System. **339**

Which Solution Is Best for You? 341

Your Responsibilities 343

Before You Do Anything 345

This Is Your Backup System 345

Consider TCO, Not Just Acquisition Cost 347

Picking a Solution 349

Find Any Showstoppers 350

Prioritize Ease of Use 350

Prioritize Scalability 351

Prioritize Future Proofing 352

Takeaways 352

Index. **355**

Foreword

As an IT storage technology journalist, I've been learning and writing about the data protection market for 20 years or more. In that time, the backup market and supplier landscape has developed in new directions and grown enormously. We have seen the rise of server virtualization, the provision of centrally-managed endpoint backup, the incredible growth of public clouds, and data protection within those clouds.

Suppliers have devised data protection for applications delivered as a service, such as Salesforce and Microsoft 365. The growth of containerization and cloud native applications has added a new dimension to both on-premises and public cloud backup and restoration. A further and highly important dimension has arrived with the ransomware threat and the need to make backups immutable through physical and virtual air gaps.

We have seen the arrival of data management suppliers who use backup as a means of protecting data, and of ingesting it for subsequent reuse and analysis. Data sovereignty has become an important subject of interest in the data protection sphere. And another quite recent development is the SaaS approach: data-protection-as-a-service (DPaaS).

Throughout this time, one authority has remained constant: W. Curtis Preston. He has always seemed to have a clear line of sight to all of these developments, and insight into their implications on users and data protection processes, procedures, and planning.

His latest book is necessary because so many developments are happening concurrently that the industry needs someone to step back and cast a perceptive and knowledgeable eye across the field to bring all the strands together and provide a clear and coherent picture of what is going on. There is no one better qualified than Curtis to do this, and you will find this book an invaluable aid in helping you understand the new data protection landscape.

— Chris Mellor, Editor, Blocks & Files

Preface

This is the book I've wanted to write for over 10 years. The commercial data protection space is a complicated one, and I know of no other book that covers it at this scale. I tried very hard to cover all the things you need to back up, archive, restore and retrieve; all the methods, software, and services you could use to do so; and all the hardware you'll use to store those backups and archives.

The fact that the coverage is so broad does mean that I can't cover each topic that deeply. It would have been easy to write a separate book on each of these chapters. In fact, when the folks at O'Reilly first saw my outline, their first comment was that this looked like a 2000-page book!

Even so, I guarantee that there are topics covered in this book that are found nowhere else. I also settle a lot of arguments that come up in this space: like the real place for tape, the difference between backup and archive, and whether or not you need to back up software-as-a-service (SaaS) offerings like Microsoft 365 and Salesforce. The book covers important foundational concepts that you can use to make your own decisions. A perfect example is how the 3-2-1 rule can be used to determine whether something is being properly protected or not. (If you're not familiar with this rule, trust me. You will be by the time you finish this book.)

I also help you understand all of the various backup methods and technologies, along with the pros and cons of each. I tried really hard to be evenhanded here, as every technology type has both advantages and disadvantages. Understanding each one will help you make your own decisions about what's right for your environment.

I'd like to say one more thing about the coverage in this book. I do work for a company that offers a data protection service, so you might expect me to push my employer's way of doing things. Nothing could be further from the truth. For those unfamiliar with my career, this is actually my first vendor in an almost 30-year career. I therefore know as much about our competitors as I do about our own offerings. My employer put absolutely zero pressure on me to put its products in a positive light. Instead, they simply told me to make sure I wrote a helpful book. But because I do work for a vendor, I did go out of my way to be evenhanded when I explained competitive offerings. I also specifically asked my 36 technical editors to point out if they thought I was going too easy or too hard on any product category. Most of these technical editors actually work directly with these products or for the companies that offer them.

The Work Continues

The fun thing about writing technical books is that they are out of date as soon as they're published. That's why I use my blog and podcast to provide updates on things that change after the book. If you care about data protection, feel free to check out my blog at *backupcentral.com*, or look for the *Restore it All* podcast at your favorite podcatcher.

Conventions Used in This Book

The following typographical conventions are used in this book:

Italic
    Indicates new terms, URLs, email addresses, filenames, and file extensions.

`Constant width`
    Used for program listings, as well as within paragraphs to refer to program elements such as variable or function names, databases, data types, environment variables, statements, and keywords.

This element signifies a tip or suggestion.

This element signifies a general note or a quote.

This element indicates a warning or caution.

O'Reilly Online Learning

 For more than 40 years, *O'Reilly Media* has provided technology and business training, knowledge, and insight to help companies succeed.

Our unique network of experts and innovators share their knowledge and expertise through books, articles, and our online learning platform. O'Reilly's online learning platform gives you on-demand access to live training courses, in-depth learning paths, interactive coding environments, and a vast collection of text and video from O'Reilly and 200+ other publishers. For more information, visit *http://oreilly.com*.

How to Contact Us

Please address comments and questions concerning this book to the publisher:

O'Reilly Media, Inc.
1005 Gravenstein Highway North
Sebastopol, CA 95472
800-998-9938 (in the United States or Canada)
707-829-0515 (international or local)
707-829-0104 (fax)

We have a web page for this book, where we list errata, examples, and any additional information. You can access this page at *https://oreil.ly/modern-data-protection*.

Email *bookquestions@oreilly.com* to comment or ask technical questions about this book.

For news and information about our books and courses, visit *http://oreilly.com*.

Find us on Facebook: *http://facebook.com/oreilly*

Follow us on Twitter: *http://twitter.com/oreillymedia*

Watch us on YouTube: *http://www.youtube.com/oreillymedia*

Acknowledgments

So many people to thank...it's really hard to know where to start. I am where I am in my life and my career because of so many people. This book was only made possible by the efforts of dozens of them.

I will start with my family. Thanks to Mom and Dad, who always encouraged me to be my best.

Thanks to my wife, two daughters, their husbands, and my granddaughter for keeping me grounded. To them I'm just Curtis, Dad, and Papa. They think my dad jokes are horrible, and my articles and books are boring. They also agree on my brisket, though. My brisket is amazing, or as Lily calls it, "famous."

Thank you to Lou Hoffmeister for giving me my first job in backup, for Susan Davidson for not firing me when I had my first restore failure, and for Joe Fitzpatrick for saving my butt when that happened. Thanks to Ron Rodriguez for handing me the backup reins at MBNA. I never did learn how to log into that VAX, though.

Thank you to all those who helped me in my career. Thanks to *SysAdmin Magazine* (may she rest in peace) for publishing my first article, and for O'Reilly for taking a chance on an unknown author over 20 years ago. I hope Gigi Estebrook eventually recovered from being my editor. Mike Loukides seems to be doing just fine. O'Reilly is a classy organization and I'm super proud to be a part of it.

Thanks to my friend and podcast cohost Prasanna Malaiyandi, for offering a completely different perspective on many topics, while also keeping things fun. He's also one of the very few tech editors that read this book cover to cover. Also, if you're working on a project—any kind of project—ask him about it. Chances are he's watching a bunch of YouTube videos on it, even if he's never attempted it himself.

I need to thank Dan Frith and Jeff Rochlin for the chapter that each of them wrote. It's always nice to get wisdom from the real field. I'm trying not to resent the fact that Dan's chapter had the fewest grammar edits of any of the chapters.

I want to thank my 36 technical editors! Some of you read only one chapter, while others read the entire book. Some of you just said, "Looks great!" while others drove me crazy with edits and comments on every chapter. (You know who you were.)

- Andrew Cates
- Bob Bakh
- Bob Smolenyak
- Brian Greenberg
- Dan Frith
- David Barker
- Edwin Danso
- Eric Harless
- Franciso Amaro
- Jeff Rochlin
- John Baldauf
- John Stoffel
- Jorge Fragoso
- Juan Pablo Silva
- Julie Ulrich
- Kamran-Bijan Pechrak
- Kirk Kirkconnell
- Kurt Buff
- Kyle Shuberg
- Larry Blake
- Laura Silva
- Marc Selwan
- Matt Leib
- Matt Starr

- Michael Barrow
- Mike Bush
- Prasanna Malaiyandi
- Rob Worman
- Russell Cantwell
- Scott D. Lowe
- Shalabh Goyal
- Stan Horwitz
- Stephen Manley
- Stephen Quan
- Stuart Liddle
- Zoë Rose

I am going to thank O'Reilly again for taking a chance on me with another book. I especially want to thank Mary Preap, Melissa "Ravenclaw" Potter, Kristen Brown, and Kerin Forsyth for being my editors. Thanks also to Cassandra Furtado for her help as well.

This book was written almost entirely while walking on an Xterra treadmill using Dragon Professional running on a Dell laptop, with a SpeechWare FlexyMike Dual Ear Cardioid microphone—so I'm giving a shout out to those folks. I sure hope Dragon stays around. It should be more popular than it is.

Thank you to Jaspreet Singh, CEO of Druva, for giving me the green light when I told him that I wanted to write my next book, and for Thomas Been, CMO of Druva, for pushing me to actually get it done. Not every CEO and CMO would understand why an employee of theirs should publish anything that might say something positive about the competition, but both of you were in lockstep agreement that I should write exactly the same book that I would have written if I didn't work at Druva. Kudos to you.

Finally, I want to thank those of you that read my books, blogs, and articles, listen to my podcasts, and keep this important topic going. Backup may be where many of us get our start, but it is also where some of us have found a home. My props to the sysadmin who has to maintain a backup system with open source software and no budget, while also administering databases, networks, or servers. Shout out to those of you in big environments that have to deal with the cutting edge of this industry, and keep pushing employers like mine to make things better.

To everyone that simply cares that all your data is protected, I say, "3-2-1 rule forever!"

CHAPTER 1

Risks to Your Data: Why We Back Up

You might think you don't need this chapter. You know why we back up data, and you don't need someone convincing you that backing it up is an important thing to do. Nonetheless, there might be a few reasons for backing up that you might not have thought of. These will be helpful in meetings that start with the question, "Why do we spend so much money on backup and disaster recovery?"

 No one cares if you can backup. Only if you can restore.

—Mr. Backup

This chapter covers a variety of reasons why we need backup and disaster recovery (DR), listed in the order they are most likely to happen. Let's start by looking at the most common reason why you'll find yourself looking for your backup manual: Someone did something wrong. A natural disaster might not be likely in your case, but a human disaster most certainly is.

The One That Got Away

"You mean to tell me that we have absolutely no backups of *paris* whatsoever?" I will never forget those words. I had been in charge of backups for only two months, and I just knew my career was over. We had moved an Oracle application from one server to another about six weeks earlier, and I missed one crucial part of the move. I knew very little about database backups in those days, and I didn't realize that I needed to shut down an Oracle database before backing it up. This was accomplished on the old server by a cron job that I never knew existed. I discovered all of this after a disk on the new server went south. (I cover Oracle backup in detail in Chapter 7.)

"Just give us the last full backup," they said. I started looking through my logs. That's when I started seeing the errors. "No problem," I thought, "I'll just use an older backup." The older logs didn't look any better. Frantically, I looked at log after log until I came to one that looked as if it were OK. It was just over six weeks old. When I went to grab that volume, I realized that we had a six-week rotation cycle, and we had overwritten that volume two days ago.

That was it! At that moment, I knew that I'd be looking for another job. This was our purchasing database, and this data loss would amount to approximately two months of lost purchase orders for a multibillion-dollar organization.

So I told my boss the news. That's when I heard, "You mean to tell me that we have absolutely no backups of *paris* whatsoever?" Isn't it amazing how I haven't forgotten its name? I don't remember any other system names from that place, but I remember this one. I felt so small that I could have fit inside a 4-mm tape box. Fortunately, a system administrator worked what, at the time, I could only describe as magic. The dead disk was resurrected, and the data was recovered straight from the disk itself. We lost only a few days' worth of data. Our department had to send a memo to the entire organization, saying that any purchase orders entered in the past two days had to be reentered. I should have framed a copy of that memo to remind me of what can happen if you don't take this job seriously enough. I didn't need to, though; its image is permanently etched in my brain.

Some of this book's reviewers said things like, "That's pretty bold! You're writing a book on backups and you start it out with a story about how you messed up. Some authority you are!" Why did I include it? Through all the years, and all the outages, this one sticks in my mind.

Perhaps it's because it's the only one that almost got me. Had it not been for the miraculous efforts of a wonderful administrator named Joe Fitzpatrick, my career might have been over before it started. I include this anecdote because:

- It's the one that changed the direction of my career.
- I learned several valuable lessons from it, which I discuss in this book.
- It could have been avoided if I had had a book like this one.
- You must admit that it's pretty darn scary.

Human Disasters

The majority of restores and disaster recoveries today are executed because of humans doing something, accidentally or on purpose, that damages your computing environment. This can be anything from a simple fat-finger mistake to a terrorist attack that takes out your whole building. Since this activity is so common, it's what your backup and DR systems should be really good at recovering from.

First, I'll describe a group of disasters that are caused accidentally, and then I'll move on to more malicious acts that want to harm your data as well. I'll then round out this section with how to protect against the threat to your data from the inside.

Accidents

People make mistakes. Sometimes you copy the wrong file into the wrong place and overwrite a good file with a bad file. Sometimes you're trying to make room for new data and you delete a bunch of files and clear out the trash can—only to realize seconds later that you deleted something you didn't mean to.

As a person who has been working at a keyboard for most of his life, I can't tell you the number of times I have fat-fingered something and done an incredible amount of damage with just a few keystrokes. This is what some of us call PEBKAC, as in, "Problem exists between keyboard and chair."

Often when we think about what we call *user error*, we tend to think about what our industry calls the *end user*, or the person or persons who are actually using the systems and databases that the IT department provides. It's really easy to think that all user error comes from them, not from us. But the reality is that system, network, and database administrators are also quite fallible.

In fact, not only do administrators make mistakes just like everyone else, but their mistakes can have much greater ramifications. I have seen hundreds of examples of this in my career. Here's just a quick list off the top of my head.

- Drop the wrong table in a database.
- Format the wrong drive, erasing a perfectly good file system.
- Perform a restore of a development database onto a production database.
- Write a script designed to delete orphaned home directories but that actually deletes *all* home directories.
- Delete the wrong virtual machine (VM).

Those of us with administrator privileges wield a mighty sword. A slight swing in the wrong direction can be deadly. *We* are another reason we back up.

That's Not What I Meant!

I was administering a QA group for a major software organization. When the software is installed, it typically creates an install directory in `$HOME/foo`, which would be a subdirectory in the home directory of the user installing the software. A QA person was doing the install as root, so it should have created a directory called *foo* in root's home directory. Instead, it created an actual directory called `/$HOME/foo`—literally

---

$HOME was the directory name. The user submitted the bug fix and decided to get rid of the useless directory using the following command:

```
# rm -rf $HOME
```

(This was on a standard Unix system, where $HOME for root was still /.)

Once I finally stopped laughing, I used the install media and rebuilt the machine (there was no golden image for that one that I could use to reinstall everything. Nor were there any backups for the various QA servers). Fortunately, most of the critical data was on the network file system (NFS) server.

Bad Code

Bad code can come from anywhere. It can be something as simple as a shell script that gets overzealous and deletes the wrong data, or it could be an actual bug in the core software that silently corrupts data. These stories don't usually make the news, but they happen all the time.

Perhaps it is an in-house developer who doesn't follow basic rules, like where to place their code. I remember years ago when an entire development team of a dozen or so in-house developers stored their entire code tree in /tmp on an HP-UX system, where /tmp was stored in RAM. The code was wonderful until someone rebooted the server and /tmp was cleaned out along with everything else in RAM.

Commercial software developed by a professional team of developers is not immune, either. Once again, not only is their software often run at a privileged level and therefore able to do a lot of damage, the same software is being run in hundreds or thousands of organizations. Sometimes a mistake isn't noticed until it has done quite a bit of damage.

My favorite story to illustrate this is about a version of a particular commercial backup software package whose developer wanted to make it faster to put an electronic label on the front of each tape. There were two complaints about the old process, the first of which was that a tape that was being reused—and therefore being electronically relabeled—required multiple button presses to ensure that you really did mean to overwrite this tape with a new electronic label. The second was that the process only used one tape drive at a time, even if there were several tape drives in the tape library. The latest version of the software introduced what they called the "fast-and-silent" option. This meant it would label as many tapes as you wanted, without prompting you about overwriting them, using as many available tape drives as you had.

This new feature came with a new bug. Previously, when you saw a list of tapes and you double-clicked one tape, it would pull up a dialog box and ask you whether you wanted to overwrite *that tape*. But now, double-clicking a single tape pulled up a dialog box that listed *every tape in the tape library*.

Like the combination of user error and bad code that caused me to lose a version of this chapter, a user who thought they were overwriting one tape would find themselves two mouse clicks away from overwriting every tape in the tape library without being prompted—while using every available tape drive to make this process go as quickly as possible.

I was at a customer meeting sitting next to a consultant who was sent by the vendor providing the software, who did just that. He wanted to relabel a single tape in the customer's tape library, so he double-clicked that tape, probably just like he always did. He saw the new fast-and-silent option and chose it. It was several minutes before he realized what he had done, which was to overwrite every tape in the customer's tape library, rendering them useless. Yes, the customer had off-site copies of all these tapes, so they didn't lose any data. No, they were not very understanding.

This is a good place for me to tell you about the *3-2-1 rule*, which is: three versions of your data, on two different media, one of which is stored somewhere.

 The 3-2-1 rule is the fundamental rule upon which all backups are based. I'll cover it in more detail in Chapter 3, but you'll see it mentioned in almost every chapter.

People make mistakes. Sometimes good people do bad things that either delete or corrupt data, and this is yet another reason we back it up.

Malicious Attacks

Now let's take a look at the second type of data risk: bad people doing bad things. Malicious attacks against your datacenter have sadly become quite common. This is why the true enemies of the modern datacenter are bad actors bent on doing your organization harm via some type of electronic attack. Steel yourself; this can get a bit choppy.

Largest Electronic Attack in History

As I wrote this chapter, the United States was experiencing its largest electronic attack (of which I am aware). At the time, the full extent of the damage, and the timescale involved, was unclear. It seemed that the malware in question was inserted in a Trojan horse provided by a commercial software organization. Malicious code was inserted into the vendor's software without its knowledge, and then distributed to its entire customer base. We're not entirely sure how it happened at this point, but two lessons you should take from this are that you literally never know where an attack can come from, and every software update should be validated for security vulnerabilities. You also don't know how long it might be between the infection and the execution of the attack, so you may need to hold your backups a little longer than you are currently doing.

Terrorism

Someone may choose to target your organization purposefully and cause physical damage in some way. They may attempt to blow up your buildings, set them on fire, fly planes into them, or commit all sorts of physical terrorist actions. This could be for political purposes, such as what happened on 9/11, or for corporate sabotage. The latter is less likely, mind you, but it can and does happen.

Protecting your infrastructure from terrorism is outside the scope of this book. I simply wanted to mention that terrorism is yet another reason why the 3-2-1 rule exists. Get backups of your data and move them far away from the data you are protecting.

Unfortunately on 9/11, several organizations ceased to exist because they failed to follow the 3-2-1 rule. They did have backups. They even had DR hot sites that were ready to take over at a moment's notice—in the other tower. This is why when we talk about the "1" in the 3-2-1 rule, we mean far away. A synchronously replicated copy of your database sitting on a server a few hundred yards away is not a good DR plan.

Electronic Attacks

The more common event that your organization is likely to experience is an electronic attack of some sort. Although this could be via someone hacking your firewall and opening up a backdoor into your datacenter, it's more likely that it will be some type of malware that got into your computing environment. That malware then opens the door from the inside.

I watched a speech from a security expert who did live demonstrations on how to hack into organizations. None of them were via exploited firewalls, or anything of the sort. Every single one exploited some human vulnerability to get you to open the backdoor for him. It was honestly quite scary.

Such malware is typically introduced via some type of phishing and/or social engineering mechanism that results in someone in your organization downloading the errant code directly into your computing environment. It could be an email, a hacked website, or even a phone call to the wrong person. (In the previously mentioned speech, one attack vector was a phone charging cable that deployed malware if you plugged it into a computer that enabled data on that USB port.) Once that initial penetration happens, the malware can spread through a variety of means to the entire organization.

Ransomware

The most common malware that is running amok these days is what we call *ransomware*. Once inside your system, it silently encrypts data and then eventually offers you a decryption key in exchange for a financial sum (i.e., a *ransom*). This ransom could be a few hundred dollars if you are a single individual or millions of dollars if you are a big organization.

Ransomware attacks are on the rise, and ransom demands have only gotten larger. This trend will continue until every organization figures out the simple response to such an attack: a good DR system.

This is why I discuss ransomware in more detail in Chapter 11. I think ransomware is the number one reason you might actually need to use your DR system. You are much more likely to be struck by a ransomware attack than by a natural disaster or a rogue administrator deleting your data. And the only valid response to such is a DR system with a short recovery time.

Malware and ransomware have been a problem for a while. This is partly because ransomware attacks were limited to those with the technical wherewithal to pull them off, but that is no longer the case. It is changing with the advent of ransomware-as-a-service (RaaS) vendors, who make it much easier to get into the ransomware game.

You specify the target and any information helpful in gaining access to said target, and they execute the attack. These criminal organizations are doing this solely for profit, because they take a significant share of any profit from the attack. They have little interest in other uses for ransomware or theftware.

RaaS is relevant to this discussion because it bolsters my claim that this is becoming a greater danger to your data than anything else. Skilled hackers that are hacking your organization for altruistic or corporate espionage reasons have existed since computers came on the scene, but they were limited in number. For you to be susceptible to such an attack, you would need someone with enough incentive to attack you and enough knowledge of how to do so. The existence of RaaS removes that last requirement. The only knowledge an attacker needs now is how to get on the dark web and contact such a service.

My point is this: In addition to natural disasters becoming more common than ever before because of climate change, RaaS will make ransomware attacks a greater risk to your data with each passing day. They are yet another reason why we perform backups.

External threats such as natural disasters and electronic attacks are not your only problem, though. You must consider the risk from your own personnel. Let's take a look at the internal threats to your data.

Internal Threats

Many organizations do not properly prepare for attacks that come from within, to their detriment. Information security professionals repeatedly warn that many attacks come from the inside. Even if an attack isn't initiated from within, it could be enabled from within, such as by an innocent employee accidentally clicking the wrong email attachment.

The most common internal threat is an employee or contractor with privileged access who becomes disgruntled in some way and chooses to harm the organization. The harm may be anything from damaging operations or data simply out of spite, to using their access to facilitate a ransomware attack.

This is typically referred to as the *rogue admin* problem. A person with privileged access can do quite a bit of harm without anyone knowing. They can even plant code that will do damage after they leave.

I'm thinking of Yung-Hsun Lin, the Unix administrator who installed what was referred to as a "logic bomb" on 70 of his organization's servers in 2004. The script in question was set to destroy all data on the servers as retaliation if he was laid off. Although his fears of being laid off turned out to be unfounded, he left the logic bomb in place anyway. Luckily it was discovered before it was set to go off and never actually did any damage. He was convicted in 2006.

I'm also thinking of Joe Venzor, whose premeditated attack on his organization's data resulted in weeks of backlog for a boot manufacturer. Fearing that he might be fired, he put in a backdoor disguised as a printer. He was indeed fired, and immediately activated his malware. It shut down all manufacturing within one hour of his termination.

While researching for this section, I came upon an online discussion in which a snarky person said that what Joe Venzor did wrong was doing things in such a way that allowed him to get caught. What he should have done, this poster said, was to put the attack in place and have it continually check for this person logging in. (He could have used a variety of scheduling tools to accomplish this.) If the person did not log in for more than a month, the attack would be initiated and accomplish whatever the attacker wanted to do to punish the organization.

This illustrates the power that system administrators can have if you allow them to do so. This is why you really must do your best to limit the blast radius of those with privileged access.

Unrestricted access to the administrator account in Windows, or the root account in Unix and Linux, or similar accounts in other systems, can easily allow a rogue administrator to do damage with zero accountability. Do everything you can to limit people's ability to log in directly as these accounts, including all of the following ideas.

Use named accounts for everything
Everyone should log in as themselves all the time. If you have to use root or administrator privilege, you should log in as yourself and then obtain such privileges via a logged mechanism. Limit or eliminate tools that must be run as root or Administrator.

Don't give anyone the root password
I have worked in organizations that set the root or administrator password to a random string that no one records. The idea is that if you need administrator or root access, you can always grant yourself that access through systems like sudo or Run as Administrator. This allows you to do your job but records all of your activities.

Delete or disable programs with shell access
This is more of a Unix/Linux problem, but there are many commands (e.g., vi) that support escaping to the shell. If you can run vi as root, you can then run any command as root without it being logged. This is why those concerned about this problem replace vi with a similar command that does not have such access.

Allow superuser login only on the console
Another way to limit unrestricted superuser access is to allow only such access from the console. This is less than ideal, but it is better than nothing. Then make sure that any physical access to the console is logged. This works just as well in a virtual console world where people must log in to the virtual console when accessing.

Off-host logging
Any access to a superuser account (authorized or not) should be logged as a security incident, and any related information (e.g., video surveillance or virtual console logs) should immediately be stored in such a way that a hacker could not remove the evidence. That way, if someone does compromise a system, they can't easily clean up their tracks.

Limit booting from alternate media

As much as you can, remove the ability to boot the server or VM from alternate media. The reason for this is that if you can boot from alternate media, any Linux or Windows admin can easily boot the server, mount the boot drive, and edit any settings that are in their way.

I'm focusing on things that a data protection person should do to help protect the data. You should also work with an information security professional, which is another discipline entirely, and outside the scope of this book.

Separation of powers

Once you make it the norm to log on as yourself when doing administrative work, the next hurdle to overcome is that too many people have access to all-powerful tools that can do as much harm as good. For example, if an employee has the ability to log in as administrator—even via sudo or the like—they can do a lot of damage before being stopped. If that same person also has access to the backup system, they can hamper or remove the organization's ability to recover from their actions.

This is why there is a good argument to be made to separate such powers as much as possible. The backup and DR systems should be your last line of defense, and it should be managed by a completely different entity that does not also have the ability to damage the infrastructure it's protecting.

Role-based administration

A manifestation of the concept of separation of powers can be seen in the *role-based administration* features of many data protection products. The idea is to have different parts of the data protection system managed by different people who actually have different powers that are defined as *roles*.

One role might be day-to-day operations, so you can only execute predefined tasks. For example, this role can monitor the success of backup policies and rerun a given backup policy if it fails. What it *cannot* do is change the definition of that backup in any way. Another role would have the ability to define backup policies but not have the ability to run said policies. Separating backup configuration from backup operations minimizes what one person can do.

A completely different role might be one having to do with restores. In a perfect world, such a role could be limited in such a way that it would only allow data to be restored back to the place it was backed up from. Alternate server and alternate directory restores would require special authorization to prevent this person from using this feature to exfiltrate data from the organization.

Backup products that have the concept of role-based administration built into them have defined these roles already, and you simply need to assign them to different people. My point is simply to suggest that you think long and hard about how to do this. The easy thing to do would be to assign all roles to a single person, just like it's easier to give everyone the root/admin password; however, the best thing from a security perspective is to give several people a single role within the backup system. They would need to work with another person in the organization to do something outside of their role. Although this does not completely remove the idea of an inside job, it does significantly reduce the chances of one.

Least privilege

Once you have enabled role-based administration, make sure that each person and each process has only the level of access they require to do their job. One example of this is not to grant full admin access to the backup agent you are installing. Find out the lowest level of access it needs to do the job, and use that role or level of access. The same is true of any operators or administrators. They should have only the level of access necessary to accomplish their job—and nothing more.

Multiperson authentication

As long as I'm on the idea of protecting your organization from insider threats, I'd like to introduce a concept not found in most backup products: multiperson authentication. It's a take on multifactor authentication that requires two people to authenticate a particular activity. This is sometimes referred to as *four-eyes authentication*, because it requires two sets of eyes. (Although as a person who must wear glasses, this term is not my favorite.) This feature could be enabled on parts of the backup system where security is a concern.

If you're going to do something nefarious, you might want to delete all previous backups for a given server or application, reduce the retention period for any further backups, and even delete the backup configuration altogether. In most backup environments, you could do all of that without setting off any alarms! The same thing is true of restores. If someone wants to steal your data, they can easily use the backup system to restore all of that data to a location from which they can easily remove it. This is why some products require two-person authentication for restores, changes in a backup policy, or a reduction in the retention period of an existing backup.

Just like everything else discussed in this chapter, two-person authentication is not foolproof. A hacker who has gained access to your communication system could easily intercept and circumvent additional requests for authentication. There is no IT without risks; the job of the data protection system is to reduce those risks as much is possible. That, my friends, is why we back up.

Mechanical or System Failure

When I entered the data protection industry in the early nineties, this was the number one reason we would actually use our backup system for its intended purpose. File systems and databases sat directly on physical hard drives, and when one of those hard drives decided to take a dive, it took its data along with it.

Things are very different today for a variety of reasons, the first of which is that most mission-critical data now sits on solid-state media of some sort. Almost all edge data is also stored on such media, including laptops, smartphones and tablets, and Internet of Things (IoT) devices. The result is that the average IT person today simply has not experienced the level of device failure that we experienced back in the day.

In addition to storage devices becoming more resilient, redundant storage systems such as RAID and erasure coding have become the norm in any datacenter that cares about its data. Disk drive manufacturers also appear to build integrity checking in their devices' firmware that errs on the conservative side to prevent loss of data better due to a failed disk. This means that a restore is almost never conducted due to the failure of a hard drive, but that is not to say that such things do not happen.

Even in a RAID or erasure coding array that can handle multiple simultaneous disk failures, such failures can happen. Power supplies can still go awry, or some firmware may cause failure on multiple drives. It is incredibly rare for simultaneous disk failure to take out a RAID array, but it is not unheard of. This is why RAID and/or erasure coding does not take away the need for backup. Restores due to such failures are rare, but they do happen.

Power Disruptions

As much as I hate to continue to use where I live as an example, we are currently experiencing what we call rolling blackouts. We are in fire season, and power companies use rolling brownouts to help reduce the possibility of fires.

This is something you can easily design for, and you should be able to survive from a data protection perspective. Any datacenter of a decent size has redundant power and a large generator. You can weather a reasonably large power disruption, assuming you know it's coming.

What might happen, however, is an *unexpected* power interruption. If all the power coming into your datacenter simply stops without notice, all your servers will stop working. Data will not be properly saved and some of it could become corrupted. Most structured data should be able to survive due to built-in data integrity features, and *most* unstructured data should survive, except a few files in the process of being written at the moment of the outage. In addition, whereas a database may survive due to its data integrity features, the media recovery process (covered in Chapter 7) may take longer than a full restore.

There are multiple shoulds in the previous paragraph, which is why we back up. Sometimes databases don't come back up after a server crashes. Sometimes the file that was being written when the power went out was a really important file that people have been working on for multiple days. This is why we back up.

There Is No Cloud

As big a fan as I am of the public cloud, it's really just packaging and marketing. There is no such thing as a cloud; there is only someone else's computer. Yes, they have done all sorts of programming to make the cloud easy to provision and administer and to make it more resilient in general. But the cloud is not magic; it is just a bunch of computers providing you a service. Those computers can still fail, as can the drives within them.

It's also important to realize that not all storage within the cloud is the same from a data protection standpoint. Although object storage is typically replicated to multiple locations and can therefore survive a number of calamities, most block storage is simply a logical unit number (LUN) on a virtual drive from a single storage array in a single datacenter. It offers no redundancy whatsoever and therefore must be backed up. Redundant block storage is available in the cloud, but most people do not use that option. In addition, as will be discussed later in this chapter, redundancy does not solve issues caused by humans.

System Failure

Whether we are talking about a single server with a single storage array, a metro cluster spanning multiple datacenters and geographic locations, or a service being used in the cloud, nothing is perfect. Programmers make mistakes and bad things happen. This is why we back up any data that actually matters.

In an irony to end all ironies, a programming error combined with user error caused me to lose the first version of this chapter completely. As mentioned in other parts of the book, I am writing this book using Dragon dictation software while walking on a treadmill in the middle of a pandemic. The default setting in Dragon is to save the audio of your dictation automatically, along with the document itself, and it makes saving the document take much longer. Since I had never used the audio, this particular morning I decided to change the setting and tell it to ask me before saving the audio.

I dictated for roughly two hours as I walked on the treadmill, and then suddenly remembered that I had not been saving as I went along, as I normally do. I said, "Click File...Save," which triggers the saving process. A dialog box popped up that asked me if I wanted to save the document, but for some reason I thought it was asking me if I wanted to save the audio. I responded, "No," and it proceeded to close the document without saving it. There went two hours of dictation.

I should have paid closer attention when responding to the dialog box, and it shouldn't have closed the file that I didn't tell it to close. I simply told Dragon to save it and then told it not to save it; I never told it to close it. My point is that software and hardware might not do what you expect them to do, and this is why we back up. This is a bad example, because backup would not help in this case; the entire document was simply in RAM. Even a continuous data protection (CDP) product would not have helped the situation.

 Most of the advice given in this book should apply to any commercial, governmental, or nonprofit entity that uses computers to store data vital to the functioning of that organization. This is why, whenever possible, I will use the word *organization* when referring to the entity being protected. That could be a government, a nongovernmental organization (NGO), a for-profit private or public company, or a nonprofit company.

System and storage resiliency being what it is these days, data loss due to physical system failure shouldn't happen too often. However, there is little your organization can do to stop the next threat to your data that we will discuss. If a natural disaster hits your organization, you'd better be ready.

Natural Disasters

Depending on where you live, and the luck your organization has, you may have already experienced one or more natural disasters that tried to take out your data. In fact, due to the incredible level of resiliency of today's hardware, you are much more likely to experience a natural disaster than a mechanical or system failure.

Natural disasters are one big reason the 3-2-1 rule is so important, and why this will not be the last time I discuss it in this book. It is especially important if you're going to use your backup system for DR.

The key to surviving a natural disaster is planning and designing your DR system around the types of disasters that may have an impact on your area and, therefore, your data. Let's take a look at several types of natural disasters to see what I mean. I apologize in advance to my international audience; all my examples will be based in the United States. I'm assuming you have similar natural disasters where you live.

Floods

Floods can take out your datacenter and occur for a variety of reasons. Perhaps your building sprinkler system malfunctions and floods your building with water. Perhaps your roof leaks and there's a solid downpour; there go your servers. Or perhaps you live in a floodplain, and a giant river overflows and takes your building with it. The result is the same: Computers and water do not mix.

I cut my first backup teeth in Delaware, right next to the Delaware River. We weren't *too* concerned about hurricanes, except that one coming up the coast could cause a large storm that could cause a flood in the Delaware River. Our datacenters were on the ground floor, and that was a problem. Combine that with the fact that our off-site media storage facility was in a World War II bunker that was actually underground.

When it comes to floods, high ground is a beautiful thing. Like the other regional disasters mentioned earlier, the key is to make sure that your DR site is completely outside of wherever there might be a flood. Depending on your locale, this actually could be relatively close but on higher ground. Like everything else here, consult an expert on such things before making a decision.

Fires

We have four seasons in California: fire, flood, mud, and drought. It's a desert climate, and it doesn't take much to start a wildfire. Once out of control, those wildfires are their own living thing and are nearly impossible to stop. I have evacuated due to fire at least once, because a large wildfire was burning out of control and heading straight for my house. (If you looked at the map of that fire, it was shaped like a giant triangle. The point of that triangle was pointed directly at my house.) Fire got within a few miles of us, but we eventually got lucky.

It might not be a wildfire that takes out your datacenter, though. It could be something as simple as an electrical short in a single box. This is why we have breakers, but they don't always work. Perhaps someone stores too many oily rags in the wrong place and you get spontaneous combustion. Perhaps someone throws a cigarette out the window and it creates a fire near your building before you stop it. Fires are incredibly damaging to a datacenter. Just as water and computers don't mix, neither do computers and smoke.

There are a variety of methods outside the scope of backup and DR to survive a datacenter fire. But most likely, if you have one, you'll be wanting a solid backup and DR plan. Fire is therefore yet another reason we back up.

Earthquakes

I live in southern California, so I am very familiar with earthquakes. For those of you who do not live here, please understand that most earthquakes are incredibly minor and merely feel like you're sitting on a big vibrating bed for a few seconds. I can't remember the last time an earthquake in my area was strong enough to knock anything off the shelf, let alone do any real damage. The Northridge quake in Los Angeles (100 miles from me) is the most recent major earthquake in history, and it was in 1994.

The key to surviving an earthquake is preparation. Buildings are built to survive minor earthquakes, and building codes require things inside those buildings to be strapped down. Even within my home, for example, my water heater requires a strap. Datacenter racks are put on shock mounts that allow the rack to move around a little bit if the floor shakes. This probably sounds completely foreign if you don't live here, but it is a very standard part of building and datacenter design in California.

You also have to think about how much damage an earthquake can do and make sure the DR copy of your data is outside the blast radius of that damage. This is actually not that hard to do, because earthquakes tend to be very localized. Consult an earthquake expert, and they will advise you in this regard.

Hurricanes, Typhoons, and Cyclones

Hurricanes, typhoons, and cyclones are deadly storms forming over water. (Hurricanes are called typhoons in the western North Pacific, and cyclones in the Indian Ocean and South Pacific Ocean.) I grew up in Florida, and I've spent a good amount of time on the Gulf Coast of Texas, so hurricanes are also something I know a little bit about. My family members and I have been in the midst of multiple hurricanes and on the fringes of many more. Unlike a typical earthquake, the great thing about a hurricane is that you do get a little bit of advance warning. You also have a solid understanding of the types of damage a hurricane can do, depending on where you live. You may be dealing with storm surge, which causes flooding. You may be dealing with roof or building damage. You simply need to design around these issues with your DR plan.

The real key to surviving a hurricane is to make sure that your DR plan is based on using a system that is completely outside of the path of any potential hurricane. This means not putting your DR site anywhere along the southeast coast of the United States or anywhere along the Gulf Coast. Hurricanes can be incredibly unpredictable and can go anywhere along the coast in those regions. As we will cover in the DR chapter, I think the best option to survive a hurricane is a cloud-based DR system, because it would allow you to have your DR site anywhere else in the country—even somewhere else in the world.

Tornadoes

Tornadoes are deadly swirling windstorms of extremely concentrated power. In the United States, we have something called *tornado alley*, where tornadoes are a frequent occurrence. It includes parts of nine states, starting with northern Texas and stretching up to South Dakota. For those unfamiliar with a tornado, they are incredibly concentrated events that can completely remove all evidence of one building while leaving the building next door completely untouched. They combine the worst powers of a hurricane with the unpredictability of an earthquake, because a tornado can actually touch down out of nowhere in a matter of seconds.

Like hurricanes, the key to surviving tornadoes is a DR site that is located nowhere in tornado alley. You can perhaps argue that tornadoes are such concentrated events that a DR site in, say, South Dakota can protect a datacenter in, say, Kansas. I just don't know why, given the choice, you would do that. My personal opinion would be to have it somewhere very far west or east of where you are.

Sinkholes

I have a lot of arguments with my parents over which state has the worst natural disasters: Florida or California. I mention to them that every single year there are hurricanes that hit Florida, but major earthquakes are incredibly rare in California. They counter with the fact that hurricanes give you some advance notice and allow you to prepare, whereas earthquakes just strike without warning. The trump card is sinkholes. Not only do they strike with little to no warning, they can do an incredible amount of damage in a very short period. They combine the surgical-strike nature of tornadoes with the zero-warning aspect of earthquakes. Tornado survivors tell you it sounds like a freight train as it is happening; sinkholes are completely silent—except for the massive damage they cause. Talk about scary!

For those who are unfamiliar with this phenomenon, which is quite common in Florida and not unheard of in other parts of the world, it comes from having a foundation of limestone sitting on top of giant underwater reservoirs. These underground rivers and lakes run throughout Florida and are often tapped as a source of freshwater. If you drain all the freshwater out of a particular reservoir, you create a weak point in the limestone. It's a house of cards and can instantly take something as small as a bedroom or as big as several city blocks.

I watched a documentary that talked about people's beds being sucked into sinkholes while they were sleeping. It also mentioned the most infamous sinkhole that happened 15 minutes from where I lived: the Winter Park sinkhole of 1981. One afternoon, several city blocks just sank into the earth hundreds of feet below, never to be seen again, taking a house, the community swimming pool, and a Porsche dealership along with it.

At the risk of repeating myself, make sure your DR site is nowhere near your primary site. Sinkholes are relatively rare from a sinkhole-per-square-mile perspective, but they happen all the time. It's yet another reason to make sure that you follow the 3-2-1 rule, which I'll spell out in Chapter 3.

Takeaways

There are countless reasons to back up our important data and ensure that it is protected from damage. The first reason is that what has not been backed up cannot be restored. Remember, they don't care if you can back up; they only care if you can restore.

The world has not been kind to those who do not back up. Natural disasters, terrorists, hackers, and simple accidents by our own staff are all on the list. In addition, as reliable as compute and storage have become over the past few decades, neither reliability nor resilience stops a hurricane or a hacker. All that resilient hardware protects you from is hardware failure, not things that attack the data itself or blow up the entire datacenter.

In short, backup, recovery, and DR are now more important and more complex than ever before. This is why it's more important than ever to get our requirements right before designing a data protection system, and that's why the next chapter is about doing just that.

CHAPTER 2

Gathering and Determining Service Levels

 This chapter was written by Jeff Rochlin, who spent many years working in an organization that did work for the Department of Defense (DOD) and strictly followed Military Standard 480B (MIL-STD-480B) regarding what they call *configuration control*. I first met Jeff while consulting for that company over 20 years ago. I learned so much about change control, working with Jeff in this environment, that I could think of no one better to write this chapter.

The purpose of this chapter is to explain the business and political aspects of the process of building or enhancing your data protection system. Equally important to designing a good technical solution is getting buy-in from everyone who will either benefit from it or pay for it. For more on the technical aspects of designing or refining your data protection system, see Chapter 16.

Data protection is not the sexy part of IT. It reminds the organization that it is vulnerable to various risks that often have nothing to do with IT's core competency. The resources that need to be applied are costly and, in most cases, don't show up in the final product you are selling to your customers. You are selling your organization on an insurance policy that, deep down, no one wants to buy. It might not be easy, but the truth remains that your data protection plan will be one of the most important investments you will make in any organization.

Before you go off and spend big chunks of a budget on data protection, make sure what you build properly covers the needs of the organization. After all, there is no sense in having an insurance policy if it won't cover your losses if the unthinkable happens. So, in these next pages, let's put structure to a process and develop the tools to build an effective plan.

What Does Your Organization Do?

To do this right, it will not be enough to be a strong technologist with vast knowledge of what goes into a data protection system. You need to understand the purpose of your organization, as well as any external requirements that may be placed on you via laws and regulations.

- Are you a governmental organization? If so, what services do you provide and what functions do you serve that IT makes possible?

- Whether you are a governmental organization or a commercial or nonprofit company, does your organization provide products and services through an e-commerce model?

- Do you work for a commercial business that produces a physical object that has to go through a research and development (R&D), prototyping, and manufacturing cycle before it goes to market?

- Are there external requirements for data protection that may also drive your design, such as regulations or laws that require you to store (or not store) certain data types in certain ways?

Each part of this complex system will have differing requirements. You as the data protection person will need to architect the best solution that protects everything for everyone.

Start with an understanding of the organization and the services or products you provide to understand the importance of your organization's data. Find someone in the organization who is willing to take the time to answer any questions you have about what the organization actually does and the full portfolio of products or services you are providing, as well as how they are delivered to your customers. Having the full picture will help you drive the journey you've undertaken.

Before you can begin processing the information you will gather, you will need to build yourself a framework designed to process it as well as a document system to record the information. This framework will be the basis of your new system, and it is the purpose of the next section.

Build Yourself a Framework

Data protection has an impact on all aspects of the organization. You will need input and approval from many groups, both technical and nontechnical. With that in mind, you should prepare to recruit a few teams of people and involve them in a series of review boards. These boards will participate in providing requirements and feedback on the design and operation of the service you are building.

As you meet with these groups, you will need to generate documentation that informs the process and ultimately acts as your future reference. Here are some standards you should adhere to when building these documents.

Document Templates

Start out with a template for all documentation you will be creating in this process. There are some basics in the structure of each document you create.

Purpose statement at the top
Explain the purpose of the document as concisely as possible, in no more than one or two paragraphs.

An executive summary
If the document is designed to provide a design or the conclusions arising from testing, make sure the people who will need to provide approval actually get the information to make their decision. We all know they won't read the entire document.

A revision history
All documents should be treated as living documents and, therefore, like life, will be subject to constant change. Especially during certain active periods in the project, those changes could be happening multiple times in a week (or even a day). A small table that notes a document revision number, the date of the revision, the author of the revision and a couple of bullet points on what changed in the revision will help you keep track of what document you are looking at and how you got there.

A sign-off page
Accountability is critical when developing a program that will be as critical to your organization as data protection. You want to make sure that all the critical approvers and subject matter experts (SMEs) are willing to commit to the plan by putting their signature on the final version of the document. Having this sign-off will also signify the completion of the content (until it needs to be updated again).

Policy/scope
The policy or scope of work being addressed can also be valuable to define the specific subjects the document is meant to address.

Glossary
A glossary to clarify any terms that the document addresses is particularly helpful for the non-SMEs involved in the approvals process.

Appendices

Any other material or supporting information that relates to, but is not necessarily directly part of, the document should also be attached to the end of the document.

Review/Advisory Boards

As I write this, I'm thinking about the two dozen or so technical editors who will review everything in this book. It's amazing how that many points of view can affect a project. A good review structure for your system will help ensure success by bringing in diverse viewpoints that prevent you from missing some critical components or requirements. There will be several iterative phases in this process, including the following.

Requirements review

The requirements review will include members from various departments, including a senior management sponsor, to make sure there is overall approval for the project from the organization. The Chief Information Officer (CIO) is a good choice for this, because they understand both technology and the strategy for how the organization uses technology.

Design review

The design review board (DRB) will include members for the technology-specific teams that could provide insight into the way technology is implemented in the organization. (Some organizations may call this an architecture review board [ARB]. The purpose is the same.) If you are a large organization, make sure to include systems engineering, database engineering, storage and network engineering, and cybersecurity. They will be able to review the infrastructure design and make recommendations on how to improve the integration and operation of the new service. The design review process should include a preliminary design review (PDR), where the plan is first reviewed against the requirements to make sure all is effectively covered, and a production readiness review (PRR) when it is all built and final testing is conducted. The purpose of the PRR is to get everyone to take a last look and make sure nothing was left out.

Operations review

You should pull together the operational teams that will run the service in production and allow them to understand fully what they are being asked to do. When the operations review is finished, you should have a runbook that will act as the user manual for the system.

Change review

Finally, there should be a change advisory board (CAB) that exists as part of the technology organization and reviews all changes before they go into production, where they can have an impact on the daily operation of the organization. The CAB acts as the gatekeeper for all changes, to protect the integrity of the organization. After the operations review is completed, it should be reviewed by the CAB before it goes live.

Project management

Using sound project management practices will help you coordinate the work, provide the available resources, and help get the work scheduled. It will also keep you accountable to the scheduled deliverables, and help ensure a smooth rollout to production.

Bring in the project management office at the very start. These are the folks that track and gate all the work that happens in most technology organizations.

Collecting Requirements

If you work in an outfit with five people, all sitting in the same room, it will be easy to look across the table and ask them what is really important to getting the job done, but most of you aren't living in that world. So first and foremost, it is going to be critical to identify your key stakeholders and understand what they need to function effectively.

What Are RPO and RTO?

Two critical metrics drive any data protection plan: the recovery point objective (RPO) and the recovery time objective (RTO). Both topics are covered extensively in Chapter 4, but a short version is that RTO is how quickly you need to recover operations after a disaster, and RPO is how much data you agree you can lose in the event of a disaster.

Find the Subject Matter Experts

From your knowledge of your organization's services or products, create a list of all your internal customers by department. (By the way, if you are in data protection, everyone in the organization is a customer.) Build a list of the SMEs who can best describe what each group does, what they need to have protected, and how critical it will be to have it online. They will fall into a couple of broad categories.

Data creators

Where does your data come from? What departments is it from? Is it generated by intelligent systems used in a manufacturing process best understood by operations and people on the manufacturing floor? Is it created by a team of highly skilled artists, writers, and editors at a substantial hourly rate? Does it come from a sales department, customer service, or any other department that is directly facing the customer? Understanding which groups are generating the data is the first step in understanding how complicated it would be to re-create the data from scratch.

Data creators will come from your production and operations teams, product management, organizational and business intelligence, and data services. You should include a representative of the compliance and cybersecurity teams as well, since they also have crucial requirements on how data is stored and used.

Remember, there are multiple entry points for your data. You may have to worry about the customer, service, product, inventory, order, and historical sales databases at the same time. Each changes at a different rate, based on the internal workflow of the organization. It could become impossible to keep all the data always protected and online at once without taking very costly measures to protect it, so it is critical to work with the data creators to understand what the RPO looks like. That will give you the picture of what a restored system actually looks like. (For example, we can't recover to the moment of failure, but maybe to failure minus one hour).

Be sure to ask questions about how many events or transactions they deal with in an hour or day, so you get an understanding of the churn rate of data in the systems. When talking to the database and data services teams, remember to collect the information on where data is stored and how much actual space it uses.

Executives

You will need to talk to members of the executive staff because they will have the best insight into the speed your organization is operating at. Understanding timelines for expected deliverables is critical, and the nontechnical leadership (i.e., department heads) are the ones who can best share that.

Any self-respecting executive will tell you they want everything protected all the time, but they will be the best at helping you understand the ebb and flow of the organization, which will help you determine priorities based on your discussions with the data creators.

Be prepared. These good people will tell you that no downtime is acceptable for the organization (that is, until you present them with the bill for a fully redundant, always active system that is geographically diverse across multiple datacenters, and keeps data synced to all sources in real time). So be prepared to have a serious discussion about what costs the organization can support, with an understanding that money is always an object in the discussion. Armed with this knowledge, you will be able to determine your RTO.

Compliance and governance

Make sure that whatever you are doing with data protection also complies with any laws and regulations that pertain to your organization. Privacy has become a major issue that is being addressed by new government legislation around the world. The General Data Protection Regulation (GDPR), the legal framework implemented by the European Union, requires an organization to be able to delete a user's information completely upon request; this would also include information stored on backups and archives. The California Consumer Privacy Act (CCPA) requires an organization to be able to report back all data that contains customer information in all systems, including backups. Seek out an SME from legal or governance teams of your organization to help make sure that your design follows the rules to be able to access data as needed in backups and archives. For example, your organization may have a data protection officer (DPO), who handles compliance with the GDPR in the European Union. They would be a natural SME for this area.

Solicit Requirements

Armed with your list of SMEs across the organization, set up an interview with each one to get their views on the organization's requirements. Keep in mind that you will be talking to both technical and nontechnical folks, so be sure you have someone there who can act as translator in case the specifics get too deep for your audience. SMEs are not usually generalists, but (as the title implies) experts on specific areas of the organization.

Be prepared: when you go into the meetings, take with you whatever documentation and diagrams you'll need to explain the concepts, in order to enable them to answer your questions. Try giving them an example, using their processes, and then tell them a piece of it is now gone. How would they handle it? Your S:\ drive or OneDrive is gone. How would that affect your operations? That gives them an easy way to wrap their heads around what you are asking.

Be respectful of their time and make sure you schedule appropriately. (For some it may be better to have three or four twenty-minute meetings than to have one two-hour meeting.) Never forget that although your job is critical to the long-term success of the organization, they have day jobs that are critical to the immediate success of the organization.

Meet with the groups individually so their views and requirements are not immediately influenced by any others. There will be time to hash it out at the requirements review later.

Review Requirements

Once you have made the rounds and collected all the requirements that each department believes are critical to survive a data loss, you need to get everyone on the same page. You should have enough information at this point in the process to figure out where the data in your organization lives, and how much of it there is. Don't be afraid to go back to the SMEs if you need additional clarification. This is really important stuff, so you want to get it right.

You should also start to have an idea of how quickly data is being generated and how quickly it is changing. (Note: The data services team told you this.)

You should have an understanding of how long services or products take to create or deliver, so you can understand the tolerance for a partial or full organization outage. (Note: The management team told you this.)

Put the copious notes you gathered into a presentation and then invite the key stakeholders to review them. These will be representatives from the management team to advocate for the organization and data creators, along with some key members of the technology teams that run the infrastructure, who will speak to the data. It's best that this happens around a table so everyone can ask and answer clarifying questions.

Start out by defining the problem you are trying to solve, and then lay out the requirements you've heard from each of the various departments in a presentation that shows each team's expectations. You are not designing the solution yet, but you are clarifying what each part of the organization believes is critical to protect to keep things running in the event of a disaster.

Microsoft PowerPoint is your friend, but don't get too flashy. Keep the slides high level, and be prepared to spend more time talking about them than asking others to read them and come to their own conclusions. Remember, this is about verifying their requirements and showing the best blending of it all into something unified. Try very hard to avoid having this discussion turn into a solution session. Too many chefs spoil the soup.

Although it isn't necessary to have a budget and quotes at this point in the process, it is a good idea to have a ballpark idea of what things will cost so you can help your audience understand how requirements translate into costs.

Service-level agreements

This is a good place to lay out the service-level agreements (SLAs) you will be establishing to meet the RPOs and RTOs you agreed to. Remember that data protection will include heavy use of network resources, storage devices (solid state and otherwise), and possibly even tape. These are all resources that have some form of physical constraint that will cause your service to take time and money. Keep in mind, too, that data protection typically uses more network bandwidth than any other service in your organization.

For example, if you copy your data to the public cloud to protect it, it must move across a wide-area network (WAN) that will have some bandwidth restraints. Once there, the cloud can become expensive if you use a lot of it, so you may want to figure out a point in time to move data to a slower tier or even delete it. When you need to restore it to meet your RTO, you have to balance the amount of time it will take to restore the data physically, as well as what data will need to be discarded for congruency, against a higher cost to reach your goals. Be sure to do your homework and define what that means to the service level you are guaranteeing for your customers so that you set their expectations properly.

Talk about a charge-back model

A *charge-back model* means that a given department will be held financially responsible for the amount of the service it uses. You should introduce this as a topic of discussion during the requirements review. It will have an impact on the design of your solution.

For example, the marketing department may generate hundreds of gigabytes of user data in the course of its work, and typically not take the time to clean up files it doesn't need after processing. If the requirements expect that all data must be protected, knowing that it will be held accountable on the budget to pay for that space can help it decide whether it really needs it all protected. A charge-back model helps drive home the reality that all this infrastructure to protect the data isn't free and should lead to a discussion about data classification.

Data classification

It may become necessary to take time in this process to classify the data that is being protected. Not all data is created equal, and it is likely that a fair portion of that data can be thrown away without affecting the normal operation of the organization. Taking the time to complete an exercise that determines what data is critical, important, nice to have, and expendable will have a direct impact on your RPO and RTO. Having said that, many data protection systems have been designed with a single data classification of "important," so don't be surprised if that happens to you.

But be sure to emphasize that even if it costs them money to protect their data, they shouldn't leave anything out that they really need protected just to reduce costs. Remind them that job one is about saving the organization in the event of a problem, and if it isn't protected it can't be recovered.

Wrapping up the requirements review

Check your ego at the door. Each person at the review will have their own opinion, and will also be approaching the problem from the perspective of their part of the organization. Do not let leading questions or unfortunate comments feel like a personal attack on you or your work. This is likely the first time they are hearing the priorities of other parts of the organization, so there will most likely be spirited discussion to clarify any misconceptions about what is best for the organization overall. If everything is top priority, then nothing is top priority, so remember you are guiding them through a process of understanding. Allocate at least 10 minutes for each person you invite to the meeting for the discussion, and make sure everyone understands that the conversation will determine the requirements of the organization.

Take good notes. If the consensus of your conclusions needs to be revised, be prepared to update the presentation and meet to review it again. Iterate as often as is necessary to get it right. You are setting the ground rules for how the organization will protect itself and recover in the event of a data loss, so it's important to get it right.

Once the requirements review is completed, put the conclusions into the document template and pass it around to get a physical signature from everyone who attended the review. (You can do this through a system like SharePoint as well, so long as it captures an official digital signature and freezes the document.) It is very important that you take this step. People will take an extra moment to make sure they understand the information in front of them when they will be held accountable for the results, and nothing says accountability like putting your signature on the dotted line.

The last thing to do with the requirements review document is ask for people to participate in the DRB. Odds are that you will need less senior management and more technology and data creator types for the design reviews. It is always valuable to have people who helped develop the requirements involved in reviewing the design.

Throughout this whole process, your role is to suggest things to others and see what they think. This is how you build consensus. You ask them questions to solicit their requirements, and then you tell them what you think they said their requirements were. Once you all agree on that, your next step will be to suggest possible ways to meet those requirements. In other words, *it's time to actually try to build this thing*.

Design and Build Your System

Now that you have everyone's requirements and have made sure they know that you understand them, it's time to move forward in the process and actually try to build something that meets those requirements. Don't worry; you won't be doing this alone, either. As you go through the design phase, your goal is to get their consensus on a design, just as you did when gathering requirements. This will start with having multiple ways to meet their requirements, each with different advantages and disadvantages.

Draw up Multiple Designs

You are going to draw up multiple ways to meet their requirements—different designs with different price points, different actual recovery times (RTAs) and actual recovery points (RPAs), and different levels of requirements for those who will use them. (Some will be easier to use, and others not so much.) Your job is to draw up these designs and guide the interested parties to a consensus around one choice.

Your first plan should always be a "pie in the sky, money is no object" solution that achieves the RPO and RTO defined in the requirements. This is your blueprint and the best example to show what a perfect solution would actually cost.

Then value engineer it into a second-best solution that still meets the objectives but has some built-in caveats. Reduce up-front costs as a trade-off to the extra expense needed on the backend when executed.

For example, say your organization makes animated movies. Your creative teams (data creators) will generate thousands of files and run complex compositing and rendering processes against them to create thousands of final images. In the process, you will create millions of small files that go into producing those images. It may be sufficient to save only the files created by the creative team to meet your RPO, but will you need to re-create the millions of others to get to where you were before the data loss, and land at your RTO? The computer and human time to reprocess those files will add a cost, but it may ultimately be cheaper than the extra effort and cost to capture the millions of files in the initial backups.

Keep in mind that failures are rarely clean and orderly events, so the effort to clean up the restored files to a state that allows you to flip the switch and get back to pre-failure state may actually be more prohibitive than just reprocessing some lost files.

Be sure to list and explain the trade-offs that come with being fiscally conservative. Be prepared to demonstrate that the cost delta between the perfect system and other options should account for the extra cost needed to clean up and reprocess data to get back to a steady state.

Your time to get back to business (RTO) will have to justify the amount of data you have to restore and clean up (RPO), so be prepared to make the sales pitch. The truth always lies somewhere in the middle of two viewpoints, so be prepared to cover all the scenarios in your solution.

Review the Designs

You've studied the white papers and industry best practices. By the time you get to the stage where you are reviewing designs, you will have read Chapter 16 of this book, which goes into detail about the technical aspects of designing or updating your backup system. You've reached out to potential vendors and sat through the dog-and-pony shows and received budgetary quotes. You've thought about it a little bit and finally produced a beautifully written 50-page document complete with scenarios, diagrams, data flows, cost analysis, and a final recommendation. It's time to get some validation that the solution makes sense to everyone involved in operating and building it.

Time to call together the DRB. Remember, the DRB includes members from the technology-specific teams that could provide insight into the way technology is implemented at your organization, including systems engineering, database engineering, storage and network engineering, and cybersecurity. You will also want to find the SMEs from the world of the data creators as well. Look to your production and operations teams for this.

Start out with a summary of the final requirements document and go deeper into the woods with this presentation by getting into the specifics of where data is being stored, how it is being encrypted, how much bandwidth you expect the system to consume, and how it will need to be operated. Be sure to note your expectations for the RPO, and what additional work will be required to get to RTO. None of us know everything about everything, so the input you take from the technical folks will help you refine the design. Bring your sharpened pencil, because your SMEs will provide great feedback.

Iterate the feedback again. If you came away with a major change to the design, architect it and run it past the DRB again. If you do some sandboxing or a full proof of concept and things turn out to be different than expected, document it and run it past the DRB another time. When you have the final design that you're prepared to move ahead with, fully document it per your framework and send it around for sign-off.

Select and Build the System

This is the fun part. You get to buy a whole bunch of things and make them work together. You'll configure the system to look at the datasets and process them. You'll meticulously time everything to certify that you are meeting your SLAs defined in the requirements document. You'll run it in parallel for a few weeks or a month, and then you'll build and run a full-scale test that will prove you have achieved your RPO and RTO goals. (Remember that achieving the recovery goals is really the only reason you're going through this process.)

Congratulations. You have a data protection system. Now it's time to build your operational plan and documentation.

Document and Implement the New System

No job is complete until the paperwork is done. If you design the most beautiful data protection system, but no one but you knows how to run it, you haven't done your job. You must document the system in such a way that people who didn't design it can run it without your intervention.

Defining Operational Responsibility

Everyone must know their responsibilities in the new system. Start by making a *responsible, accountable, collaborator, informed* (RACI) chart that will delineate which teams are responsible for the different tasks associated with the operation of the service.

Responsible
> Those who do the work to complete the activity.

Accountable
> Those who are held accountable for the completion of the task or deliverable.

Collaborator
> The person responsible for the activity, who must collaborate with others to complete the activity.

Informed
> Those who are kept up to date on the progress of the activity.

You'll define the various tasks that need to be carried out by the different teams. Table 2-1 is a typical RACI chart. It makes it very easy to see who is responsible, accountable, and collaborating, and who should stay informed.

Table 2-1. Typical RACI Chart

	Systems Admin	Data Ops	NOC	Head of IT
Run Nightly Job	R	A	C	I
Data Outage Incident Mgmt	A	C	R	I
Quarterly Testing	R	A	C	I

Defining and securing approval from the responsible teams in advance of rollout will go a long way toward making sure things go smoothly. Be sure to pull together the operations review board (ORB) to review the RACI chart and answer any questions or concerns about how your new system will affect the organization.

Operations Review and Documentation

Once you have a working system that you want to start using against your organization's critical production data, it is time to make sure all the documentation is up to date and all your audiences are addressed. You already have the requirements document and the design document, so it's time for the operations manual, runbook, or standard operating procedures (SOPs). These are all different names for the same thing. They enable people to understand how this fits into the day-to-day running of the organization. It's time to get an operations document in place, and as the designer of the system, you're in the best place to make that happen.

Be sure to meet with each team defined in the RACI chart, such as systems administration or the network operations center (NOC), and collect some requirements from them on what they need documented to take on the operational responsibility for the service. It will probably be really helpful to you and them to bring over someone from each team, train them on their responsibilities, and have them take a first pass at writing a manual. Having the perspective of the person who will incorporate the task into the day-to-day activity is invaluable.

Documentation Is Good

Let's take a moment to discuss that giant elephant in the middle of the room. No one likes writing documentation. We all have more fun things to be doing at our jobs. It's just easier to manage the system yourself than to document it so others can run it.

You will have to be a salesperson on this journey, so be prepared to explain that documentation is critical to the efficient and orderly operation of the system, and a runbook, manual, or SOPs written from the eye of the person doing the task will always be more effective than one written by someone who never has to do that. The following paragraph is your sales pitch to get people to write documentation:

> So, here is why the greatest thing you can do for yourself is to write your documentation…. You want to go on vacation? Take a day off work? Sleep through the night? Get promoted to a new and better job? You can't do any of those things if you are always the one they need to call when something isn't working. If you are under the impression that it gives you job security, I can assure you that every single one of us can be replaced on a moment's notice with the proper application of capital resources. So why not actually make your life easier and help build the documentation that will allow an operator on the graveyard shift to solve the problem before waking you up?

Runbooks

The operations runbook (i.e., SOPs, operations manual) should incorporate the same template as the design and requirements documents. As a matter of fact, be thorough and attach them as appendices, so a curious operator can learn more about the service. There should be a service summary, a revision history, and a sign-off page for every department that will be participating in the operation of the service.

In addition, the runbook should be made up of checklists that define the regular tasks by the frequency with which the operations folks will carry them out. They should be formatted like a checklist so that a busy operator can always grab a copy and check the boxes when they have it completed.

There should be a frequently asked questions (FAQ) section that goes into depth on any process that can get complicated.

Be sure to include a contact list that includes all the major vendor support contract information in the event of a component failure, as well as a list of the responsible members of the various groups that can be affected by the service, and the executives that need to be kept informed. You should have mobile phone information and be sure to note how they prefer to be contacted in an emergency.

Finally, there should be a section in the runbook for the operator to list any incidents that take place, with a brief summary and resolution. Leave room to refer to the tracking support ticket. This will be especially helpful for an operator to see whether something has happened before and how it was dealt with.

My personal opinion is that at least one copy of the runbook should be on paper in a binder where your operations folks can find it. We live in a world of cloud-based services and wikis to hold our documentation, and none of them are guaranteed to be available in the event of a system or network failure when you need the runbook for restoring your services. It may feel like a waste of trees to print it, but you will feel much better about it when you are standing in the darkened machine room and need to remember the order in which your servers and storage need to be rebooted to bring the services back online.

Implement the New System

Now that the system is designed, tested, and documented, it's time to make it part of the official computing environment. The CAB is going to have something to say about that.

If your technology organization doesn't have a CAB that meets regularly to review changes before they go into production and potentially affect customers, they should. Having a process like this will dramatically increase overall uptime by asking a few simple questions:

- What are you changing?
- Has it been thoroughly tested?
- What services can or will be affected by the change?
- How do we back the change out if something goes unexpectedly?
- When is the change scheduled to be made and how much time will it take to be implemented?

A CAB will provide visibility to anyone in the organization to any changes, so that problems can be noticed faster and rolled back in a timely manner if they cause issues. If you don't have a CAB, create one. Also helpful would be a change manager whose sole responsibility is the CAB and everything it oversees.

When you are ready for production, bring your complete documentation set to the CAB, especially the runbook, and be prepared to review it all. If you've done your work well, many of your CAB members will have been on various review boards and will already understand what you are bringing online.

This is also an iterative process, so follow the queues of the CAB members. If they have concerns and need more data, collect it and review it with them again. If they tell you to hold changes due to other changes on the slate, be patient. It's always harder to find the root cause of a problem when you make too many changes at the same time. Once blessed, go live.

Anytime you need to make a change in your service, such as a software upgrade or a restore test, make sure the CAB has been informed as well. Trust me on this; they are your best friend for organizational stability.

Takeaways

Congratulations. You have built and implemented a world-class data protection service for your organization that protects its critical assets and accounts for the necessary requirements that keep the doors open. Plus, you have done it using a methodology that has produced a thorough set of documents that will be useful for the life cycle of the service. You have made life easier for the operations crew, so running it and troubleshooting problems will be clearer and require less experience. You have proper documentation to support the needs of the cybersecurity team when analyzing data anomalies and repairing damage after potential breaches, and have satisfied the compliance groups when they need to confirm that the organization is properly supporting its Sarbanes-Oxley Act (SOX) or the GDPR data protection and exclusion rules.

By thoroughly understanding the organization, its requirements and all the components of a good data protection solution, you will build one of the most important, and often ignored, components of a solid, successful technology department.

Now that you have a thorough understanding of your organizational requirements, you know what needs to be backed up and what needs to be kept for very long periods. Now what you need to know is the different types of data protection systems you can use to do just that. This means knowing the difference between backup and archive, which is the purpose of the next chapter.

CHAPTER 3

Backup and Archive Are Very Different

This chapter starts with what many will consider a basic question: What's the difference between backup and archive? It might be a basic question but it's one I'm continually having to explain. I then explain other important concepts about how to keep your backups and archives safe: the 3-2-1 rule, immutability, encryption, air gaps, and disaster recovery plans.

Before you embark on designing, building, or maintaining a data protection system, you really need to have a solid understanding of these terms and concepts, especially those that are often confused with each other or overlooked in the rush to decision. So although you might be tempted to skip this chapter, I would recommend you not do so. There's probably some gold in them thar hills.

Before We Get Started

I take a very hard line on the difference between backup and archive. To me they are two very separate actions that serve two very different purposes. Having said that, my main goal is to have you understand the different *purposes* of these actions, because that's what matters. There are indeed a few products that satisfy both backup and archive needs—*and I'm fine with that*.

What I'm not fine with is using a product or service that is very obviously a backup product—and only a backup product—but also trying to satisfy archive needs with it. Unfortunately, that is what happens every day at organizations around the world. As I will explain over the next several pages, using a backup product as an archive product exposes the organization to additional risk and cost.

I am well aware that I will not change the world, and this is not a battle that I will ultimately win. The generic term *archive* is so ingrained in our vernacular that I won't fix this problem with a few pages on what backups and archives actually are, any more than I can convince you that *golf* is a noun and not a verb.

One does not "go golfing." One *plays golf*—just like you play tennis and football and baseball. You do not "go tennising," footballing, or baseballing. You go running, swimming, or jumping; hunting; or shooting, because those are *verbs*. You don't "play run" or "play shoot." See how silly that sounds? So why do you "go golfing?" Golf is a noun and I'm sticking to that. But no one cares and life moves on. Just do me a favor and don't say the phrase, "archiving a backup," or, "let's go golfing," while I'm within earshot. It hurts my ears.

I also urge you to learn the true differences between these concepts. If your product or service truly satisfies both needs, then fine. But if you're one of the millions of organizations doing one thing and calling it another thing, I urge you to reconsider that action.

What Is Backup?

Many of the terms and concepts in this chapter can be confusing, because they often have generic meanings outside of IT, and nowhere is this truer than in the terms *backup* and *archive*. Think of the various uses of these terms in popular culture, and you will see what I mean.

If you watch police dramas, you know they always tell the officer to wait for backup. People often talk about making sure that they have a backup available, when what they mean is a second instance of the item in question. For example, my wife's car is my backup car.

The term "backup" is also used in IT in ways that don't fit the traditional definition I will be giving in a few paragraphs. We talk about making a backup copy of the file, when technically what we are referring to is making a *copy* of the file that sits right next to the file it is a backup for. (As you will see later in this chapter, this violates the 3-2-1 rule, so it's a copy, not a backup.)

We also talk about virtual snapshots—usually used in network-attached storage (NAS) filers—as backups, even though they aren't even *copies*! They are *virtual copies* that rely on the original—so they are even less of a backup than the previous example of a copy of a file sitting right next to its original. I would call these *convenience copies*, because they are convenient and can be used for what we would typically use a backup for, but I wouldn't really call them backups.

A backup is a copy of data stored separately from the original and used to restore that data to its former state, usually after the data has been deleted or damaged in some way. Let's take a look at a few elements of this definition that are essential to understanding its meaning.

Just a quick note from the backup grammar police. Backup is a compound word, consisting of *back* and *up*. When used as a verb, it is two words. It has to be that way, or it won't conjugate properly. I back up. You back up. She backs up. He backed up. When it is a noun, it is one word. When I back up, I make a backup. You're welcome.

"Copy"

A copy is a byte-for-byte reproduction of the original that contains the same content as the original. When you use the `cp` command in Linux or the `copy` command in Windows, you create a copy. When you copy and paste a file in File Explorer in your operating system's user interface, you are creating a copy. When you run a backup command of any sort (e.g., `tar`, `dump`, `cpio`, Windows backup or any commercial backup software) and create another instance of the original, that is a copy. A true copy of a file will include all metadata, especially security and permissions settings. Whether a copy is also a backup will be based on whether it meets the rest of the definition.

It's just as important to say what is *not* a copy. As previously mentioned, virtual snapshots created in the file system or storage system are not copies, because they do not contain the contents of the original. They actually reference the original for most of their data. Examples of such snapshots include those created in NAS filers, snapshots in XFS, Volume Shadow Copy Services (VSS) snapshots in Windows, or snapshots made in hypervisors such as VMware or Hyper-V. Any "copy" that needs the original to function is not a real copy; it is a virtual copy. This means that it does not meet the first part of the definition of a backup.

It is also important to state that if you copy that virtual snapshot to another system, it does become a real copy and is just as much a copy as if you had copied the original data directly to the other system. In fact, replicating a snapshot to another system makes a superior copy, since all data in that volume will be from the same point in time, even if it takes hours to replicate the copy. (I explain all of this in more detail when I cover snapshots in Chapter 9.)

Snapshots are a wonderful source for very good backups. Take a filesystem snapshot after putting your database in backup mode or take a VSS snapshot that will do the right thing with the database, and copy that snapshot to your backup system. That is a very sound backup design. It's just important to realize that the original snapshot relies on the original thing it is a snapshot of and, therefore, is not a copy until it is actually replicated (i.e., copied) somewhere else.

Just to make things more confusing, a few things in the IT world are referred to as snapshots that are actually copies. Examples of this include AWS Elastic Block Store (EBS) "snapshots" and similar snapshots taken in AWS and other cloud vendors. I would call these *image copies*, not snapshots, because they are actually byte-for-byte copies of whatever they are backing up. Some database products call their backup a snapshot when it is also an image copy.

"Stored Separately from the Original"

If your copy is stored in the same file system, computer, or database, I would call it a convenience copy, not a backup. A copy that can be destroyed by an action that destroys the original isn't backing up that original; it's just sitting next to it. This is why we say that to be considered a backup, something needs to be stored on media separate from the original. I will cover this concept in more detail in "The 3-2-1 Rule" on page 42.

"For the Purposes of Restoring"

This is really where the rubber meets the road, because archives are also copies stored separately from the original. *It is why you created the copy that makes it a backup or an archive.* If you made the copy so that you can restore the original if it gets damaged, then it is a backup. This part really isn't that hard to understand. (As you will see later in this chapter, archives are not made for restores. They are made for *retrievals*, which is different.)

Suppose the original file, drive, server, or even datacenter that you copied has been damaged beyond repair. You accidentally deleted it or made changes to the file that you didn't want to make, and saved the file anyway. You dropped a table in a database that you did not mean to drop. You accidentally formatted the wrong drive and managed to wipe out an existing file system instead of making a new one. (I actually did that just a few weeks ago.) You had a triple-disk failure in a RAID-6 array. Triple-disk failures happen. I remember one server that lost six disk drives in one night. (Yes, I had a backup.) Or perhaps your entire datacenter has gone up in flames, is covered in water, or was taken out by some type of ransomware attack. The thing you reach for to fix all of this is a *backup*. If that is the reason you made your copy, then you made a backup.

What Is a Restore?

I have already defined a restore as the action you perform when you use a backup to return the original to its former glory. Let's drill down into that concept to differentiate it from a *retrieve*, which is what you do with an archive.

First, restores are usually designed to return a server or file system to a relatively recent point in time. In fact, backups are almost always used to restore to yesterday, and more recent than that if you can. You almost always use the most recent backup to restore whatever you are restoring. With exceptions that I will discuss, you don't restore your file system to the way it looked six months ago. You definitely do not restore your production database to the way it looked even two weeks ago. You would lose weeks of transactions and whatever business was associated with those transactions. You almost always want the most recent backup of the file, server, or database that you have available.

You may be shaking your head right now and saying, "Of course," and wondering why I'm making this point. Stay with me, I will show the relevance shortly.

There are exceptions to the "recent" concept. Perhaps you just discovered that the file you need to restore was deleted six months ago, so you'll need backups from six months ago to restore that file. Perhaps you found out that you had been infected with ransomware a long time before it actually executed its payload, so you want to restore it to a point in time prior to the actual infection. You might want to take a backup from a production database from a previous point in time and restore that database to a test or development area where you might actually want an older version of the database to compare it against the current version of the database. (Perhaps you made big changes in the database schema and you suspect that it is the cause of your current performance problems. To accomplish this, you restore a version of the database before you made the schema change and compare the performance of the two databases.)

There are rare cases when you might want to restore a slightly older version of a backup. There are even fewer cases when you might want a version that is *very* old—like nine months or a little over a year. Beyond that, you will start to have problems with how backups work.

How Does a Restore Work?

To do a restore, you need multiple pieces of information that indicate where the backup came from: server or VM name (unless we're talking containers), application name, the appropriate credentials for the server or VM in question, and some kind of subset name. For example, this might be the name of a filesystem (e.g., H:\ or /data), a directory (e.g., /data/data1), a table in a database (e.g., the users table), a bucket in object storage, or something like that. It is the next level of detail required after VM/server/application. You usually also need to know the *name* of the thing you want to restore, such as filename, database record, or object. (You do not need this last piece of information if you mean to restore the entire VM site server/application; you just need the name of the VM, server, or app.)

Finally—and this is crucial—*you need to know the date when the item in question was in the desired state that you want to restore*. For example, you know you fat-fingered the file this morning, so you want the most recent version of the file prior to this morning. You know you dropped the database table five minutes ago, so you want the most recent backup of the database prior to five minutes ago.

You want from one to many items from within a single area (database, filesystem, directory, bucket) from a single server, VM, or application from a single point in time prior to some bad event.

Attorneys and those who like to argue are at this point saying, "But sometimes I need to restore all of the servers." Yes, that is true. But for the purposes of this definition, what you're actually doing in that case is dozens or hundreds of individual restores of separate servers. What you are *not* doing is restoring several versions of the same server, database, file system, or file.

Even if you are restoring several versions of something, you are still doing several individual restores (from a definition perspective), and what you are most likely doing is a fishing expedition, because you actually don't have all the pieces of information you need to do a proper restore. You don't know when the file or database was in a good condition, or you don't know in which directory the file was located when you lost it, or (God forbid) you don't know the name of the file.

A restore returns a single thing to a single point in time. That's it.

This is so different from how an archive and retrieve works that it's not even close. As I will explain later in this chapter, a retrieve returns many things from a big date range. Hold that thought for now.

The 3-2-1 Rule

This section of the book is probably referred to more times than any other part. I will probably refer to the 3-2-1 rule in every single chapter of this book, and hardly an episode of my *Restore It All* podcast[1] goes by without me referencing it. The funny thing is that I spent many years of my career following the rule without ever actually realizing that it existed, so I want to prevent that from happening to you.

The 3-2-1 rule is the fundamental rule upon which all backups are based. It is to backup design what $E = mc^2$ is to physics. If you are ever in doubt that your design is a proper one, one very good thing is to verify whether it complies with this rule.

Simply stated, the 3-2-1 rule says that you should have at least three versions of your data on two different media, one of which should be somewhere else. Let's take a look at the three parts of this rule.

---

1 The Restore It All podcast is available on *BackupCentral.com* and all the usual podcatchers.

Three versions of your data

In my understanding of this rule, this means three *additional* versions of your data. In fact, whenever I am talking about the 3-2-1 rule, I never include the original in any of my calculations. The idea of having three versions is that it allows for a series of bad mistakes, like you corrupted your file at some point but didn't realize it. Then the corrupted file got backed up, so restoring the most recent backup version would restore a corrupted file. Hence the need for at least three versions.

Because of so many changes in how backup and recovery is done, it's actually pretty normal to have many more than three versions of your data, and I would encourage you to do so. Three is a *minimum,* not a maximum. In fact, many modern office productivity applications create many versions throughout the day, allowing you to undo numerous changes. Transaction logs of databases essentially create thousands of versions of your database throughout the day, allowing you to undo or redo quite a bit of work. Finally, it's common to back up laptops throughout the day—as often as every minute—so that you always have every version of every file that you are currently working on, enabling you to recover from a mistake that you didn't realize you made 30 minutes ago.

On two different media

You don't want all your backups stored on the same media. You definitely do not want your backups stored on the same media as the original. My favorite example of this is Mac OS Time Machine, which I like a lot. It is possible to go into the disk manager in Mac OS and partition your root drive to create what appears to the operating system as two drives. You could then configure Time Machine to back up the first hard drive to the second hard drive. I hope you immediately see how silly this is. Yes, you would have many versions of the data sitting on the first drive, and you will be able to restore any of those versions anytime you want—as long as the reason you're restoring it *isn't* that the drive actually failed.

If the drive actually failed, the fact that you stored your backups on a partition of that drive means that you actually don't have *any* backups. You need to store your backups on a different drive than the original. You need to store your backups in a different computer than the original. I would prefer your backups to be physically nowhere near the computer they are backing up. Like many opinions in this book, I have felt that way for a long time. Make sure to read the next sidebar, "You Can't Get There from Here".

You Can't Get There from Here

Years ago, when I had my first job as backup guy at MBNA, we had a tape library. By "tape library," I mean we had an actual device that housed nothing but tape. We had backup software tapes, we had nine-track tapes that held actual banking data from the mainframe, and we had about 15 robotic tape libraries that held DDS and AIT tape drives and tapes.

This was done for many reasons, one of which was the 3-2-1 rule. But it also allowed us to apply different security to that room, limiting the number of people who had access to backup tapes. Anyone in IT had access to the datacenter, but not everyone had access to the tape library.

The servers these tape libraries were backing up were two doors and roughly a little over 100 feet away. In those days, those servers only shipped with SCSI-2 buses. My memory of the specifications of SCSI-2 has faded, but suffice it to say that it did not allow me to have tape libraries 100 feet away.

To go that far, we needed Ultra-wide SCSI, which we called fast and wide SCSI, and neither the servers nor the tape drive supported that. We only had what we began to call "slow and skinny SCSI" on both ends. How did I do it, then? A company called Paralan sold bridges between these two protocols, and I bought two bridges for each cable, converting SCSI-2 to Ultra-wide SCSI and then converting back to SCSI-2 on the other end. I remember my tape library vendor telling me that this was not supported, and I remember telling them that if there was ever a communication problem, I would move the tape library in question back over to the server room to prove that it was or wasn't my funny little boxes. I never once had a problem.

The "two media" part of the 3-2-1 rule is one of the reasons I refuse to accept versions stored inside *software-as-a-service* (SaaS) offerings as a valid backup. Examples include Microsoft 365 Retention Policies and Google Archive. These are all just additional versions of email and files stored in exactly the same system they are protecting. They do not follow the 3-2-1 rule, so they are not backups. My story will change when their configuration changes.

"One of which is somewhere else"

This used to read "one of which is off-site," because that used to be the world: on-site and off-site. Today's world is so much more complicated. The idea is that at least one of your copies of data should be located a very safe distance away from the thing being protected. Historically, this meant storing your backups on tapes given to a "man in a van[2]" that was being driven to Iron Mountain or the like. This kept these tapes safely away from the things they were protecting, and you could easily recall the tapes in case of disaster. But the core concept here was to separate the disaster recovery copy from any type of disaster.

Sadly, there were some companies that ceased to exist on 9/11 because they failed to follow this part of the rule. They actually had very sophisticated redundant systems that were being synchronously replicated throughout the day to a hot site—in the other tower. Although no one foresaw the possibility that both towers could come crashing down at the same time, I hate to say that it should have been obvious that you don't store your hot site so close to the site it is protecting. Manhattan is an island, and the Hudson River could flood. Even if a tragedy hadn't taken out both towers, something could have made getting to either tower for work impossible. Your disaster-recovery copy, and definitely your hot site, should be somewhere that will not be subject to whatever types of disasters might potentially take out the main site.

Because of what happened on 9/11, there was an attempt at some legislation to say that financial trading firms had to have a synchronously replicated copy of files over 300 miles away. Although this sounded like a good idea, the speed of light got in the way, and they eventually backed down on having the copy be so far away *and* synchronously replicated. They would have to settle for asynchronous replication that would not have an impact on the performance of the original application.

In the world of the cloud, you need to remember that you're not just trying to separate the backup from the building where you happen to work. Make sure that backups of any application are stored in a different geographical area from the thing you are backing up. Find out where your cloud solution is actually hosted geographically and back up your data to cloud storage located in a different region.

If you are using an IaaS/PaaS vendor, you will know exactly which region your application is running in, and, by default, all backups created in your account will be stored in the same region and the same account they are protecting. You need to think about the things that could go wrong with your cloud account and separate your backup from those things. Although most services in such vendors are actually highly available services and able to survive many typical failures, a single hacked account with the wrong permissions can delete your entire application—and possibly your organization with it.

---

2 Don't blame me for the phrase. It's an old one left over from days gone by. "Person in a van" is more appropriate now, but it just doesn't have the same ring to it.

There's a New One

In 2014, there was a company called codespaces.com. It advertised itself as a safe place to put your code. It offered triple redundancy for all data and numerous backups. It sounded like a good design, but its backup system failed to follow the 3-2-1 rule. All backups were stored in the same account in the same region.

Somehow, a hacker gained access to a privileged account, partly because the company had not enabled multifactor authentication for its accounts. The hacker said the company needed to pay them a ransom or the hacker would delete the account. Instead of paying the ransom, the company tried to lock the compromised account out of its cloud account. The hacker realized what the codespace's people were trying to do and deleted everything. They deleted the VMs. They deleted their object storage. They deleted their databases. And because their backups were stored in the same account, they deleted their backups, too.

In an actual case of massive irony, the safe place to store your code turned out to be a very bad place to store your code. Feel free to check the internet archives for previous versions of the company's website, but you can see that after 2014, the company ceased to exist. *The 3-2-1 rule matters.*

I cover this story in more detail in the sidebar "Well, That Would Never Happen" on page 173.

My best advice when backing up a cloud resource is to create a separate account in a separate region whose only purpose is to hold backups, and perform cross-region backups from every other account to that account. You then need to lock up the keys to this really important kingdom. As of this writing, I am unaware of any major cloud vendors that support the concept of *multiperson authentication*, but if such a feature exists, you really should use it for this account. This would require two people to log in to do anything like delete backups or any other potentially damaging activities. This is like what they do in missile silos, where two keys must be turned at exactly the same time and they locate the keys far enough apart that it requires two physical people to turn the keys. This should be the electronic equivalent of the same. I will say they do support immutable storage, which I cover later in this chapter, and it can serve the same purpose.

From an authentication perspective, the best you can do if you do not have multiperson authentication is to simulate it using a standard *multifactor authentication*, but then divide the two factors between two people. One person has the email account and password, and the other person has the second authentication device. That way, the person with the email would not be able to log in without physically compromising the other person. The person who has only the secondary authentication device wouldn't know the account password and would not be able to reset it, because the other person is the only one who can log in to that email account. This isn't a perfect system, but it's the best you can do under the circumstances.

I'll sound like a broken record, but the versions stored in SaaS products, like Microsoft 365, Google Workspace, and Salesforce, are stored in the same place and therefore also do not comply with the last part of the rule. That's my story, and I'm sticking to it.

Now that we know what backups are, we need to look at archives and what distinguishes them from backup. They seem so similar in many ways, but their purpose makes them actually quite different.

What Is an Archive?

The term *archive* is also well used in popular culture. People talk about "going into the archives," which just means a big dusty room with a lot of boxes. When I think of archives in popular culture, I think of the warehouse at the end of *Raiders of the Lost Ark*, or the file room in *Cold Case*.

But it is in IT where the term *archive* is really misused. People talk about any old data as an archive, when an archive is actually something very specific. But when people call old backups "archives," I get truly bothered. They are not archives; they are old backups. Moving a backup from an expensive storage medium to a less expensive medium that is designed for long-term storage is not *archiving a backup*. There is no such thing as archiving a backup; you are moving a backup into long-term storage.

Old backups do not magically turn into archives any more than old grape juice turns into wine. If you want wine, you need to set out to make wine. If you want archives, you need to make archives. Stop treating old backups as archives, because they almost always are really bad at being archives. How long something is stored does not determine whether it's a backup or archive; it's why and how it was stored that makes it so. Now that we've covered what isn't an archive, let me explain what an archive actually is.

An archive is a copy of data stored in a separate location, made to serve as a reference copy, and stored with enough metadata to find the data in question without knowing where it came from.

The first two parts of this definition are the same as a backup. Just like a backup, you need to store an archive in a separate location or it's not really an archive, and it needs to be a complete copy that does not require the original to function.

What differentiates an archive from a backup is the purpose for which it was stored, the purpose for which it will be retrieved, and the manner in which it will be stored and retrieved.

To Serve as a Reference

Archives are not used to restore a server or file to its original glory. They are typically used to find data for purposes other than for which it was originally created. It may be a related purpose, but it is almost always a different purpose.

For example, suppose you are a satellite manufacturer and you archive a CAD drawing for a particular model of a satellite so that it may be looked at many years later. The reason someone might retrieve the CAD drawing is probably not to make an identical satellite, but it might be to make a similar satellite. Or it might be because the satellite fell from the sky and we need to go look at the design to figure out why. These purposes are related to the original purpose of the drawing but are not quite the same.

An email archive is usually used for e-discovery purposes, not email. Besides that, an archive is not stored in a way that will easily restore your email database, it's not really how you search against an email archive. You are generally looking for email that matches certain patterns, such as if they contain certain phrases or are from certain users, not just all emails that were on the server yesterday. That's what the backup is for.

This is one of the many reasons I do not consider Microsoft 365 Retention Policies and Google Archive to be a backup of Microsoft 365 or Google Workspace. They are an archive of your email and other data; *they are not a backup*. Their purpose is to be there for your reference, usually for e-discovery purposes, not to restore your database. Therefore, the way that you would query this archive is completely different from the way you would query a backup of the same. *In other words, in the same way backups make lousy archives, archives (what Microsoft 365 and Google Workspace do) make lousy backups.*

Stored with Additional Metadata

Sometimes the additional metadata in question is actually already contained in the thing being archived. For example, the metadata stored in an email archive includes the sender, addressee, and subject and date that the email was sent. The additional metadata needs to be stored in such a way that you can easily query it in order to find the reference information you are looking for.

All of this information is also stored in a backup, but it is not usually stored in such a way that it can be accessed other than by restoring the entire email system. As I mentioned previously, there are types of systems that serve a dual purpose and do store this additional metadata in a way you can query it. But if your "archive" requires you to know the name of the server or the database name to query it, it's not really an archive. With almost all products, the line between the two is usually very thick, but some software packages and services can meet the full definition of both backup and archive, and I'm fine with that. I'm not a monster.

Sometimes you also add additional metadata, such as when you create an archive of an inactive project. You put all the files, emails, pictures, and drawings that are part of the project in an archive and name the archive after the project. This metadata may or may not be in the actual files themselves, but it definitely needs to be stored outside the files for someone to query against the project name.

Sometimes archive systems can also extract the plaintext information from the thing being archived to search against that as well. When an archive system supports this, you see phrases like *fulltext search*. Such a feature is necessary if you intend to search for information based on the content of the files or emails themselves, versus just their metadata (e.g., subject line of an email, not its body).

The reason all of this matters so much is that a retrieve is very different from a restore. A restore doesn't need to query all this metadata easily. More important is that when performing a typical retrieve, you do not have the information you need to do a restore. So if your system is only capable of performing a restore, you will have a very hard time performing a retrieve.

What Is a Retrieve?

A retrieve is very different from a restore. As mentioned previously, a restore needs the name of a server, directory, database, filesystem, filename, tablename, and actual date that you want to restore the system to. When doing a retrieve, *you typically have none of that information.*

A retrieve gathers a group of related information based on its content and associated metadata. You are typically retrieving from multiple servers and applications, as well as across a range of dates. It is literally the complete opposite of a restore. And a proper archive system is typically as bad at doing a restore as a typical backup system is at doing a retrieve.

You might be doing a retrieve years or even decades after the original information was created. You might have a vague idea of the types of servers that might have contained the information you're looking for, but there is no way you're going to know the server, VM names, database names, and so on.

Try to think of the name of the email server that you used five years ago. If you do still remember it, it's either still in production or it probably caused you a lot of pain. I remember the database server that launched my career, which was *paris*. I remember it because I thought I was going to get fired that day. Make sure to read "The One That Got Away" on page 1.

When you are doing a retrieve, you are usually looking for *information,* not a server or file. You are more interested in the content of that file. You are looking for all emails with the word *Apollo* in them. You are looking for all emails sent from Stephen Smith to Jane Collins in the past three years, regardless of which email system they came from or went to. You are looking for all the versions of the particular piece of code that John Stevenson worked on—five years ago.

Perhaps you have a vague memory of some projects from several years ago that you think might be relevant to a project today. Your brain is saying, "This reminds me of that widget project three years ago." So you go to the archive system and search for the widget project from three years ago, and there it is. All the files and emails from that project are available with the simple click of a button. (Assuming you knew where all this information used to be, you could restore this with a backup system, but it would take several restores and require a lot more information than you would typically have in such a scenario.)

I'll go into more detail on the different types of archives in Chapter 10.

Both backups and archives are important. If you create either a backup or archive (or both), you'll want it to remain intact and not destroyed, corrupted, or tampered with. The following is a discussion of various techniques that organizations use to make sure that backups and archives survive anything that might damage them.

Protecting Backup and Archive Data

I covered a number of things in Chapter 1 that may damage (or attempt to damage) your backup and archive data. Just like your primary data, data protection data can be damaged by equipment failure, natural disasters, and things that people may do accidentally or maliciously to harm such data. Let's talk about what you can do to help mitigate these risks.

Encryption

The best thing you can do to prevent your data protection data from being inadvertently accessed is to encrypt it. Any modern backup device supports hardware encryption and third-party key management. Any modern backup software or service supports encrypting data in flight as well as at rest.

Encryption will not prevent a bad actor from deleting or stealing your backups, but it can prevent them from reading them. This would prevent a bad actor from using your backups as a means of extortion. They could literally steal your entire backup system and be unable to read anything if they are unable to authenticate into the system.

This is why the concepts I discussed in Chapter 1 around multifactor and multiperson authentication are extremely important. A bad actor can immediately defeat any encryption system if they are able to log in as a privileged user.

This Is Why You Encrypt Backups

As I was editing the book, another data breach happened, this one caused by bad security around backups. Bonobos, a Walmart company, announced that someone had accessed and published its 70 GB customer database and had done so by accessing a cloud backup of it.

Very few details were provided, but we know that someone who wasn't supposed to access this backup did so, and we know that they were ultimately able to read it. We know the latter because they published the plaintext information online, and the private information of 400,000 customers was released to the public. The data was limited in scope, such as only exposing the last four digits of the SSNs rather than the entire SSN, and the passwords that were leaked were encrypted with SHA-256. But for reasons that are outside the scope of this book, someone used brute-force techniques to decrypt about a third of those passwords anyway.

One thing I will say is that that is what happens when people who are not cloud experts start using the cloud to store their backups. They don't properly secure the backups and they don't encrypt them, either. Nothing other than their backup program should have been able to access that backup, and if someone did access it anyway, it should have been encrypted and unreadable. Please make sure that any backups you create are encrypted. It would have stopped this attack.

Air Gaps

The term *air gap* literally refers to a gap of air between the protected system and the protection system. If there was some type of rolling disaster or attack that affected both the primary and secondary systems, creating an air gap between those systems would effectively stop the event from taking out the only thing designed to allow you to recover from such an event. We talk a lot in data protection about limiting the blast radius. The best way to do that is to separate as much as possible the protection copy from the protected system, both geographically (as I discussed in "The 3-2-1 Rule" on page 42) and electronically. The bigger and thicker the air gap between the two systems, the better.

This idea originated way before we even had internet-connected datacenters. A software bug might cause what we call a *rolling disaster*, when one system infects another system, which infects another system, and so on. If your primary system and secondary system used exactly the same code, an error in that code could cause you to lose data on both sides and, therefore, permanently lose your organization's data that you are supposed to be protecting.

Now that we have internet-connected datacenters, and ransomware is on the rise, the idea of a piece of code that can attack both the primary and secondary system is far from a bogeyman. It is a reality for many organizations.

Just read various stories about ransomware attacks when they talk about the backup system also being infected and therefore unable to help. Read about the ransomware attack that took out hundreds of dentists' offices in the United States[3]. Not only did it take out the primary and backup systems, it used the backup system *as the means of attack*. There are plenty of stories of people who stored their encrypted backups on Windows-based backup servers along with the encrypted primary systems. This happened because the backup system in question did not include an air gap.

Please do not interpret this statement as me being anti-Windows. I am at this very moment using a Windows laptop and Dragon Professional to dictate this book. I am simply stating that the primary attack vector for ransomware, as of this writing, is Windows-based laptops and desktops. Once a single laptop or desktop is infected and inside the datacenter, it uses protocols found within the Windows world, such as the Remote Desktop Protocol (RDP), to attack the rest of the datacenter. If your backup server is directly accessible via your local area network (LAN), and is running the same operating system as the compromised system, there is a risk that it may be attacked by the same ransomware.

In addition, as mentioned in "Target Deduplication Appliances" on page 272, if the backups are directly accessible via a directory on that Windows-based backup server, they may be infected along with your primary systems. The bad actor may then be able to force you to pay the ransom because you have no recourse via your backup and recovery system.

Physical air gap

In the old days, we always had an air gap. Even if the backup server and primary server ran the same operating system, we backed up to tape. Then we handed copies of those tapes to a man in a van who took them away. Not only was there a very large gap of air between these copies, there were additional layers of security that kept track of and secured the air-gapped copy.

We kept track of every piece of media via a barcode. These tapes were scanned by our personnel as well as the vaulting vendor's staff. Tapes were scanned into a box when they left and then scanned out of the box when they were put on a shelf in the vault. We had a system that would check that the tapes we put into the box had shown up in

---

3 Enter "Ransomware Attack Hits 400 Dental Offices" in your favorite search engine.

the vault, and the tapes that they took out of the vault showed back up in our datacenter. A regular rotation schedule brought expired tapes back on-site after two weeks.

Any access to off-site tapes outside of the regular rotation schedule was highly regulated and well-documented. We required two-person authentication to have a tape shipped back on-site outside of the normal schedule. This may sound like a pain, but it really didn't happen very much. We always had an on-site copy and an off-site copy, so the only time we would need the off-site copy is if the on-site copy had been damaged. Therefore, the only usual reason we were doing such a thing was for a full-fledged DR test.

We would also conduct penetration tests against the vaulting vendor. We would visit them and ask them to see some of the tapes, which, of course also required two-person authentication. We would try to concoct a scenario that would get us inside the vault where the tapes were kept, hopefully unattended. I do not recall even once being left unattended with our own tapes. Kudos to the vaulting vendor.

Virtual air gap

The logistics of how backups were done back in the day simply required an air gap, but most of us don't even make tapes anymore when we make backups. Many of us never even see the system we are backing up or the system to which we are backing up. Most important, every single system is internet-connected. Therefore, the attack face is much larger and the possibility of an attack hopping from system to system is much higher.

Can we create a digital equivalent of an actual air gap? Can we create a copy of backups that is unreachable electronically or otherwise? If they are reachable electronically, can we ensure that they are immutable, that an attack cannot encrypt or delete both the primary and the backup?

The answer to all of these questions is yes, but this old tape guy still likes to refer to this as an "air gap," with quotes around it (finger quotes if I'm talking). I have also taken to calling this a *virtual air gap*, which seems appropriate since everything else is virtual.

You can accomplish a virtual air gap between your primary systems and your backup system in a variety of ways. Please use as many of the following methods as you can, based on your environment:

Disable or impair Remote Desktop Protocol
RDP is one of the most common attack vectors ransomware attackers use. Either disable RDP or lock it down, especially on the backup system. Configure it so that it can only be accessed via a certain network, such as a virtual private network (VPN). Require multifactor authentication to enable it. RDP should not be required for day-to-day activities, so requiring a few extra steps to connect to the

console of your backup server shouldn't be that much of an inconvenience. (If RDP *is* part of your day-to-day activities, address that immediately.)

Different operating system

If possible, use a different operating system for your backup server than you do for your primary computing servers. In most modern datacenters, this means using Linux for the backup server, since most of your primary servers are based on Windows. Some of the backup products that require a Windows-based backup server might support a Linux-based media server. Since it is the media (i.e., backups) that we're trying to protect here, see whether you can use a different operating system for your media servers. By the way, my recommendation stays the same even if you are running this backup software in the cloud, if the cloud-based servers are made to appear as if they're in the datacenter (i.e., by using a VPN). If they look like they're in the datacenter, they are in the datacenter from an attack-surface perspective.

Separate the storage

As mentioned in "Target Deduplication Appliances" on page 272, most environments that are doing on-premises backup are backing up to a purpose-built target deduplication system. (I'll go into more detail on deduplication later in Chapter 5.) The easiest way to connect such a system to your backup server is to use a network file system (NFS) or server message block (SMB). *Please do not do that.* Investigate the options with your backup software and target deduplication vendors for connecting the two systems via some other protocol that does not require mounting the target deduplication system as a directory on the backup server. Whatever you do, do not simply have a local disk drive mounted as a drive letter or mount point that is directly accessible via the operating system of your backup server. I am well aware that some vendors sell backup appliances with this very design; it is my opinion that those backups are vulnerable to ransomware and other attacks. This is especially true if those appliances are running Windows.

Use object storage

If your backup system supports writing to object storage instead of just a regular file system, use that feature. By changing the protocol you use to store your backups, you again obfuscate the backups from a typical attack. Even an on-premises, object-based storage system is more secure than one reachable through NFS or SMB.

Use immutable storage

Some storage systems support the concept of immutable storage, in which you specify that anything written to that system is kept for a certain period of time and *even you are not allowed to delete it*. (I cover the concept of immutability in more detail later in this chapter.) It is even better if said storage is in the cloud and not physically accessible in your datacenter. If your backup system supports writing to such a storage system, do so. Even if it doesn't support doing it directly, it is possible that you can do it in a roundabout way. For example, you might be able to create a bucket in an object-storage system with the immutable feature turned on. If the retention is set for all backups written to that bucket, you can accomplish this even if your backup software system doesn't support it.

Use tape

There is no better air gap than a tape copy sitting on a shelf in a completely different physical location than your datacenter. I know it's old-school, but it's worth mentioning. Even if you do this only every once in a while. Don't forget to encrypt the tapes as they are being written. That way, a lost tape is worthless to anyone who gets it, because they won't have the keys.

Use a backup service

There are backup services in which even an authorized system administrator never gains access to a backup server that they can log in to. If you are not able to see it and log in to it, it will be harder for a hacker or ransomware product to do so. However, not every backup service is designed in the same way. When examining such systems, make sure to look into the internal architecture of the systems behind the service. If it's exactly the same software as you would run in your datacenter, it is possible the system is still vulnerable to an attack, even if you do not see the system directly. Look for services that completely separate the backups from all network connectivity as much as possible.

Immutability

As discussed in Chapter 1, you must prevent accidental and malicious erasure or damage to your backups and archives. Besides all the usual security best practices discussed earlier, as well as other information security practices not mentioned there, there is a concept that can ensure that no one—including privileged personnel or someone impersonating such personnel—can delete, encrypt, or otherwise damage your backups and archives. That concept is immutability.

Immutability is a very straightforward concept. Something that is immutable cannot be changed by anyone or anything, including privileged personnel. If you place something in an immutable storage system and specify that it must be immutable for 90 days, you cannot change your mind. You cannot come back later and say you meant 45 days and have anything older than 45 days deleted.

You can change your retention period, of course. The new retention period will be in effect for data stored after the change was made. It will not affect backups or archives written before you made the change. They will remain unchanged for as long as you specified when they were written.

There are a few very important things I think you should know about the concept of immutability, besides that I think it will become a much more important feature in the backup and archive communities than it has ever been before, mainly due to the significant increases in ransomware attacks I mentioned in Chapter 1.

Nothing is truly immutable

Any data written to any storage can somehow be destroyed. Write-once-read-many (WORM) tapes and optical media are not impervious to fire. Immutable storage offered in the datacenter and the cloud is still subject to the laws of physics. The idea is to remove as many risks as you can and mitigate remaining risks as much as possible.

Immutability requires many controls

It used to be that the only immutable storage was optical media; now optical media is almost never used. Many people do use write-once-read-many (WORM) tape, though, which provides the same benefit. Disk-based immutable systems use object storage to address immutability. Each object stored in such a system has a hash value based on its contents; change the contents, and the hash automatically changes. This feature can easily be used to show that an object has not changed since it was placed in the system. You then need to harden the system, shutting off every way that objects could be deleted outside of the supplied APIs. You also need to control physical access to the system to prevent some other kind of access. The final check and balance is provided by how object storage works. You can easily prove an object hasn't changed by recalculating its hash. If the hash is the same, it hasn't been changed.

The most recent change in immutability is the introduction of cloud storage. It helps address a lot of the concerns around physical access and has all the same features as the on-premises systems. My personal opinion is that cloud-based immutable storage offers the current best option for immutability. Cloud-based object storage is typically replicated to multiple locations, offers immutability as an option, and ensures that even a physical breach of your datacenter wouldn't put this data at risk.

Immutable does not mean impervious

An immutable system can prove that a given object has not ever been changed. It still doesn't remove the issues around physical access or other possible damage. If a tape catches fire and melts, it won't matter that it was a WORM tape. It will be just as worthless. So continue to look at ensuring that you have multiple copies of data that are supposed to be immutable.

A lot of things are mislabeled immutable

Some backup and archive vendors call their backups immutable when they really mean "protected against attacks." They will explain the protections they put in place to protect your backups from hackers or viruses so that you understand that a virus or ransomware attack cannot affect your backups. However, if a backup administrator can reduce the retention of a backup after it has been created, that is not *immutable*. This matters because sometimes hackers do gain access to privileged accounts, even backup admin accounts. Although they may not be able to encrypt or corrupt your backups, if they can change your retention to zero days and effectively delete all your backups, they have accomplished their goal. Ask your backup vendor who claims immutability whether a backup admin can delete (or prematurely expire) backups. If the answer is yes, those backups are not immutable.

Takeaways

A proper understanding of the difference between backup and archive is crucial for proper backup and archive system design. There are products and services that can do both with a single product, but they are rare. Please don't make the mistake of thinking that keeping backups for several years is a good idea, unless your backup system is also good at retrievals, not just restores. Similarly, do not make the mistake of thinking the archive features built into SaaS products are also backup products, because they aren't. They are made for e-discovery and retrievals, not for restores. In addition, they don't even follow the 3-2-1 rule, which is essential for a process to even be called a backup.

Any good backup will follow the 3-2-1 rule. You will have at least three versions of everything, on at least two different media, at least one of which is stored somewhere else. If your backup doesn't meet this definition, then, frankly, it's not a backup.

Backups and archives are also your last lines of defense. Just as in war, the enemy (e.g., physics, hackers, etc.) will target your stronghold; you must protect it from such attacks. Separating it from such attacks, encrypting it, and even configuring it so that even you aren't allowed to change or delete it are all good methods of securing your backup and archive data.

The next chapter dives deeper into the idea of backup, starting with some metrics important to any good backup system. I also cover some important backup concepts, such as how backups are selected and retained, as well as the idea of backup levels. I also explain two ways backup data is stored (e.g., image and file level), and a few myths about backups.

CHAPTER 4

Backup and Recovery Basics

Now that I've defined what backup and archive are and how to keep them safe, we need to drill down further into some basic backup and recovery concepts. I'll start with discussing the all-important concept of recovery testing, followed by the concept of backup levels. I then look at many backup system metrics, especially the concepts of RTO and RPO and how they (more than anything else) determine backup design. I then talk about image-level versus file-level backups and how the contents of backups are selected. The first, and possibly most important basic backup concept, however, is that all backups must be tested.

Recovery Testing

There is no more basic concept of backup and recovery than to understand that the only reason we back up things is to be able to restore them. And the only way you'll know whether you can restore the things you're protecting is to test your ability to do so. Regular recovery testing should be a fundamental part of your backup system.

Besides testing the validity of the backup system and its documentation, regular testing also helps train your personnel. If the first time they're executing a big restore is when they're doing it in production, such a restore will be a much more stressful situation and more likely to be error prone. If they've done such a restore multitudinous times, they should just be able to follow their usual procedure.

You should regularly test the recovery of anything and everything you are responsible for. This includes small things and very large things. The frequency of testing of each thing should be related to how often a restore of such a thing happens. A few times a year might be appropriate for a big DR test, but you should be restoring individual files and VMs at least once a week per person.

The cloud has made all of this much easier, because you don't have to fight for the resources to use for recovery. You just have to configure the appropriate resources in the cloud and then restore to those resources. This is especially true of large DR resources; it should be very easy to configure everything you need to do a full DR test in the cloud. And doing this on a regular basis will make doing so in production much easier. Tests should also include restoring common things in SaaS services, such as users, folders, and individual files or emails.

A backup isn't a backup until it's been tested!

—Ben Patridge

Backup Levels

There are essentially two very broad categories of what the backup industry calls backup levels; you are either backing up everything (i.e., full backup) or you are backing up only what has changed (i.e., incremental backup). Each of these broad types has variations that behave slightly differently. Most of the backup levels are throwbacks to a bygone era of tape, but it's worth going through their definitions anyway. Then I'll explain the levels that are still relevant in "Do Backup Levels Matter?" on page 67.

Traditional Full Backup

A traditional full backup copies everything from the system being backed up (except anything you specifically told it to exclude) to the backup server. This means all files in a filesystem (unstructured data) or all records in a database (structured data).

It requires a significant amount of input/output (I/O), which can create a significant performance impact on your application. This is especially true if you are pretending that your VMs are physical machines, and you happen to be performing multiple, simultaneous, full traditional backups on several VMs on the same hypervisor node.

Figure 4-1 shows a typical weekly full backup setup, with three types of incremental backups that I will discuss next.

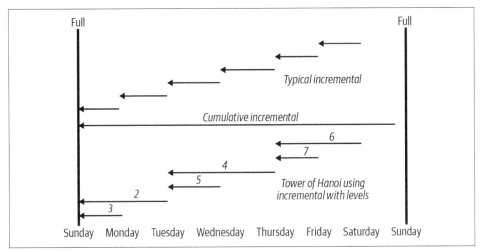

Figure 4-1. Full and incremental backups

Traditional Incremental Backup

A traditional incremental backup will back up all filesystem files or database records that have changed since a previous backup. There are different types of incremental backups, and different products use different terminology for the different types. What follows is my best attempt to summarize the different types.

Unless otherwise specified, incremental backups are *full-file incremental backups*, meaning the system will back up a file if the modification time has changed or its archive bit has been set in Windows. Even if the user changed only one block in the file, the complete (i.e., full) file will be backed up. Block-level incremental and source-side deduplication backups (both of which are discussed later in this chapter) are the only incremental backups that do not behave this way.

Typical incremental backup

A *typical incremental* backup will back up all data that has changed since the previous backup, whatever type of backup it happened to be. Whether the previous backup was a full backup or another incremental backup, the next incremental backup will back up only data that has changed since the last backup. This is the most common type of incremental backup. You can see this behavior in Figure 4-1.

Cumulative incremental backup

A *cumulative incremental* backup backs up all data that has changed since the last full backup. This requires more I/O of the backup client than a typical incremental, and requires more bandwidth to transmit and more storage to store (assuming you're not using deduplication). The advantage of this type of backup is that you only need to restore from the full backup and the latest cumulative incremental backup. Compare this with the typical incremental backup, when you need to restore from the full backup and each subsequent incremental backup. However, the advantage of this type of incremental really goes by the wayside if you are using disk as your backup target.

In Figure 4-1, you can see a cumulative incremental backup being run on Saturday night. It backs up anything that has changed since the full backup on Sunday. This would happen regardless of which night it is run.

This type of backup is often called a differential, but I prefer not to use that term, because some backup software products use that term to mean something very different. Therefore, I use the term *cumulative* incremental.

Incremental backup with levels

This type of incremental backup uses the concept of *levels*, each specified by a number, where 0 represents a full backup, and 1–9 represents other incremental backup levels. An incremental backup of a certain number will back up everything that has changed since a previous backup one level down. For example, if you run a level 2 backup, it will back up everything that has changed since the last level 1 backup. You can mix and match these levels for various results.

For example, you might do a level 0 (i.e., full backup) on Sunday and then a level 1 every day. Each level 1 backup would contain all data that has changed since the level 0 on Sunday. You could also do a level 0 backup on the first day of the month, a level 1 every Sunday, and a series of backups with increasing levels the rest of the week (e.g., 2, 3, 4, 5, 6, 7). Each Sunday's backup would be a cumulative incremental (i.e., all data changed since the level 0), and the rest of the backups would behave as typical incremental backups, just like in the top half of Figure 4-1.

An interesting idea that uses levels is called the *Tower of Hanoi* (TOH) backup plan, which is illustrated in the bottom half of Figure 4-1. It's based on an ancient mathematical progression puzzle of the same name. If you're still backing up to tape and are worried about a single piece of media ruining a restore, TOH can help with that.

The game consists of three pegs and a number of different-sized rings inserted on those pegs. A ring may not be placed on top of a ring with a smaller radius. The goal of the game is to move all the rings from the first peg to the third peg, using the second peg for temporary storage when needed.[1]

---

1 For a complete history of the game and a URL where you can play it on the web, see *http://www.math.toronto.edu/mathnet/games/towers.html*.

One of the goals of most backup schedules is to get changed files on more than one volume while reducing total volume usage. The TOH accomplishes this better than any other schedule. If you use a TOH progression for your backup levels, most changed files will be backed up twice—but only twice. Here are two versions of the progression. (They're related to the number of rings on the three pegs, by the way.)

0 3 2 5 4 7 6 9 8 9

0 3 2 4 3 5 4 6 5 7 6 8 7 9 8

These mathematical progressions are actually pretty easy. Each consists of two interleaved series of numbers (e.g., 2 3 4 5 6 7 8 9 interleaved with 3 4 5 6 7 8 9). Please refer to Table 4-1 to see how this would work.

Table 4-1. Basic Tower of Hanoi schedule

Sunday	Monday	Tuesday	Wednesday	Thursday	Friday	Saturday
0	3	2	5	4	7	6

As you can see in Table 4-1, it starts with a level 0 (full) on Sunday. Suppose that a file is changed on Monday. The level 3 on Monday would back up everything since the level 0, so that changed file would be included on Monday's backup. Suppose that on Tuesday we change another file. Then on Tuesday night, the level 2 backup must look for a level that is lower, right? The level 3 on Monday is not lower, so it will reference the level 0 also. So the file that was changed on Monday, as well as the file that was changed on Tuesday, gets backed up again. On Wednesday, the level 5 will back up just what changed that day, since it will reference the level 2 on Tuesday. But on Thursday, the level 4 will not reference the level 5 on Wednesday; it will reference the level 2 on Tuesday.

Note that the file that changed on Tuesday was backed up only once. To get around this problem, we use a modified TOH progression, dropping down to a level 1 backup each week, as shown in Table 4-2.

Table 4-2. Monthly Tower of Hanoi schedule

Su	0	Su	1	Su	1	Su	1
Mo	3	Mo	3	Mo	3	Mo	3
Tu	2	Tu	2	Tu	2	Tu	2
We	5	We	5	We	5	We	5
Th	4	Th	4	Th	4	Th	4
Fr	7	Fr	7	Fr	7	Fr	7
Sa	6	Sa	6	Sa	6	Sa	6

If it doesn't confuse you and your backup methodology,[2] the schedule depicted in Table 4-2 can be very helpful. Each Sunday, you will get a complete incremental backup of everything that has changed since the monthly full backup. During the rest of the week, every changed file will be backed up twice—except for Wednesday's files. This protects you from media failure better than any of the schedules mentioned previously. You will need more than one volume to do a full restore, of course, but this is not a problem if you have a sophisticated backup utility with volume management.

Block-level incremental backup

A *block-level incremental* only backs up bytes or blocks that have changed since the last backup. In this context, a *block* is any contiguous section of bytes that is less than a file. The key differentiator here is that something is tracking which bytes or blocks have changed, and that tracking mechanism will determine which of these blocks, bytes, or segments of bytes are sent in an incremental backup.

This requires significantly less I/O and bandwidth than the full-file incremental approach. It has become much more popular with the advent of disks in the backup system, because it creates many smaller backups, all of which have to be read in a restore. This would be very problematic in a tape world, but it's no big deal if your backups are on disk.

The most common place where block-level incremental backup occurs today is in backing up hypervisors. The hypervisor and its subsequent VMs maintain a *bitmap* containing a map of all bits that have changed since a given point in time. Backup software can simply query the bitmap for all bytes that have changed since the specified date, and the hypervisor will respond with the results after it queries the bitmap.

Source-side deduplication

Source-side deduplication (or just source deduplication, to differentiate it from target dedupe) will be covered in more detail in Chapter 5, but it is technically a type of incremental. Specifically, it is an extension of the block-level incremental backup approach, except additional processing is applied to the new or changed blocks before they are sent to the backup server. The source dedupe process tries to identify whether the "new" blocks have been seen before by the backup system. If, for example, a new block has already been backed up somewhere else, it won't need to be backed up again. This might happen if you are backing up a file shared among many people, or if you back up the operating system that shares a lot of files with other

---

2 This is always the case for any recommendation in this book. If it confuses you or your backup methodology, it's not good! If your backups confuse you, you don't even want to try to restore! Always Keep It Simple SA . . . (K.I.S.S.).

systems. This saves time and bandwidth even more than block-level incremental backup does.

Synthetic full backups

The traditional reason for periodic full backups is to make a typical restore faster. If you only performed one full backup (with a traditional backup product), followed by incrementals forever, a restore would take a very long time. Traditional backup software would restore all data found on the full backup, even if some of the data on that tape had been replaced by newer versions found on incremental backups. The restore process would then begin restoring new or updated files from the various incremental backups in the order that they were created.

This process of performing multiple restores, some of which are restoring data that will be overwritten, is inefficient to say the least. Since traditional restores were coming from tape, you also had to add the time required to insert and load each tape, seek the appropriate place on the tape, and eject the tape once it was no longer needed. This process can take over five minutes per tape.

This means that with this type of configuration, the more frequent your full backups are, the faster your restores will be because they are wasting less time. (From a restore perspective only, full backups every night would be ideal.) This is why it was very common to perform a full backup once a week on all systems. As systems got more automated, some practitioners moved to monthly or quarterly full backups.

However, performing a full backup on an active server or VM creates a significant load on that server. This gives an incentive for a backup administrator to decrease the frequency of full backups as much as possible, even if it results in restores that take longer. This push and pull between backup and restore efficiency is the main reason that *synthetic full backups* came to be. A synthetic full backup is a backup that behaves as a full backup during restores, but it is not produced via a typical full backup. There are three main methods of creating a synthetic full backup.

Synthetic full by copying. The first and most common method of creating a synthetic full backup is to create one by copying available backups from one device to another. The backup system keeps a catalog of all data it finds during each backup, so at any given point, it knows all the files or blocks—and which versions of those files or blocks that would be on a full backup if it were to create one in the traditional way. It simply copies each of those files from one medium to another. This method will work with tape or disk as long as multiple devices are available.

The big advantage of this method of creating a synthetic full backup is that this process can be run any time of day without any impact to the backup clients, because the servers or VMs for which you are creating the synthetic full backup are completely uninvolved. When complete, the resulting backup usually looks identical to a traditional full backup, and subsequent incremental backups can be based on that full backup.

There are two downsides to this method, the first of which is that the process of copying data can take quite a bit of time but, as already mentioned, you can do it anytime, even in the middle of the day. The other downside is that it can also create quite an I/O load on disk systems being used as a source and target for this backup. This wasn't so much of a problem in the tape world, because the source and target devices were obviously separate devices. But if you have a single target deduplication appliance, a synthetic full backup created with this method is the I/O equivalent of a full restore and a full backup at the same time. How much this affects your appliance will depend on the appliance.

Virtual synthetic full.   There is another approach to synthetic full backups that is only possible with target deduplication systems (explained in more detail in Chapters 5 and 12). In a target deduplication system, all backups are broken into small chunks to identify which chunks are redundant.[3] Each chunk is then stored as a separate object in the target dedupe appliance's storage, resulting in each changed file or block being represented by many small chunks stored in the target deduplication system. This means that it is possible for this appliance to pretend to create a full backup by creating a new backup that simply points to blocks from other backups.

This method does require integration with the backup product. Although the dedupe system may indeed be able to create a full backup without the backup product, the backup product wouldn't know about it and wouldn't be able to use it for restores or to base incremental backups on. So the backup product tells the target deduplication system to create a *virtual synthetic full* backup, after which it creates one pretty much instantaneously. There is no data movement, so this method is very efficient, but it may be limited to certain backup types, such as VMs, filesystem backups, and certain supported databases.

Incremental forever.   The idea of a synthetic full backup is to use various ways to create something that behaves like a full backup without actually having to do another full backup. Newer backup systems have been created from the ground up to never again need another full backup, synthetic or otherwise. Although early implementations of this idea did occur in the tape world, the idea of *incremental forever* (also called forever incremental) backups really took off in the world of disk backups.

A true incremental forever is only feasible when using disk as your primary target, because the backup system will need to access all backups at the same time for it to

---

3 A chunk is some collections of bytes. Most people use the term *chunk* versus block, because blocks tend to be a fixed size, and chunks can be any size. Some dedupe systems even use variable-sized chunks.

work. Another change is that backup cannot be stored inside an opaque container (e.g., tar or a proprietary backup format), as most backup products can. (Please do not confuse this term *container* with Docker containers. I just don't have a better word.) Instead, the backup system will store each changed item from the latest incremental backup as a separate object, typically in an object-storage system.

This will work whether your incremental forever backup software product backs up entire files, parts of files, or blocks of data (as discussed in "Block-level incremental backup" on page 64). Your backup software would store each object separately—even the smallest object (e.g., file, subfile, block, or chunk)—allowing it to access all backups as one big collection.

During each incremental backup, the backup system will also see the current status of each server, VM, or application it backs up, and it knows where all the blocks are that represent its current state (i.e., the full backup). It doesn't need to do anything other than hold on to that information. When it's time for a restore, it just needs to know where all the objects that represent a full backup are and deliver them to the restore process. This means that all backups will be incremental backups, but every backup will behave as a full backup from a restore perspective, without having to do any data movement to create that full backup.

This backup method creates a full backup every day without any of the downsides of doing that, or doing it with synthetic full backups. The only real downside to this approach is that it needs to be built into the backup system from the beginning. It only works if the backup system is built from scratch to never again look for a full backup, synthetic or otherwise..

Do Backup Levels Matter?

Backup levels are really a throwback to a bygone era, and they matter much less than they used to. When I first started my backup job in the early '90s, backup levels mattered a lot. You wanted to do a full backup every week and a cumulative incremental (all changes since the full) every day if you could get away with it. Doing backups that way meant you needed two tapes to do a restore. It also meant that much of the changed data was on multiple tapes, since each cumulative incremental was often backing up many of the files that were on the previous cumulative incremental. This method was popular when I was literally hand-swapping tapes into a drive when I needed to do a restore, so you really wanted to minimize the number of tapes you had to grab from the tape drawer (or bring back from Iron Mountain), because you had to swap them in and out of the drive until the restore was done. Who wanted to do that with 30 tapes (what you would need to do if you did monthly full backups)?

Move forward just a few years, and commercial backup software and robotic tape libraries really took over. I didn't have to swap tapes for a restore, but there was one downside to a restore that needed a lot of tapes. If the robot had to swap 30 tapes in and out for a restore, it would add about 45 minutes to the process. This was because it took 90 seconds on average to load the tape and get to the first byte of data. I modified my typical setup to use a monthly backup, daily typical incremental backups, and a weekly cumulative incremental backup. This meant a worst-case restore would need eight tapes, which would add about 12 minutes instead of 45. And that's how things were for a really long time.

For those who have moved on from tape as a target for backups, most of the reasons we did various levels of backups no longer apply. Even doing a full backup every day doesn't waste storage if you're using a good target deduplication system. There is also no loading of 30 incremental backup tapes when all your backups are on disk. Finally, there are newer backup systems that really only do one backup level: block-level incremental. This is all to say that the more you are using disk and other modern technologies, the less the previous section should matter to you.

What Is the Archive Bit in Windows?

The archive bit is a flag set on files in Windows. If the "ready for archiving" bit is set on a file in Windows, it indicates that a file is new or changed and that it should be backed up in an incremental backup. Once this happens, the archive bit is cleared.

The first problem I have with the archive bit is that it should be called the backup bit, because, as I mentioned in Chapter 3, backups are not archives. But the real issue I have is that the first backup program to back up the directory will clear the archive bit, and the next program will not back up the same file. If a regular user uses some third-party backup tool to back up their own files, it will clear the archive bit, and the corporate backup system in charge of backing up those files will not back them up. They don't appear to be in need of backup, because the archive bit is not set. So any user can defeat the purpose of the entire backup system.

I've never been a fan of the archive bit. The good news is that it's pretty much a non-factor in most datacenter backups, because backups are running at a VM level. The archive bit is not being used to decide what gets backed up. #Winning

---

Metrics

You need to determine and monitor a number of metrics when designing and maintaining a data protection system. They determine everything from how you design the system to how you tell whether the system is doing what it's designed to do. Metrics also determine how much compute and storage capacity you are using and how much you have left before you have to buy additional capacity.

Recovery Metrics

There are no more important metrics than those having to do with recovery. No one cares how long it takes you to back up; they only care how long it takes to restore. There are really only two metrics that determine whether your backup system is doing its job: how fast you can restore and how much data you lose when you do restore. This section explains these metrics and how they are determined and measured.

Recovery time objective (RTO)

The recovery time objective (RTO) is the amount of time, agreed to by all parties, that a restore should take after some kind of incident requiring a restore. The length of an acceptable RTO for any given organization is typically driven by the amount of money it will lose when systems are down.

If a company determines it will lose millions of dollars of sales per hour during downtime, it will typically want a very tight RTO. Companies such as financial trading firms, for example, seek to have an RTO as close to zero as possible. Organizations that can tolerate longer periods of computer downtime might have an RTO measured in weeks. The important thing is that the RTO must match the needs of the organization.

Calculating an RTO for a governmental organization, or a nonprofit company, can be a bit more problematic. They will most likely not lose revenue if they are down for a period of time. One thing they might need to calculate, however, is the amount of overtime they may have to pay to catch up if a prolonged outage occurs.

There is no need to have a single RTO across the entire organization. It is perfectly normal and reasonable to have a tighter RTO for more critical applications and a more relaxed RTO for the rest of the datacenter.

It's important when calculating an RTO to understand that the clock starts when the incident happens, and stops when the application is completely online and business has returned to normal. Too many people focused on backup think the RTO is the amount of time they have to restore data, but this is definitely not the case. The actual process of copying data from backups to the recovered system is actually a small part of the activities that have to take place to recover from something that would take out an application. A hardware order might have to be placed, or some other contract or logistical issue might have to be resolved before you can actually begin a restore. In addition, additional things might have to happen after you perform your restore before the application is ready for the public. So remember when determining your RTO that it's much more than just the restore that you have to make time for.

Remember that RTO is the *objective*. Whether you can meet that objective is a different issue explained in "Recovery time actual and recovery point actual" on page 70. But first we need to talk about RPO, or recovery point objective.

Recovery point objective (RPO)

RPO is the amount of acceptable data loss after a large incident, measured in time. For example, if we agree we can lose one hour's worth of data, we have agreed to a one-hour RPO. Like the RTO, it is perfectly normal to have multiple RPOs throughout the organization, depending on the criticality of different datasets.

Most organizations, however, settle on values that are much higher than an hour, such as 24 hours or more. This is primarily because the smaller your RPO, the more frequently you must run your backup system. There's not much point in agreeing to a one-hour RPO and then only running backups once a day. The best you will be able to do with such a system is a 24-hour RPO, and that's being optimistic.

Negotiating your RPO and RTO

Many organizations might want a very tight RTO and RPO. In fact, almost every RTO and RPO conversation I have participated in started with a question of what the organization wanted for these values. The response was almost always an RTO and RPO of zero. This means that if a disaster occurred, the business/operational unit wants you to resume operations with no down time and no loss of data. Not only is that not technically possible even with the best of systems, it would be incredibly expensive to do.

Therefore, a response to such a request should be the proposed cost of the system required to meet that request. If the organization can justify an RTO and RPO of 0—or anything close to those values—they should be able to back it up with a spreadsheet showing the potential cost of an outage to the organization.

There can then be a negotiation between what is technically feasible and affordable (as determined by the organization) and what is currently happening with the disaster recovery system. Please don't just take whatever RTO and RPO you are given and then just ignore it. Please also don't make up an RTO and RPO without consulting the business/operational units because you think they're going to ask for something unreasonable. This conversation is an important one and it needs to happen, which is why Chapter 2 is dedicated to it.

Recovery time actual and recovery point actual

The *recovery point actual* (RPA) and *recovery time actual* (RTA) metrics are measured only if a recovery occurs, whether real or via a test. The RTO and RPO are objectives; the RPA and RTA measure the degree to which you met those objectives after a restore. It is important to measure this and compare it against the RTO and RPO to evaluate whether you need to consider a redesign of your backup-and-recovery system.

The reality is that most organizations' RTA and RPA are nowhere near the agreed-upon RTO and RPO for the organization. What's important is to bring this reality to light and acknowledge it. Either we adjust the RTO and RPO, or we redesign the backup system. There is no point in having a tight RTO or RPO if the RTA and RPA are nowhere near it.

 Consecutive backup failures happen a lot in the real world, and that can affect your RPA. One rule of thumb I use to ensure backup failures don't impact my RPA is to determine backup frequency by dividing the RPO by three. For example, a three-day RPO would require a backup frequency of one day. That way, you can have up to two consecutive backup failures without missing your RPO. Of course if your backup system is only capable of performing daily backups as the most frequent, that would mean that your RPA would be three days if you had two consecutive backup failures that were not addressed. Since consecutive backup failures often happen in the real world, the typical RPO of 24 hours will rarely be met unless you are able to back up more often than once a day.

—Stuart Liddle

Testing recoveries

This is a perfect time to point out that you must test recoveries. The reason for this is that most organizations rarely get to fire their backup system in anger; therefore, they must pretend to do so on a regular basis. You will have no idea how your backup system actually performs if you don't test it.

You won't know how reliable your backup system is if you don't test it with recoveries. You won't know what kind of resources a large-scale recovery uses and how much it tasks the rest of the environment. You won't have any idea what your RTA and RPA are if you don't occasionally perform a large restore and see how long it takes and how much data you lose.

I will be talking about success metrics in a few pages. Backup success is an important metric, but there will always be failed backups. If your system is doing what it is supposed to be doing, frequent restores will show a restore success of 100% (or at least close to it). Advertising this metric will help build confidence in your recovery system.

Having participated in a few large-scale recoveries where I didn't know the system capabilities very well, I can tell you the first question you are going to get is, "How long will this take?" If you haven't been doing regular test restores, you will not be able to answer that question. That means you'll be sitting there with knots in your stomach the whole time, not knowing what to tell senior management.

Be as familiar with restores as you are with backups. The only way to do that is testing.

Capacity Metrics

Whether you use an on-premises or cloud-based system, you need to monitor the amount of storage, compute, and network available to you and adjust your design and settings as necessary. As you will see in these sections, this is one area where a cloud-based system can really excel.

License/workload usage

Your backup product or service has a set number of licenses for each thing you are backing up. You should track your utilization of those licenses so you know when you will run out of them.

Closely related to this is simply tracking the number of workloads you are backing up. Although this may not result in a license issue, it is another metric that can show you growth of your backup system.

Storage capacity and usage

Let's start with a very basic metric: Does your backup system have enough storage capacity to meet your current and future backup and recovery needs? Does your DR system have sufficient storage and compute capacity to take over from the primary datacenter in case of disaster? Can it do this while also conducting backups? Whether you are talking about a tape library or a storage array, your storage system has a finite amount of capacity, and you need to monitor that capacity and the percentage of it that you're using over time.

Failing to monitor storage usage and capacity can result in you being forced to make emergency decisions that might go against your organization's policies. For example, the only way to create additional capacity without purchasing more is to delete older backups. It would be a shame if failure to monitor the capacity of your storage system resulted in the inability to meet the retention requirements your organization has set.

This is a lot easier if the storage you are using in the cloud is object storage. Both object and block storage have virtually unlimited capacity in the cloud, but only object storage automatically grows to meet your needs. If your backup system requires you to create block-based volumes in the cloud, you will still have to monitor capacity, because you will need to create and grow virtual volumes to handle the growth of your data. This is not a requirement if you are using object storage.

Besides the downsides of having to create, manage, monitor, and grow these volumes, there is also the difference in how they are charged. Cloud block volumes are priced based on provisioned capacity, not used capacity. Object storage, on the other hand, only charges you for the number of gigabytes you store in a given month.

Throughput capacity and usage

Typical backup systems have the ability to accept a certain volume of backups per day, usually measured in megabytes per second or terabytes per hour. You should be aware of this number and make sure you monitor your backup system's usage of it. Failure to do so can result in backups taking longer and stretching into the work day. As with storage capacity utilization, failure to monitor this metric may force you to make emergency decisions that might go against your organization's policies.

Monitoring the throughput capacity and usage of tape is particularly important. As I will discuss in more detail in "Tape Drives" on page 257, it is very important for the throughput of your backups to match the throughput of your tape drive's ability to transfer data. Specifically, the throughput that you supply to your tape drive should be more than the tape drive's minimum speed. Failure to do so will result in device failure and backup failure. Consult the documentation for the drive and the vendor's support system to find out what the minimum acceptable speed is, and try to get as close to that as possible. It is unlikely that you'll approach the maximum speed of the tape drive, but you should also monitor for that.

This is one area where the cloud offers both an upside and a downside. The upside is that the throughput of the cloud is virtually unlimited (like cloud-based object storage), assuming the cloud-based product or service you are using can scale its use of the bandwidth available to it. If, for example, their design uses standard backup software running in a VM in the cloud, you will be limited to the throughput of that VM, and you will need to upgrade the type of VM (because different VM types get different levels of bandwidth). At some point, though, you will reach the limits of what your backup software can do with one VM and will need to add additional VMs to add additional bandwidth. Some systems can automatically add bandwidth as your needs grow.

One downside of using the cloud as your backup destination is that *your* site's bandwidth is not unlimited, nor is the number of hours in a day. Even with byte-level replication or source-side deduplication (explained later in this chapter), the possibility is that you might exceed your site's upload bandwidth. This will require you to upgrade bandwidth or, potentially, change designs or vendors. (The bandwidth required by different vendors is not the same.)

Compute capacity and usage

The capability of your backup system is also driven by the ability of the compute system behind it. If the processing capability of the backup servers or the database behind the backup system is unable to keep up, it can also slow down your backups and result in them slipping into the work day. You should also monitor the performance of your backup system to see the degree to which this is happening.

Once again, this is another area where the cloud can help—if your backup system is designed for the cloud. If so, it can automatically scale the amount of compute necessary to get the job done. Some can even scale the compute up and down throughout the day, lowering the overall cost of ownership by lowering the number of VMs, containers, or serverless processes that are used.

Unfortunately, many backup systems and services running in the cloud are using the same software that you would run in your datacenter. Because the concept of automatically adding additional compute was really born in the cloud, backup software products written for the datacenter do not have this concept. That means that if you run out of compute on the backend, you will need to add additional compute manually, and the licenses that go with it, yourself.

Backup Window

A traditional backup system has a significant impact on the performance of your primary systems during backup. Traditional backup systems perform a series of full and incremental backups, each of which can take quite a toll on the systems being backed up. Of course, the full backups will take a toll because they back up everything. Incremental backups are also a challenge if they are what are called *full-file incrementals*, meaning the system backs up the entire file even if only one byte has changed. It changes the modification bit in Linux or the archive bit in Windows, and the whole file gets backed up. Since the typical backup can really affect the performance of the backed-up systems, you should agree in advance on the time you are allowed to run backups, referred to as the *backup window*.

Back in the day, a typical backup window for me was 6 p.m. to 6 a.m. Monday to Thursday, and from 6 p.m. Friday to 6 a.m. Monday. This was for a typical work environment where most people were not working on the weekends, and fewer people were using the systems at night.

If you have a backup window, you need to monitor how much you are filling it up. If you are coming close to filling up the entire window with backups, it's time either to reevaluate the window or redesign the backup system.

I also feel that you should assign a window to your backup products and just let it do the scheduling within that window. Some people try to overengineer their backup system, scheduling thousands of individual backups with their external scheduler. I have never found a situation in which an external scheduler can be as efficient with backup resources as the included scheduler. I think it's more efficient and a whole lot less tedious. But I'm sure someone reading this will feel completely different.

Organizations that use backup techniques that fall into the incremental forever category (e.g., continuous data protection [CDP], near-CDP, block-level incremental backups, or source-side deduplication backups, all of which are explained elsewhere in this book) don't typically have to worry about a backup window. This is because these backups typically run for very short periods (i.e., a few minutes) and transfer a small amount of data (i.e., a few megabytes). These methods usually have a very low performance impact on primary systems or at least less of a performance impact than the typical setup of occasional full backups and daily full-file incremental backups. This is why customers using such systems typically perform backups throughout the day, as often as once an hour or even every five minutes. A true CDP system actually runs continuously, transferring each new byte as it's written. (Technically, if it *isn't* running completely continuously, it's not a continuous data protection system. Just saying.)

Backup and Recovery Success and Failure

Someone should be keeping track of how many backups and recoveries you perform and what percentage of them is successful. Although you should shoot for 100% of both, that is highly unlikely, especially for backup. You should definitely monitor this metric, though, and look at it over time. Although the backup system will rarely be perfect, looking at it over time can tell you whether things are getting better or worse.

It's also important for any backup or recovery failures to be addressed. If a backup or restore is successfully rerun, you can at least cross the failed one off your list of concerns. However, it's still important to keep track of those failures for trending purposes.

Retention

Although not technically a metric, retention is one of the things that are monitored in your backup and archive system. You should ensure that the defined retention policies are being adhered to.

Like RTO and RPO, the retention settings of your data protection system should be determined by the organization. No one in IT should be determining how long backups or archives should be kept; this should be determined by legal requirements, organizational requirements, and regulatory requirements.

Another thing to mention when discussing retention is how long things should be kept on each tier of storage. Gone are the days when all backups and archives were kept on tape. In fact, most of today's backups are not kept on tape; they are kept on disk. Disk has a variety of classes from a performance and cost perspective. Retention should also specify how long things should be kept on each tier.

Once you determine your retention policies, you should also review whether your data protection system is adhering to the policies that have been determined. (I'm referring here to the organization's policies, not the settings of the backup system.) Determine what your retention policies are and document them. Then periodically review your backup and archive systems to make sure that the retention policies that have been set within these systems match the policies that you determined for your organization. Adjust and report as necessary.

The Right to Be Forgotten

Closely related to retention is the idea of the *right to be forgotten* (formally, the *right to erasure*), which was popularized by the EU's GDPR and the CCPA. The concept is relatively simple: Your personal information is yours, and you should have the right to say who can have it. If you withdraw your consent from a company, or if it never had it to begin with, it is supposed to erase all of your personal information from its systems.

Here's food for thought: How do you address that in a backup system? Backup systems are made to remember, and you're asking it to forget. I brought this issue up when the GDPR first went into effect, but I've never seen guidance on what this means. Are backups excluded from the right to erasure? How, exactly, would you go about deleting such data from backups? If you can't delete such data from backups, how do you address restores? What happens if you accidentally restore a database that has deleted people in it?

I don't yet have answers to most of these questions. At this point, I just think the questions need to be asked. It would be nice if the GDPR Commission and others requiring erasure would clarify this issue.

Using Metrics

One of the ways you can increase the confidence in your backup system is to document and publish all the metrics mentioned here. Let your management know the degree to which your backup system is performing as designed. Let them know how many backups and recoveries you perform, and how well they perform and how long it will be before they need to buy additional capacity. Above all, make sure that they are aware of your backup and recovery system's ability to meet your agreed-upon RTO and RPO. Hiding your RTA and RPA will do no one any good if there is an outage.

I remember knowing what our company's RTO and RPO were and knowing our RTA and RPA were nowhere near those numbers. We had a four-hour RTO and I could barely get tapes back from our vaulting vendor in that time. The restore itself for a full server was usually longer than four hours, and I knew that the restore couldn't start until we replaced the hardware that had been damaged. I remember that we all just laughed at these metrics. Don't do that. Figure 4-2 spells this out perfectly.

Figure 4-2. Don't be a Curtis

Be the person in the room bold enough to raise your hand in a meeting and point out that the RTO and RPO are nowhere near the RTA and RPA. Push for a change in the objectives or the system. Either way, you win.

Speaking of meetings, I'd like to dispel a few myths about backup and archive that you're likely to hear in them. I hope these will allow you to respond to them in real time.

Backup and Archive Myths

There are many myths in the backup and archive space. I have argued every one of the myths in this section countless times with people in person and even more people on the internet. People are convinced of a particular idea and, often, no number of facts seems to change their mind, but this is my response to these myths:

You don't need to back up RAID.
> Redundant disk systems do not obviate the need for backup. You would think that this wouldn't have to be debated, but it comes up way more often than you might think. RAID in all of its forms and levels, as well as RAID-like technologies like erasure coding, only protects against physical device failure. Different levels of RAID protect against different types of device failures, but in the end, RAID was designed to provide redundancy in the hardware itself. It was never designed to replace backup for one very important reason: RAID protects the volume, not the filesystem on top of the volume. If you delete a file, get ransomware and have the file encrypted, or drop a table in a database that you didn't mean to drop, RAID can do nothing to help you. This is why you back up data on a RAID array, no matter what level.

A friend of mine was using NT4 Workstation on a RAID1 array, but didn't have any backups, because it was RAID1, and therefore "safe". He was a database administrator (DBA), and a semi-professional photographer, with many thousands of photos on the same partition as the OS. A patch for the OS corrupted his filesystem due to a driver incompatibility, but his drives were fine. He lost all of his photos to this myth. I tried to help him recover, but the tools I had available were of no use.

—Kurt Buff

You don't need to back up replicated data.

The answer to this is really the same as the section on RAID. Replication, no matter how many times you do it, replicates everything, not just the good things. If bad things happen to the data sitting on your replicated volume, the replication will simply copy those things over to another location. In fact, I often make the joke that replication doesn't fix your error or stop the virus; it just makes your error or the virus more efficient. It will replicate your mistake or virus anywhere you told it to. Where this comes up these days is in multinode, sharded databases like Cassandra and MongoDB. Some DBAs of these products mentioned that every shard is replicated to at least three nodes, so it should be able to survive multiple node failures. That is true, but what happens if you drop a table that you didn't mean to drop? All the replication in the world will not fix that. This is why you must back up replicated data.

You don't need to back up IaaS and PaaS.

I don't typically get into too many arguments with people who think they don't need to back up their public cloud infrastructure. IaaS and PaaS vendors often provide facilities for you to be able to do your own backup, but I don't know any that back up on your behalf. Cloud resources are wonderful and infinitely scalable. Many of them also have high-availability features built in. But just like replication and RAID, high availability has nothing to do with what happens when you make a mistake or are attacked, or the datacenter becomes a crater from an explosion.

The main point I want to make here is that it is really important to get your cloud backups out of your cloud account and the region where they were created. Yes, I know it's harder. Yes, I know it might even cost a little bit more to do it this way. But leaving your backups in the same account that created them and storing them in the same region as the resources you are protecting doesn't follow the 3-2-1 rule. Read the sidebar "There's a New One" on page 46 to learn what can happen when you don't do this.

You don't need to back up SaaS

I argue this myth two or three times a week at this point. Everyone seems to think that backups either should be or already are included as part of the service when you contract a SaaS vendor like Microsoft 365 or Google Workspace. But here's a really important fact: such services are almost never included in the major SaaS vendors. If you doubt me, try to find the words *backup, recovery*, or *restore* in your service contract. Try also to find the word *backup* in the documentation for the product. I have searched for all of these, and I find nothing that meets the basic definition of backup, which is the 3-2-1 rule. At best, these products offer *convenience restore* features that use versioning and recycle bins and things like that, which are not protected against a catastrophic failure or attack. This topic is covered in more detail in "Software-as-a-Service (SaaS)" on page 166.

Backups should be stored for many years

Chapter 3 gives a solid definition of backup and archive. Backup products are not usually designed to do the job of archive. If your backup product requires you to know the hostname, application name, directory name and tablename, and a single date to initiate a restore, then that is a traditional backup product and not one designed to do retrievals. If you can search for information by a different context, such as who wrote the email, what words were in the email or the subject line, and a *range* of dates—*and you don't need to know the server it came from*—then your backup product can do retrievals, and you can go read a different myth.

But most of you are dealing with a backup product that only knows how to do backups and restores, which means it doesn't know how to do archives and retrievals. (Again, if you don't know the difference, you really need to read Chapter 3, which goes into this topic in detail.) If your backup product doesn't know how to do retrievals and you're storing backups for several years, you are asking for trouble. Because if the data is accessible to you and you get an e-discovery request, you will legally be required to satisfy that request. If what you have is a backup product and not an archive product, you are looking at a potentially multimillion-dollar process to satisfy a single e-discovery request. If you think I'm exaggerating, read the sidebar "Backups Make Really Expensive Archives" on page 81.

Most restores are from the past 24 hours. I've done an awful lot of restores in my career, and very few of them have been from any time except the past few days, and even fewer were older than the past few weeks. I personally like to set the retention of the backup system to 18 months, which accounts for a file that you only use once a year and didn't realize it was deleted or corrupted last year.

After that, things get a lot more complicated. Server names change, application names change, and you don't even know where the file is anymore. The file might also be incompatible with the current version of software you're running. This is especially true in database backups.

If you have an organizational need to keep data for many years, you need a system that is capable of that. If you are one of the rare organizations using a backup system that is truly capable of both backup and archive, go in peace. But if you are one of the many organizations using your backup system to hold data for seven years or—God forbid—forever, please seriously reconsider that policy. You are asking for trouble.

Tape is dead

I haven't personally used a tape drive to make a backup in several years. I haven't designed a new backup system to use tape drives as its initial backup target in at least 10 years, probably more. With very few exceptions, tape is pretty much dead to me as an initial target for backups for all the reasons discussed in "Tape Drives" on page 257. (I will consider using it as a target for a copy of a backup, which I go into in Chapter 9.)

I don't have this opinion because I think the tape is unreliable. As I discuss in the aforementioned "Tape Drives" section, I think tape is fundamentally incompatible with how we do backups today. Tapes want to go much faster than typical backups run, and the incompatibility between these two processes creates the unreliability that some people believe tape drives have.

The irony is that tape drives are actually better at writing ones and zeros than disk is; they're also better than disk at holding on to ones and zeros for longer periods. But trying to make a tape drive that wants to go 1 GB a second happy with a backup that is running a few dozen megabytes per second is simply impossible.

And yet, more tape is sold today than ever before. Giant tape libraries are being sold left and right, and those tape libraries are storing something. As I said elsewhere, the worst-kept secret in cloud computing is that these big cloud vendors buy a lot of tape libraries. So what is all this tape being used for?

I think the perfect use for tape is long-term archives. Don't try to send an incremental backup directly to tape; you are asking for trouble. But if you happen to create a large archive of a few terabytes of data and you have it stored on disk right next to that tape drive, you should have no problem streaming that archive directly to tape and keeping that tape drive happy. The tape drive will reliably write that data to tape and hold on to that data for a really long time. You can create three or more copies for next to nothing and distribute those copies around the world as well.

Tape is an incredibly inexpensive medium. Not only is the medium, and the drives that create it, incredibly inexpensive, the power and cooling of a tape library costs much less than the power and cooling of a disk system. In fact, a disk system would cost more *even if the disks themselves were free*. (Over time, the power and cooling costs of the disk drives will outweigh the power and cooling costs and the purchase cost of the tape drives.)

You are probably using more tape than you think if you are using very inexpensive object storage in the cloud. I don't know this for a fact, but the behavior of many of these systems sounds an awful lot like tape. So although tape may be retiring from the backup and recovery business, it has a long life in the long-term storage business.

I have one final thought on the subject. I had a conversation recently with a fellow IT person. He was explaining to me how they had datacenters on a Caribbean island that didn't have good internet, so they did not feel that cloud-based backup was a way to safeguard their data, because they just don't have the bandwidth for it. Thus, they use disk backups to create an on-premises backup that is then replicated to an off-premises array, which is then copied to tape and sent to Iron Mountain. I said the chances that they would ever actually use that tape are next to none, and then he reminded me of a hurricane that just took out that entire island not that long ago. Tapes were all they had. Like I said, tapes are not dead.

Now that those myths are out of the way, let's continue our journey through the basics of backup and recovery. The next thing to think about is the unit you will be backing up. Will you back up individual items (e.g., files) or entire images?

Backups Make Really Expensive Archives

I worked with a customer many years ago who received a single electronic discovery request for emails that matched a particular set of criteria during a period of three years. This customer didn't have an email archive system, but they did have a weekly full backup of Exchange for the past three years.

If they'd had an email archive, they could've done a single request that said something like this: show me all the emails for the past three years written by Curtis that say the phrase "3-2-1 rule." They would soon be presented with a downloadable PST file that they could hand to the lawyers.

But they didn't have an email archive system; they had a backup system. So here's what they had to do:

1. Set the restore time frame to 156 weeks ago (three years).
2. Perform an alternate-server Microsoft Exchange restore (a very complicated task indeed) of the entire Exchange server from 156 weeks ago.

3. Search Curtis's Sent Items folder for any emails written in the past week with the phrase "3-2-1 rule."

4. Subtract 1 from the current number of weeks (156 −1 = 155).

5. Repeat steps 2–4 *155 more times*.

We were able to do three restores at a time. Each restore took a long time and had to be executed by someone who really knew what they were doing. (Alternate server Exchange restores are no joke.) A team of consultants, hired specifically for the task, worked 24 hours a day for several months to accomplish it. It cost the client $2 million in consulting fees.

Like I said, backups make really expensive archives.

Item- Versus Image-Level Backups

There are two very different ways to back up a server: *item-level backup* and *image-level backup*. Item level is usually called file level, although you are not always backing up files. (It might be objects.) Image level is currently most popular when backing up virtualized environments. They both come with their own advantages and disadvantages.

Item-Level Backup

An item-level backup backs up discrete collections of information that are addressed as individual items, and the most common type of item is a file. In fact, if this section were being written several years ago, this would most likely be called *file-level backup*.

The other type of item that might be included in an item-level backup is an object in an object-storage system. For many environments, objects are similar to files in that most organizations using object storage are simply using it to hold on to what would otherwise be files, but since they are being stored in an object storage system, they are not files, because files are stored in a filesystem. The contents are often the same, but they get a different name because they are stored differently.

You typically perform item-level backup if you are running a backup agent inside the server or VM itself. The backup agent is deciding which files to back up by first looking at the filesystem, such as `C:\Users` or `/Users`. If you are performing a full backup, it will back up all the files in the filesystem. If you are performing an incremental backup, it will be backing up files that have changed since the last backup. You are also performing an item-level backup if you are backing up your object-storage system, such as Amazon S3, Azure Blob, or Google Cloud Storage. The idea of whether to back up object storage is covered in "Object storage in the cloud" on page 161.

The advantage of an item-level backup is that it is very easy to understand. Install a backup agent in the appropriate place, and it will examine your file or object-storage system, find all the items, and back them up at the appropriate time.

Image-Level Backups

An image-level backup is the result of backing up either a physical or virtual device at the block level, creating an *image* of the entire drive. This is why, depending on your frame of reference, image-level backups are also referred to as drive-level, volume-level, or VM-level backups. The device could be storing a variety of information types, including a standard filesystem, block storage for a database, or even the boot volume for a physical or virtual machine. Within an image-level backup, you're backing up the building blocks of the filesystem rather than backing up the files themselves.

Prior to the advent of virtualization, image-level backups were rare because backing up the physical drive was a lot harder and required unmounting the filesystem while you backed up the blocks. Otherwise, you risked a contaminated backup, where some of the blocks would be from one point in time and some of the blocks would be from another point in time. Virtual snapshot technology, such as is found in Windows Volume Shadow Services (VSS) or VMware snapshots, solved this underlying problem.

Backing up at the volume level became much more popular once VMs came on the scene. Image-level backups allow you to perform a backup of a VM at the hypervisor level, where your backup software runs outside the VM and sees the VM as one or more images (e.g., VMDK files in VMware).

Backing up at the image level has a number of advantages. First, it provides faster backups and much faster restores. Image-level backups avoid the overhead of the file- or object-storage system and go directly to the underlying storage. Image-level restores can be much faster because file-level backups require restoring each file individually, which requires creating a file in the filesystem, a process that comes with quite a bit of overhead. This problem really rears its ugly head when restoring very dense filesystems with millions of files, when the process of creating the files during the restore actually takes longer than the process of transferring the data into the files. Image-level restores do not have this problem because they are writing the data straight to the drive at the block level.

Once the changing block issue was addressed with snapshots, backup systems were presented with the second biggest challenge of image-level backups: incremental backups. When you are backing up at the drive, volume, or image level, every file is a full backup. For example, consider a VM represented by a virtual machine disk (VMDK) file. If that VM is running and a single block in the VM changes, the modification time on that image will show that it has changed. A subsequent backup will then back up the entire VMDK file, even though only a few blocks of data might have changed.

This challenge has also been solved in the VM world via *changed-block tracking* (CBT), which is a process that keeps track of when a previous backup was created, and the blocks that have changed since that last backup. This allows an image-level backup to perform a block-level incremental backup by using this protocol to ask which blocks have changed and then copying only those blocks.

File-Level Recovery from an Image-Level Backup

This leaves us with one final disadvantage of backing up at the image level, and that is the lack of item-level recovery. Customers do not typically want to restore an entire VM; they want to restore a file or two within that VM. How do you restore a single file from a VM when you backed up the entire VM as a single image? This is also a problem that has been solved by many backup software companies. For example, in the case of a VMware VM, they understand the format of VMDK files, which allows them to do a number of things.

One option that some backup products allow you to do is mount the original VMDK files as a virtual volume that can be made available by the file explorer on the backup server or any client where the backup software runs. The customer can then drag and drop whatever file(s) they are looking for from that image and tell the backup software to unmount it. In this case, the image is usually mounted read-only, facilitating these drag-and-drop type restores. (Mounting the VM image read-write and actually running the VM from that image is called *instant recovery* and is covered in Chapter 9.)

Other backup software products can index the images ahead of time, so they know which files use which blocks within the image. This allows these products to support regular file-level restores from these images without requiring the customer to mount the image and manually grab the files. The customer would use the same workflow they always use to select files for restore, and the backup system would do whatever it needs to do in the background to restore the files in question.

Combining Image- and File-Level Backups

Most customers are performing image-level backups of their VMs while still retaining the ability to perform both incremental backups and item-level restores. They also want block-level incremental backups, which are actually much more efficient than item-level incremental backups.

Backing up at the VM level (i.e., image level) also comes with the potential to restore the VM easily as a single image. This makes what we used to call *bare-metal recovery* so much easier than it was. You get all the bare-metal recovery capabilities you need without having to jump through hoops to address the changing block issues historically found in image-level backups.

We even have image-level backups of physical Windows servers, since most people are using Windows VSS to create a snapshot of each filesystem prior to backing it up. This allows the backup software product to back up at the image level without risking data corruption.

Once you've decided what you're backing up, you need to know how the things to be backed up are selected by the backup product. This section is very important, because picking the wrong method can create significant gaps in your backup system.

Backup Selection Methods

Understanding how systems, directories, and databases are included in the backup system is the key to making sure that the files you think are being backed up are indeed being backed up. No one wants to find out the system or database they thought was protected wasn't protected at all.

One caveat, though. Your backup selection methods only work once your backup system knows about the systems being backed up. That means the first step toward this goal is making sure servers and services you want backed up are registered with your backup and recovery system.

For example, if you start using a new SaaS such as Salesforce, the backup system will not automatically notice that addition and start backing it up for you. If you are fully virtualized on VMware and your backup system is connected to vCenter, systems will automatically notice if you add a new node to the configuration. But if you start using Hyper-V or kernel virtual machine (KVM), the backup system will not automatically notice there is a new hypervisor in the datacenter and start backing it up. And of course your backup system will not notice you installed a new physical server. So these selection methods come with this caveat.

Selective Inclusion Versus Selective Exclusion

There are two very broad categories of how items can be included in a backup system: *selective inclusion* and *selective exclusion*.

In selective inclusion, the administrator individually specifies which filesystems, databases, or objects the backup system will back up. For example, if an administrator says they want to back up just the D:\ drive, or just the Apollo database, they are practicing selective inclusion.

In selective exclusion, AKA *automatic inclusion*, an administrator specifies backing up everything on the server except what is specifically excluded. For example, an administrator might select all filesystems except for /tmp on a Linux system or a user's iTunes or Movies directories on a Windows laptop.

It's very common for administrators to think they administer systems in such a way that there is no point in backing up the operating system. They know they want to back up C:\Users on a Windows laptop, /Users on a MacBook, or something like /data or /home on a Linux system. They see no point in backing up the operating system or applications, so they manually select just the filesystems they want to back up. The same is true of databases. They might not want your backup test databases, so they selectively include which databases to back up.

The problem with selective inclusion is configuration changes. Every time a new database or filesystem with data is added to a system, someone needs to change the backup configuration; otherwise, the new resource will never be backed up. This is why selective inclusion is much less safe than selective exclusion.

With selective exclusion, the worst possible side effect is that you might back up some worthless data (assuming you forgot to exclude it). Compare this to the worst possible side effect of selective inclusion, in which important data is completely excluded from the backup system. There is simply no comparison between the two. Selective inclusion may appear to save money because less data is stored, but it's much riskier.

It is easy to exclude data that you know to be worthless, such as /tmp or /temp on a Linux system. If you see no reason to back up the operating system, you might also exclude /, /user, /usr, /var, and /opt, although I would back up those directories. On a Windows system, you could exclude C:\Windows and C:\Program Files if you really don't want to back up the OS and application programs.

One thing to consider, though, is the effect deduplication might have on this decision. It's one thing to know you are backing up hundreds or thousands of filesystems that have no value, and wasting valuable storage space on your disk array or tape library. But what if the operating system that you are spending so much time excluding is actually only stored once?

Deduplication would ensure that only one copy of the Windows or Linux operating system is actually stored in your backup system. Considering this, perhaps you could just leave the backup system at its default configuration and not worry about excluding the operating system, because the cost to your backup system will be very small.

Tag-Based and Folder-Based Inclusion

Another way to add backup data to the backup system automatically is by tag-based and folder-based inclusion. This has become popular in the virtualization world, where each new VM or database that is created can be given one or more tags (or placed in a particular folder) that can be used to classify the type of VM or database.

For example, all new database servers might be given the *database* tag or put in the database folder, indicating to multiple other processes that it is a database-related VM. This might tell certain monitoring systems to monitor whether the database is available. It might also automatically apply certain security rules and firewalls to that VM. And in many backup systems, it can also automatically apply a database-centric backup policy to that VM as well.

One important thing to note when using this method: You need a default backup policy. You should create a backup policy that your backup software automatically uses if no appropriate tags are found, or if a VM is not in a particular folder. Then make sure to monitor that default policy for any new systems that show up, because it means that the data on those systems might not be getting properly backed up. If your backup software product does not support a default backup policy when used with this method, it might be best not to use this functionality, because it comes with the risk of new VMs or databases not being backed up.

 We have our server build process automated and VMs are backed up by an SLA added to the folder the VMs go in. For database backups, we need to add an agent and add them to our backup software and add an SLA. This is all done during the server build when DB is checked. That way we hopefully don't miss a backup that we weren't aware of.

—Julie Ulrich

Takeaways

If you're designing or operating a backup system for which you do not have an agreed-upon SLA for RTO and RPO, you are asking for trouble. Take the time now to document one, and remember that it should come from the organization—*not from IT*. In addition, if you have a documented RTO and RPO and you know your RTA and RPA are nowhere near it, now is the time to speak up.

As to the backup myths, all sorts of them say you don't need to back up X, Y, or Z. That is almost never true. If you have a system that truly does have backup and recovery as part of its feature set, make sure to get that in writing.

As to backup levels, I think most people don't need that entire section. Most modern backup products are doing block-level incremental backups forever and really don't use the backup levels from days gone by.

Default to selective exclusion (i.e., automatic inclusion). Spend your valuable time on other administrator activities, without having to worry whether your new database is being backed up. Backup priorities should always be safety and protection first, cost second. No one ever got fired because their backup system backed up too much data, but plenty of people have been fired for not backing up enough data.

The next chapter is dedicated to the way most people back up today: disk as their primary target. I'll cover the different ways people use disk in their backup systems and follow that up with different ways people recover.

CHAPTER 5

Using Disk and Deduplication for Data Protection

In this section of the book, I've covered some important conceptual terms and practices, starting with the very important concept of the difference between backup and archive and what makes something a backup (versus a copy). Then I dug a bit deeper into backup, looking at metrics (especially RTO, RPO, RTA, and RPA) along with backup levels and how things are included (or excluded) from backups. Now I want to look at how the typical data path of backup has changed over the past 20 years, as well as how these changes have affected the choices we have when it comes to recovery.

Disk has evolved from hardly being used in backups at all to becoming the primary target for most backups today. (It is also used with archives, but less so, because the economics are different.) There are two primary reasons for the increased use of disk; the first was when vendors started creating disk arrays, using AT attachment (ATA) and serial AT attachment (serial ATA, SATA) disk drives. Prior to this, you really only saw those disk drives in consumer computers and not in the datacenter. Using SATA disk drives made disk significantly less expensive than it used to be.

However, the technology that really made disk feasible was deduplication. It reduces the cost of disk by at least an order of magnitude, and it makes a number of other technologies possible as well. Let's take a look at this extremely important technology.

Deduplication

Deduplication (also called *dedupe*) is the identification and elimination of duplicate data within a dataset that can include many backups taken from many places over time. A very basic representation of dedupe is shown in Figure 5-1, where the number of blocks needed to store data is reduced by 66% by using dedupe. It can eliminate duplicate data found between multiple files, even if they are stored in different directories. Some dedupe systems can even find duplicate data across multiple hosts and datacenters. (More on that later in this chapter, in "Dedupe scope" on page 94.)

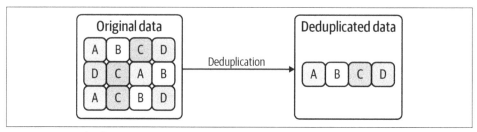

Figure 5-1. Deduplication overview

What Can Dedupe Do?

Dedupe can reduce, by an order of magnitude or more, how much disk is needed to store backups. A few examples should help you understand how dedupe works. Let's consider the history of a single file over time:

Versions over time

In Figure 5-2, you can see that Curtis edits a spreadsheet each day and it is backed up each day, storing many versions of the same file over time. Most of the data in each version is the same as the previous version. Dedupe will eliminate the duplicate data between versions and store only the data unique to each version. Look at the difference between the amount of storage needed in the backup system before and after deduplication.

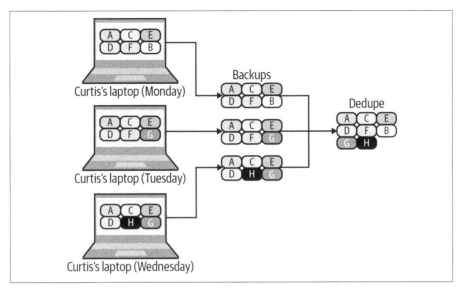

Figure 5-2. Versions over time

Same file multiple places

The same file can also exist in multiple places, as shown in Figure 5-3. Curtis was so proud of his spreadsheet that he stored it on the company file server. A good dedupe system would recognize these duplicate files and only backup one of them. The same thing happens when you back up hundreds of VMs that contain the same OS. A dedupe will recognize the part of the image backup that contains the same bits as other image backups, storing the OS only once.

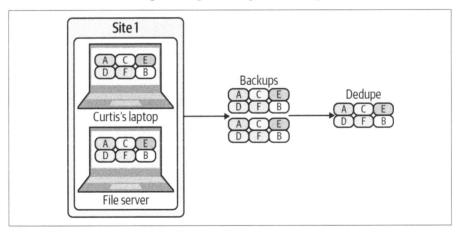

Figure 5-3. Same file, multiple places

Hidden duplicates

Curtis also emailed his spreadsheet to Steve, who also stored it on his office's file server. As you can see in Figure 5-4; that means it's on Curtis's laptop, Curtis's Sent Items folder on his email server, Steve's Inbox on his email server, and on two company file servers that happen to be in multiple sites. The dedupe system could see and eliminate these duplicate files even in email backups, because it contains the same data already backed up from someone's laptop.

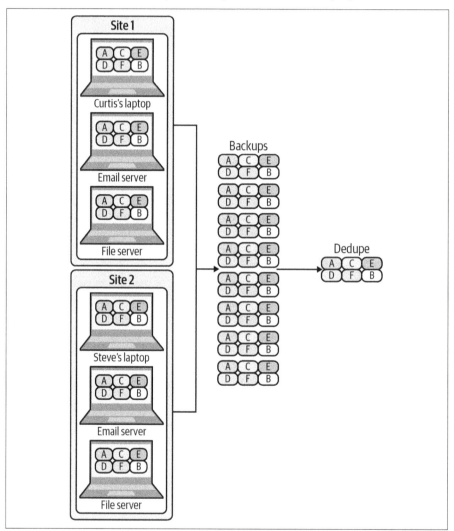

Figure 5-4. Hidden duplicates

The amount of data reduction achieved by a deduplication system is variable and is the result of multiple factors, including the deduplication technology itself, the redundancy within a single dataset, and the configuration of the backup system. For example, you could get a 100:1 deduplication ratio by performing a full backup of exactly the same data 100 times. You can also guarantee a 1:1 deduplication ratio by turning on your backup software's encryption feature and encrypting the data *before* handing it to a deduplication system. This is usually not a problem if your backup and dedupe software is from the same company; it knows in which order to do it. The problem lies in using backup software from one company and dedupe hardware from another company. If you encrypt your backups before sending them to the third-party appliance, you will get no dedupe. In addition, you can encrypt deduped backups; you just need to do it in the right order.

How Dedupe Works

The following is a simplistic explanation of how deduplication works under the covers. A typical dedupe system will slice the data it is given into smaller pieces, often called *chunks*. The size of these chunks ranges from a few kilobytes to a few hundred kilobytes, depending on the deduplication system in question and a customer's choices when configuring the system. The chunks can also be of a fixed or variable size, depending on the system in question.

Each chunk is run through a cryptographic hashing algorithm, such as SHA-1, SHA-2, or SHA-256. In a process that mirrors the way unique IDs (UIDs) are created for objects in an object-storage system, the algorithm creates an alphanumeric sequence that uniquely represents that data. The sequence cannot be used to re-create the data, but it is a sequence that is unique to that content.

Just for example's sake, the following alphanumeric string represents a SHA-1 hash for the sentence, "The quick brown fox jumps over the lazy dog."

```
408D94384216F890FF7A0C3528E8BED1E0B01621
```

If you type the same sentence, with the capital T and the period into any online SHA-1 hash generator, you should get the same result. Even a tiny change in a chunk can result in a completely different hash. For example, change the T to lowercase, and you'll see this value instead.

```
21D5E0A8782D7921B284F615E59460730EC4C21A
```

The deduplication product maintains a database, often referred to as a *hash table* or *dedupe index,* of all hashes that the program has previously seen. The next step is for the dedupe system to perform a lookup in the hash table to see whether it has seen the hash before. If the hash is already in the hash table, the chunk is deemed redundant, and the hash table is updated with a reference to a new occurrence of the same chunk. If the hash is *not* found in the hash table, the chunk is deemed unique and the new hash is added to the hash table.

If the chunk is new and is to be written to disk, the new chunk is usually compressed beforehand. Compression is a completely different data reduction method, so it often reduces the size of the chunk enough to warrant running all chunks through the compression process. The overall reduction in the size of the incoming data is a combination of redundancies identified by the hash deduplication process and further reduction provided by the compression process.

Dedupe scope

Not all deduplication systems are created equal, and not all dedupe systems can compare the same amount of data. Consider the following dedupe scopes to understand what I mean. The farther down this list you go, the more duplicate data you are likely to find and eliminate. In addition, the farther down this list you go, the more resources you will need to accomplish the job.

Backup set

> Some backup products can only dedupe within a backup set. The backups of a database are only compared against other backups of that database and so on. The backups of the OS or database application software on the same host as that database will not be compared to the backups of the database itself.

Host

> In host-level dedupe, the backups of a host are only compared with other backups of that host. This dedupe scope is barely larger than the backup set scope mentioned earlier, because it would compare the backups of a database with other data on the same host. This matters if you are backing up an entire VM image and a database running on that VM, which is actually a common occurrence. Without host-level dedupe, you would end up storing the database twice unless you can exclude it from the VM backup in some way.

Appliance

> This is the most common level of dedupe scope. All backups sent to a given backup appliance are compared against all other backups sent to that appliance. If you have multiple appliances, they do not share the same scope. Backups are not compared across appliances.

Site

> Functionally equivalent to appliance-level dedupe, all backups from a given site are compared to other backups from that same site. Backups from multiple sites are not compared against each other.

Global

> All backups sent to a given backup system are compared against all other backups sent to that system, even if they are from multiple backup types, hosts, and even multiple sites. This could be a backup system backing up data directly from

multiple sites or multiple appliances replicating their backups to a single, larger appliance off-site. When multiple dedupe appliances (with an appliance-level dedupe scope) replicate their backups to a central appliance, the central appliance typically dedupes their backups against each other.

It's also important to understand that most deduplication systems have an upper limit of the amount of data that can be duplicated within a single dedupe scope. This is usually based on the maximum size of the hash table. If a hash table gets too big, lookups take too long, and performance suffers. Therefore, most dedupe systems enforce an upper limit so that they don't run into this problem.

Having said that, some dedupe systems seem to have broken through this barrier and are able to deduplicate data globally, regardless of location or size and without creating the problem of a *single point of failure*. The ability to deduplicate all backups against each other should provide significant savings for their customers, in the amount of bandwidth necessary to send backups off-site and the amount of storage they must pay for to store their backups.

Do not compare dedupe ratios

A very common question when evaluating deduplication systems is to ask what a vendor's advertised deduplication ratio is, and I cannot think of a more worthless question to ask a vendor. This is because any advertised deduplication ratio is based on lab conditions with artificially generated data that rarely reflects real-world use. And since each vendor is creating their own data for testing purposes, you cannot compare their dedupe ratios against each other.

Another challenge is when you are comparing dedupe ratios between target deduplication systems with source deduplication systems. Since the source dedupe systems eliminate the data before it gets to the backup server, their dedupe ratios actually look much smaller. What matters is not the ratio; what matters is how much disk each system uses when it finishes backing up the same datasets.

An SE I knew for a large-target dedupe vendor once told me how he tested systems for potential or new customers. He told the customer to do all full backups. Do 30 full backups to the same appliance. Look how much storage you saved! You got a 30:1 dedupe ratio! Amazingly, customers fell for it. Do not be impressed by the ratio; be impressed by how much disk is used to back up your data in the way you would normally back it up.

This is not to say that different systems do not reduce the amount of stored data by different rates. Nothing could be further from the truth. The point is that the only way you can determine how well a given system will deduplicate your data is to run it in your datacenter with your data. Even then, do not compare dedupe ratios; compare the amount of disk each product uses.

Chunk size matters

A friend of mine once told me a joke that Stanford had done a study on deduplication. The results were that there were really only two unique bits of data, and everything else was actually metadata. This joke illustrates a point. The smaller you can slice the data, the better the deduplication results you are likely to get. However, the smaller you slice the data, the more hashes you will have to create and look up. Creating hashes requires a significant amount of compute power, and the size of your hash table would also increase and cause problems there. Therefore, every deduplication implementation has to manage a trade-off between performance and deduplication effectiveness.

File-level dedupe

Object storage—assuming what you are storing would otherwise be called files—is essentially a file-level deduplication system. Every incoming object is run through a hashing algorithm, which is then checked against the hash table. The hash is used both as a unique identifier and to determine whether the object has ever been stored in the object-storage system before. That is, essentially, a file-level deduplication system.

Such technologies can be used inside many storage systems, especially in archive systems to reduce the storage necessary to store emails and other documents. In addition to reducing the storage requirements, it can also be used to identify possible data corruption, because silent data corruption would cause the unique ID to change because its hash would change. This is covered in more detail in "Object storage in the cloud" on page 161.

Target Deduplication

A *target deduplication* system is one that deduplicates backups once they have been received by the deduplication system. Typically, the deduplication process runs in an appliance that is being used as the target for all backups, hence the term *target* deduplication. Typically, a target deduplication system connects to the backup software via an NFS or SMB but can also connect as a virtual tape library (VTL). The backup server can also use a proprietary protocol to communicate with the target deduplication appliance, which comes with security and performance benefits. (See "Target Deduplication Appliances" on page 272 for more information on that.)

The popularity of target dedupe

Target deduplication systems have become quite popular over the past two decades, primarily because they require very few configuration changes from those responsible for backups. You could literally unplug your tape library and plug in the new target deduplication system and point your backups at it. Everything else works exactly the same way, except that you could kiss your tape problems goodbye.

Please note that not all target deduplication systems consisted of a backup server (that knows nothing about dedupe) and a dedupe appliance. Some backup software products also perform target dedupe inside the backup server or media server. This is usually the approach taken by *hyper-converged backup appliances*, which are covered in Chapter 15.

A typical target deduplication system could also replicate backups to another target deduplication system of the same brand. This allowed people to have on-site backups and off-site backups without ever touching a tape. Unfortunately, most organizations found the purchase of two target deduplication systems too expensive for their budget, and they adopted a hybrid system, using target dedupe on-site and tape for off-site.

They would use the target deduplication system as the initial target for their backups and then use their backup system to copy backups to a tape library to create off-site copies of those backups. This has easily been the predominant backup architecture of the past 10 years. The nice thing about the hybrid configuration of a target dedupe appliance and tape was that it confirmed what I have said in this book and elsewhere about how reliable tape drives are: They're great if you send them a stream of data fast enough to make them happy. The target deduplication system acted as a giant cache to the tape system. Copying backups from the target deduplication system to tape allowed the copy process to run at full speed and keep the tape drive happy. Everybody wins.

Inline versus post-process deduplication

When discussing target deduplication systems, a somewhat religious debate will always come up about when the appliance dedupes the data. It can have significant cost and performance ramifications.

Target deduplication systems fall into two types of appliances: inline or post-process. An *inline deduplication* system performs deduplication in-band, in-memory, and in the CPU before data is ever written to disk. A *post-process deduplication* system, also known as *asynchronous deduplication*, performs the deduplication process out of band after backup data has been written to disk. The deduplication process is also called asynchronous because it may actually be running at the same time as backups are coming in, but it is running against backups that have already been written and not backups that are still being transferred into the box.

There is quite the rivalry between the two camps, and I remember many years ago giving a speech version of the comparison I'm about to give here, and both sides came up and told me afterward that I had obviously been bought out by the other side. I'll take that as a win.

The good thing about inline appliances is that they don't waste I/O cycles writing previously known data to disk. That means once they write a backup to disk, it's immediately ready to be replicated somewhere else. There are a few concerns, however, starting with the fact that they must have a more powerful CPU to perform deduplication as data is coming in, without slowing down the incoming backup. Lots of examples in the field show how the inline/in-band process slows down the backup as it's processing the data. The comeback to that concern is that at least with an inline vendor, when the backup's done, it's done. A post-process vendor still has work to do.

Post-process vendors first write the incoming backup to a landing zone that serves two purposes. This is where the dedupe process will read and dedupe new backups. New chunks are copied from the staging area to the deduped pool, and the latest backup is kept untouched in its native format, which brings us to the second advantage. Restores and copies coming from the latest backup will also likely be faster than an inline system would be, because the inline system will have to *reduplicate*, also known as *rehydrate*, the backups as they are being copied or restored. This just means that in an inline system, the disk will likely do as many seeks as it does reads, resulting in slower performance during a restore.

This latest backup stored in native format comes in particularly handy if you are going to use it in a random access fashion. Most restores read backups in a serial fashion, because they are throwbacks to the days when backups were stored on tape. However, some modern backup systems support the concept of instant recovery, where you need to mount the backup in a read/write fashion. If you intend to write back to the backup, and read it in a random-access fashion, it would be very helpful for it to be stored in its native format. Inline systems cannot do this, and their performance during such restores shows it.

One downside of the post-process approach is the cost of this landing zone. You essentially need enough extra disk for one full backup. This limitation, however, can often be addressed in a competitive bidding situation. The additional steps of "write everything," "read everything," and "delete most of the data since it's redundant" also require much more I/O overall than the inline approach.

Which approach is right for you depends on how you intend to do, make, and use your backups. If you're more concerned with the initial backup time, or want to do a lot of instant recoveries, you will probably be happier with the post-process approach. If, however, you want your dedupe process to be over as soon as your backup is over, and for your dedupe system to be able to start replicating backups the second they are written to disk, then the inline approach would be more helpful.

Source Deduplication

Source deduplication (also called *client-side* or *source-side deduplication*) gets its name from the fact that the deduplication process happens at the very beginning of the backup process (i.e., the *source*, or the *client*). By its nature, this process must be done by the backup software system itself. The data reduction process begins with the backup software product doing whatever it can to reduce the size of the data that it must process with the deduplication system, which typically takes the form of block-level incremental forever backups wherever possible, with typical incremental backups used only when necessary.

Once the backup system identifies the files, blocks, bytes, or bits from a bitmap that appear to have changed since the last backup, its next step is to determine whether this new data is actually unique. To accomplish this, it follows the same process discussed earlier, slicing each new file or block of data into smaller chunks and then creating a hash and looking that hash up in the hash table to determine whether the chunk is actually new and unique. If the chunk is unique, it is transmitted across the network and stored in the backup system. If it is not unique and has been seen before, the hash table is simply updated.

Target Versus Source Deduplication

Target and source dedupe have been around a long time and have advantages and disadvantages. The following is my best attempt to compare and contrast these pros and cons.

The biggest advantage of the target deduplication approach is its evolutionary approach, versus the revolution that the source dedupe approach requires. One of the biggest downsides to source dedupe is that to get its benefits, you most likely have to replace your current backup software and disk, a significant change to such an important system. With target dedupe, you usually have to change very little, and the thing you were usually throwing out (or at least demoting) was the tape library that you probably hated anyway. (As I discuss in "Tape Drives" on page 257, I personally think tape has gotten a bad rap, but many people blame their tape drives for their backup problems.)

Proponents of target deduplication would argue that the restore performance of their appliances is greater than the restore performance of the typical source deduplication implementation. I believe this is a problem with some implementations of source dedupe, not of the concept itself. There are source deduplication systems that can restore at speeds equal to or greater than target deduplication systems.

Target dedupe's ability to slip into virtually any datacenter is because it will work with pretty much any backup system. All backups are sent to the appliance: full backups, cumulative incremental backups, and incremental backups. Customers send filesystem backups, image-level backups of VMs, and backups of databases of all sorts. It is even quite common for an individual customer to send multiple backup formats, including multiple commercial formats, as well as open source formats or the native formats of their database products.

The downside to this approach, however, is that to accomplish any dedupe, the target dedupe system must crack the format, meaning open up the backup container (e.g., `tar`, `dump`, or commercial formats). Source dedupe systems don't have to do that because they *are* the backup product, and they are looking directly at the files, images, bytes, or bits that need to be deduped. Cracking the backup format requires quite a bit of development work for each format, and then a lot of compute cycles every time a backup is read. You're also typically reading a full backup (synthetic or real) on a regular basis, only to delete almost all of it. That's a lot of work to get to the same place in the end. The source dedupe system only has to slice and dice files and images, and only the ones that need to be on the next incremental backup.

Target dedupe also requires all those full backups and full-file incremental backups to be unnecessarily sent across the network. This might not be a big deal in a datacenter, but it is a big deal when backing up remote data. Target dedupe proponents would put a target dedupe appliance (often virtual) in the remote site, which then would replicate back to a central site. A source dedupe approach needs no remote appliance, only a backup client on the system being backed up. Proponents of source dedupe say all of this means it is the more efficient, modern, revolutionary approach that all backups should eventually migrate to. But its biggest downside is still the amount of change it requires of a customer to use source dedupe.

Proponents of target dedupe say that another disadvantage of source dedupe is that the system being backed up has to do more work to participate in the deduplication process. It has to perform the process of slicing incremental backup data into chunks and then has to create the hash that will be used in the hash table lookup. (The lookup typically happens elsewhere.) Each of these is a process that the backup client would otherwise not be doing. Proponents of source deduplication say any increase in the use of CPU and RAM by the deduplication process on the client is offset by a significant reduction in packets that have to be sent across the network, and a backup window that runs in a few minutes rather than a few hours.

Hybrid Dedupe

Hybrid dedupe is not really a term anyone uses, but I don't know what else to call it. Vendors that offer this style of dedupe would probably market it as source dedupe, but I think it's something slightly different—hence this separate section describing it.

Some target deduplication systems support source deduplication in a limited fashion. The way it works is by a special driver that you install on the backup client where you want to deduplicate on the client side, which creates a virtual device to which you point the client's backups. This driver then performs source deduplication on the backup client before the data is transferred across the network. I am calling this method hybrid dedupe.

This approach is only supported with backup products that can use the special device and only on OSs on which the special driver can be installed. When this technology can be used, it does behave very much like a source deduplication system and minimizes the amount of data transferred across the network.

This approach makes sense if you already have a target deduplication system and you want to add this functionality. It allows you to add some of the benefits of source deduplication to your existing backup system without having to replace it with an actual source deduplication system. However, there does not appear to be an advantage to this architecture over an actual source deduplication system, and it is likely to be more expensive. One reason for the increased price is that backup software products often charge more for using a device like this on a backup client that would otherwise send its data across the network.

Selecting the Right Dedupe for You

Before doing anything, you should first check to see whether your backup software vendor supports either source or target deduplication in the product. If it does, then at a minimum, you should be testing its capabilities against any potential new product.

If you know you'll buy something new, this decision comes down to how much of a change you are willing to make. If you are simply looking to replace your current disk system or frontend your tape library system with a deduplication system, you should select a target deduplication system. Once you have made that decision, you will need to decide between an inline and a post-process system. If you plan to back up to a target deduplication system and replicate to another target system, and you want that entire process to finish as quickly as possible, that design possibly favors the inline approach, because inline systems begin deduplicating and replicating as soon as backups start arriving at the appliance. If, however, you plan to mount a lot of VMs from your backups, you will find the post-process approach more amenable to that activity, for reasons previously mentioned in "Inline versus post-process deduplication" on page 97.

If you are looking to make a more wholesale replacement of your backup system, the decision is a lot harder, because there are so many more choices. You will probably be less likely to end up with a target deduplication system if you start from scratch. Target dedupe systems are designed to enhance an existing data protection system. If you were designing from scratch, you would be more likely to choose a system based on source deduplication, forever incremental, snapshots and replication, or even a backup-as-a-service offering.

Having said all this, the best advice I can give you is to test everything. I can think of no area in IT where the results vary so much based on the environment in which the product is used. Your data is very different from any other organization's data, and how you back it up is also different. All of that influences the behavior of the deduplication system. Test backups and restores. Test as close to production as possible. Then if you decide on a particular product, buy a small version of it and do a small rollout of it into production. You really cannot tell how a dedupe system will perform until it is in the wild.

Hopefully, this overview of deduplication is helpful. I cover the topic again in Chapter 12, in context with all the targets you can use to back up your data. Now that you understand how important dedupe is, and the role it plays in a backup system, it's time to talk about disk. The use of disk for backups, primarily enabled by dedupe, has driven many advancements in backup. Let's take a look at the many ways disk is being used for backups today.

Using Disk in Your Backup System

It's important to understand that most of the designs discussed in the section are datacenter designs, meaning that these are methods you would employ in a backup system that is running in the datacenter. There is no such thing as *disk-to-disk-to-tape* (D2D2T) in the cloud, at least not as this writing.

As I'll cover in "Tape Drives" on page 257, the problem with tape in a typical backup and recovery system is that it is fundamentally incompatible with the way backups work. Specifically, most backups are incremental backups, and most of them run at a few megabytes per second to a few dozen megabytes per second. Meanwhile, tape drives want to go hundreds of megabytes per second, and they cannot go slower than that. Sending a backup that is running at 10 MB per second to a tape drive whose optimal speed is 700 MB per second is setting up your backup and tape drive to fail. (For more detail on this problem, see "What Tape Is Bad At" on page 262.)

Disk Caching

One approach to solving this tape speed mismatch problem (while keeping your tape drives) is to put a little bit of disk in front of your tape library. Buy enough disk to hold your biggest night's worth of backups—and this does not need to be a deduplication system—since you're only going to store one night's worth of backups. (Some people take this a little further and buy enough disk to hold one full backup and a week's worth of incremental backups.)

Since you will only use it as a cache, the worst-case scenario is that you lose last night's backups. Choose your disk array based on that risk profile. You will most likely be choosing between an array based on SATA or shared access signature (SAS) disk drives. You could use solid-state disk (SSD); it's just that they're probably too expensive for this purpose.

SATA, SAS, and SSD all have different performance and reliability characteristics: SAS being better than SATA, and SSD being better than SAS (and their price reflects that). One important consideration is whether you are looking at implementing instant recovery (covered in more detail in Chapter 9), when you will mount VMs directly from your backups. If so, that might help justify the cost of SAS or SSD for your disk cache.

Any standard disk array will likely be less expensive than a target deduplication appliance. This is what distinguishes this particular approach from the rest of the approaches in this section; you do not need to buy a target deduplication system and pay the dedupe tax that comes with that. You are only using disk as a staging area for tape.

Once the disk array is configured, send all your backups to that array. Some backups will go faster and some backups will go slower, and that's fine. That's the beauty of sending backups to a random-access device. Each backup can go at its own pace without affecting the performance of other backups.

Once all backups are complete, copy those backups to two sets of tapes. One set of tapes will stay on-site in your tape library, and the other set of tapes will be given to a man in a van. (This makes this design conform to the 3-2-1 rule mentioned in Chapter 3: two copies of every backup, one of which is off-site.)

The final step in this process is to expire (delete) the backups stored on disk before the next set of backups comes in. (If you are keeping a week's worth of backups in the staging area, you would be deleting backups from a week ago.) Do your best to leave backups on disk as long as possible, because they will also be helpful during a restore. A good backup system should help you automate this process so that the backups expire just prior to you running the next night's backups.

Disk staging helps address the speed mismatch problem with backups. It doesn't really help during restores, unless you have enough disk for a full and a set of incremental backups against that full. It actually is possible to do that, but it's a lot more complicated, so most people do not try. Except for something you are restoring from the disk cache, all restores will come from tape. That makes the primary benefits of this method cost and ease of implementation. It allows you to keep your current tape library system, your current backup software, and simply make all of that a little bit better at a relatively inexpensive price.

Disk-to-Disk-to-Tape (D2D2T)

The next disk-based backup method that people use to enhance their current tape library system is called disk-to-disk-to-tape (D2D2T), and the difference between this method and the disk staging method is that instead of buying enough disk for one night's backups, you buy enough disk for your current backup retention, which means you'll be probably be using deduplication to make this affordable. At a minimum, you buy enough deduplicated disk capacity to store at least one backup cycle (full backups accompanied by a series of incremental backups).

In this method, all backups are sent to deduplicated disk and then copied to tape; however, in this case the deduplicated disk system will act as your primary source for all restores. The purpose of your tape is to create the off-site copy and, possibly, long-term retention. Therefore, most people using this design only create one tape copy which is given to a man in a van. The tape copy is the just-in-case copy that they hope they never need to use, but they make just in case.

This method is typically associated with target deduplication (discussed in more detail later in this chapter). Target deduplication is often many people's first use of deduplication in a backup system, because many environments do not have enough budget to support the two appliances that a *disk-to-disk-to-disk* (D2D2D) approach would require. However, there is no reason this approach cannot be used with a source-based deduplication system. There are some backup software products that support both source deduplication and tape drives. You can use these systems to follow the same approach.

One concern, though, with using tape behind a source-based deduplication system is that some systems support copying deduplicated data to tape. (Most systems rehydrate or reduplicate the data when copying to tape.) Storing deduplicated data to tape would mean that you would potentially need many tapes to restore a single file, so I have personally never been a fan of this approach. Tape is so inexpensive that I do not think it warrants the additional risk that storing deduplicated data on tape brings. The best approach when copying to tape from deduplicated data is to rehydrate it first. The day you need the tape copy of your backup system is going to be a bad enough day; deduplicating your tapes is going to make that day way worse.

Disk-to-Disk-to-Disk (D2D2D)

You can also have a fully disk-based backup and recovery system, which is also called disk-to-disk-to-disk (D2D2D). This approach can also be done with either target or source deduplication. First you back up to a disk system, using deduplication, and then you replicate the deduplicated backups to another system from the same vendor. (This is always the case in deduplication; you cannot mix and match deduplication vendors.)

If you are using a target-based deduplication system, the replication process can be managed by either the appliance or the backup software product. Managing the replication process with the appliance makes it invisible to the backup product in good and bad ways. It's good, in that the replication process just happens, and you do not need to configure it or manage it in the backup process. You simply configure the two appliances and say that one appliance replicates to the other appliance. You can also cross-replicate, where both appliances replicate any backups sent to them to the other appliance. This works really well with multiple locations, with each location backing up to its local deduplication appliance and then replicating its backups to the other deduplication appliance in the other location. This is how a lot of organizations provide both on-site and off-site backups without involving a service provider.

The downside of managing the replication process with the appliance is that the backup software product doesn't know about the replicated copy. This means that if you ever need to use the other copy, you will need to make it look like it is the original. Using either a VPN or physically moving the off-site system on-site, you then mount it in the same place as the old system. It also means that this "invisible" replication process won't be observed and therefore reported by the process that you use to monitor and report on the success of your backup system.

A potential disadvantage of having the backup system manage the replication process is that it needs to know it is replicating deduplicated backups, or it will actually rehydrate the backups to copy them. This is because it will simply copy them as if they were any other backups, rehydrating them and making the process take much longer and require much more bandwidth than if they stayed deduplicated during replication. This is why if you're going to use the backup system to manage the replication process, you want to do so with the support of the target deduplication vendor, which provides an application programming interface (API) that allows the backups to direct the process that is actually then managed underneath via a deduplicated replication process.

Finally, another advantage of having the backup system manage the replication process is that you can have different retention between the different appliances. You could perhaps have a larger appliance off premises that has a longer retention than the on-premises, faster, more expensive appliance. This will allow you to keep backups for longer periods than you otherwise would.

Most of these concerns don't really apply if you are doing this with a source deduplication system—another advantage of source dedupe. Since the source deduplication is being done by the backup software itself, it will obviously be managing the replication of the backups. It will also know that the backups are deduplicated and not try to replicate rehydrated data. It can also manage multiple retention periods for different backup destinations. These are all additional reasons that I offered in the previous section, "Selecting the Right Dedupe for You" on page 101; I think it's unlikely you would choose a target deduplication system if you were designing your system from scratch.

Direct-to-Cloud (D2C)

Another design choice is called *direct-to-cloud* (D2C) backup; it requires a source deduplication system. In this model, all backups are deduplicated at the backup client, and new, unique chunks are sent directly to the cloud, which is both an advantage and a disadvantage. The cloud provides unlimited pay-as-you-go capacity, and the source dedupe approach means you can back up from anywhere without requiring local hardware, as a system using target deduplication would require. The biggest disadvantage of this model is the first backup and any large restores. You need to talk to any prospective service provider about how it handles these two issues.

The first hurdle to overcome is the first backup, also called the *initial seed*. In a source deduplication system, incremental backups typically back up less than one percent of the overall size of the dataset they are backing up, so day-to-day backup does not require too much bandwidth. However, the first backup does have to back up everything, and that can take quite some time, given the amount of bandwidth you may have. This is why most D2C backup products and services support the concept of seeding via common carrier. (You back up to a portable appliance that you ship back to the carrier.)

D2C vendors address the large restore concern via a variety of methods. They might use a local cache or reverse seeding (i.e., the opposite of the previously described seeding process). They also might support DR in the cloud, where you recover to cloud-based VMs running in native VMs offered by AWS, Azure, or Google Cloud, or perhaps to VMware Cloud.

Disk-to-Disk-to-Cloud (D2D2C)

Another common disk-only design is to back up to a disk system on premises and then replicate some or all of those backups to storage in the cloud. The *disk-to-disk-to-cloud* (D2D2C) approach is different from D2C in that it sees the cloud as a place to store copies of backups or older backups. They see the on-premises copy as the primary copy. If a backup product or service sees the cloud as the primary copy, it's really a D2C vendor.

That means the D2D2C approach is generally taken by traditional backup vendors that can back up to deduplicated disk on-site and want to help their customers use the cloud as their just-in-case copy. In this design, the cloud is essentially taking the place of Iron Mountain or a similar vendor; it is replacing tape with a copy of backups in the cloud.

Usually in this design, backups are copied to an object-storage system (e.g., S3) and are typically stored in rehydrated format. This is not always the case, because some people use cloud versions of their deduplication appliance and replicate to that.

The object-storage approach will appeal to those who want to have the bulk of their backup data in an on-premises system for fast restores, and see the cloud as a cheap place to store backups, but not as a way to achieve disaster recovery. The cloud version of a deduplication appliance approach appeals to those who want to continue using their target deduplication system, but don't want to buy a second device just for backups. They can pay for the cloud device as they use it.

Now that I've covered deduplication and the use of disk in backups, it's time to talk about recovery. As I've said elsewhere in this book, no one cares if you can back up; they only care if you can recover. In addition to understanding all the foregoing backup architectures, you need to understand how these architectures would affect recoveries. Let's take a look at that now.

Recovery Concepts

Much of the content of the last few chapters was dedicated to backup concepts, although I did try to explain the recovery aspects of each of them where appropriate. This section will be dedicated exclusively to concepts and terms that we use during restores or recoveries. It's paramount to understand all these options before looking at the backup system options in the coming chapters. Backup system design determines which recovery options are available to you; therefore, recovery requirements drive backup system design.

Image Recovery

Earlier in this chapter, I discussed the term *image backup*, and it's important to understand what that is prior to discussing *image recovery*. In short, it is a backup of a disk image rather than the files on the disk. The most common place you will see an image backup today is in the backup of a VM at the hypervisor level. When you back up a Virtual Machine Disk (VMDK) file in VMware or a Virtual Hard Disk (VHD) file in Hyper-V, you are backing up an image of the virtual hard drive(s) that represent(s) that particular virtual machine. There are also image backup software products that can create a disk image from a running physical machine.

An ISO image is another type of image backup that you might be familiar with. It is a file that actually represents the raw contents of a CD or DVD. You can mount it just like you would mount any other disk drive in your operating system, after which you can use it just like any other filesystem. The ISO image illustrates what an image backup is; it is a direct copy of a raw device, whether that device is physical (e.g., disk drive, CD drive) or virtual (e.g., VMDK/VHD file).

An image recovery is when you restore an image backup directly to a device. One image restore that you might be familiar with is restoring a VM by restoring its virtual disk images. With all the virtualization going on, it can sometimes obscure what you're actually doing, which is restoring an image of a virtual raw disk to another virtual raw disk, which can then be mounted inside your hypervisor as a virtual disk. A new VM can also use it as its boot drive.

The main thing to understand about image restores of all types is that they get around the issues having to do with the filesystem. Performing an image restore of a 20 TB disk (virtual or otherwise) will typically take far less time than restoring the same amount of data with a file-level restore. This is especially true if the filesystem is very dense—that is, if it has a lot of files per TB.

I remember a 2 TB volume a customer had that consisted of millions of HTML files. HTML files are small, so imagine how many of them are in a 2 TB volume. If we tried to restore the millions of files with a file-level restore, it would take forever. However, if we backed up and restored this volume with an image-level recovery, the restore would hardly take any time at all. The main downside to image restores is that they are an all-or-nothing approach. You generally restore all of a given device or none of it. (For more details on recovery options from image-level backups, please see "Image-Level Backups" on page 83.)

Another thing to keep in mind is that because you are restoring at a lower level than the filesystem, you do need to do this in the place where the restored hard drive will be usable. For example, suppose you are restoring an image backup of a drive that contains a disk drive from a Mac. If you are not restoring it to a Mac, nothing will be able to mount that drive and use that information.

Outside of the VM world, the main place you see image restores is in bare-metal recovery. If you have an image backup of the boot drive and you can restore it directly to a new boot drive, you can use the restored drive as the new boot drive and recover your machine from bare metal. I won't be covering bare-metal recovery too much in this book because it has become much less *en vogue* with the advent of virtualization. If you are interested in more information on this topic, see my other book, *Backup and Recovery* (*https://oreil.ly/backupRecovery*). It's a little dated, but the information on bare-metal recovery is still solid.

File-Level Recovery

Most of the recoveries you will perform with your backup and recovery system are file-level recoveries. In fact, almost all restores are the recovery of a single important file. Even if you are recovering an entire filesystem due to the loss of multiple disk drives in a RAID array, you are still most likely performing a file-level restore. There are three ways this is generally performed.

Direct restore

The most common way that a file-level restore occurs is that you select one or more files in the user interface of your backup and recovery software, and then it communicates with the agent running in the physical or virtual machine you are restoring to and transfers the data directly to the selected filesystem. You are typically given choices during a restore, such as whether you want to overwrite conflicting files. Another choice might be to restore the selected files to a different directory (or subdirectory of the directory to be restored) so that you may look at them before determining what to do with them.

The challenge with this type of restore in today's computing environment is that many of the machines to which you might restore data are not machines at all; they are virtual machines. Because they are VMs, a backup client is not likely to be installed inside them. You are probably backing them up at the hypervisor level and so do not have to load a backup client in them to accomplish backups. This also means there is no client through which you can accomplish direct restores. However, if you have a particular VM on which you are doing a lot of file-level restores, such as the file server for your department, you might consider loading a backup client on that VM to facilitate these restores.

Restoring with an SMB/NFS mount

There is another workaround if a backup client is not installed in a VM. Both Linux and Windows have the ability to share their hard drives to other systems. Windows does this with the SMB protocol and Linux does it with the NFS protocol. It is possible to configure these protocols to allow the backup server to write to an SMB or NFS mount via the network.

It is possible to restore data this way, but configuring your entire network to have writable SMB or NFS shares isn't exactly the most secure configuration. Therefore, I would recommend using this method sparingly—only on demand. For example, if you need to restore a large number of files to a VM, you could configure this share just for that restore and then deactivate it afterward.

SMB and NFS can also be used as a source for restores. The backup system can present, to any system it wants, an SMB or NFS to mount a point from which it can grab any files it would like. This is more common and is more secure than the previously mentioned method, because it does not open the share with writeable permissions. Having said that, this share should only be open to the appropriate users at the appropriate time. Making all backups available with an SMB or NFS mount to anyone in the organization makes no sense at all from a security perspective.

Restore via image mount

Often, the backups that are available to do file-level restores are not file-level backups, such as those from when you back up VMs at the hypervisor level. What you have is a backup of an image that represents a virtual hard drive. This backup contains the files you need, but they are not readily accessible as files.

One technique in this scenario is for the backup software to make this image mountable as a drive, very much in the way that you can mount an ISO image as a filesystem. Once it is mounted, you can use it as a source for restores. The most likely way you would do this was mentioned in the previous section: mount that filesystem as a shared drive in the system that you want to restore. Once mounted as a shared drive, it looks like any other filesystem, and you can drag and drop the files you would like to restore into the place where you would like to restore them.

Recovering SaaS data

I spend more than a few pages in this book explaining why you need to back up SaaS applications such as Microsoft 365, Google Workspace, Salesforce, GitHub, and other SaaS applications like them. Usually there is a partnership between the SaaS vendor and the backup software vendors that provides a two-way API for backups and restores. That means that most recoveries of SaaS data are relatively straightforward. You select the item you would like to restore in the user interface of your backup software, and it uses the authentication you have provided and the API provided by the SaaS product to restore the appropriate data right back to where it came from.

Unfortunately, this is not always the case. Not all SaaS vendors provide APIs for backup and recovery. Sometimes backup vendors are forced to use workarounds to access your data and back it up. A perfect example is Microsoft 365, where backup vendors must use Outlook Web Access to access user data to back it up. No API is provided specifically for backup. There are also parts of Microsoft 365 where backup can't back up the data, such as Yammer or Planner. (One can hope this will change one day.) Other parts of Microsoft 365 can be backed up but not restored! As of this writing, Microsoft refuses to supply a way to restore conversations within Teams channels. So even though many vendors have figured out a way to back up this information, they do not have a way to restore it.

I mention all this so that those of you who do believe that you should back up SaaS applications can help put pressure on vendors like Microsoft to provide such APIs. Perhaps if you vote with your dollars and stop giving money to a company that will not allow you to back up and restore your own data, it might change this practice.

Instant Recovery

The idea of instant recovery is a good byproduct of disk-based backups, because it is simply not possible with tape. The idea is relatively simple: mount an image of the boot drive(s) of a VM in a read/write fashion and boot that VM by using the mounted drive(s) as a replacement for a VM that has been damaged or corrupted in some way. You have essentially instantaneously recovered the VM without having to do a traditional restore, which is why this is often called instant recovery.

One way to accomplish this is if the backup system in question stores the image backups in their native formats without putting them in some type of proprietary container (e.g., tar, commercial backup format). If the backup of the hard drive image is stored in its native format, it could easily be mounted as a hard drive at any time. (It is a bit more complicated than that, since these virtual hard drive images are actually a combination of full backups and block-level incremental backups, and the backup software in question will have to represent all of those backups as a single virtual disk image for this to work.) The main advantage of this approach is that you do not have to decide in advance which VMs you want to do instant recovery for, and it does not require any extra storage.

Another way to accomplish this is if the backup software prepares such a virtual hard drive in advance. This is what vendors who store the backup in a different format are required to do. You select which VMs you want to be able to support instant restore for, and it will prepare their images in advance and keep those images up to date after each backup. The advantage of this approach is that the restore image will probably be more contiguous than the virtual image mentioned in the previous option, but it also comes with the disadvantage of needing to decide in advance the VMs you will protect, as well needing extra storage for the images that will be used for instant recovery.

Finally, some hyper-converged data protection appliances (covered in Chapter 15) get around this limitation by storing some backups on flash. The high performance of flash helps ameliorate the issues with deduplicated backups being used for instant recovery.

Storage matters

In the discussion about inline versus post-process target deduplication systems, I mentioned that the post-process method works much better with instant recovery, because you are running a VM from a virtual disk image that happens to reside in your backup system. Backup systems, especially inline deduplication systems, have historically been designed with streaming in mind. They are designed to make a typical streaming backup or restore faster. These activities are serial in nature, because they are not typically any different from what would happen if you were reading from a tape drive. Mounting a virtual hard drive with read/write access is very different from a streaming backup or restore and requires unfettered random access to your backup data.

If you are using an inline target deduplication system, it will constantly have to rehydrate data as it reads, and deduplicate data as it writes any changes back to the system. It will work, but it is unlikely to offer much in the way of performance. This also means that you should probably limit the number of VMs that you do this with at a time. Most people I have talked to who have done this have said that one VM is slow; more than a few is abysmal.

By design, a post-process target deduplication system holds the most recent copy of data in native format on regular disk. This means that if you mounted it read/write, it would perform just like any other system on that type of hard drive. You will still most likely find that the hard drives in such systems are SATA drives, not SAS or SSD drives. But it will still be way faster than you can do with an inline deduplication system, and the more VMs you run at the same time, the more true that will be.

Use cases

Instant recovery is not a replacement for a disaster recovery plan, nor should it be considered a critical element of one. None of the currently shipping systems that support instant recovery would recommend that you try to boot all of the VMs in your datacenter instantly from the backup system. It is meant more as a convenient way to easily bring up a VM or two in use cases when availability is more important than performance.

The degree to which these statements are true will of course vary from vendor to vendor. Some vendors supporting instant recovery can support no more than one or two VMs at a time, whereas others can support dozens of running VMs without suffering performance degradation. It's very important to have a conversation in advance, before you rely on this feature for anything very important. What matters more than anything is for you to have realistic expectations for this feature.

One use case I can think of is to bring up a VM quickly to take the place of a single VM that has been damaged or is malfunctioning. You could instantly boot that VM from your backup system and either compare and contrast that with the malfunctioning VM, or actually have it stand in the place of the damaged VM while you perform an actual restore. You could also use features like Storage vMotion to copy the affected VM from the instantly recovered VM to the real one that will run in production. This offers the advantage of bringing up the VM instantly and allowing it to continue to function while you immediately begin the real restore that will be accomplished via vMotion. This is probably the most realistic, useful application of the instant recovery concept for recovery purposes.

Another use of instant recovery is to pull up another instance of a working VM for the purposes of testing or development. Keeping in mind that the running system will not be a high-performance system, and that leaving it running for long periods of time may adversely affect the performance of your backup system, bringing up another version of a production VM in a lab environment can be very useful.

You might ask why you wouldn't just restore the VM in question to another location if the purpose of the restore is testing and development, and that would be a very valid question to ask. One answer might be that you just want to do something very quickly and you don't want to go through the process of fully restoring the VM in question. The biggest advantage of this is that it doesn't take up any disk other than a few megabytes of changed data that is written while it's running.

Choosing a Recovery Type

Like many other things in this book, your choice of recovery type will often be made for you because your backup product or service will likely support only one method. But assuming you have all choices available to you, I'd consider this train of thought.

Most of the time, you will be choosing a file-level restore, because that is the most likely restore to happen unless there is a reason not to. If you can perform a direct restore, choose that. Then you can try whichever other method is most appropriate to your situation.

If you have a filesystem with high file density (i.e., millions of files per gigabyte), you should investigate the possibility of an image restore. This will require prior planning and changing how you do backups for the filesystem, but it will render very useful restores. If the filesystem in question is in a VM, you're in luck. Most restores of VMs will be image-based.

Speaking of which, if you are backing up a VM, you will want to choose an image-level restore if you are restoring the entire VM. Otherwise, you will have to rebuild the VM in question from scratch and then restore its data, unless, of course, time is of the essence and instant recovery is available to you. If so, recover the VM via instant recovery and then use your hypervisor's tools to move the running VM to the public.

Takeaways

It's hard to overemphasize the degree to which disk and deduplication have changed the backup and recovery world since I joined it in 1993. Backups and, much more important, restores are so much more reliable than they were when I joined the industry. There are so many recovery options as well. The most recent recovery choice, instant recovery, simply isn't possible without disk as your backup medium. It requires a random-access device. If you are one of the last five people who haven't added disk to your backup system, well, it's time.

So far, I've covered a lot of important concepts about what backup and archive is and many important foundational concepts like RTO, RPO, the 3-2-1 rule, and how much backup has changed over the past few years. Now it's time to look at the things we need to back up, starting with servers and virtual servers, which is the topic for the next chapter.

CHAPTER 6

Traditional Data Sources

Understanding where all of an organization's data lies is a lot more complicated than it was when I started my backup and recovery career. If someone asked me back then where all my company's data was, all I had to do was walk them down the hall and point. "There. There's all my data," I would say, as I pointed at the datacenter. All servers were physical, laptops were rare, and even desktops were not that common. As hard as it is for a modern IT person to grasp, we used what we called dumb terminals to connect to the servers that were in the datacenter. (Lotus 1-2-3 ran on AT&T 3B2s, and a curses version of WordPerfect ran on DEC Ultrix servers.) All data was in the datacenter; that's why it was called the *datacenter*.

Compare this with the infrastructure of a typical organization today. Servers are rarely physical, and they are often not even located within the confines of the buildings where the organization lives. Laptops are ubiquitous and even mobile phones and tablets are used to create and store the organization's data. Data is often created and stored on servers and services that no one in the organization will ever physically see. In short—*the datacenter is no longer the center of data.*

That's why this chapter (and the next two chapters) exists. Although some of these data sources will be obvious, others are not. Even some of the obvious ones might come with a few surprises.

This chapter will be dedicated to what I now think of as traditional workloads (i.e., data sources) that need to be protected: computers. These include physical servers, virtual machines (VMs), desktops, laptops, and mobile devices.

Physical Servers

Back in the day, we just called physical servers *servers*; *physical* was assumed. Today I must specify that I am speaking of a single physical server running a single operating system, such as Windows, Linux, OpenBSD, or one of the various commercial Unix operating systems. This also includes any specialized servers, such as NAS filers. Servers can serve various purposes, such as an Active Directory server, a DNS server, a file server (i.e., NAS), an application server, or a database server. When backing up a server, you need to consider two types of backups.

 A physical server could also be a mainframe or a minicomputer, but I am not including them in this book for various reasons, the first of which is that I have spent my entire career without having to interact with such computers. But I thought it was important at least to acknowledge their existence. Mainframes and minicomputers are not dead. A colleague once said that after a nuclear apocalypse we will still see mainframe and tape drive salespeople.

Standard Backup

Standard backup is what most people think of when they think about backing up a server: backing up and recovering the data from whatever service this server provides. This would include backing up the filesystems, the directory service, DNS configuration, or the data from a database running on the server. To accomplish this backup, you typically install an agent from your favorite backup software and configure the appropriate scheduled backup. Details on how these different backups take place will be covered in a later section.

 This book assumes that you will spend some money on your data protection system; therefore, it will not cover the myriad native backup tools available on your physical servers (e.g., `dump`, `tar`, `cpio`, Windows Backup). We will also not be covering open source backup tools such as BackupPC, Bacula, Amanda, and so on. If you're curious about those, I have already covered them in another book, *Backup & Recovery*.

Bare-Metal Backup

A bare-metal backup focuses on recovering the physical server itself. This is perhaps one of the biggest concerns with legacy physical servers: If something happens to the server itself, you have to replace the hardware along with the operating system and its configuration, which is much more complicated than simply restoring data. The biggest difficulty lies with collecting and storing the boot-level information from the server's boot drive, because this information lies underneath the filesystem. The previously mentioned agents typically run at the filesystem level and do not attempt to access such information. This is not to say it can't be done from a filesystem-level backup, but it is not typically done by these tools.

A well-executed, bare-metal recovery process would involve replacing the hardware, executing the bare-metal recovery process to restore the underlying operating system, possibly then executing a separate recovery of the application and its data, and rebooting the server. If done properly, the new server should simply take over where the previous server left off. The only data that would be lost would be any that was created after the last backup, and the only downtime would be how long it took you to replace the server and execute the restore.

Bare-metal recovery was starting to come into its own when virtualization took off and the idea of recovering a physical server became much less *en vogue*. There are commercial backup software products that do support bare-metal recovery, so if you're interested in that support, just ask for it when talking to prospective vendors. If you're curious about how to do bare-metal recovery on the cheap, I cover that concept in another book called *Backup and Recovery* (*https://oreil.ly/backupRecovery*).

Backing Up NAS

NAS filers are specialized physical servers found in many datacenters that typically require special handling from a backup and recovery perspective. The challenge is that they do not typically support installing the typical agent one would install to back up a given server; therefore, you must do something different to back up these servers. There are three choices: using a proxy, using the network data management protocol (NDMP), or using replicated snapshots to a second NAS filer.

NAS filers can also act as block devices connected to other servers. For the purposes of this book, I'm not going to treat those block devices any differently than any other storage arrays. Just to summarize, though, the data on these block devices can either be backed up via the host and/or application writing data to them, or they can be replicated to another filer.

Using a proxy

The two main file sharing protocols for NAS servers are NFS (for Unix/Linux) and SMB (for Windows). When filers (a generic term for NAS file servers) first came on the scene, the only way to back them up was to install a backup client on a standard server that would mount the NFS or SMB share and then back up the data from there.

There are advantages and disadvantages of this approach. The advantage is that the files look like any other files in the backup system and can be restored anywhere. It also makes things simpler for the backup companies, because they don't have to write specialized code for filers.

The big disadvantage is that backup traffic looks the same as user traffic. Although backups are running, the filer cannot distinguish between the two and prioritize user traffic. This means that backup systems backing up via a proxy can have a negative impact on the performance of other users more than a backup via some other mechanism, such as NDMP, which I cover in the next section.

One concern is when you have multiprotocol volumes or shares that are available via NFS and SMB at the same time. The metadata behavior between the two is not exactly the same, so if you back up the data via NFS, you will not get the SMB metadata and vice versa. Customers concerned about this issue either have to back up the data both ways or use some other method, such as NDMP.

There are also some file restore issues if you are an advanced user. For example, there isn't a way to restore a stub file that points back to another object, such as what you would find if you were using a hierarchical storage management (HSM) solution. There may be other limitations, depending on your file vendor.

NDMP

NDMP was created by and for the NAS industry, specifically to give you a way to back up filers, a generic term for NAS file servers. It creates an API that allows backup software products to communicate directly with the filer as a filer, and request a backup. This backup can be sent directly to a tape drive attached to the filer or remotely to another tape drive supporting the NDMP protocol. This could be a tape drive on another filer or one connected to an appliance supporting this protocol. An example of that would be a VTL, such as I discuss in Chapter 12. Since the VTL is typically disk behind a Linux OS, the appliance vendor can write an NDMP agent that accepts NDMP backup traffic as if it were a filer. This gives the advantage of using disk for a protocol that typically only understands tape.

The big disadvantage to NDMP is that it allows the filer vendor to determine the backup format, and they are all different native protocols. One might use `dump`, another `tar`, and still another `cpio`. This means you cannot restore backups from one vendor's filer to another vendor's filer. This means that your backup method could keep you tied to a particular filer vendor even if you want to change vendors, especially if you need to keep legacy data around for a long time. One backup vendor managed to work around this issue by cracking the backup formats, but the core issue remains.

I was a fan of NDMP for a long time because it seemed to be the official way to back up filers. Now I look at this concept of data portability, as well as backup simplicity, and prefer using an NFS/SMB proxy for those reasons.

Snapshot replication

The truly official way to back up a NAS filer is to use that vendor's snapshot system to create snapshots on one filer and replicate those snapshots to another filer. I say "truly official" because this is the one the filer vendors like best; it sells more filers. This typical configuration is shown in Figure 6-1.

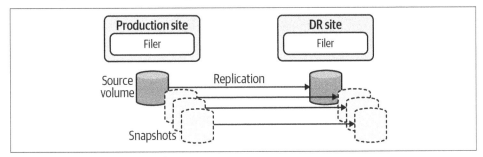

Figure 6-1. Replicating snapshots

It's also the best way from a restore-speed perspective. It's hard to beat a replicated copy of the original for recovery speed. You can easily push a few buttons and have the replicated copy take over for the source copy in a matter of seconds. And byte-level replication is also incredibly efficient from an I/O and network perspective.

The one concern I've always had with a pure implementation of this is the concern of a rolling disaster that takes out all three copies. I would feel better if there were at least one copy in at least one other method.

My favorite thing to do here would be to use snapshot replication to get the data to another filer and then use some kind of backup system to get that data off-site. The best thing from an efficiency perspective would be to use a source deduplication system to back it up to another site without needing any local appliance other than the second filer you're replicating to. With this combined setup, you get the best of both worlds: a locally ready-to-go copy and a remote just-in-case copy.

Now that I've explained the various ways to back up physical servers, let's talk about the servers that are much more common these days: virtual servers. I've talked to many sysadmins who told me they are 100% virtualized; the only physical servers they have are VMware hosts. This is for a lot of reasons, backup and recovery being one of them. Let's take a look.

Virtual Servers

Virtual servers are more commonly known as VMs, which is simply an abbreviation for virtual machine. A VM is essentially something pretending to be a physical machine; in fact, the operating system still thinks it is running on a physical system.

In reality, there is a physical server upon which you run a specialized operating system called a *hypervisor*, which does the job of pretending to be one or more physical machines. Examples of hypervisors include vSphere, Hyper-V, KVM, Xen, and Acropolis Hypervisor (AHV).

There are a few ways to back up a VM. This section takes a look at these various methods, which basically break down into two broad categories: pretend the VM is a physical machine or do something special for backup because it's a VM. We'll also need to look at the concept of Windows' Volume Shadow Copy Services (VSS), because it is crucial to understanding hypervisor-level backup.

As Figure 6-2 shows, *hypervisor* technically refers to the software pretending to be many physical hosts; I use the same term to refer to the host where the hypervisor runs. For example, I refer to a single physical host running vSphere as a hypervisor. Others may call this the host computer, host node, hypervisor node, and so on, but I refer to the entire collection of what you see in Figure 6-2 as the hypervisor. *You may be right; I may be crazy. OH, but it just may be a lunatic you're looking for.*

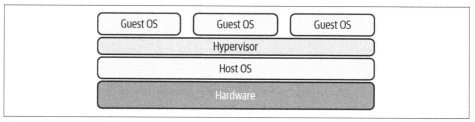

Figure 6-2. A typical hypervisor

VM-Level Backups

When VMs first came on the scene, pretending they were a physical machine was really the only choice, because the hypervisor-level backup method discussed later in this chapter hadn't been developed yet. There really was no way for backup software to interface with a VM's operating system (referred to as the *guest OS*) without pretending the VM was a physical machine.

VM-level backups are done by installing into the guest OS whatever backup software agent you would typically install in a physical server and do the same kind of backups you would do if it were physical. Although this is better than nothing, it can be quite problematic.

The real problem with pretending a VM is a physical machine is the amount of I/O a backup typically generates—especially a full backup. It's one thing to bring the I/O system of a physical machine to its knees while you are running a full backup; however, it is an entirely different thing when you have multiple VMs doing that at the same time—especially when they happen to be running on the same hypervisor. This creates a significant amount of I/O that slows down everything. Backups take forever and it affects the performance of every VM running in that hypervisor. (This is referred to in hypervisor circles as the *noisy neighbor* problem.)

Even the amount of I/O from a full-file incremental backup (i.e., one that backs up an entire file even if only a few bytes have changed) can be significant when it's being performed on 20 or 50 virtual machines at the same time on the same hypervisor. This is why hypervisor vendors received a lot of pressure to provide an API for hypervisor-level backups.

What Is VSS?

Before continuing, it's important to understand the Windows Volume Shadow Copy Service (VSS). It is a specialized snapshot system in Windows that enables backup software systems to back up an *application-consistent* view of filesystems or applications running in Windows. It is a supported way to back up all typical Microsoft applications, such as SQL Server and Exchange, as well as some third-party applications such as Oracle.

There are two types of backups when it comes to backing up something that is changing while you are backing it up: *crash-consistent* and *application-consistent*. Crash-consistent backups are as consistent as a crash; they are equivalent to flipping the power off on the server and then backing it up. They are usually OK from a data protection standpoint, but an individual backup can be corrupted beyond repair, and you won't know until you need it. Application-consistent backups are consistent in a way that the application can always use to recover from something. They are the more desired of the two types of application backups.

A backup of any server or VM takes a certain amount of time, and the bigger the VM, the longer it takes to back it up. If the data on a server is constantly changing, the data backed up at the beginning of the backup will be from a completely different point in time than the data backed up at the end of the backup. In the Windows world, this can be challenging when backing up filesystems, but it is really challenging if backing up something like SQL Server or Microsoft Exchange.

VSS solves this by allowing the backup system to request a snapshot prior to running a backup. Each application that wants to be supported by VSS creates what Microsoft calls a *VSS writer*. As shown in Figure 6-3, when a backup system starts a backup, it is a *requestor* that asks VSS whether any VSS writers are on the selected server or VM. The VSS system responds with the appropriate writers (e.g., SQL Writer), and the backup system requests a snapshot for each VSS writer. Each VSS writer, which knows what to do for the application it supports, does the appropriate thing for that application and then takes the snapshot by requesting one from the OS or from a VSS-integrated hardware provider. These two options are in the bottom of Figure 6-3.

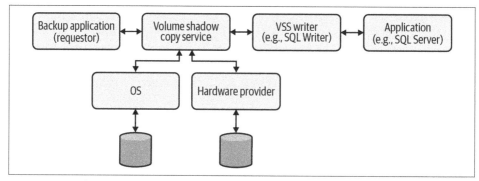

Figure 6-3. Volume Shadow Services (VSS)

Once all the VSS writer snapshots are taken, the backup system uses those snapshots as consistent images to back up from. This means the backup is accessing data all from the same point in time, no matter how long the backup takes. Once the backup is complete, it notifies the VSS system, which then instructs the VSS writers that they can delete their respective snapshots.

VSS can accomplish other backup-related tasks as well, such as truncating the transaction logs in SQL Server and Exchange after a backup. This feature just needs to be supported by VSS and requested by the backup application. It is very common to truncate logs after a backup, so backup software products can request a VSS snapshot, perform the appropriate backup, and then truncate the transaction logs with VSS.

Specialized Backups for Hypervisors

There are a variety of ways to perform backups at the hypervisor level. They require a partnership between the hypervisor and the backup software vendor, a storage vendor, or other specialized hardware. The hypervisor vendor provides an API, and these other vendors have to program to that API. The options available to you will vary based on which hypervisor you are using, and the hardware and software you are using for backups. The following is a list of those options.

VADP

The most well-known such API is the *vSphere Storage APIs for Data Protection* (VADP), which runs in all versions of VMware, including vSphere on premises, and VMware Cloud, which runs in many providers. Vendors who develop software that utilize this API can perform full backups and block-level incremental backups against the VMs running on a vSphere hypervisor. VMware also enables the backup software to interface with Windows VSS in each Windows VM to make sure that the image it is backing up is application-consistent. This is really important because of how backup software products would typically back up a database or application, which would be to install the appropriate database agent in the operating system where the database is running. Although it is possible to do that in this scenario, it is not desirable for the previously mentioned reasons (i.e., massive performance implications).

Therefore, it's necessary to give the backup software product a way to interface with the application running in the Windows VM, without actually installing software in the Windows VM. The way this happens is VSS. In Figure 6-4, you can see the same VSS configuration you saw in Figure 6-3, but this time inside a VM in a VMware hypervisor. The backup software product interfaces with VADP, which in turn interfaces with VSS inside the guest OS, which in turn interfaces with the appropriate VSS writer for the application in question. This can even include truncating SQL Server and Exchange transaction logs in the guest OS.

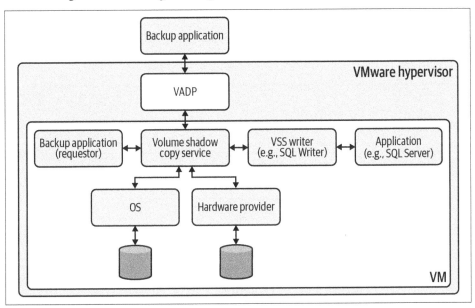

Figure 6-4. vSphere VADP

There is no similar functionality for Linux-based VMs. When a backup product backs up a Linux VM running in VMware, it still calls VADP; however, there is no VSS equivalent in Linux. The best VMware can do in this case is to try to sync anything in RAM out to disk before taking the snapshot. This reminds me of when we would always enter sync;sync;reboot to make sure everything in RAM had been written to disk before rebooting. VADP is essentially doing the same thing before taking a snapshot.

Hyper-V and VSS

Whereas vSphere is a specialized application running on top of a Linux-like operating system, Hyper-V is a specialized application running in Windows. This means that it has access to the VSS system running in Windows, which means Hyper-V has a VSS writer.

You can see that Figure 6-5 is similar to Figure 6-4, except the backup application now interfaces with the VSS provider in the Hyper-V hypervisor. The backup application requests a VSS snapshot from VSS in the Windows server that is running Hyper-V. The Hyper-V VSS writer acts in a similar fashion to vSphere's VADP, and interfaces with VSS in each Windows guest to request that the Windows guest perform its own snapshot. Once a snapshot has been taken in each Windows guest, Hyper-V can create a snapshot of the filesystem where the Windows guest disk images are stored, and the backup software can back up that snapshot and know that it has an application-consistent image of whatever applications are running in the guest OSs.

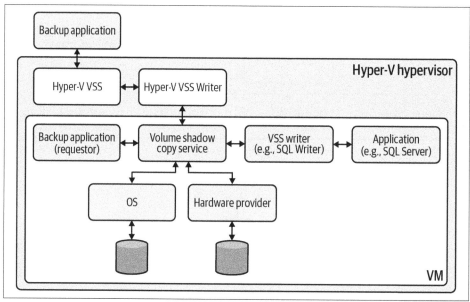

Figure 6-5. Hyper-V VSS Writer

Snapshot-based backup

Some storage products have connected hypervisor-backup APIs with their snapshot capability as a backup methodology. All customers need to do is put their data store on the storage system in question and provide the appropriate level of authentication in the hypervisor. At the agreed-upon schedule, the snapshot system interfaces with the hypervisor, places the various VMs in the appropriate backup mode (i.e., creating a hypervisor-level snapshot), and then takes a storage-level snapshot. The snapshot takes only a few seconds to make, and then the VMs can be taken out of backup mode and the hypervisor snapshot deleted. This is faster than the previous backup method and has a lower impact on hypervisor performance.

Any virtual snapshots need to be replicated to another storage system to be considered a valid backup, and this can happen in a variety of ways. Such replication typically requires very little bandwidth and CPU and is relatively easy to accomplish. This allows organizations using this backup method to have both an on-premises and an off-premises copy without ever having to perform what most people consider to be a backup.

Hyper-converged infrastructure (HCI)

Some organizations run hypervisors on hyper-converged infrastructure (HCI) systems, which are specialized hardware specifically designed to run hypervisors with integrated storage. When backing up VMs running on such a system, one can use the same backup interface that you would typically use to back up the same hypervisor (e.g., VADP or VSS). However, some HCI products offer additional ways to back up the VMs running on their platform. This integrated data protection functionality is often sold as a reason you might run their hypervisor on the HCI product versus running it on your own hardware. HCI customers may also have additional backup challenges, depending on the HCI vendor and hypervisor they have chosen.

The functionality provided by these different tools varies, but the most common method is snapshots. Snapshot-based backups, as long as they are replicated to another location, offer some of the fastest RTOs and RPOs in the industry. (RTO and RPO are discussed in detail in "Recovery Metrics" on page 69.) One usual downside to using the snapshot-based backup method discussed in the previous section is that it typically requires a separate storage product, one that might be quite expensive.

HCI systems take care of this downside by bundling compute, network, and storage in a single package that also typically includes snapshot-based data protection mechanisms. This allows their customers to use the snapshot-based backup method, without requiring a separate storage system. This single, integrated system makes it easier to create and manage VMs while also making sure that backups are happening as well with the HCI's integrated snapshot-based backup system. Instead of compute, networking, storage, and backup systems from four vendors, the HCI world offers a single vendor that accomplishes all of that. This is one of the reasons many organizations, especially smaller ones, have really taken to HCI.

Some HCI vendors take integrated data protection even further and integrate these backups into the cloud, providing a DR function as well. This allows you to recover your entire datacenter to the cloud, without ever running a traditional backup or replicating data the way you would in a typical DR scenario. For more information on this, see "DR-as-a-Service" on page 246.

What About Converged Infrastructure (CI)?

Converged infrastructure (CI) products are also purpose-built systems designed to run hypervisors; however, they are typically much larger systems composed of products from several vendors rather than a single system provided from one vendor. More important to this book, CI products tend to use standard hypervisors and the data protection tools that work with them, so they do not need separate coverage.

What about lesser-known hypervisors?

Some HCI vendors do not use Hyper-V or VMware. For example, Scale Computing uses the KVM hypervisor and Nutanix uses the Acropolis Hypervisor (AHV), although Nutanix does also support VMware. The potential concern here is whether these hypervisors have the same level of data protection APIs offered by VMware and Hyper-V and whether backup vendors write to those APIs.

Customers using HCI vendors that use less-known hypervisors have two basic choices for data protection: find a backup software vendor that supports the hypervisor or use the integrated data protection features available in the HCI product. (You could, of course, back up the VMs by pretending they are physical machines, but I've already explained why that's a bad idea.) A few vendors address the backup needs of this market. The integrated snapshot-based backup systems available in both Scale Computing and Nutanix are on par with the snapshot-based backup systems mentioned in other HCI platforms.

The integrated data protection and disaster recovery features from some HCI vendors meet or exceed what is possible using third-party tools. Such vendors argue that it's simply one more thing they are simplifying, and that's a solid argument. If a single product could meet your virtualized compute, networking, and storage needs while also making sure you're protected in case of an outage or disaster, that's a compelling offer.

The technology for protecting VMs is now relatively mature. A number of options are available to you; they depend on your choice of hypervisor and the hardware you choose to run it on. Now let's leave the world of virtualization and get back to something much more real: desktops and laptops.

Desktops and Laptops

You would think in this cloud-centric world that people no longer feel the need to back up laptops and desktops, but that really isn't the case, at least not for everybody. The question really comes down to whether data is being stored on the device.

Laptops as a Cache

It is true that some laptops never store data, or at least not for very long. They are used only as a mechanism to create data in the cloud. Chromebooks are a perfect example of this; they are really just a device used to access Google Workspace. The hard drive is used to boot the OS and perhaps store an offline copy of the document you are working on. It's really just an interface for Google Workspace. If your laptop never has any data on it—and I mean never—even I don't see the need to back it up.

Here's something that may surprise you: I do not back up the laptop that I am currently writing this book on! I'm a Mac person and this is not a Mac. (I absolutely back up my Mac in multiple ways.) This is a Dell laptop running Windows, because that is the only operating system where I can run Dragon Professional, which is the voice dictation software I have used for at least 15 years. I used to do it in Parallels on my Mac, but I found this perfectly good laptop that I could dedicate to the purpose. I dictate directly into DragonPad (which is Dragon's built-in notepad) for a few minutes, and then I copy and paste the results into Google Docs. I could dictate directly into Google Docs, but the features are better in DragonPad. So I live on the edge in a world where I might lose the last 15 minutes of talking. I am never using the local versions of Microsoft Word or Excel or PowerPoint—or any other app—to create any data. If that's how you use your laptop, you have my permission to forget backing it up.

Having said that, you're still taking a risk. I mention in "Mechanical or System Failure" on page 12 that Dragon did indeed fail me and I did lose some of my dictation. But as I also said in Chapter 1, backup wouldn't have fixed that problem, since the real problem was that I didn't follow my own process and save often. Nobody is perfect!

Please note: I am not describing people who actually do create data on their laptops and then use sync-and-share programs like Dropbox, OneDrive, or Google Drive to synchronize their data to a cloud provider and use that as some type of backup. That is something entirely different, and I discuss how different it is in "File sync and share" on page 129.

Normal Desktop and Laptop Usage

Modern laptops are much more reliable than previous laptops, especially due to SSDs, but they still aren't impervious to damage. They are also not invulnerable to human error. Have you ever worked on a document for many days or weeks and accidentally deleted it?

What about ransomware? Installing a malware prevention system to try to stop ransomware, and a backup software system that can detect it if you get it is the best one-two punch that you can give ransomware. Modern backup software systems can detect changes in user behavior by using machine learning, notify you that your laptop has become compromised, and stop things before they get worse. They can, of course, also recover data after it's been corrupted.

Backing up a laptop also makes upgrading your laptop much easier, especially in the current world of much more remote work. Upgrading (i.e., replacing) a laptop is quite a lot of work for an IT department and usually results in a lot of extra work on the part of the person whose laptop is being replaced. However, if you use a backup system that is designed to back up both the data and the user's profile, it becomes an extremely easy thing to do. Simply install the backup agent on the laptop and ship it to the user. They can authenticate themselves and then restore all data and settings in one single step. It makes upgrading the OS or the hardware so much easier than without it.

I understand that you may have been in the IT industry for a long time. You may have tried backing up desktops and laptops before and found that it was horrible. The good news is that those bad products of days gone by are mostly gone and have been replaced by a new generation of software and services that back up laptops and desktops in a way that is completely transparent to the end user and easily manageable by an IT person. So let's take a look at some of the options for backing up these devices.

Desktop and Laptop Backup Options

There are a few options for backing up laptops, some of which I would not want you to use. Honestly, my opinion is that only one option really makes sense in today's computing world. I'll explain the others mainly to say why not to use them.

Portable hard drive backup

The usual way people back up their own desktop or laptop is to use a portable hard drive. Short of not backing up your laptop at all, this is a very bad option. It violates the 3-2-1 rule, since your backup is almost always right next to the thing you're backing up. I would also say of all the disk drive failures I've had in my life, most of them have been portable hard drives. They get banged around a lot, and as a result are very unreliable.

I should also add that this method is really bad from an IT perspective. There is no centralized control or reporting over the backup process, but the real issue is the risk of hundreds or thousands of unencrypted copies of corporate data. It's super easy to mount that portable hard drive to another laptop and read all its data; therefore, portable hard drives should *never* be used to back up corporate data.

File-level incremental backup

Traditional backup software that backs up data at the file level will work for desktops in a LAN but will not work for laptops. Traditional incremental backups, which I discuss in more detail in Chapter 4, use far too much bandwidth to be used on a laptop. You need a backup system that can back up over slow, unreliable, and insecure connections. (Traditional backup software also does not typically encrypt data in transit.)

File sync and share

This is another solution, like portable hard drives, that might sound OK for an individual user, but is a really bad idea from a corporate perspective. Some people use services like Dropbox or OneDrive to sync their laptop to a cloud copy of their data. The biggest risk for a personal user is the idea that a bad actor could easily encrypt or delete all copies of your data, and these actions would simply be replicated to the cloud copy.

The first concern for an IT department tasked with this responsibility is the same ransomware concern times many, desktops and laptops. File sync-and-share products are not designed to be backup tools; they are collaboration and data accessibility tools. Like the discussion of the difference between backup and archive that I had in Chapter 3, you will only truly appreciate how bad an idea this is if you are hit with a large ransomware attack that also infects your sync-and-share installation. Getting you back to a good point in time will prove to be quite a lot of work.

The second challenge with sync and share as a backup method is that there is no centralized control or reporting on the process that IT can use to ensure that backups are working. A user can accidentally or maliciously disable the sync process, causing their backups to stop, and IT will have no idea this happened.

Sync-and-share products also only typically sync a single folder. If a user puts anything outside that folder, it will not be synced and will therefore get lost if the user loses their laptop or something damages their desktop hard drive.

Sync and share's only redeeming value to some is that it is something they are already paying for. They are already a Microsoft 365 or Google Workspace customer, and both of these services offer this functionality. Some customers think that although it is clearly not a backup product, it allows them to tell management that desktops and laptops are being protected, without having to pay extra for it. My personal opinion is that if you have desktop and laptop data that need protecting, it deserves a product that is actually designed as a centralized corporate backup system. You'll thank me if you ever get a large ransomware attack targeting your end-user devices.

Source-side dedupe to a backup system or service

This is really the only valid option for backing up desktops and laptops. Source-side dedupe reduces, as much as possible, the amount of data that must be transferred to back them up, so it has very little impact on the performance of the end-user device.

(A good source-side dedupe backup system should essentially be invisible to the user of the device being backed up.)

This can be done via purchasing and maintaining backup software designed for this purpose, or by using a service designed for backing up end-user devices. The big requirements to be successful in this part of the industry are: a low-impact or invisible backup process to the end user, source-side dedupe to reduce bandwidth requirements, end-to-end encryption, and protection against ransomware.

Please look into backing up your desktops and laptops. Yes, it costs money. You might be surprised, however, how much you can save when it comes time to upgrade or replace everyone's desktop or laptop. You'll also be really glad you did do this if a ransomware attack hits you. Now let's look at a group of devices that are even more on the edge: mobile devices such as smartphones and tablets.

Mobile Devices

We live in a world where virtually everyone has a smartphone in their hand, running Android OS or iOS. These devices have an incredible amount of computing and storage capacity compared with devices of just a few years ago. In fact, my latest smartphone has the same storage capacity as the datacenter of the $35 billion company I joined almost 30 years ago.

My comments on mobile devices will basically be the same as those about the desktop and laptop. If it's just a cache to the cloud, don't worry about backing it up. But if data valuable to the organization is created and stored on mobile devices, those mobile devices need to be backed up.

If, however, all apps you are using on these mobile devices immediately send any data they create to a secure location in the cloud, I am less worried about backing up those devices. The only data on my smartphone is pictures of my family and the occasional smoked brisket I make. Every picture I take is immediately synchronized to iCloud by the built-in application and then synchronized back down to my laptop. In fact, my settings are such that what is stored on my phone is actually a low-resolution version of the pictures, and the record of authority is actually the cloud. Even though I am creating the data on my device and my device gives the impression that it is storing the data I'm creating, it's actually being stored in the cloud.

Another reason many people do not back up their smartphones or tablets is that it's actually quite hard to back up anything other than the base applications that come with the operating system. The security model is such that each application can only see the data created by that application; therefore, you cannot install a backup application and have it back up data of other applications unless they give it permission to do so, which is highly unlikely. This is why each application, and especially any applications that are creating data for your organization, needs to make sure that its data is actually being stored in the cloud, and any difficulties getting that data into the cloud is reported to someone who can fix that problem.

With the previously mentioned caveats, there are things you can do to protect corporate data on mobile devices. Let's take a look at them.

Cloud Sync

The most common way that people back up their devices is to make sure they only use apps that sync their data to their mobile device vendor. If the only thing your device does is create content that is immediately sent to the cloud, and you use only apps that work like that, this is not too much of a concern. This is similar to what I said about cloud-based notebooks like Chromebook.

Physical Sync

Another option that some still use is to sync their phone to another device, like a laptop, and then back up that device. This is less-than-optimal for multiple reasons, starting with the fact that you have to remember to do it, which means it won't happen very often, if ever. But the problem from an IT perspective is that you have zero control over that process. There is no good reason I can think of for an IT department to adopt that as its method of backing up such devices.

Mobile Device Backup

There are also services and software that specialize in backing up mobile devices. These are a corporate-controlled version of the previously mentioned cloud sync option. The advantage of this is that the protected data is controlled by the corporation to which the data actually belongs. The challenge with this method, however, was already mentioned in the introductory section: You typically can access the core apps only when running backup software on an iOS or Android device unless you *root* it. (Rooting is essentially hacking the phone to give you root access to the device. This is not recommended as a corporate practice.)

Mobile Device Management (MDM)

Mobile device management (MDM) is the option that most organizations prefer if there is actually corporate data on a device. A specialized app on the device holds all corporate data, requiring the user to put any corporate data in that app. This is easily controlled, because the corporate apps where a user would be creating data are running inside or on top of this specialized app.

The app then controls what happens to that data, which includes encrypting it when it is stored on the phone and replicating it back to a central location to be protected using other means. An MDM-based system will also allow you to delete any corporate data remotely from a device that has it. This way, the data itself is protected (from a backup perspective), and it's protected from theft via the remote-wipe concept.

Takeaways

This chapter talked about traditional sources of data, which I decided meant physical things that might contain data, even if some of those physical things are actually virtual things pretending to be physical things. Every one of these data sources can (and probably does) contain corporate data that must be protected, and you must adopt a backup method that works for each of them. You might also think about some kind of archive solution as well, because much of this data could be subject to e-discovery.

You might choose as a company not to back up desktops, laptops, and mobile devices. Many companies do just that, or they use the sync-and-share method that I described as a bad idea. Just realize that you are adopting a risk profile that is greater than you would have if you treated that corporate data the same way you did physical and virtual servers. The data on these devices is not safe if you're not backing them up like other data. If you know that and choose not to, that's your call. All I ask is that you give it serious consideration.

Now it's time to talk about another traditional data source that you will find in your datacenter and perhaps in the cloud: databases. Databases contain some of the most mission-critical data in your organization, and they can also be some of the most challenging to back up. The next chapter takes a look at the challenges and methods used to back up this important data.

CHAPTER 7

Protecting Databases

The life blood of most organizations is stored in some kind of database or an application that stores its data in a database. And yet, as I look back on the past three decades of work, most of the truly difficult backup and recovery problems I've had were with databases. I therefore think this may be the most important chapter in the book.

There are 13 types of database and 300 database products listed on db-engines.com, and each of them has a unique backup and recovery process. Some have entire manuals and books dedicated just to the best ways to back up those databases. Given the variety of types of database and the different ways they are backed up, the best I can do in this chapter is point you in the right direction.

My goal is to help you understand why databases are so hard to back up, explain the database architectural concept that someone tasked with backup should know, and describe the various ways that people back them up, including my opinion on the pros and cons of each method. I will then examine what I know of how these databases are backed up and offer my opinions there as well. My goal is to push you in the right direction and to give you enough knowledge to evaluate the details of your database backup methodology and potentially make improvements.

Before we start looking at the challenges and solutions of database backup and recovery, we need to talk about several categories of database. The first way that databases are delineated is how you would deploy them or how they are delivered to you. These delivery models will determine how much of the underlying data protection challenges are yours.

Database Delivery Models

The database world has significantly changed in the past decade or so. Just like what has happened in the computing world, things have moved from physical servers to virtual servers and cloud computing, and the database world has made a similar shift. Gone are the days when you could assume that a database would be a piece of software you installed on a server or VM you also administered. In fact, we are quickly entering a world where that is becoming the exception. Let's take a look at the three ways databases are delivered to you.

 Defining databases is quite hard, because it's very difficult to avoid using an undefined term when defining another term. If you see a term you're unfamiliar with, make note. That term will probably be defined in the following pages.

Traditional Database Software

The traditional database software model is the way all software was delivered until a few years ago. You buy a license for a product, download the software, and install it on a server or VM of your choice. You are responsible for everything, including the security and administration of the server, the storage, the application itself, and (of course) the backup of the database.

Backing up databases that are running on a server or VM you administer means you have a variety of choices to make, some of which will be *completely invalid ways to back up a database*. This is because databases behave in a particular way that makes them not so easy to back up using typical methods. The following three concepts apply to almost all on-premises databases.

Moving target
> The data in databases is generally stored in *data files*, which you can see in the filesystem of the server or VM where you are hosting the database. These files are constantly changing as long as something is making updates to the database, which means you cannot just back them up like any other file. The resulting backup of this moving target would be worthless. I should know; this fact launched my career. Make sure to read "The One That Got Away" on page 1. This moving target aspect of data files means you have to do something to get them to stand still while you're backing them up, or back up the database via its APIs.

Point-in-time backups and restores
> If you do back up the database, using a supported method, that backup will only be able to restore the database to that point in time. Most backups of on-premises databases will occur on a daily basis, although some are able to back up more often than that. If you are only backing up the database once a day, that means that without some assistance from the database (as I will explain next), the *best* RPO you can meet is 24 hours. Your actual RPA will often be greater than that due to other factors.

Rolling forward (or backward) from a point in time

Most databases have a journal of transactions that can be replayed after a point-in-time restore to move the point in time up to a more recent point that you specify. This is how you can take a nightly backup, restore the database to a point in time, and then use this log to roll the database forward in time to a few minutes before whatever happened to make you restore the database. This log can also be used to roll back transactions if the database crashes and comes up in an inconsistent state (i.e., some transactions are only partially written to disk).

Those three general concepts are behind almost all databases running on servers or VMs you administer, although there are exceptions to every rule. Data files are sometimes block devices and not files at all, and they sometimes do not change, even if the database is changing. The key to getting the backups of your database right lies in understanding how your database solves these three challenges.

 Please note I say "all servers or VMs you administer," which includes databases running in VMs in the cloud, or even in servers or VMs in a colocation facility. If you have root or administrator privilege to the server, that database is using the traditional delivery model.

Platform-as-a-Service

A second way that databases are delivered is the platform-as-a-service (PaaS) model, where you see only the application and have limited to no access to the infrastructure behind it. Some traditional databases are offered this way, and other database products are only available as a service.

With a PaaS database, you do not need to worry about how storage or servers will be provisioned, but you do specify what should be provisioned. For example, you may specify how many replicas or partitions a database may have or how much storage capacity should be provisioned on your behalf. All of that will then be handled automatically. Amazon Relational Database Service (RDS) is an example of a PaaS offering, and it can be configured to provide Oracle, MySQL, PostgreSQL, and MariaDB, and Aurora databases. Azure doesn't have a brand that covers all PaaS databases, but also offers SQL Server, MySQL, PostgreSQL, and others in a PaaS configuration.

Backup options for a PaaS database are usually pretty straightforward. Each PaaS offering provides a mechanism that supports backup. This either happens automatically, or you are given documentation on what you need to do to set it up. You simply follow the documented process.

Like a lot of things in the as-a-service world, it's simpler than managing your own infrastructure; however, this simplicity often comes with reduced control in some areas. Many see this reduction in control or functionality as a feature. Think of it as the difference between a stick shift and an automatic. You get a lot more control over exactly how your car drives with a stick shift, but driving an automatic is a lot easier, especially in traffic. It also doesn't require the kind of specialized training I had to give my two daughters as they got to driving age. (I still live in the world where everyone should know how to drive a stick.)

In addition to delivery models, there are also different ways databases store and process the information they are tasked with. How such information is queried is also different between different database types, referred to as *database models*, and there are many such models. The one most people are familiar with (including me) is the *relational database management system* (RDBMS), but that is one of many such models. Understanding the model of a database is crucial to figuring out how to protect it, so let's take a look at the different database models.

Serverless Databases

Serverless databases take the PaaS concept one step further, removing even more administration requirements from the customer and creating an even easier-to-use platform. As already mentioned, with a PaaS database, you don't have to provision it, but you do have to decide what should be provisioned for you. Typically, you are specifying how many replicas and partitions and how much storage you will need.

With a serverless database, you don't have to specify any of that. You literally just start putting in data. The compute and storage resources, as well as database partitioning decisions, will automatically be decided and provisioned for you.

As will be discussed later in this chapter, some databases are *partitioned* across hundreds or thousands of nodes. If that's happening in a serverless database, you will have no idea, and that's perfectly fine. You will know only about the records you are adding to the database. In fact, with serverless databases, you do not even have full administration rights for the database itself. You will only see the part of the database you have control over, and even then only through the management interface and APIs they offer you.

Like PaaS databases, the backup methods are dictated by the vendor offering the database. Amazon Web Services (AWS) DynamoDB is an example of a serverless database. AWS Aurora is PaaS, but there is AWS Aurora Serverless as well, where it scales as your data scales.

The delivery model of your database is one of the ways it may differentiate itself from the competition. Another way it's likely to differentiate itself will be how it stores, queries, and retrieves data. Understanding the various database models (i.e., storing and querying methods) is one of the first steps to understanding how to back up your database, so let's look at them now.

Database Models

According to db-engines.com there are at least 13 database models or designs. Some databases support only one model, whereas others can run multiple models. I've chosen to discuss the five most popular database models, along with a few whose popular databases have generated a lot of backup questions. Figure 7-1 shows the popularity of the various database models according to db-engines.com.

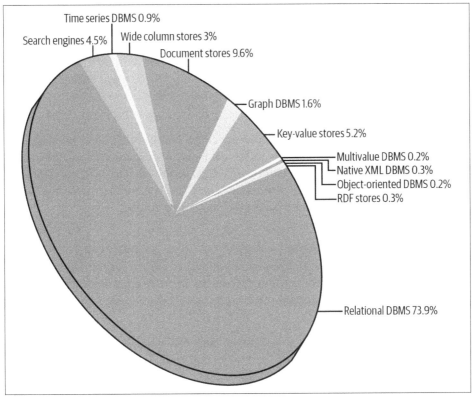

Figure 7-1. Popularity of database models (courtesy of db-engines.com)

One advantage of understanding these different database models is that it will be easier to have conversations with your DBAs and to create a relationship with them during this process. Asking questions like, "Is this a relational database?" will establish credibility with them and help establish a trust level that can be very helpful in this process. I will also say that db-engines.com is very helpful in understanding the different database models and the common database products that use them.

Relational

A relational database management system (RDBMS) *is* your parents' database, and (as you can see in Figure 7-1) is easily the most popular model. It is a series of tables that have a defined *schema* (i.e., layout). It consists of records (i.e., rows) of one or more *attributes* (i.e., values). The tables relate to each other via interesting, predefined values. Examples of relational databases include Oracle, SQL Server, DB2, MySQL, and PostgreSQL. To query these databases, you use the structured query language, or SQL. This is why these databases are often called *SQL* databases, to distinguish them from databases that are not-only-SQL (NoSQL).

Key value

This is a database management system (DBMS) with a simple schema, consisting of keys and values, where you can look up the value if you know the key. (The schema may be simple, but the underlying architecture of most such databases is anything but simple.) A key-value database is one of many NoSQL database models. Popular examples are Redis and DynamoDB.

Time series

A NoSQL database is specifically designed to handle time data, because each entry has a time stamp. Whereas other database models are used for time series data, the structure and query abilities of a time series database will be customized for time-series use cases. The Prometheus database is a popular time-series database and is used quite a bit in Kubernetes implementations.

Document

A NoSQL DBMS is designed specifically to store documents. Records do not need to conform to any uniform standard and can store very different types of data. JSON is often used to store documents in such a database. MongoDB is easily the most popular database that supports only the Document model.

Graph

Graph databases are gaining popularity and use graph structures for queries instead of the traditional concepts of tables and rows. Explaining how these databases work is outside the scope of this book, but I wanted to include it here because of their rise in popularity. Neo4j is the most popular graph-only database, and Amazon Neptune is a multimodel graph database that supports this model.

Search engine

This is a NoSQL database optimized for search. It enables complex indexing and searches, such as you might type in a search engine. Elasticsearch and Splunk are two popular search engine databases.

Wide column

This is another schema-free NoSQL DBMS that can store very large numbers of columns of data, without a preschema. Column names and keys can be defined throughout the database. Cassandra is the most well-known database of this type.

Most readers will be most familiar with relational databases, just as I am, but other database models have grown significantly in popularity, especially with the addition of the PaaS databases. You do not need to be an expert in each type, but being aware of the database model will be very helpful when talking to DBAs.

Another really important way databases are different from each other is how they keep their data consistent, especially in databases running on multiple nodes. This is an incredibly important thing to understand when deciding how to back up and recover a particular database.

Consistency Models

There are two very different ways in which views of inserted or updated database data are kept (or not kept) consistent for all viewers of the database, and this *consistency model* can affect how you think about the backup and recovery of that database. Consider what happens immediately after an insert of a new record. Will all users immediately see that inserted record? The answer to that question is what determines whether the database supports immediate consistency, eventual consistency, or a hybrid of the two.

Immediate consistency

> *Immediate consistency*, also referred to as *strong consistency*, ensures that all users will see the same data at the same time, regardless of where or how they view the data. Most traditional (i.e., relational) databases follow this model. Immediate consistency leads to fewer bugs and troubleshooting issues, so it is preferred over eventual consistency, but it can limit performance, especially in a multinode database. This is why many large, multinode databases use the eventual consistency model described next.

Eventual consistency

> The term *eventual consistency* comes from the idea that, provided no changes are made to the entity in question, all reads of that entity will return the same value eventually. A great example of eventual consistency is the DNS system. It can take a few minutes to many hours for a DNS change to propagate across all DNS servers in the world, but eventually that change will make it to all servers, and they will all return the same value.

Hybrid consistency

> *Hybrid consistency* is a consistency model often used in NoSQL databases that supports eventually consistent writes, but allows you to specify on a per-API-call basis the level of consistency you need on a read. For example, DynamoDB users can tell DynamoDB they want a strongly consistent read and it will always read from the leader (where the write was initially made, even if it is still being replicated elsewhere). DynamoDB, MongoDB, Couchbase, and a few others support

this hybrid model. Backup processes can use this feature to specify that they want fully consistent data.

The reason the consistency model can affect your data protection method is that you need to be sure you are backing up (or have the ability to restore) consistent data. If you, for example, backed up an out-of-date database node, your backup would be out of date. And if one node had part of the data, and another node had another part of the data *from a different point in time*, you could not get a consistent backup of all data by backing them both up at the same time. You would have what is called *referential integrity* issues between the two servers if you restored them to two different points in time. Table 7-1 shows which databases support which consistency models.

Table 7-1. Database consistency models

Database	Oracle MySQL SQL Server DB2 PostgreSQL	MongoDB DynamoDB	Cassandra Neo4j
Consistency model	Immediate	Hybrid	Eventual

The consistency model your database product supports affects how it will be able to survive various failure scenarios; therefore, it's an important part of the design. The following section discusses this idea.

Most databases have the ability to survive many common failures. Traditional availability features can survive a storage failure and compute node failure or the failure of both storage and compute. Which of these it could survive would depend on whether you were replicating (or sharing) the storage or computer. And how a database survives these failures tends to spring from the consistency model they employ.

Traditional Databases Running in Your Datacenter

A database supporting immediate consistency that was only concerned with surviving node failures would have two highly available hosts sharing a single storage array. The storage array might have redundancy inside it as well, but it's still just one storage array. This design could survive a node failure but not a full storage array failure.

A fully redundant system using immediate consistency would use a fully redundant system with a *shared-nothing* architecture, meaning nothing (including storage) is shared between database nodes. All data is immediately replicated to all members of the cluster, although there are typically only two nodes in a cluster. You can even configure things so that a transaction would not get its write acknowledgment (i.e., ACK) until an update had been successfully recorded to both nodes. Although this would have an impact on performance, it has the highest level of data integrity. This model could survive either a node failure or a storage failure, because any part of the cluster has an entire up-to-date copy of the database and can act on behalf of the rest of the cluster at any time. The big disadvantage to this approach is that it only scales so far.

Databases using eventual or hybrid consistency use a very different availability configuration. Their tables can be sharded across dozens to thousands of nodes, and replication works similarly to the way object-storage replication works. A given update will be recorded immediately on the node in which it was received and then propagated to as many replica nodes as the design specifies. A typical number would be three replicas for every record.

In addition to providing redundancy, replicas can also assist in the backup and recovery process. For example, an organization using three replicas can stop the replication process, flush any memory to disk, split one replica of each node, and then take a backup of that replica. This has two advantages: Backups are not affecting the performance of the main database, and it gives the backup system a consistent image to back up, solving any referential integrity issues that can be caused by backing up that many nodes.

PaaS and Serverless Databases

The level of failure PaaS and serverless databases can survive will be specified in the service agreement and the service level you choose. Serverless databases typically have a very high ability to survive most any type of outage. PaaS databases may or may not have such an ability, depending on the level of redundancy you're looking for.

Either way, the technology designed to overcome failure is integrated with the offering and is hidden from the view of the customer. You get the benefit of all this technology without having to worry about its implementation.

 Please note that just like everything else in data protection, the protections mentioned in this section only protect against hardware failure. If a DBA accidentally drops a crucial table, or a bad actor deletes or encrypts your database, your fancy replication will only make it more efficient. It will immediately replicate whatever happened everywhere else. This is why we back up databases, too.

Another helpful thing when talking to DBAs would be to use the right terminology when talking about the database in question. Using the right terminology at the right time can again be very helpful in establishing credibility and ensuring that everyone is on the same page. This next section talks about traditional database terminology that applies mainly to traditional databases hosted in your datacenter or cloud VMs and, sometimes, to PaaS databases. Most of these terms are not applicable to server-less databases.

Traditional Database Terminology

The following section covers a list of common database terms found in traditional (mostly SQL) databases, along with what popular databases call the same term. Some (but not most) of them will also apply to newer databases. This will allow you to better understand any documentation you read, sound more knowledgeable when talking to your DBAs, and will assist you in designing your backup and recovery process.

The goal of this section is not to make you an expert on all databases. It is designed to give you enough knowledge for you to talk to your organization's DBAs without sounding like you have no clue.

 If you only use serverless, modern, NoSQL databases, you might as well skip this database terminology section. Most of the terms are probably not relevant to you. In addition, the complexity of restoring such databases is so much simpler, partly because you don't need to know all these terms. That is why those databases are not listed in Table 7-2.

Table 7-2 gives you a summary of the terms I'll define, as well as the relevant terms (where applicable) for various popular database products. Feel free to refer to this when talking to your DBA friends.

Table 7-2. Traditional database terminology

	Oracle	MySQL	SQL Server	DB2	PostgreSQL
Cluster	Cluster	Cluster	Cluster	Cluster	Cluster
Instance	Instance	Instance	Instance	Instance	Instance
Database	Database	Database	Database	Database	Database
Table	Table	Table	Table	Table	Table
Index	Index	Index	Index	Index	Index
Row	Row	Row	Row	Row	Row
Attribute	Attribute	Attribute	Attribute	Attribute	Attribute
Datafile	Datafile	Datafile	Datafile	Container	Datafile
Tablespace	Tablespace	Tablespace	Filegroup	Tablespace	Tablespace
Partition	Shard	Partition	Partition	Partition + Shard	Partition
Master database	Control file	MySQL database	Master database	Catalog	System tables
Transaction	Transaction	Transaction	Transaction	Transaction	Transaction
Transaction log	Redo log	Binary log	Transaction log	Transaction log	Write Ahead Log

Instance

An *instance* is a set of processes on one or more machines, through which the databases attached to that instance communicate with shared memory. There often can be multiple databases within an instance, and a database also can be distributed across multiple instances on the same machine or on separate machines within a cluster. Therefore, an instance and a database are two entirely different concepts. Historically, an instance ran within a server, but modern database platforms have instances that span multiple servers and nodes.

If an instance needs to be shut down and restarted for any reason, all databases within that instance are unavailable during the shutdown. Perhaps this helps explain the original definition, since all the databases within an instance have a single connection to shared memory, which is provided by the instance. If the instance is shut down, that connection is no longer available.

Database

A *database* is a collection of database objects. It may be a very simple database on one node with one table and no indexes, or it could contain many (or no) tables, indexes, or other database objects, and might be split across many nodes, even hundreds of them.

Table

A *table* is a grouping of related information in a database. (That is why it is called a *relation* in formal database terminology.) In a relational database, it will have a well-defined schema before any data is added to the table, and information is typically grouped in such a way that data is not replicated between tables except when necessary. NoSQL databases may have a bit more free-flowing format and not really think of it as a table.

Index

An *index* is a special-purpose object that allows for specialized table lookups. This might mean quicker access or access from a different view than offered by the table (e.g., sort order). It could even be an index of a subset of the table (referred to as a *sparse index*). A table is indexed by the value that you usually would use to look up a record (row). For example, the customer database might be indexed by last name if customers frequently call in and do not know their account number. Indexes have a unique status when recovering a database, since you can often re-create an index from an existing table instead of recovering it. You may still choose to recover it along with the rest of the database, but if you can't, you could simply rebuild it.

Row

A row is a collection of related attributes. For example, there may be a row that contains all the basic information about a customer such as their name, address, account number, and phone number (this is also similar to a row in a spreadsheet). Each row typically has at least one unique attribute, such as the account number, to distinguish it from other rows. A row is also sometimes called a record. Most NoSQL databases do not use the concept of rows. For example, MongoDB, DynamoDB, and Neo4j do not use this concept. You could think of a key and its associated value in a key-value pair database as a row, but they don't really use that term. DynamoDB, for example, calls it an *item*.

Attribute

An *attribute* is the basic element of data within a table. It is a single value, such as a customer's name or zip code. An attribute may be very small, such as a zip code, or very large, such as a document. An attribute is the value that a database user changes when performing a *transaction*. (Transactions are covered later in this chapter.)

Data File

A *data file* is where the data is stored. This may be a *raw device* (e.g., /dev/sd1 in Linux) or a *cooked file* (e.g., /oracle/data/dbs01.dbf or c:\database\some file.dbf) that will reside in a local filesystem or a network drive from a NAS filer. Some products require the use of raw partitions, whereas others merely suggest it. Some products allow a mixture of raw and cooked files. The only real difference to the DBA is how they are initially created and how they are backed up. Other than that, they look the same within the database.

Tablespace

A *tablespace* is a collection of one or more data files and is the space into which you insert tables. A table is created in a tablespace (e.g., create table in tablespace alpha). When creating an instance in most database products, you specify which data file will be the main (or system) tablespace. The database product then creates this tablespace for you automatically. Tablespaces are another thing that serverless customers don't have access to or have to worry about.

Partition

One of the biggest advancements in database technology is the ability to spread, or *partition*, a table across multiple resources. Historically with RDBMSs, a table had to be contained within a tablespace, as described before. Most modern database products now allow you to partition a table and store it across multiple tablespaces. A table can be partitioned horizontally or vertically. Vertical partitioned tables put some attributes in one tablespace and other attributes in another one. Horizontal partitions, which are more common, are split by rows, placing certain rows in various tablespaces. Sharding takes partitioning to another level by placing the pieces (i.e., shards) of a table on different nodes. This is done with large, scale-out databases that run on dozens or hundreds of nodes. Serverless databases are almost certainly sharded across tens of thousands of nodes, but like most other pieces of database architecture, such sharding is neither visible nor something you need to worry about.

Master File

Most traditional and PaaS databases have some way of keeping track of all elements within a given installation; however, as with many other elements of database architecture, it is hidden from your view if you are running a serverless database. There also may be no centralized control in some database architectures. If there is a centralized system for keeping track of all the storage elements that it has at its disposal, I'm calling it the *master file*. This master file might be a JSON file, a text file, or even a database that keeps track of all the pieces of the database and their status. If multiple databases are allowed, it needs to keep track of them as well. Oracle has what it calls a *control file*, which keeps track of this information. Other databases often have a similar concept, such as a JSON file or an actual database (e.g., SQL Server's Master Database).

Transaction

A *transaction* is any activity within a database that changes one or more attributes in the database. There are two types of transactions, a *simple transaction* and a *complex transaction*. A simple transaction is done in one statement (e.g., `update attribute X in table Y to 100`). A complex transaction may be much longer, and opens with a begin transaction statement and closes with an end transaction statement. For example, consider a bank that is debiting money from one account and crediting it to another account. The debit and credit must both happen, or neither can happen. The system would begin a transaction, debit one account, credit another account, and then end the transaction. That way, if anything happens in the middle of that transaction (e.g., a crash), the database would undo the entire transaction to return the database to a consistent state.

Transaction Log

Consider the transaction example in the previous paragraph. How would the database know after a crash that there was a partially completed transaction that must be rolled back? That is the job of the transaction log, something that is found in all RDBMSs but not in all NoSQL databases.

Such a log can also be helpful when restoring the database from backup. Suppose that a system were to crash in such a way that it needed to be recovered from your latest database backup. If there were no way to redo the transactions that have occurred since the last backup, all such transactions would be lost. A *transaction log* records each transaction and the records it changed. This information is used in case of a system crash that requires reentering those transactions. The master file knows which state each data file is in, and it looks at each of them upon starting up. If it detects any that are corrupt beyond what it can repair with the transaction log, you have to restore those data files from your backup.

After a point-in-time restore, the master database looks at the data file and realizes it was restored from an earlier point in time. It then goes to the transaction log to redo all the transactions that have been recorded since that time. Uncommitted transactions are also rolled back. The actual order of this process differs from product to product. However, the main purpose remains the same. The rollback and transaction logs work together to ensure that all pages are returned to their proper state after a crash or reboot.

Now that you know a variety of traditional database terms, we can apply them in the rest of the chapter. We've also talked about different database models, so you should know that different database types act differently in a number of ways. I also covered different consistency models and how that determines how they work around hardware failure.

Now let's talk about how to back up these important receptacles of corporate data. How you back up your database will most likely be driven by your delivery method. Backing up a traditionally delivered database (i.e., one hosted in your datacenter or VMs that you manage) will be much more complex and present many more options. Both the backup and restore of PaaS or serverless databases will be significantly easier for many reasons. Let's take a look at your choices for backing up databases.

Backing Up Traditionally Delivered Databases

This section is talking about databases that you installed in a server or VM you control, as I discussed in the previous section, "Traditional Databases Running in Your Datacenter" on page 140. This has nothing to do with how old or new a given database product is; it's about whether it is running in the servers or VMs that you manage, as opposed to a PaaS or serverless database.

If you want to back up a traditionally delivered database, you will have several choices. Not all methods discussed in this section apply to all databases, and sometimes you might use a combination of these methods.

You may remember that the problem with backing up databases is that although they may look just like regular (albeit big) files just sitting in the filesystem, you cannot back them up like other files. This is because they are constantly changing while you would be backing them up. You must address this issue if you are to back them up directly. Let's take a look at your choices.

Cold Backup

The simplest way to make sure the data files are not changing as you are backing them up is to shut down the database instance and directly back up the data files. This is referred to as a *cold backup*. It is an extremely safe way to back up most databases, but it is usually considered operationally inconvenient.

Split Replica

Some NoSQL databases support a concept similar to cold backup, a *split replica backup*. The idea is relatively simple: ensure that the replica is up to date, split the replica from the rest of the configuration, and then back up the replica. Since the replica is no longer changing, it is essentially the same as a cold backup even though the database is still up and running.

Hot Backup Mode

Some databases support the idea of placing the database in *hot backup mode*, allowing you to back up the data files directly even though they are still changing as you are backing them up. This works by doing something special with the database while you are backing it up to deal with the fact that the datafiles are changing.

The most well-known database that does this is Oracle. You can issue the command `alter database begin backup`, and it will start doing extra logging to the redo logs that will allow it to overcome the previously mentioned issue with the data files changing while you are backing them up. If your database supports the concept of a hot backup mode, you can take as long as you need to back it up once you have placed it in hot backup mode.

If you want to limit the amount of time in hot backup mode, you can place it in hot backup mode, take a snapshot, and then take it out of backup mode. This is how some people do backups of Oracle inside VMs. For this method to work, there must be a command to put the database into this special mode.

Snap and Sweep

A *snap-and-sweep* backup is very similar to the hot backup snapshot method mentioned in the previous paragraph, the difference being that instead of placing the database in a special mode, you use a snapshot command provided by the database itself that can produce a consistent snapshot for you to back up. From a backup perspective, it's almost the same. It's just that the database is doing both operations for you: putting the database into the appropriate mode and making the snapshot. You just have to issue one command.

Once the snapshot is taken, you can take as long as you need to back it up (i.e., sweep), because you're being presented with an application-consistent image for that purpose. This method is used by some modern, multinode, sharded databases. To use this method, there should be a supported snapshot command that interfaces with the database. Simply taking a filesystem snapshot that does not interface with the database is not sufficient.

One really big thing to keep in mind when backing up multinode databases is that you need to do everything you can to back up all nodes of the cluster at the same time. If you just back up each node one at a time, it can take a very long time for the recovered node to be made consistent with the rest of the nodes, because such databases use an eventually consistent model. Stories of consistency processes that take days are common. The best way to do this is to get a snapshot of all nodes at the same time and then back them all up together. This should minimize the time distance between nodes.

Another snap-and-sweep method is when the database is running in a Windows VM, your hypervisor supports VSS, and the database in question has a VSS writer. As mentioned in "Specialized Backups for Hypervisors" on page 122, your backup software will talk to VSS, which will in turn talk to the database product and tell it to go into backup mode. A VSS snapshot will then be taken, after which your backup software will back up that snapshot. Voilà! You have a hot backup without having to write any scripts.

Dump and Sweep

The most popular way of backing up traditionally delivered databases is referred to as *dump and sweep*, because you first run a database backup (i.e., *dump*), and then you run a regular filesystem backup to back up the results of the database backup (i.e., *sweep*). One reason this is so popular is that it does not require the purchase of commercial backup software or the installation of any sort of database backup agent. It's also somewhat universal, in that it does not require the backup product in question to support the database in question officially. It does, however, require the equivalent of a dump command, such as Oracle's RMAN, MySQL's mysqldump, and so on. Not all databases have such a command.

Here is one important aspect of this backup method. Be sure to include enough storage to hold two copies of your backup. That way, you can always have the most recently completed backup ready for a restore, even if you're in the middle of making a new backup. Each time, just delete or overwrite the oldest backup with the next backup. That will leave the previous backup untouched and ready for recovery.

Stream-to-Backup Product

Streaming directly to the backup product will most likely be the recommended backup solution if you are running a traditional RDBMS and you look at its manual for the official way to back it up. You do this by installing the appropriate backup agent and having your backup software kick off the backup process. When the backup is performed this way, the backup creates a stream of data that is then passed directly to your backup product, which then stores it wherever your backup product or service stores its data.

The best part about this method is that it doesn't require custom scripting on your part. That means that your backup system should come with great error reporting and you won't have to worry about the previously mentioned issues with scripting.

It is possible that your backup software product or service might charge extra to back up the database in question. It is also possible that your favorite database is not supported by your favorite backup product. It is also highly likely that your DBAs will not like the idea of installing a backup agent on their database server or VM. Therefore, although this method is easily the best method for backing up many databases, it is also the least likely to be used.

Transaction Log Backup

In addition to backing up the data files, most database products also need you to back up their transaction logs. In fact, although you may back up your database once a night, you may also back up your transaction logs throughout the day. The transaction logs will be very useful during a recovery, as I will cover in the next section. Make sure to investigate how to back up your database's transaction logs. The options to back up the transaction logs are essentially the same as the options to back up the data files themselves: cold and hot backups, snap and sweep, dump and sweep, and streaming to your backup product. Investigate the methods available to you and make sure to back up the transaction logs.

 When backing up some transaction logs, some databases have the concept of truncating (i.e., deleting) the logs you just backed up. If you have and use that feature, understand that only one process can back up your transaction logs, or things can get very confusing when it comes time to restore things.

Modern, multinode, eventually consistent databases also have a transaction log, although they may call it something different (e.g., journal). If you're using a serverless database, such a log is usually not available to you.

Master File

If there is a file that keeps track of all of the pieces of a given database (e.g., Oracle's control file), it must be backed up too. This might be listed as a JSON file, control file, master database, or something like that. Read the backup section of your database product manual to find out if your database has this type of database and then make sure to back it up.

Now that we've looked at how to back up traditionally delivered databases that run on your own servers and VMs, we can look at the much simpler job of backing up those that are provided as a service.

Backing Up PaaS and Serverless Databases

Like every other service running in the cloud, PaaS and serverless databases must be backed up. Unlike all major SaaS offerings, though, the backup will be included as part of the package. The good news is that it's most likely much easier than those you have to do with traditionally delivered databases.

On one hand, the choices are the same as you might have with a traditionally delivered database: dump and sweep, and near-CDP. How these work, however, is quite different. In the end, there's usually only one valid choice for each platform. Let's take a look at these options.

Dump and Sweep

It is rare that this will be the only option available to you for backing up a PaaS database; however, a smaller PaaS offering might not offer integrated backup and require you to perform your own. It will provide a scheduler and a place to send a dump file that you can then back up however you would like. All the pros and cons for this option mentioned in my previous discussion on it apply here as well. If your database platform also has transaction logs, you will also have to dump and sweep them.

Interestingly enough, some PaaS platforms support backup of some databases, using that database's dump program, but they do not support restore with that tool! An example would be (as of this writing) the AWS RDS version of Oracle that supports RMAN backup but does not support RMAN restore. I believe they should do both or neither.

Integrated Backup-as-a-Service

Many PaaS and serverless vendors support a process by which the database service creates frequent image copies, which are often referred to in that world as *snapshots*. (I discuss in "Infrastructure-as-a-Service (IaaS)" on page 160 why I do not like that term in that context.) These snapshots are actually image copies of the database and are typically stored in a separate storage system to comply better with the 3-2-1 rule. (Although, as I will discuss in a few paragraphs, these backups do not fully conform to this rule.)

This is similar to the snap-and-sweep method previously mentioned in this chapter, but it takes it just a little further. Like this process, the traditional snap-and-sweep method supports creating a snapshot of a running database that can then be used as a source for backup. The difference here is that the snapshot is automatically copied out to another storage system, whereas the other method required you to do that.

Such snapshots allow you to take a very quick backup of your entire configuration, so this can be a great way to back up a large multinode database. If the database in question is a PaaS or serverless database, it is often the *only* way to back it up.

Check your PaaS or serverless database manual for how to enable this feature. Sometimes it is turned on by default, automatically creating a backup every few hours. At other times, you simply need to turn it on, or sometimes you will need to turn it on and configure its options, such as how often to back it up, and so on.

Test your backups

Although I believe this book has been pretty consistent in saying that everything that matters should be tested, I want to reiterate that here. Some backup methods available to you in the SaaS/serverless world simply don't work, at least not the restore part of the backup, anyway. Make sure you fully test whatever backup method you choose.

3-2-1 rule

I love how simple the backups are with PaaS and serverless databases. The one thing I think you should ask them is how well they conform to the 3-2-1 rule. At least one copy of your backups should be somewhere else. Storing the backup in object storage in the same account isn't good enough. Look what happened to codespaces.com when a hacker deleted its entire account in seconds. You should not be storing your only copy of database backups in the same account the database runs in. Ask your PaaS or serverless database vendor how to address this concern.

Now that we've looked at all the various ways you can back up databases, it's time to look at them by product. The next section discusses several popular database products and the various ways to back them up.

Preferred backup methods

Each major database product has one or more backup methods that the vendor or its users prefer to use. Given the size of this book and this chapter, this list will only be a quick summary, but what I can do is provide you with some of my thoughts on the various options. Hopefully, you can use these thoughts about the pros and cons of the various methods to make your own decision on the best way to back up your own database.

Oracle

Oracle has many options for backup, but the official answer for backing Oracle would be Recovery Manager (RMAN), which is also the name of the actual command that invokes it. It can perform full or incremental backups of all or part of the database and its redo logs by streaming data directly to a backup product or service, or to disk for a dump-and-sweep operation. RMAN also supports an image option that can merge older incrementals into the full backup, which would give you multiple recovery points without having to make multiple full backups. I think that's the most efficient dump-and-sweep option. Some customers also still use the `alter database begin/end backup` commands to put Oracle into/out of hot backup mode before/after backing up the data files with their backup tool of choice. This option works with anything and doesn't require a disk staging area, but it does require extensive scripting knowledge. On Windows, Oracle can also be backed up hot via the VSS method discussed in Chapter 6. There's nothing wrong with that option either.

SQL Server

The `backup database` command can be used to automate full or incremental backups of the database or its transaction logs to disk (for a dump and sweep), to Azure (for cloud backup), or to stream them directly to a third-party backup tool. SQL Server can also be backed up hot with the VSS method discussed in

Chapter 6. The VSS method is more easily integrated into VM backups and doesn't require a disk staging area.

DB2

The `backup database` command can be used to perform full or incremental backups of all or part of a DB2 database and its transaction logs to disk (for a dump and sweep) or stream them directly to a third-party backup tool. The command also supports a `snapshot` flag that integrates with storage devices that support snapshots, and can be used to create an application-consistent snapshot of a database. Like other snapshots, you should replicate that snapshot somewhere else once it is created.

MySQL

MySQL customers have a number of backup choices, mainly because the different types of tables (e.g., MyISAM and InnoDB) support different options. Customers of MySQL Enterprise Edition can use the Enterprise Backup feature that allows them to place the database in a hot backup mode before backing up its data files. This option is more efficient than using the `mysqldump` command; however, it is really only fully supported on InnoDB tables. Writes to MyISAM tables are halted during a backup. It works but is not as elegant as what happens to InnoDB tables. If you are using InnoDB tables and the Enterprise Edition, this is the best option. The `mysqldump` command is more universal and is available to all customers, but it is quite slow for large databases. Most people use it in a dump-and-sweep fashion; however, it can only perform full point-in-time backups and can be rather slow for larger databases. MySQL offers several other backup methods, though, including copying table files, incremental backups using the binary log, filesystem snapshots, and using a split replica to back up. MySQL customers should test all these backup options to see what works for them. Make sure to test the recovery speed of each method as well.

PostgreSQL

The usual method with PostgreSQL is the `pg_dump` command that creates a full SQL dump to disk, for a dump-and-sweep setup. It can back up the entire database or selected tables. If you'd like a tighter RPO than your `pg_dump` frequency, you should enable the continuous write ahead log (WAL) and then put the database into and out of hot backup mode, using `pg_start_backup` and `pg_stop_backup` before and after a filesystem backup. During a recovery, you start by restoring the filesystem, and then you use the WAL files to replay transactions that occurred after the backup. This option is efficient and mirrors the tight RPO recovery options of more expensive databases.

MongoDB

If you are using MongoDB Atlas (the PaaS version of the product), the best backup method would be continuous cloud backup with point-in-time recovery. You specify how far back you want to be able to recover, and Atlas automatically performs the backups it needs to perform to be able to restore your cluster to any point in time within the window you specified. There are some caveats that you should investigate, like not guaranteeing casual consistency. If you're hosting your own MongoDB installation, you can use MongoDB Cloud Manager (SaaS) or Ops Manager (on-premises software). Cloud Manager supports various SLAs at different price points and seems the obvious choice if you are not using Atlas. If you're running MongoDB 4.2 or greater, you can also just back up the underlying filesystem while `mongod` is running, and MongoDB will detect dirty keys after a restore and address them. The `mongodump` option is also available to use in a dump-and-sweep fashion, but it is only recommended for small deployments. One big reason is that `mongodump` cannot guarantee the atomicity of transactions across shards.

Cassandra

Your backup options with Cassandra vary widely based on whether you are using the open source version, the Enterprise version, or Astra (PaaS). Remember not to confuse the resilience of Cassandra with backup; resiliency will not protect you if someone accidentally dropped or truncated a table. The typical backup tool in Cassandra is called `nodetool snapshot`, which is a snapshot-like system that creates an entirely separate copy of all the data of all or certain keyspaces or tables, using hard links. It can create a full or incremental backup. This copy can then be used in a snap-and-sweep configuration to copy this data elsewhere. There are a number of challenges with this option, including storage usage, as well as RTO and RPO issues. Customers running any version of Cassandra on a cloud vendor can take the opportunity to create a cloud snapshot of their entire cluster at once. This provides much better restore options than can be done with the `nodetool snapshot` command. Datastax also has an offering called *DSE Backup and Restore Service* for Enterprise users, designed to back up and restore the entire cluster. Datastax Astra customers are automatically backed up every four hours.

Backing up DynamoDB

Since DynamoDB is only offered as a service, the choices for backup are relatively straightforward. AWS offers automated backups you can enable that support point-in-time recovery of all or part of your table in DynamoDB. All you have to do is enable point-in-time recovery and AWS will manage everything for you. AWS also offers on-demand backups that you can control, but they do not offer point-in-time restore.

Backing up Neo4j

Neo4j databases can be backed up using the `neo4j-admin backup` command to perform full and incremental backups of one or more online databases for use in a dump-and-sweep configuration. Offline (i.e., cold) backups are also supported but not required, and do not support incremental backups. It's recommended to configure the backup to run from a read replica, which lessens the performance impact of the backup process.

Select one of these backup methods to back up your important database, and then it's time to try restoring them. The restore process can be simple or complicated. Practice makes perfect. Let's look at a summary of what it's like to restore most databases.

Recovering Traditional Databases

Recovering traditional databases is a relatively simple process if you have practiced the various scenarios that can go wrong. Just make sure that a real database outage is not the first time you are testing whether your backup system has all the appropriate pieces to support an effective restore. Here is a very high-level summary of the various steps necessary to restore a database:

Identify what's wrong

This may seem very obvious, but it's not. Each database product has a sequence of steps you can go through to identify exactly why your database is no longer running. Sometimes it is obvious, because you know that you had a double disk failure on your RAID array. Or perhaps you accidentally deleted the database in question and know that you have to restore the entire thing. But if your database is just no longer running and you don't know why, learn how to try to start it up in phases to see which parts aren't working.

You may save a significant amount of time and effort in the recovery phase. For example, if you identify that the only thing wrong is your Oracle control file, a very simple small recovery of the control file and a restart of the database, using its backup control file, is all you will need to do. It will take you less than a minute. Imagine restoring your 5 TB Oracle database only to find out that the only thing that was wrong was a control file.

Restore data files

You need to restore the data files from wherever you backed them up. If you used the cold backup, hot backup, snap and sweep, or stream-to-backup product method, you just need to go to your backup product and restore the files directly in place. If you use the dump-and-sweep method, you will need to identify whether the backup that you need is still sitting where you typically run the backup. If it is there, you can just issue the restore command. If it is not there, you will need to restore your dump file from your backup system before you can issue the database restore command. (This is another disadvantage of the dump-and-sweep method; you might have to do a two-phase restore.)

Apply media recovery

If your database product supports it, and you have the transaction logs, you can usually replay them against a database restored from an older point in time. This will replay the transactions that have occurred since you backed up the database, bringing the database back to the point in time before the outage occurred. Media recovery is also a necessary step if you used the hot backup or snap-and-sweep methods, because it will be used to bring all the data files up to the same point in time, since you backed them up at different points in time.

Start the database

If you performed all of the foregoing steps correctly, you should be able to start the database at this point. If you cannot start it, go back to step one and figure out what happened.

Hopefully, this overview will be helpful when determining which steps you will need to restore your database. If you won't restore data files and apply transaction logs, your recovery will be very different from what I just discussed. The next section talks about some more modern ways of recovering databases.

Recovering Modern Databases

The recovery process for a modern database, especially one sharded across many nodes, will really depend on how and what you backed up and whether it is an immediately consistent or eventually consistent database. The overall process may be similar to the previously mentioned method for traditional databases, but the details will be quite different. Please investigate and test various backup *and recovery* methods of your chosen database before you actually need to use it. The cloud makes testing even the largest database so easy that there is no excuse. The following is a brief summary of some of the options:

Point-in-time recovery without media recovery

Some backup methods, especially PaaS and serverless databases, do not provide point-in-time recovery in the same manner as traditional databases (e.g., restore from point-in-time backup and then roll things forward from the transaction log). Some newer databases support point-in-time recovery by simply performing very frequent snapshot-based backup. A recovery to a point in time is done simply by selecting the appropriate snapshot, issuing the restore command, and starting the database.

Table-based recovery

Some of the backup options for modern databases only back up data at the table level; therefore, the restore of these databases will be at the table level as well.

Node-level recovery

In a multinode, sharded database, it may be necessary to recover a single node. In most such databases, this can be done without a restore. Simply issue the appropriate commands to create a new replica of data already in the database.

Cloud-level snapshot

If your database is running in a cloud vendor, it is possible you can perform frequent snapshots of any volumes where the database resides. Recovery here is very similar to the just-mentioned point-in-time recovery. Simply use one of those storage-level snapshots to restore all LUNs or filesystems where the database is running, and start the database.

Eventually consistent restore

There are some restore scenarios that, depending on how data is restored, will need to be brought consistent with the rest of the database. Depending on how out of date it is, how big the cluster is, and how good the performance of the cluster is, this process can take from a few minutes to several weeks.

Work with a specialist who understands your database product, learn the scenarios most likely to damage your database, and practice those recovery scenarios so you know exactly what to expect when the worst happens. What will it look like if you lose multiple nodes? How will you recover if you lose all members of a replica set? What if something horrible, such as a fire or explosion, takes out all nodes in your cluster? What about human mistakes or attacks? How will you respond if someone drops or truncates a table? Make sure you are prepared for all scenarios. Failure to be prepared can result in job losses, especially yours.

Takeaways

Databases can be difficult to back up and recover, but it is not impossible. Learn enough about them to talk to your DBA and develop a plan. They will most likely see things from a different point of view, so understand that. Try to make them your ally and not your enemy. I spent too much of my career trying to convince DBAs to do things my way. Don't let perfect be the enemy of good. Bad is no backups at all, which means anything is better than that.

All databases aren't the same. Just because dump and sweep is the best option for one database doesn't mean it's the best option for another one. Learn the advantages and disadvantages of the various backup methods for each database and select accordingly.

Finally, database recoveries can be very complicated, depending on what went wrong. Use the cloud to practice various recovery scenarios so that you and your DBAs are pros at recovering your databases. Please don't let a major recovery be the first time you're testing how to recover your database.

Now it's time to cover more modern workloads. Let's talk about things running in the cloud, in containers, and even services that hold corporate data. The cloud is not magic, and bad things can happen there as well. So let's talk about how cloud data needs to be protected, too.

CHAPTER 8

Modern Data Sources

The first chapters were about protecting data sources that very few people would argue about. There are exceptions, of course. Everyone agrees we need to back up servers and databases. Not everyone agrees we should back up laptops, and some people still try to say that some scalable databases are so resilient they don't need backup. (They're both wrong.) But with the data sources in this chapter, I constantly find myself arguing with people who either don't realize they need to be backed up or adamantly say they really don't need backup.

I can't state this strongly enough. *The cloud is not magic! There is no such thing as the cloud; there is only someone else's computer.* The cloud, SaaS, and (most recently) Kubernetes, do not change the fundamental rules of data protection and data ownership. It's your data and your responsibility to back it up, and unless you have it in writing that someone else is doing it for you, you have to do it. Even if you have it in writing that they're doing it for you, it is your job to test that fact.

With all this in mind, let's take a look at these modern and ever-developing workloads. If you're using them and not backing them up, you can't say I didn't tell you.

The Public Cloud

Several large service providers provide compute, storage, networking, and other services to organizations around the world and are referred to as infrastructure-as-a-service (IaaS). These services are giant datacenters that run specialized hypervisors and other processes to provide you with a series of services that offer nearly infinite scalability both up and down. If all you need is a single container for 30 seconds or a VM for a few days, these vendors can make it happen. If you need to move your organization's entire computing infrastructure into their datacenter, they can do that too.

Many huge organizations run most or their entire computing infrastructure inside the public cloud. Perhaps the best-known example is Netflix. They started out in AWS, experimented with doing some of their own infrastructure, and eventually moved everything back into AWS. Netflix is the perfect example of the kind of application that can leverage the cloud both to increase its service level and reduce cost at the same time.

The amount of computing resources necessary to provide a service like Netflix is directly proportional to the number of people watching Netflix at any given moment. The number of people watching Netflix changes month to month, day to day, and even hour to hour. As of this writing, we are in the midst of a global pandemic; the number of people watching Netflix has skyrocketed, and they didn't skip a beat.

The reason Netflix has done so well both financially and technically is that it built its system to take advantage of how the cloud works. Its software automatically scales its computing, network, and storage usage as its needs change. It can automatically add more resources when more people are watching Netflix and take away those resources when they are no longer watching. This happens automatically throughout the day. It's truly an amazing way to do IT infrastructure.

Infrastructure-as-a-Service (IaaS)

Examples of IaaS are AWS Elastic Compute Cloud (EC2) and Elastic Block Storage (EBS). Microsoft, Google, Oracle, and others all have similar versions of such products, but I will stick with AWS for examples, since it's the most well-known provider. EC2 is a specialized hypervisor that provides VMs of various sizes that are available to run for minutes, hours, or even permanently. For a VM to exist, it needs block storage, which is where EBS comes into the story.

Most people using IaaS services know that no backups are provided. They may provide the ability to back up your data, but you must initiate and manage any backups, and you must protect them against anything that might damage them. Make sure to read "You Need to Protect the Cloud" on page 172 later in this chapter.

Customers using IaaS services typically have two choices when it comes to backing them up. As with traditional VMs, cloud VMs can be backed up by simply installing a cloud-friendly version of a backup software product or service and backing up those VMs in the same way you would back up a remote physical server. Because you typically pay for outgoing traffic (often referred to as egress charges), it would be advantageous for you to use a backup method that is very bandwidth-friendly. For example, you could use a block-level, incremental forever backup method such as snapshot and replication-based backup, or a source-side deduplication backup system, both of which are discussed in Chapter 9. Even if you use a backup service provider that incorporates those fees in its pricing, those fees are still there.

The more common way to back up IaaS services is to use the native tools provided by that vendor. Each IaaS vendor provides anything from APIs that you or a third-party product can call, to full-fledged, scheduled backup services. Most people use these native tools to back up in the public cloud because the tools typically are designed for the environment in question. They utilize the native capabilities of that cloud vendor and provide extra functionality that is difficult to get without the integration they offer, because they are provided by the cloud vendor.

Block storage in the cloud

AWS, for example, provides basic to advanced backup services for EC2 VMs running on EBS. You can perform them manually in the AWS interface, schedule them to happen automatically, or use a third-party product to manage the process for you. The first backup of an EBS volume creates a byte-for-byte image copy of the source volume (or all of the source volumes attached to a given EC2 host you are backing up), and this copy is stored in a completely different storage system, which happens to be the AWS Simple Storage Service (S3).

AWS calls this an *EBS snapshot*, although it is very different from what I mean when I talk about snapshots. In Chapter 9, I define snapshots as virtual images of a volume that rely on the source volume for most of the data. In this case, the snapshot is a full copy of the protected volume, which is quite different. That's more of an image copy than a snapshot. Subsequent snapshots will store only the bytes that have changed since the previous backup and will also be called EBS snapshots.

You can restore the original protected volume(s) from any point in time from which one of the snapshots was taken. If you are interested in this method of backup, make sure to look into the speed of the restore and how different configuration choices you make can affect that speed.

One advantage of EBS snapshots is that they do not incur egress charges when they are created, because the data is not leaving Amazon. Another advantage is that EBS snapshots for EC2 VMs can interact with VSS in the VM if it happens to be running Windows, allowing you to perform application-consistent backups of VSS-supported applications running in a Windows VM in EC2, without having to install an agent inside that VM. These are a few of the reasons many AWS customers prefer these integrated snapshots. As I mentioned earlier, just be sure to follow the advice mentioned later in this chapter in "You Need to Protect the Cloud" on page 172.

Object storage in the cloud

Another type of storage found in IaaS vendors is object storage. Examples include AWS Simple Storage Service (S3), Azure Blob, and Google Cloud Storage. Object storage is very different from block or file storage, but it is easier to describe it by comparing it with file storage.

A filesystem stores files on block storage, and each file is identified by its filename and the directory in which the file is stored. For example, resume.doc in /home/ Curtis is considered a completely different file from resume.doc in /home/Steve. This is true even if the contents and basename (resume.doc) of these two files are exactly the same. They are considered two different files because they are in two different directories; their contents are not compared against each other. Nor is there any ability to know whether the contents of any of these files have been changed.

 Some people might think that you could detect a change in a file by watching its modification time, but remember that there are facilities in most OSs to modify the modification time, which allows a smart hacker to reset the modification time back to whatever time it was before modifying the file. Another change that modification time won't detect is bit rot, which is the degradation of the file in magnetic storage over time.

Object storage also stores files on block storage, but they are not called files for multiple reasons, the first of which is that files are stored in a filesystem. An object-storage system stores objects. Objects may be what a typical user would consider a file, such as resume.doc. But they can also be anything else, including a disk image of an EBS volume. (The previously mentioned EBS snapshot is stored as an object in S3, which is an object-storage system.) An object can also be part of something. For example, deduplication systems usually slice everything they store into small chunks of data, often referred to as *shards*. Some deduplication systems store each shard as an object in an object-storage system.

A filesystem is a hierarchical storage system, using a series of directories and subdirectories to identify the files therein. An object-storage system, by contrast, is completely flat. Every object in the "buckets" of an object-storage systems are stored in the same namespace. Many buckets can be in an account, but they are also all at the same level. They are therefore not akin to directories and subdirectories. Figure 8-1 shows a typical filesystem with the hierarchy of directories, subdirectories, and files.

Unlike files, objects are identified by their contents, not by an arbitrary name given to them by their creator. Each object is run through a cryptographic hashing algorithm (e.g., SHA-1) that creates an alphanumeric value referred to as a hash. The following is a SHA-1 hash of the phrase *hello world*: 2AAE6C35C94FCFB415DBE95F408B9 CE91EE846ED.

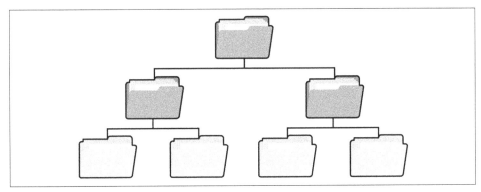

Figure 8-1. Filesystem

This hash is unique to each object because it is based on the contents of that object; therefore, the hash becomes the unique identifier (e.g., UID) for that object. When you store an object in an object-storage system, it responds with the UID that it just stored for you. You then must store that UID and use it whenever you want to request that object. Figure 8-2 shows an object-storage system in which there are several types of self-describing objects, each storing completely different types of data and each directly accessible via its UID.

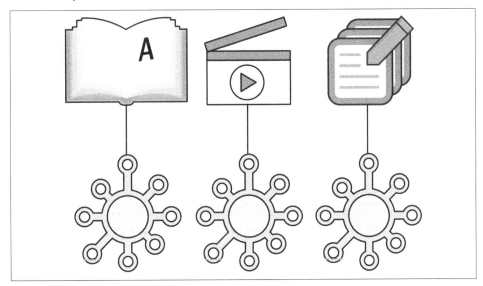

Figure 8-2. Object-storage system

If you've ever interacted with a cloud-based object-storage system, you might be thinking that you can name stored objects, because that's what you do in the UI you're using. In reality, what you are seeing is a translation layer between the object-storage system and you. You tell it what filename you want to store, it stores that file in object storage, and then records the UID of the object and associates it with the filename you specified.

Another difference between object storage and filesystems is that objects never change. Although it is normal to open a file, modify it, and save it again, using the same name, this cannot happen with objects. If you think about how objects are created and identified, you can see why this is not possible with object storage. If you were to change an object and save it again, you would change its content and therefore its UID, which is based on that content. Therefore, if you need to modify an object, you simply store a new version of that object and, optionally, store the previous version of that object for versioning purposes.

Don't confuse a filesystem interface to object storage, *with* object storage. Yes, filesystem translation services exist that give all the features of a typical filesystem (e.g., directories, modifying files) and store their data in object storage. In reality, when you modify a file in such a system, it is storing the modified object as a new object.

Data protection features are built into object storage. The most obvious feature is that at any time you can verify that each object in the system is the same as it was when it was stored. You do this by recalculating the hash and comparing it against the current hash. If the hash is the same as it was when it was originally stored, the contents have not been changed, either by a hacker or by magnetic degradation (bit rot). This is a great feature for proving chain of custody, immutability, and identifying bit rot in the underlying storage. (Bit rot is discussed in "Long-term retention" on page 260.)

Another feature built into most object-storage systems is a way to specify how many times each object is stored. For example, the AWSs S3 standard stores every object in "a minimum of three availability zones, each separated by miles across an AWS region," according to the S3 documentation. These extra copies can be used to survive natural and man-made disasters as well as recover an unmodified version of an object if the integrity check mentioned in the previous paragraph identifies a corrupted object.

Object storage provided by IaaS vendors is used by many organizations as an inexpensive place to store certain types of data that do not need storage that can be constantly changed, like block or file storage. For example, many organizations store their backups or archives in S3, Azure Blob storage or Google Cloud Storage.

Many data protection features in popular object-storage systems meet the backup requirements specified in the 3-2-1 rule. There are three copies of the data in three locations. You can even enable a write-once-read-many (WORM) feature that will prevent even you from deleting your data. This would protect your data against a hacker that might gain access to your account. It is also self-healing in that it can detect and repair silent data corruption caused by bit rot.

Because of these data protection features, many organizations do not feel the need to back up object storage. If you do not back up your object storage, please do what you can to protect it. Make sure you programmatically search your organization's entire account for open buckets, which are object-storage buckets that anyone can read. Do not be the next organization with an open bucket. Make sure you enable multifactor authentication and store important backup data in a separate account in a separate region. Be sure to read "You Need to Protect the Cloud" on page 172 and follow its advice.

Let's take things up one level from infrastructure and look at database platforms. They are also available as a service and are the next modern data source we need to look at. Like IaaS, they need to be backed up, but the vendors that offer them provide you with the capability to do so.

Platform-as-a-Service (PaaS)

In addition to providing infrastructure services such as compute and storage, most cloud vendors also offer platform-as-a-service (PaaS) services. These can be database platforms (e.g., MySQL, Oracle), application platforms, or even virtualization platforms (e.g., VMware Cloud). The PaaS customer selects the service they want and configures it to meet their needs.

For example, they might use AWS Relational Database Service (RDS) to specify the version of MySQL they need, the size of the database, and the identities of the administrators. (Dozens of configuration options might be provided at the initial creation of a particular offering; I'm just listing these as an example.) Once the customer specifies how they want the platform provisioned, it will be provisioned automatically, and then the customer can start using the service.

These services are for those who are fine with managing the platform but are not interested in the typical system administration side of things. They know they want a 1 TB database; they don't want to provision it themselves.

What is important, though, is that just like the IaaS services mentioned in the previous section, any PaaS offering that creates data needs to be backed up. Like the IaaS offerings, many of these offerings provide automated backup services. AWS RDS is a PaaS and offers integrated backup. It works quite similarly to the EBS volume backup described in the previous section. It will take an application-consistent snapshot of the database in question and store that snapshot as a full byte-for-byte copy in S3. Subsequent snapshots will store only the bytes changed since the last backup.

The same is true for VMware Cloud and Hyper-V Cloud. They need to be backed up just as much as an on-premises version of the same software, but you are responsible for doing so. In this case, you will need to connect a backup system capable of backing up these hypervisors.

 As of this writing, AWS does allow Oracle RDS customers to use RMAN to create backups of their RDS Oracle database, but it provides no facilities to restore an Oracle RDS database from such an RMAN backup!

In many cases, integrated backups of PaaS offerings are the only way to create a backup of that data, because there is nowhere to install a backup agent. Please use this functionality to create a backup and then protect that backup against hackers and natural disasters by following the advice listed in "You Need to Protect the Cloud" on page 172.

Serverless Services

Some applications are offered purely as a service at a further abstraction layer above PaaS. In such applications, you simply use the application and don't have to configure or manage *anything*. A perfect example of that would be Amazon DynamoDB, which is a straightforward key-value database with a very easy-to-understand structure. Authenticate yourself to DynamoDB and start storing key-value pairs—no storage or database configuration needed. (The database is already running, and you are actually only creating a table in said database, but you don't see any of this. You just see your table containing your key-value pairs.) Put one pair in there or ten billion of them; you won't have to configure anything. DynamoDB will automatically scale the backend to meet your (and other customers') needs. Just like everything else in the cloud, this service is very resilient, but you still need to back it up.

Each service like this typically offers a way to back up such data. DynamoDB, for example, can be configured for very frequent backups that are stored in your AWS account. It's simple to back up and restore, but it's still your responsibility to ensure that it's configured and running.

Software-as-a-Service (SaaS)

The final type of service that we need to talk about is software-as-a-service (SaaS). Although some might see products such as AWS RDS as SaaS, that is not really what most people mean when they use the term. Generally speaking, SaaS applications are full-blown, purpose-built applications that accomplish a specific purpose. SaaS applications tend to have a few things in common.

You are most likely familiar with several SaaS applications. Microsoft 365, Google Workspace, Salesforce, Slack, and GitHub are all purpose-built SaaS applications.

No infrastructure required

The infrastructure necessary to provide the service in question is not your responsibility, either from a management or cost perspective. It may be myriad servers and applications that all work together to accomplish the service's purposes, but you don't have to worry about any of that. This is what differentiates SaaS from subscription-based software. With subscription software, you are simply paying for the software via a recurring bill; you are still responsible for the infrastructure upon which that software runs. When you pay for a SaaS product, you should never know or care about the infrastructure that makes it happen. That means no servers or storage to provision or protect.

Frequent automatic updates

Most SaaS applications have developed the agile development model and come out with new features that are simply rolled into the product on a very regular basis. You do not need to worry about maintaining or upgrading the service, because that is simply handled for you. You just need to learn about and use any new features.

Pay-as-you-go model

Typical hardware and software products are purchased as large capital purchases based on guesses of how much capacity you will need, and you pay for everything up front, regardless of whether you ever use it. To make sure you have enough resources, most such products are overprovisioned, and you often end up paying for hardware and software you never actually use. A SaaS system allows you to pay for what you use, such as a number of users or gigabytes backed up. Many SaaS services may still ask you to pay for a year or so in advance, but then what you actually pay is based on actual usage.

Backup is not included

As discussed in "You Need to Protect the Cloud" on page 172, backup is not included in any of the major SaaS applications discussed in this chapter. There may be backup-like features such as the recycle bin or versioning, but nothing that matches the basic definition of backup: something that follows the 3-2-1 rule. See Chapter 3 for a definition of this very important rule.

The following is a brief overview of various SaaS services, the types of things that you might want to back up from them, and whether that can be done within the product.

Salesforce

Salesforce Datacenter (SFDC) is a customer relationship management (CRM) service. Salespeople put all their leads and contacts here, as well as keeping track of all their sales and potential sales with this service.

SFDC is essentially a giant special-purpose database, but since you do not have typical database access, you use slightly different terminology than you would for a typical database product. For example, instead of tables, SFDC has *objects*. This can be confusing, given that objects are used for so many very different things in IT. But in SFDC parlance, an object is the same thing as a table.

The *users* object stores all the users, their passwords, and what things they have access to in SFDC. A potential customer is typically first recorded in the *leads* object and then moved to the *contacts* object after they become a customer. Hopefully, a potential sale will be recorded in the *opportunities* object, which will then be recorded as *won* or *lost*. All communication with this customer will be stored in one or more related objects that are all tied together via the unique record ID of each user, lead, or object it belongs to.

Hundreds of third-party applications also integrate with SFDC to do many things, including automated billing, commission management, emailing and retargeting on the web, and so on. All these applications use SFDC as the *source of record*; they get their authoritative information from SFDC and then record any of their activities directly into the appropriate leader contact record as well.

SFDC is an incredibly integral part of so many organizations, and yet many of them do not back up this important resource. Salesforce has unfortunately confused the issue with mixed messages, as I will explain in the following paragraphs.

Salesforce provides a just-in-case recovery service that costs $10,000 and takes six to eight weeks to provide you with a download link for comma-separated values (CSV) files, each of which represent a full backup of one Salesforce object (e.g., users, leads, contacts). These CSV files would then need to be imported one at a time in a particular order to effect a restore properly.

Salesforce initially withdrew this service in July 2020, saying that it wasn't living up to the expectations it set for its products (I agree!), and declared that it is the user's responsibility to back up their own data. (That's at least one nice thing; not every SaaS vendor has been so forthcoming.) Then in March 2021, it reversed this position and is now again offering what I can only describe as the worst backup and recovery service I have ever looked at. A six to eight–week RTA with no recovery guarantee and that requires an incredibly manual restore process? Why would anyone pressure Salesforce to put this service back into production?

Salesforce users have a few tools they can use to back it up. Unfortunately, none of the free tools are automated. A Salesforce admin can go into the Salesforce interface and tell it to perform a backup. After a certain period of time, based on the number of records in your account, you will be presented with a file that you can download as your backup. This is a very manual process that cannot be automated.

Some users use their sandbox as a backup method. Assuming your license allows it, you have one free sandbox that you can use to perform a complete copy from your production database. This also cannot be automated, and there is no way to restore from the sandbox directly to production. You again have to download from the sandbox and then use these CSVs to restore your production instance.

As of this writing, Salesforce claims to be developing an actual native backup and recovery offering that's better than they currently have. I can't evaluate it because it's not released yet, but if it does not copy data out of the Salesforce infrastructure, it would not conform to the 3-2-1 rule, and I would not consider it a valid option. But if it provides a way to copy your Salesforce data automatically to a secure S3 bucket, or something like that, we could be getting somewhere.

There are a number of commercial tools to back up and restore Salesforce in a fully automated way as part of your overall organization's data protection system. My recommendation would be to use one of those software products or services.

Microsoft 365

Microsoft 365, formally known as Office 365, is a series of communication and collaboration tools, including Exchange Online, SharePoint, OneDrive, and Teams. Each of these tools represents a significant amount of intellectual property of a given organization that would be very much missed if it were to be lost. Very few people would debate the value of such important IT infrastructure.

Where people seem to differ is whether this data is already being backed up. The fact is that there really is no debate here. Just like with the other SaaS applications, nothing Microsoft is doing to protect your data would qualify as a backup by the all-important 3-2-1 rule.

At best, I would describe many of their backup features as *convenience* features. They are no different than a recycle bin on your laptop. A recycle bin is convenient, but if your laptop catches fire, that recycle bin will be of no use to you.

A perfect example of such a convenience feature is Microsoft 365 *Retention Policies*. You can create a retention policy that specifies that every version of every file and every sent or received email is saved for n days or months. Yes, it is true that every single file or email created, received, or sent via Microsoft 365 will be stored via such a retention policy. You can even specify that this copy cannot be deleted, even by you. (This is to protect against hackers and is very helpful in a chain-of-custody accusation in a lawsuit.)

The question is about what happens when you need to *restore* your data. The only way to retrieve data stored by a Microsoft retention policy is to use the e-discovery system, which should never be confused with a restore system. Suppose an account (or part thereof) was corrupted or deleted in some significant way. A normal restore would be able to restore that account to the way it looked just prior to the damage. Folders and any other organizational structures built into the account would be restored along with the data.

E-discovery systems don't know about folders and organizational structures. They are focused on retrieving data for lawsuits. Although it will be super easy to find all emails that contain a particular phrase or that were sent or received by a particular user, putting those emails or files back in the place they came from in the way they were originally stored simply isn't in the purview of an e-discovery system. What you will get after a long and complicated process is a giant pile of emails and files all stored in a single level.

An e-discovery system also doesn't understand the concept of a point-in-time restore of a mailbox or directory. It knows how to give you all the email and files created or received during a particular time range. Ask it to show you all the emails that existed (and were not deleted) on the day the outage occurred—and it will be completely unable to answer that question. This means that in addition to restoring all emails and files into one big folder, it will also restore files that were deleted.

Finally, this retention policy is also storing these extra emails and files in the same database used to provide your email and file service. If something happens to your entire account, such as was discussed in "You Need to Protect the Cloud" on page 172, these extra copies will disappear as well.

Those that would mock the idea of third-party backup of Microsoft 365 say that I am being a fear monger and that what I previously described as a nightmare recovery scenario is an edge case. They also say it's rare enough that you'd just deal with the inconveniences created by not having proper backups. My retort to that is that, whereas I admit that the odds of this happening to a given organization are very low, if it does happen to you, making the recovery that much harder makes the attack that much worse. The cost of using a third-party backup service for Microsoft 365 is small, and the potential rewards are so big. I just can't imagine taking that big of a risk with such important data.

The two most popular service levels of Microsoft 365 are E3 and E5; the main difference is some added security and e-discovery features in E5. What I really can't understand are customers who pay for E5, which costs $15 more per user per month than E3. The functionality and protection provided by E5 is significantly less than any decent third-party tool would offer and costs more than such tools would charge.

In the end, the decision is up to you. If you decided that your organization was willing to live without the benefits of a backup, that's your decision. I just want to make sure you know that nothing Microsoft is doing for you is actually a backup. My biggest concern is that people aren't backing their data up because they think it's already backed up, and that's wrong.

One other thing I'd like to add is this: look at your service agreement for Microsoft 365. Find the section that talks about backup and restore. I'll wait. That's right; there isn't one. You are counting on Microsoft to do something it isn't doing and doesn't say it's doing in the contract.

There are no tools in Microsoft 365 to back up your organization's data for free. There are some commercial tools that have freemium versions that allow you to back up a handful of accounts or a handful of gigabytes for free before paying for a commercial version. But for most organizations, the only way to back up Microsoft 365 properly is to use a commercial software product or service to automate this.

Google Workspace

Almost everything I said about Microsoft 365 is also true about Google Workspace (formerly known as G-Suite). It is a series of collaboration tools that should be backed up, but backup is not included in the suite itself. Google Vault is Google's equivalent to Microsoft Retention Policies; it is an e-discovery and retention system for Google Workspace. As with Microsoft 365, it can be used to store a copy of every email or file that went through the system, and this archive can be easily searched via the web.

Like retention policies, Google Archive is not a backup and, more important, cannot restore your mailbox or G Drive folder to the way it looked yesterday before the bad thing happened, whatever it was. If someone accidentally deleted your account, or you accidentally deleted a big part of your account, or you got ransomware in the folder you are syncing to G Drive, Google Archive cannot return whatever it was to the way it looked before it happened. That is not the purpose of an e-discovery system. At best, it can put all files and emails back that have ever existed in your account! That is far from what you would want in such a scenario.

If, however, you need to see all files or emails where you said the word "wizbang," or if you need something to show you all files or emails you created during a certain time period, Google Archive is your friend. That's what e-discovery systems do. What they don't do is restore your account to a particular point in time. The good news is that I don't know anyone trying to say otherwise, unlike what I keep seeing in the Microsoft 365 world.

The tools available for Google Workspace are similar to the ones available for Microsoft 365. There are free tools that will sync a single user to their laptop, and a few freemium versions that will back up a few accounts or terabytes of your organization's account so that you can sample their product and, hopefully, buy more. I would recommend examining one of the commercial products that can back up Google Workspace.

Slack

Slack is easily the most popular chat application available as a service, although Microsoft Teams is starting to catch up now that it is bundled with Microsoft 365. There is a free version of Slack with certain limitations (you can only search back through the past 10,000 messages, for example) and a commercial version that removes those limitations.

Because Slack is increasingly becoming the default method of communication for a lot of organizations, many are starting to see it as an important repository of organizational knowledge. It's also another thing that is targeted in lawsuits, so it would be helpful to be able to perform e-discovery against the state as well.

I am unaware of any free tools to back up Slack, but there are third-party applications that can do the job.

GitHub

The GitHub repository system, and others like it, has become increasingly important for organizations that are deploying their own applications, especially those that are doing so via Docker and Kubernetes. A quick review of "Docker and Kubernetes" on page 179, which talks about how to manage Docker and Kubernetes properly, would certainly lead the reader to believe that GitHub is a very important destination and source of very important information.

I know this will sound like a broken record, but backups of GitHub are not included in the service contract. You need to examine how you can back up GitHub, but as of this writing, third-party options for backing it up are not as easy to find as some of the other tools mentioned in this chapter.

You Need to Protect the Cloud

The cloud is not some magical place where all problems are solved. In fact, the public cloud is yet another example of the old adage, "We never fix problems in IT; we just move them." Yes, the services provided in the public cloud often take away many of the mundane tasks that a typical IT infrastructure would require. But it's really important to understand that the public cloud does not fundamentally change the nature of computing and, more specifically, data protection. Bad things can and still do happen in the cloud, and you need to protect your data from them.

As I was putting the final touches on this book, there was a major disaster at Europe's largest cloud vendor, OVHcloud. An apparent malfunction in an uninterruptible power supply (UPS) created a fire that completely destroyed one of their datacenters.

The fire was big enough that it also created smoke damage in a neighboring datacenter. Customers who had backups that conform to the 3-2-1 rule were easily able to restore operations, but some customers lost everything. Some of them believed OVHcloud was performing backups for them—and they weren't. Others made backups, but stored them in the same datacenter or in the neighboring one that was damaged by smoke. Like I said in the previous paragraph, the cloud is not magic. Bad things happen in the cloud just like they happen in real life. You must protect your data from such things.

There are many stories of data that has been lost or stolen in the cloud and never recovered because the IT people responsible failed to acknowledge the fact that data in the cloud still needs to be protected. I regularly state that I believe the security level of servers and data in the average public cloud is greater than the security level of the same in the typical datacenters that I have encountered. But even if it is the best security in the entire universe, it is not invulnerable to attack. In addition, whereas there are redundancies upon redundancies, many things can go wrong at the same time and kill every one of your redundancies. A perfect example of this is described in the next sidebar "Well, That Would Never Happen".

Well, That Would Never Happen

I had barely begun my IT career working at MBNA, a credit card company, in February 1993 when a snowstorm took out one of two hubs for the Cirrus ATM network. This network was, of course, needed for most ATM transactions in the United States.

"No problem," we said, "there is a completely redundant system in the basement of the World Trade Center in New York City."

Yes, that World Trade Center. And yes, this was the same day a truck bomb was detonated in the parking area underneath the north tower, taking out our second redundant system—and the Cirrus ATM network along with it.

That bombing took place on February 26, 1993. I took my job as the backup guy at MBNA (at the time the second largest credit card corporation in the United States) on February 23, 1993. You might say that it had a profound impact on the way I viewed redundant systems for the rest of my IT career. To this day, I laugh when somebody says, "We have fully redundant systems."

"Let me tell you about my third day on the job," are usually the next words out of my mouth.

Many stories come to mind when I think about whether data in the cloud needs to be protected, but no story comes close to the disaster that was codespaces.com. It's also an incredible example of irony. (Unlike Alanis Morissette, I actually know what irony means.) I covered it in the sidebar "There's a New One" on page 46, but I'm covering it here in more detail.

Codespaces.com was a SaaS service that advertised itself as a "Rock Solid, Secure and Affordable SVN Hosting, Git Hosting and Project Management." On June 14, 2014, its website said it offered "Rock-Solid Repository Hosting" and "Full Redundancy & Snapshot Backups." Its entire IT infrastructure was stored in AWS, the most trusted cloud service in the world. Of course it had redundancy and rock-solid hosting.

On Tuesday, June 17, 2014, the website said, "Code Spaces is down." A hacker had gained access to its AWS control panel and attempted to extort money from it with the threat of deleting its account. It attempted to lock the hacker out, and the hacker retaliated. "In summary, most of our data, backups, machine configurations and off-site backups were either partially or completely deleted."

It was later discovered that Code Spaces had not followed the usual practices of enabling multifactor authentication, which enabled the hacker to gain access in the first place. It is unknown how they got access, but it happened. And since Code Spaces had also not followed separation-of-powers practices in separating its production data from its backup data, the hacker was able to delete everything in a few keystrokes.

You could read the story and think, "I would have enabled multifactor authentication, so that would not have happened to me." So let's assume that your security practices are up to snuff and you follow all the best practices. I have another story for you. A company in Oakland, California, called Musee, Inc., managed to shoot itself in the foot, as the saying goes. A well-intentioned system administrator, attempting to delete a test account, accidentally deleted their company's G-Suite account. This company was a very cloudy company that stored all of its intellectual property in G-Suite (now called Google Workspace). In fact, it apparently didn't even synchronize its G Drive to any laptops or desktops. It simply stored data directly in G Drive.

So when its system administrator accidentally deleted its account, its entire company's intellectual property ceased to exist. It attempted to contact Google support to no avail. This may come as a surprise to you, but Google and other companies like it are not backing up your data in a way that you can use to recover it if you or someone else deletes it or corrupts it.

In the SaaS world, there is rarely anything that a backup expert would consider backups. To meet the most basic definition of backups (the 3-2-1 rule), you need to be storing backup data *in a separate system*, and these vendors are not doing that. At best, they have versioning that stores historical versions of your data in the same system your data is being stored in. It is not being stored on separate media, and it is certainly not being stored in a different geographical area.

A quick read of the description of the very important 3-2-1 Rule described in Chapter 3 will show you how a recycle bin or versioning fails to meet the 2 and the 1 from that rule. Those parts of the rule are arguably the most important parts.

I'm reminded of the car rental episode of Seinfeld when he is confronting a rental car agent who is telling him they have his reservation, but don't have a car for him. "You know how to take the reservation; you just don't know how to *hold* the reservation. And that's really the most important part of the reservation: the *holding.*"

The same is true with the 3-2-1 rule. Yes, it's important to keep at least three versions of your data, but if you store all of them in the system you are backing up, you're saving them for no reason. To plagiarize Seinfeld, "That's really the most important part of the backups: the *separating.*"

Another very important point is that the vendor is under no legal obligation to help you in a data recovery situation because there is nothing in your service contract that specifies that. In a case of confirmation bias, you may have seen phrases in your service contract that refer to things like availability, redundancy, and data resiliency and assumed that they addressed backup and recovery. But all of these speak to the hardware and software behind the service itself; none of them speaks to protecting the data itself. Look at your service agreement again. Look for words like *backup*, *restore*, and *recovery*. Look for words and phrases like *ransomware attack* or *hack*. You will not find those phrases in your service contract for your favorite IaaS/PaaS/SaaS vendor. Which means it has no legal obligation to help you if things go wrong with your data. Musee, the previously mentioned Oakland company, sued Google over their loss of data. All I can say is, "Good luck with that."

Another big incident happened in 2020, with KPMG and Microsoft 365. KPMG was using a retention policy to specify that all private chats would be held for some period such as 90 days. For some reason, the powers that be wanted to delete one person's private chat, so the administrator created a retention policy with a retention of zero days and went to move that user into that policy. The problem was that they actually did the opposite of what they intended to do, instead moving 140,000 users into the policy with no retention. Suddenly, everyone's private chats were gone. They contacted Microsoft and got the only answer Microsoft could give: there is no backup for that.

One more story should help hammer this home. In May 2019, thousands of Salesforce customers found their accounts deactivated and were given only this message to explain what happened: "On May 17, 2019, Salesforce blocked access to certain instances that contained customers affected by a database script deployment that inadvertently gave users broader data access than intended." A script run by a Salesforce employee gave every user in your organization access to every record inside your Salesforce account. Its solution was to deactivate your account and tell you to fix the problem before it would enable your account. Let me restate that. Salesforce corrupted the *users* object in thousands of customers' accounts *and then told them to go fix it.* If you had a backup of your account, you could fix it in a few minutes. Just restore the *users* object to the way it was before the error and you would be done. Without it, though, you had to edit the permissions manually on all your users. The only good thing to come out of this is that Salesforce now officially states that it is your responsibility to back up your data. I wish other SaaS apps were as up-front about that.

It is your responsibility to protect your organization's data regardless of where it resides. I would argue that point even if these vendors provided true backup and recovery services that would meet the definitions given elsewhere in this book—and of course they don't. But if they did, I would not rely on those services for my organization's data. The only way to know for sure that your backups follow the 3-2-1 rule is to back up data to a separate system or service.

Most people seem to know that they need to back up their VMs and block storage running in IaaS vendors. Most people also seem to know that they need to back up their PaaS data, such as when they use database services like Azure SQL Database or VMware Cloud or Azure Cloud.

My biggest concern is with SaaS data, because it is SaaS data where I often get the argument about backup. I'm not really sure why, but it is a very common misunderstanding about SaaS offerings that backup and recovery is part of the package. It could be because there are so many backup-like features such as versioning and long-term retention of deleted files and emails. But as I've already mentioned, these backup copies do not meet the definition of a backup; they are not stored in a separate system or location. When you delete a file or email in these systems, they are simply setting the *delete* flag and keeping the file or email around in the same place. They are not saving it anywhere.

Once you are actually backing up your cloud data, I also want to make sure that you are protecting those backups against hacker attacks like what happened to codespaces.com as well as against region-wide disasters like hurricanes or floods. Don't do what codespaces.com did and store your backups in the same account or region as your primary copy.

Ensure that your backup data is stored in a different account and region than your primary data. I think the best idea is to pick a region where you are not using any cloud services and send all of your backups to that region. Create a separate account whose only purpose is backup and recovery. Protect that account with the highest level of security you can. Use multifactor authentication and every security feature that vendor offers. If possible, multiperson authentication would be best, so that deleting data outside of the normal deletion policies requires the authentication and authorization of multiple people. A great thing to do would be to use the WORM feature of some object-storage systems to make sure your backups are not modified or deleted before their retention period is up.

I am stepping down from my soapbox, now, and getting back to describing modern workloads that need to be backed up. The next one is another where I tend to get into a little bit of an argument, and that is with what we call hybrid cloud deployments, where some hardware is on-prem and other data is in the cloud.

Hybrid Cloud Configurations

Many computing environments use what is referred to as a *hybrid cloud* model, which means that they move to the cloud those workloads that are most appropriate for the cloud and keep workloads that are more appropriate for on premises still in the data-center. In this section, we are talking specifically about combinations of hardware and software that adopt a hybrid cloud model within their design.

NFS/SMB Gateway

A perfect example of a hybrid cloud product would be one that is often described as a *cloud gateway*. It comes in a variety of forms, but the main idea is that applications and users in the datacenter get to use an on-premises appliance that to them seems like any other appliance; in reality, the appliance is storing data in the cloud. A very common version of this is a NFS or SMB server, with unlimited capacity due to the cloud. How you approach such a system from a data protection standpoint would depend on a variety of factors.

Caching or staging

The question is what role the cloud plays in the overall storage design. If the cloud is sent all data stored on the device, then the device is simply a cache. You do not need to worry about backing up cache data, and you can simply make your decisions about whether to back up the cloud copy, based on your opinions of how the cloud copy is being protected.

If, however, the cloud is being used as a storage tier, that is a very different matter. That means you have data that is on the local appliance that resides only on that appliance, and that data needs to be backed up like any other data in the datacenter.

Versioning

Does the gateway replicate the current version of files to the cloud, or does it use some type of versioning? If you modify a file, what happens to the previous version of the file? Are previous versions available via some sort of mechanism, or do they disappear forever? If the product has versioning built in, you have addressed the versioning part of the 3-2-1 rule. Whether you have met the data separation part of that rule will depend on what storage you are using in the cloud. If you are using object storage that automatically replicates all data to three locations, an argument can be made that you have provided for all aspects of the 3-2-1 rule, especially if you have activated the WORM feature in the object-storage system.

Sizing

If the appliance is sized in such a way that it can hold all current data, meaning the current version of all files in the device, then the cloud is actually the backup copy, and the primary copy is on the appliance itself. If, however, the device is sized so that it only holds active files, meaning files that are currently in use within, say, the past 30 days, that is, as we say, a horse of a different color. That means that the cloud contains the only copy of the current versions of files that are not actively being used, and you need to apply the same logic discussed in the previous list entry on versioning. Your decision will be based on your opinion of the need to back up object storage. Make sure to read "Object storage in the cloud" on page 161 to help you in this decision.

Multicloud

A less-used feature that is available in some cloud gateways is the ability to copy files to multiple cloud providers. If you are storing all versions of every file in both AWS S3 and Azure Blob, it would be very hard to argue against that design from a data protection standpoint, especially if you have activated the WORM feature. Having said that, I've never met anyone who's done that.

The reason the WORM feature in some object-storage systems is so important when considering cloud gateways is because a hacker or malicious employee could destroy your entire account with a few keystrokes. (This is what happened to codespaces.com.) If you activate the WORM feature, you can set things up so that not even you can delete your data sooner than the specified retention. This also prevents any malicious people from doing the same.

The Cloud in a Box

Some public cloud vendors are starting to provide local appliances that run their software, such as Azure Gateway and AWS Outposts. You rent the hardware from the cloud provider, and it runs some or all of the same services that you might use in the cloud, but runs them in the appliance in your datacenter.

Since these appliances are merely physical manifestations of the same services present in the cloud provider, the same rules that apply to backing up those resources should be true of these appliances. In fact, depending on the resource in question, they may be even more in need of protection. Do not assume, for example, that all service options present in these appliances are as redundant as those you can use in the public cloud.

The good news is that the appliances that have shown up so far allow you to use the same tools that you would use to protect the same services running in the normal cloud. Your datacenter simply shows up as another availability zone you can select in the usual interface you would use to perform backups.

For example, you can schedule a backup of an EC2 host, running in an AWS Outposts appliance, using the same interfaces you would use to back up a normal EC2 host. The backup of that host will be stored as an EBS snapshot in S3, which is in the cloud. That does mean that you might have to deal with bandwidth issues when backing up a local VM running in Outposts, since you will have to transfer the snapshot from your datacenter to the cloud, but at least you can use the same tools to manage the process.

In my best Monty Python voice: "And now for something completely different!" The next workload is really an up-and-coming one, and not everyone thinks it needs to be backed up. They feel that containers should be ephemeral and therefore not need backup. I would remind those people that at least their Kubernetes configuration is something they might want to protect. In addition, a lot more people are doing stateful containers than ever before. Let's talk about the super-exciting world of Docker and Kubernetes.

Docker and Kubernetes

The newest data source to frustrate data protection people is containers and orchestrators, the most popular of which are *Docker* and *Kubernetes*. My personal opinion is that Docker and Kubernetes will require more changes to typical backup and recovery processes and software than anything in a long time. Some commercial backup solutions can protect some or all of the things you should protect when using Docker and Kubernetes. You should talk to your backup vendor about what offerings it has. But since very few mature commercial solutions are available at the time of writing, I'm going to cover this topic in much more detail than many other topics in this chapter.

A simplistic definition of a container is a lightweight VM. Where a VM might perform many functions, a container typically has only one function. Instead of a hypervisor like vSphere or Hyper-V, we get the *container runtime environment*, *Docker*. Docker interfaces between running containers and the operating system (typically Linux) on the host where Docker is running. (Docker can also run on other operating systems, but Linux is by far the most prominent host OS for Docker.) Docker provides to each container the functions provided by the core OS that Docker is running on. This lightweight nature is why containers can boot so fast; they don't have to boot the OS, only the functions they are responsible for.

Whereas VMs are designed to run inside a particular hypervisor running on a particular set of hardware, containers are much more portable. Containers are designed to run on virtually any Linux system and can even run on Windows if the appropriate software has been installed. Finally, containers are designed to be much more temporary than VMs. Whereas a typical VM might run for months or even years, most containers live for less than a week.

Running a lot of containers in a production environment requires orchestration, and that's where Kubernetes (often spelled K8s) comes in. Continuing the (somewhat inaccurate) analogy of containers to VMs, the counterpart in the VM world to K8s would be VMware's vCenter or Hyper-V's System Center Virtual Machine Manager. K8s groups containers into pods, which allows them to communicate with each other easily and share storage by mounting a shared volume. K8s pods are often called *logical hosts* and are analogous to VMs; each of the processes on a VM is analogous to one or more containers in a pod.

In Kubernetes, you define an application by specifying all resources that make up an application as well as configuration information needed to init, access, and destroy those resources. Although this really does turn the configuration of backups on its head, it will eventually come with some really great advantages. I will touch on this a little more later in this chapter, in "Kubernetes: A New Path" on page 184.

How Containers Break Backups

Before virtualization, backups were accomplished by placing an agent in a server. Virtualization broke that model, so a different model was created, where the agent runs at the hypervisor level and backs up the VMs as images. Containers offer neither of these options.

Although you could theoretically place an agent inside a container image, that is considered very bad form for many reasons, so that simply isn't done. In addition, there is currently no way to run an agent at the container runtime (i.e., Docker) layer, which is analogous to the hypervisor level.

Many container advocates are quick to point out that high availability is built into every part of the container infrastructure. Kubernetes is always run in a cluster. Containers are always spawned and killed off as needed. Unfortunately, many confuse this high availability with the ability to recover from a disaster.

To change the conversation, ask someone how they would re-create their entire Kubernetes and Docker environment if something took out their entire cluster, container nodes, configuration, and associated persistent storage. If you don't have a good answer, perhaps it's time to think about backing up K8s and Docker.

Besides DR, you need to be able to duplicate the environment, such as when moving from a test/dev environment to production or from production to staging before an upgrade. Finally, you need to migrate a Kubernetes cluster more easily. The following sections discuss the things you would need to back up to recover Docker and Kubernetes in a disaster. And, of course, the applications that you are running on the K8s cluster may also need to be backed up to handle user error, software bugs, and compliance regulations. Make sure whatever solution you use protects all these things.

Dockerfiles

Docker containers are run from images, and images are built from Dockerfiles. A proper Docker configuration would first use some kind of repository such as GitHub as a version-control system for all Dockerfiles. Do not create ad hoc containers using ad hoc images built from ad hoc Dockerfiles. All Dockerfiles should be stored in a repository that allows you to pull historical versions of that Dockerfile if there's a problem with the current build. This is even true of third-party Docker images, because there is no guarantee the third party will version them. If you need to roll back to a previous version of an image, that may be up to you.

You should also have some kind of repository where you store the YAML files associated with each K8s deployment. These are text files that can benefit from a version-control system.

These repositories then need to be backed up. One of the most popular repositories is GitHub, which offers a number of ways to back up your repository. There are a variety of scripts, using the provided APIs, to download a current backup of your repository. There are also third-party commercial tools you can use to back up GitHub.

If you haven't followed the preceding advice and have running containers based on images that you no longer have the Dockerfiles for, you can use the `Docker image history` command to create a Dockerfile from your current images. Put those Dockerfiles in a repository and start backing it up! But, honestly, try not to get into this situation. Always store and back up the Dockerfiles and YAML files used to create your environment.

Docker Images

The current images used to run your containers should also be stored in a repository. (Of course, if you're running Docker images in Kubernetes, you're already doing that.) You can use a private repo, such as a Docker registry, or a public repo like Docker Hub. Cloud providers can also provide you with a private repo to store your images. The contents of that repo should then be backed up. A simple Google search such as "Docker Hub backup" can yield a surprising number of options.

If you do not have the current image used to run your containers, you can create one using the Docker commit command. You can then create a Dockerfile from that image, using Docker image history.

Kubernetes etcd

The Kubernetes etcd configuration database is very important. A backup of it can help with full cluster metadata recovery, since it stores the state of the cluster as well as its configuration. It should therefore be backed up using the etcdctl snapshot save db command. This will create the file snapshot.db in the current directory. That file should then be backed up to external storage.

If you are using commercial backup software, you can easily trigger the etcdctl snapshot save command before backing up the directory where the snapshot.db will be created. That's one way you can integrate this backup with your commercial backup environment.

Persistent Volumes

There are a variety of ways you can give your containers access to persistent storage that can be used to store or create data. Traditional Docker volumes reside in a sub-directory of the Docker configuration. Bind mounts are simply any directory on a Docker host that is mounted inside a container (using the bind mount command). For the purposes of backup, traditional volumes and bind mounts are essentially the same. You can also mount a network file system (NFS) directory or an object from an object-storage system as a volume inside a container.

The method you use to back up your persistent volumes will be based on which of these options you use for the container. However, all of them will have the same problem: If the data is changing, you will need to deal with that to get an application-consistent backup.

One way to do this is to shut down any containers using a particular volume. This is a bit old-school, but it will definitely work. Once shut down, the volume can be backed up. If it is a traditional Docker volume, you can back it up by mounting it to another container that won't change its data while it's backing up, and then creating a tar image of the volume in a bind-mounted volume that you then back up using whatever your backup system uses.

However, this is really hard to do in Kubernetes. This is one reason stateful information is best stored in a database, not in a filesystem. Please consider this issue when designing your K8s infrastructure.

Also, if you're using a bind-mounted directory, an NFS-mounted filesystem, or an object-storage system as your persistent storage system, you can use whatever is the

---

best way to back up that storage system. (Just be sure to remember that its data may be changing into your design.) You could take a snapshot and then replicate it or simply run your commercial backup software on that system.

If you are running Docker in a K8s environment, you can use the container storage interface (CSI) to simplify the use and protection of persistent volumes greatly. The CSI has been generally available (GA) since K8s 1.13 and allows you to issue a PersistentVolumeClaim (PVC) for a persistent volume (PV) that has been pre-provisioned by an administrator or dynamically provisioned by using Storage Classes. The beautiful thing about the CSI is that it is a standard plug-in that allows K8s admins to use a standard set of API calls for storage while allowing storage vendors to implement those API calls in different ways. This allows storage vendors to add their own value while still playing nicely in the K8s sandbox.

Data protection features are also built into the CSI. It supports creating snapshots of PVs that fit the standard definition of snapshots found in Chapter 9. You can also clone dynamic volumes, as long as they are the same storage class and VolumeMode setting. CSI can even support injecting a backup agent into a container, something that is otherwise impossible.

Databases

The next backup challenge is when a container is using a database to store its data. These databases need to be backed up in a way that will guarantee their integrity. Backing up a filesystem while it is changing is one thing; backing up the files of a running database while it is changing is a guaranteed way of creating a worthless backup.

Depending on the database, the method mentioned earlier might work: Shut down any containers accessing the database and then back up the directory where its files are stored. However, the downtime required by this method may not be appropriate.

Another method is to connect directly to the database engine itself and ask it to run a backup to a file you can then back up. If the database is only running inside a container, and you want to back it up in that container, you will need to use a bind mount first to attach a volume that it can back up to, so that its backup can exist outside the container. Then run the command the database uses (such as `mysqldump`) to create a backup. Then make sure to back up the file it creates, using your backup system.

Another option would be to run the database backup command in another host and point it at the database running in the container. For example, you can use the following `mysqldump` command to back up all mysql databases in the container box:

```
mysqldump -h box -u user -p password --all-databases > backup.sql
```

Finally, if you're running K8s, you can also inject a command into a database to get it to quiesce, allowing you to take a snapshot. This allows you to adopt the snap-and-sweep method of backup mentioned in Chapter 7.

What if you don't know which containers are using which storage or databases? (If this is the case, you might want to look at the preceding sections on how to configure your K8s and Docker environment properly with data protection in mind.) One solution might be to use the `Docker ps` command to list the running containers and then use the `Docker inspect` command to display each container's configuration. A section called Mounts will tell you what volumes are mounted where. Any bind mounts will also be specified in the YAML files that you submitted to Kubernetes. This is yet another argument for using Kubernetes.

Kubernetes: A New Path

Those of us who see the world from data protection eyes have had a love–hate relationship with Docker and Kubernetes, to be sure. The idea of a new product that makes it more complicated to back up data didn't exactly sit well with my friends and me. But Kubernetes has actually made some significant inroads in the data protection space, and some believe that it might just present a new way of looking at data protection.

Those of us who see the world backup first have often grumbled about being forced to back up only a server or database; we want to back up the entire application. We've known for years that the Oracle database we were backing up was only one piece of that puzzle. But Kubernetes changes that, because it presents a single place wherein one can view all the pieces of a given application and protect all of them in one fell swoop.

Data protection in Kubernetes is more than just data (volumes) or images and `etcd`. There are two ways to back up an application in K8s: application-based or namespace-based. A Kubernetes application consists of various objects like pods, secrets, PVCs (volumes), and services (like access). Some backup products allow you to capture all of those at once as an application backup. Imagine being able to know that you can back up and restore an entire application in one step.

Some products also support backing up the entire namespace, which would capture anything inside of that namespace. This would be the entire application and anything else (such as other applications) that exist in said namespace. This may be too much for some environments to do in one backup, but it could present a unique way to get a snapshot (in the general sense) of your entire K8s environment in a single backup.

Either way, Kubernetes truly presents a new path for data protection that will be interesting to follow in the coming years. Perhaps the detente between data protection people and container people can become a love fest. It's a brave new world, I tell you.

From the frying pan and into the fire. Let's leave the almost-easy-to-understand world of Kubernetes and Docker and take a look at the Internet of Things (IoT). It's creating millions of little tiny devices creating all sorts of data; does that need to be backed up?

The Internet of Things (IoT)

After covering laptops and mobile devices, here we are on the very edge of computing. The IoT is a subset of what we call *edge computing*, or devices that are at the very edge of an organization's data footprint. Prior to IoT, most edge devices were things like servers in a remote site or, more recently, smartphones and tablets. IoT devices go much further than that and are typically either data collection devices or information display devices. The latter do not create data and so are not a concern for data protection. The former, however, do create a significant amount of data that must be protected.

IoT devices come in so many forms. Governmental organizations might use IoT devices to perform data collection at places where a human was historically required. For example, an IoT device can be a smart parking meter, water meter, electric meter, and many devices that monitor and report on traffic flow. The type of IoT device an organization might use will depend on the type of organization it is. A retail store might have any number of devices to track foot traffic and interaction with products. Their point-of-sale devices would, of course, also be edge computing devices that don't really fit into the category of IoT. Typically, IoT devices are very small devices that perform a single function and collect a single type of data. They tend to be physically very small, use very little power, and usually do not have much local data storage.

Most IoT devices send any data they create immediately to some other device that actually stores the data. These systems most commonly would use some type of service in the cloud for this purpose. There would be no actual physical server that anyone needs to worry about protecting. You should examine any IoT devices in your organization to see whether they are synchronizing their data to another server or service you need to protect or whether their data is actually stored locally on the device. The latter, of course, is much more problematic, because you will need to look for creative ways to back up that data to a centralized location. If the device is running a miniaturized Linux or Windows kernel, it would be possible to use modern backup software to back up this data. You would need to make sure that you reduce the backup size by performing as much deduplication and identification of byte-level changes as you can, versus just backing up entire files. This will really help reduce the compute and I/O load of backing up such data.

If your IoT devices are not synchronizing their data to a centralized data storage device, backing up their data will probably be quite challenging. These devices don't typically have large amounts of bandwidth and yet they may actually create significant amounts of data.

A perfect storm in this case might be a high-definition video surveillance system. You really want to get that data to some location other than where the cameras are, because a thief could simply steal the video storage device, taking the evidence of their crime with them. However, HD video is not small, and replicating that data to another location can get expensive. The usual solution in this case is to use motion activation so that the cameras are only actually recording video when something is happening in front of them.

That's just one example of an edge device that can create significant amounts of data that you want to have stored somewhere else and where doing that might be quite difficult. The only advice I can give you at this level is simply to examine each of these devices and make sure you are aware of how they are storing the data.

Making Backup Decisions

The purpose of the last three chapters was really just to make sure that you are aware of all the places your organization's data might be created and stored and, therefore, all the places from which you might need to back it up. The decision on whether to back up a given piece of data is really up to you, as is the decision on how to back up the data. Consider the following concepts when making those decisions.

Criticality to the Organization

Is the data created on this device something that would cost the organization a significant amount of money to replace? Some data is virtually priceless. If you are a law firm and you hold the only evidence for an important case, it is the most critical data in the world. Loss of that data could mean the loss of someone's life if it is a criminal prosecution, or the loss of billions of dollars if it's an important lawsuit.

It might not have the same criticality as, say, the quantity of widgets sitting on a shelf in a particular warehouse. (Yes, such information is important.) But if it is lost, you can just send someone to count it again. Yes, there will be a cost to that, but it is not irreplaceable.

When making your decisions, try to attach different weights to different datasets to decide just how critical they are. This information will be very important when making design and cost decisions. For a related discussion, make sure to see what a recovery point objective (RPO) is in Chapter 4.

Remember when examining criticality to examine *time* also. Sometimes we decide to back up a given dataset, but we back it up in a way that makes it take forever to restore. Think about the cost of downtime created by a slow restore process and figure that into the criticality decision. In the criminal case mentioned in the first paragraph, maybe the judge will give you a continuance, and maybe not. Therefore, a very slow restore of this important case data might not cost someone their life, or maybe it might.

Normally, when figuring out how long a restore should take, you're not dealing with such weighty things as someone's life. Perhaps you are simply looking at how much money a prolonged restore is going to cost the organization in terms of lost revenue for the company, or fees for a governmental organization. Perhaps it will create long periods during which many of your employees cannot work, causing you to pay them overtime to catch up once the system is back up. This is another thing that determines the criticality of a given piece of data, and this is what you use to determine how quickly the restore should take. For a related discussion, see what recovery time objective (RTO) is in Chapter 4.

Consider the Source

When deciding how to back up a given data source, think about the unique aspects of that particular data source. For example, if backing up a VM, you need to consider what type of VM it is. If it is running in the cloud, you should examine cloud-based methods. If it is running in a hypervisor in your datacenter, you need to make sure that you consider how much typical backups affect the I/O performance of the hypervisor, and you should make sure to use a hypervisor-friendly backup method.

You should also consider the bandwidth available for backups. Although this is not too much of a problem in a typical datacenter, it is very much a challenge when backing up laptops, mobile devices, remote offices, and cloud resources. When considering how to back up these resources, you really need to look at bandwidth-friendly methods.

Also consider any other unique aspects of how the source behaves. For example, when backing up laptops, consider that they might not always be on. Therefore, a backup that is scheduled from a backup server that reaches out to the laptop when it is time to back it up probably won't work very well. Laptop backups need to be somewhat autonomous and run when the laptop is on.

You also need to think about how the data is changing when you are backing it up, and whether you need to treat that data in a special way while you are backing it up. The best example of this is a section on databases. Please do not just ignore the special nature of databases, back up their data files, and expect that your restores would ever work. The story that kicked off my career says otherwise. See the sidebar "The One That Got Away" on page 1.

You also must think about how a given data source needs to be restored when considering how you'll back it up. Again, laptops are a great example. If your backup methodology only works if you're in the datacenter, that's bad enough from a backup perspective. But it also means that you will be unable to restore the laptop if anyone is ever out of the office. I am writing this in the midst of the COVID-19 epidemic and have not seen my company's corporate office in six months. Make sure to take recovery needs into consideration in your design.

Takeaways

The last three chapters covered all the different workloads you need to back up. We talked about servers, VMs, desktops, laptops, and mobile devices. Then we talked about the myriad databases out there, and how difficult they can be to back up. This chapter, however, discusses the newer workloads, some of which we're still arguing over whether they need to be backed up (they do). From IaaS, PaaS, and SaaS workloads, to IoT and Kubernetes; if it's creating data, that data needs to be backed up.

Now that you know all the things to back up data from, it's time to talk about how you'll back them up. The next few chapters explain the various methods you can use to back up and archive your data.

CHAPTER 9

Backup and Recovery Software Methods

A commercial backup and recovery solution can take a variety of forms, including everything from traditional backup methods that aren't that fundamentally different from what I used 30 years ago to techniques that have only come out in the past few years. The goal of this chapter is to give you a bird's-eye view of all the options available to you and the various pros and cons of each approach.

Is Everything Backup?

There will be backup solutions discussed in this chapter that many people do not think of when they think of the word *backup*; however, I define backup rather broadly as *anything that is a copy of data stored separately from the original that can be used to restore the original system if it is damaged*. A number of technological solutions meet that definition.

When most people think about the word backup, they think of tape drives and batch backup processes of files or databases; backing up into formats like `tar`, `dump`, or a commercial format. They might expand this antiquated definition of backup to include disk as a target. But they might not think of something like replication, snapshots, or continuous data protection as having anything to do with backup. I respectfully disagree.

You will see that not everything mentioned in this chapter meets my definition of backup when used *by itself*. A perfect example of that would be both replication and snapshots. By themselves, I do not think of them as valid backup methods. (A dynamically replicated copy can easily be damaged by the same thing that took out your primary, and a snapshot relies on the original.) Together, however, they are a formidable solution referred to as *near-continuous data protection, near-CDP*. (I will explain near-CDP later in this chapter.)

Please read this chapter with an open mind regarding the term *backup*. We can all agree that we need to be able to restore our files, databases, servers, and applications to their previous state after they are damaged due to accidents, hacker or ransomware attacks, or some type of terrorist attack or disaster. How we accomplish that, however, needs to be open to change. You will have my word on one thing: Anything in this chapter that I called backup will conform to the 3-2-1 rule. If you don't know what that is, you might want to take a look at "The 3-2-1 Rule" on page 42. It is quite possibly the most important rule in backup and recovery.

To make sense of this big landscape, I need to break down backup solutions into various sections. First, I'll place all backup methods into one of two big sections, based on how the backup method type can restore your data. (Restore is, after all, the only thing that matters.)

In the first section, I describe solutions that perform a traditional restore, meaning a process that copies data from the backup solution to the system to be restored—but only once you begin a restore. The second, much larger, section contains more modern solutions that support the concept of an instant recovery, when the backup is usable as the primary for some period of time without having to perform a traditional restore before using it.

I then break down each type of restore into the various ways that backups are performed to conduct that restore. This chapter focuses only on the methods, not on packaging. Many of the backup and recovery methods mentioned in this chapter are available as software-only solutions, integrated appliances, or backup-as-a-service offerings. Those solutions will be covered in Chapters 14 and 15.

Backup Methods Supporting a Traditional Restore

A traditional restore is the obvious thing that comes to mind when you think about the word *restore*. There is a backup copy of the item you want to restore on some type of backup medium (e.g., disk, tape), and there is some type of item (e.g., file, database, or VM) that was deleted or damaged in some way and you need to bring it back to its former glory. When requested, the backup system copies the appropriate data from the backup medium to the restore medium and the item is restored. (I know all that sounds really obvious, but I'm explaining it this way to be able to contrast it with an instant recovery, which I will cover later in this chapter.)

A traditional restore will take a finite amount of time from a few minutes to many hours (or even days) from the moment you begin the restore process. How long the process takes will depend on the amount of data that must be transferred from the backup system to the system to be restored, as well as on how efficient your backup system is at performing restores. This efficiency can be affected by bandwidth, backup system performance, and restored system performance.

Multiplexing

Multiplexing isn't a style of backup, per se, but before I explain various traditional backup and recovery methods, it's important to understand this popular concept found in most traditional backup products.

Multiplexing is a method of writing data to tape that solves the tape speed mismatch problem I talked about in "Tape Drives" on page 257. The problem is simple: Tape drives want to go fast, and many backups (especially incremental backups) are pretty slow. Tape drives want to go hundreds of megabytes per second, and a typical incremental backup is only 10–20 megabytes per second.

Multiplexing interleaves many separate incremental backups, and does so to create one larger, faster backup. When the idea first came out, we used to interleave four to eight backups together. Now that number is well into the double digits. The data is often interleaved with no regard for performance during the restore.

Typically, what this means is that if you interleave, say, 36 backups together, your restore will be very slow. This is because it will read 36 backups and throw away 35 of them. Your restore speed will typically be roughly 1/36th of the total speed of the drive. This creates a shoe-shining problem in reverse.

At least one vendor decided to address this problem by using much larger chunk sizes during the interleaving process. This requires more logistics on the part of the backup software product and is probably pretty memory-intensive, but the chunks are large enough that their restore process doesn't work like the one in the previous paragraph. They can issue a seek command to get to the next chunk, read it, and then seek to the next chunk, and so on. There will still be a performance impact, but it won't be the kind of hit described in the previous paragraph.

I've spoken to customers who are using this method, and they are still using tape in production, even without disk staging. It was very interesting to see someone happily still using tape in production, all due to one minor change in how multiplexing works.

Traditional Full and Incremental Backups

The most common type of backup that will be used to perform a traditional restore is the one that you probably know very well. It will start with an initial full backup and be followed by a series of incremental or cumulative incremental backups for some period of time, after which you will perform another full backup and more incremental backups. (The different types and levels of incremental backups are covered in Chapter 4.)

Historically, people performed a weekly full backup and daily incremental backups. In recent years, many people have switched to monthly full backups, weekly cumulative incremental backups, and daily incremental backups. (I discuss backup levels in Chapter 4.) This provides a very similar restore speed to weekly full backups with a lot less data movement, which reduces the load on the backup clients as well as on the network over which you are transferring backups.

A major change to the traditional full and incremental approach has been the addition of synthetic full backups, which is a backup that behaves just like a full backup from a restore perspective, but is created without transferring another full backup from the backup client. I explain the various ways you can make a synthetic full backup in Chapter 4.

This backup design is the most popular one and has been used for decades; many commercial backup and recovery systems today use this model. The advantage is that it is simple to understand and is a tried and true method of backup and recovery.

There are many disadvantages in this approach when compared to more modern approaches to backup. Repeated full backups are a waste of energy, and the way the full and incremental backups are stored wastes a lot of time during a restore. You must restore the entire full, then each incremental backup in the order in which they were created. A significant portion of the data restored from the full backup will be overwritten with the first incremental and then overwritten again and again with each subsequent incremental. There are much faster ways to do restores today.

File-Level Incremental Forever

The next type of backup system that supports a traditional restore is a *file-level incremental forever* backup product. This type of approach has actually been around for quite some time, with early versions of it available in the 90s. The reason this is called a file-level incremental is that the decision to back up an item happens at the file level. If anything within a file changes, it will change its modification date or archive bit, and the entire file will be backed up. Even if only one byte of data was changed within the file, the entire file will be included in the backup.

To be called a file-level incremental forever backup product, a backup product needs to perform only one full backup, synthetic or otherwise, and follow that with a series of incremental backups. It will never again perform a full backup. This means that the backup product in question must be created this way from scratch.

Some commercial backup offerings are marketing themselves as incremental forever backup products because they support the concept of the synthetic full mentioned in the previous section. If a backup solution still relies on regular full backups, even if it is created synthetically, it does not qualify as a file-level incremental forever backup solution.

The reason for this distinction is that there are advantages to never again performing a full backup that go beyond the reduction in processing and network traffic on the backup client that a synthetic full backup provides. Never again doing a full backup also reduces the amount of data that must be stored in the backup system, as well as data that might be copied to other storage, including the cloud. Starting with an incremental forever approach is also a great beginning toward performing deduplication. Even synthetic full backups have to be deduplicated, which is a waste of computing power.

This system is more efficient than the traditional full and incremental method. The biggest advantage is that no wasted CPU processing, network, or storage is taken up with additional full backups. Backups also take less time.

This method is, however, even more incompatible with tape, since the biggest issue with tapes is incremental backups. (See "Tape Drives" on page 257.) Another advantage is that, by design, the system knows exactly which versions of which files need to be restored in a full restore and can restore just those files. This avoids the wasted time and effort that happens during a normal restore due to overwriting data constantly. This is a solid backup method that is not employed by very many vendors.

Block-Level Incremental Forever

Another incremental forever backup approach is *block-level incremental forever*. This method is similar to the previous method in that it will perform one full backup and a series of incremental backups and will never again perform a full backup.

In a block-level incremental backup approach, the decision to back up something will happen at the bit or block level. (This probably should be called *bit-level incremental backup*, but no one calls it that.) For this approach to work, some applications need to maintain a *bitmap* of the data and the parts which are changing, usually referred to as *changed-block tracking (CBT)*. In virtualization environments, this is typically provided by the hypervisor, such as VMware or Hyper-V. When it's time to take the next backup, the backup software will ask for the bitmap of the blocks that have changed since the last incremental backup. It will then be provided with an exact map of which blocks need to be included in the latest block-level incremental backup. Such a backup solution must also keep track of the location of each block once it has been backed up, because it will need this information when it performs a restore. Although not exclusively found within virtualization environments, that is where you tend to see such a solution.

Those familiar with concepts such as continuous data protection and near-continuous data protection (CDP and near-CDP, both of which I cover later in this chapter) might be curious about how they are different from this approach. Remember that this section of the chapter covers backup solutions that must perform a traditional restore. Since CDP and near-CDP can perform an instant recovery, they're not applicable to this section. They could also be referred to as block-level incremental backups, though. You'll see why later.

Block-level incremental forever backups significantly reduce the amount of data that must be transferred from the backup client to the backup server, so they can be very useful in backing up remote systems. Some backup solutions designed for laptops and remote offices use an incremental forever backup approach. The challenge to this approach is that something has to provide the CBT process, and not every system can do that. This type of backup process will only work with disk as the target, because an individual file could be spread out across multiple tapes if you stored it on tape, and restores would take forever. But the random-access nature of disk makes it perfect for this type of backup.

Source Deduplication

The next backup method supporting the concept of a traditional restore is *source deduplication* backup software. The concept of source deduplication (and deduplication in general) is covered extensively in Chapter 5, but a quick summary is that a source deduplication system will perform the deduplication process at the very beginning of the backup (i.e., the source). It will make the decision as the backup client about whether to transfer a new chunk of data to the backup system.

Source deduplication systems are also an incremental forever backup approach. By design, they never again back up chunks of data the system has seen before. (As discussed previously in this chapter, a chunk is a collection of bytes of an arbitrary size, created by slicing up files or larger images for the purposes of deduplication.) In fact, they can back up less data than a block-level incremental forever backup solution. The following example should help explain why that is the case.

Consider 100 Windows VMs the day after patch day, when Microsoft admins download hundreds of megabytes of patches to each VM. A file-level incremental backup would back up all those new pieces of software in their entirety. A block-level incremental backup might back up fewer blocks, because some of the patches might change just a few bytes here and there inside existing files, and those blocks will be the ones to be backed up. A source deduplication system will also back up those new blocks from the first Windows VM it backs up, and then it will never back up those blocks again, including from the 99 other Windows VMs that were updated on the same day.

That is the beauty of a source deduplication system. It is very efficient when it comes to backing up across a network. It can even help ameliorate (but not remove) some of the effects of a lot of bad data management practices. I'm of course not saying to use bad data management practices; I'm just saying that at least they won't create a lot of duplicate data in the backup system.

Since a source deduplication system will reduce the amount of data backed up from a backup client to the backup solution more than any other approach, it is even more effective than block-level incremental backup at backing up remote systems such as laptops, mobile devices, remote offices, or VMs running in the public cloud. Most of the backup solutions designed for backing up laptops and remote sites to a central location use source deduplication. The biggest disadvantage to the source deduplication approach is that you might have to change your backup software to start using it. Some of the major backup products have added support for source deduplication, but not all have done so. Table 9-1 summarizes some advantages and disadvantages of the technologies discussed in this section.

Table 9-1. Comparison of traditional restore backup methods

	Bandwidth needed	Storage needed	VM/cloud friendly	Tape, disk, or both
Traditional	4	4	4	Both
File-level incremental forever	3	3	3	Both
Block-level incremental forever	2	2	2	Both
Source deduplication	1	1	1	Disk

The numbers 1–4 (where 1 is best) in each column indicate the rank of the methods. Traditional backups get a 4 for bandwidth and storage needs, because they need the most of both. For the same reasons, source dedupe backup software gets a 1 in the VM/cloud friendly column, because it is the most friendly for VMs and the cloud, due to the significant reductions in bandwidth and CPU this approach needs. Finally, I just show that most everyone supports disk and tape, whereas a source dedupe approach pretty much requires disk.

The backup methods I've covered so far in this chapter are those that require a restore, meaning that they start copying the data from the backup source *after* you initiate a restore. This means there will be a finite amount of time (measured in minutes to days) between when you initiate the restore and when the restore is done. Many backup systems now support the concept of an instant restore, where the restored system is instantly available when you initiate the restore. Let's take a look at those options now.

Methods Supporting Instant Recovery

This section covers those backups that support the concept of instant recovery, which is described as the ability to recover from the loss of a file, filesystem, database, VM, or app without actually having to do a restore before the recovery. These types of recoveries are preferred by those with very tight RTOs.

The most common form of instant recovery is the recovery from a snapshot that requires a simple command to promote that snapshot to be the primary copy. There is no restore where data was copied from one place to another. There is just some moving of pointers, and voilà! Your filesystem is recovered.

Replication

Replication is a well-known data protection concept that has been used for decades. Everything typically starts with a volume or filesystem you want to protect (i.e., the source volume), which is either a virtual disk (often referred to as a *logical number unit* [LUN]) from a storage array or volume manager, or a filesystem. (Replication is typically done at the block level but can be done at the filesystem level.) Somewhere else, preferably in a different location, you select another volume or filesystem from another host that will be used as the target for replication (i.e., the target volume).

The next important ingredient is some type of replication system. This may take various forms and can come from the storage array vendor, the volume manager vendor, the filesystem vendor, or a third-party replication solution. You configure the source and target volumes in the replication solution, and there is an initial synchronization between the two where the target volume is made to look exactly like the source volume. Once that initial synchronization has taken place, the replication solution will ensure that every change that happens on the source volume will also be made on the target volume. This is typically done at the block level and happens continuously as changes happen. As I mentioned previously, this can be done at the file level, but it is much less efficient and not usually done that way, because file-level replication will typically replicate an entire file if any of it changes, similar to file-level incremental products mentioned in the first section of this chapter.

There are two main types of replication: synchronous and asynchronous. Synchronous provides a higher level of protection and asynchronous has less of an impact on the performance of the protected volume. Let's take a look at the advantages and disadvantages of these two methods of replication.

Synchronous replication

A synchronous replication system replicates any changes before acknowledging those changes to the application that made them. When an application writes a block of data to a volume, it waits to receive an acknowledgment (i.e., an ACK) that the write has taken place before it writes the next block. A synchronous replication system does not provide the ACK until it has replicated the newly written block to the target volume. (This is very similar to the concept of a two-phase commit in database parlance. The write to the source volume, and the copy of that write to the target volume, are seen as one *atomic* event.)

This is why it is said that synchronous replication provides a higher level of data protection. You can be assured that the source and target volumes are always 100% in sync. The main downside to this approach is that, depending on the performance of the target system and the path the replicated data has to take, it may take a significant amount of time before the application receives an ACK.

 The other downside to synchronous replication is that operator mishaps and data corruption are also 100% in sync.

—Dan Frith

A perfect illustration of the performance concerns of synchronous replication is what happened after 9/11. US regulators tried to make financial organizations synchronously replicate their data over 300 miles away because of what happened to some companies after the towers fell. (Some companies had their hot site in the other tower.) They wanted to replicate synchronously because of the importance of financial records, and they wanted it over 300 miles away to make sure that it was protected in case of disaster or attack. The latency estimator I used said that each round trip would take just under nine milliseconds (ms). That's an awfully long delay between every write, which is why they canceled these plans.

Asynchronous replication

Rather than replicating changes immediately, asynchronous replication creates a queue of changes and replicates them in the order they were received as it has time and bandwidth. The biggest advantage of this approach is that it doesn't generally affect the performance of the volume being protected. Writes are split, and one of them is sent to the replication system, which adds it to the end of the queue. Depending on bandwidth and latency, the target volume may be anywhere from a few seconds to hours behind the source volume.

The main concern with asynchronous replication is what happens when the replication process gets so far behind that it cannot catch up. At that point, some applications under some conditions can support a process known as *write coalescing*. Suppose, for example, an individual block has been updated five times. If you are too far behind to catch up, you could drop off the first four writes; that is write coalescing.

Hybrid replication

Some vendors support replication modes that they advertise as a hybrid between synchronous and asynchronous, such as for a product that is normally synchronous but is allowed to get behind the primary by a certain amount before failing. My personal opinion is that this is another binary condition. You're either synchronous or not; if you're allowed to get out of sync, even a little bit, from the primary, that's not really synchronous *in my not so humble opinion*.

Database replication

The previous section talked exclusively about block-level replication, when a source volume was continuously replicated to a target volume. A very similar concept is *database replication*, when transactions in one database are automatically replicated to another database. The big difference is that this is being done at the transaction level as opposed to the block level. Database replication is usually done asynchronously.

Limitations of replication

Replication has historically been the method of choice for those wishing to protect a mission-critical application. They knew that the backup system would take too long to restore it, so they used one of the replication methods mentioned earlier to ensure that an off-site copy was ready to go in a disaster.

I do not fault those who choose to use this method for that reason. I am concerned there are data protection limitations of using *only* replication as a backup method. The biggest limitation is that there is no back button in a typical replication system. If someone does something wrong, like dropping a table that they weren't supposed to drop, replication will simply replicate their mistake. If the database becomes corrupt in some other way, the corruption will also be replicated. This is why replication by itself cannot be the only way you are protecting your database.

Another way to put this is that replication by itself does not conform to the 3-2-1 rule. It's missing the 3! Replication has only one copy of your data, and if the source is damaged, it might damage the target along with it.

Another limitation of this approach is that it can create an additional performance load on the database or the storage beneath it. You could probably argue that this performance hit is negligible, but if you are performing both regular backups and replication, you are copying the data twice, which can have a performance impact.

Continuous Data Protection (CDP)

At one point, database administrators (DBAs) and system administrators (SAs) responsible for protecting mission-critical databases really had no choice other than to use replication to protect them. Restores from the backup systems of the past simply took far too long to use them to restore a mission-critical application. But it should be mentioned that if you have both a backup system and a replication system protecting your database, you are paying for two tools that are doing essentially the same job—just in a different way. As far as I'm concerned, they are basically two backup tools, one of which can restore the system at various points in time, whereas the other is better at restoring the system very quickly.

What if you could have both of those things in a single application? That is the goal of CDP, which is essentially asynchronous replication with a change log (i.e., a back button). This change log allows the CDP system to restore the database to either *right now* or *many hours or days ago*. The promise of CDP is a single system that does everything you need from an operational recovery and a disaster recovery perspective. It can restore the database to any point in time included in its change log, and it can do so almost instantaneously, or at least way faster than the typical backup system. (CDP customers specify how long the change log is to be retained, and that determines how far back they can use it to restore the protected system.)

There are two main types of CDP systems, the first of which is one that attempts to maintain a ready-to-go image of the application, database, or volume it is protecting. In one sense, it is essentially functioning as an asynchronous replication system that can also go back in time because it has the change log. If you need to restore to a point in time other than the current one, it will need to overwrite the blocks that have changed between the two points in time. (It only needs to change those blocks, which means the process can be fairly quick.) The advantage of this approach is that if you need the current point in time—which is the most likely recovery scenario—you can recover immediately. However, if you need to recover to a previous point in time, there will be a slight delay.

A very different approach to CDP is a system that does not maintain an actual volume for recovery, but instead stores all the various blocks it needs to present a virtual volume from any point in time that you request. The advantage of this approach is that you can be immediately presented with a volume from any point in time. The disadvantage of this approach is that this virtual volume will not have the same performance characteristics as the physical volume used in the previous method.

With CDP, you get the best of both worlds (DR and backup) and an infinite number of recovery points. That latter point is really important to understand. With any other data protection system, you get a series of recovery points, ranging from a few seconds or minutes apart to a few days apart. With CDP, you literally have a log of every write that the system performs, so you can choose any point in time that is included in the log.

Interestingly enough, the fact that it has infinite recovery points is one of the criticisms of CDP. How do you choose a point in time from an infinite set of choices? Some people found the process daunting and preferred to have a much smaller list of defined recovery points when they knew the database was in a consistent state. (CDP is often sold as the way to back up databases.)

But the real downside to CDP is the amount of resources it requires. It is very expensive in terms of I/O, CPU, memory, network, and storage resources, and the CDP software itself is not exactly inexpensive.

If you have a mission-critical database that needs an RTO and RPO at zero, you essentially have two choices. On one hand, you can pay for both a backup system for operational recovery and a replication system for DR. On the other hand, you can pay for a single system that accomplishes both. It is expensive, but so is paying for two solutions to do essentially the same job.

Insurance is never cheap, no matter how you write the policy.

–Stan Horwitz

Snapshots

There are a few things that the IT industry calls snapshots. At this point, I am now referring exclusively to virtual snapshots that rely on the primary volume they are protecting for most of their data. Such snapshots were popularized by NAS vendors, because they gave users direct access to historical versions of their directories while taking up very little space for the purpose. By the way, "very little" is a relative term, and some complain that they take up too much space; however, they definitely take up less space than most other data protection mechanisms. The main concern is that the space they occupy is on expensive primary storage.

The moment you create a snapshot, you create a virtual copy of the volume the snapshot is from. If you mount that snapshot, you will see an exact copy (albeit virtual) from the point in time when you made the snapshot. However, at the moment you take the snapshot, no actual data is copied or moved. It is merely a virtual view of the volume from the point in time when you took the snapshot. When you are reading files or blocks from the snapshot, you are actually reading most of them from the original source volume you are protecting. This is why by themselves snapshots are not a good method of backup, because if the volume the snapshot is from disappears, so does the snapshot. (It doesn't conform to the "2" or the "1" in the 3-2-1 rule; you must keep backup and original separated.)

There are three primary ways that snapshot providers handle what happens when blocks change on a volume after a snapshot has been taken. The following is a brief summary of these methods.

Copy-on-write

The copy-on-write method is the most common way snapshot software handles changes in a source volume. It gets its name from what happens when you change a block that is referenced in a snapshot. The snapshot software copies the previous version of the block and sends it to a special holding area, prior to overwriting it with the new version of the block. In other words, it *copies on writes,* hence the term. The main advantage of this method is that it doesn't require changing the underlying filesystem code to support it. The snapshot software does all the work. The disadvantage of this method is performance degradation over time. The more snapshots you have and the more changed blocks you have from those snapshots stored in the changed-block area, the worse the performance becomes on the volume. This is why most people familiar with this type of snapshot do not advise keeping them around for very long.

Redirect-on-write

In a disk system supporting the redirect-on-write method, the files in a volume consist of a series of blocks on disk, and the filesystem maintains a map of pointers that point to the various blocks that comprise each file. When you update a file, which will change one or more of its blocks, the filesystem merely writes new blocks in a different location and updates (i.e., redirects) the appropriate pointers to the new blocks. The pointer connected to the old version of each block will be used by the snapshot system. It will maintain a different map of pointers that point to the various blocks that comprise the files that existed at the point in time when the snapshots were created. The advantage to this approach is that you can have a virtually unlimited number of snapshots that you keep for an unlimited amount of time without affecting the performance of the protected volume. The disadvantage is that this only works in a filesystem that was designed from scratch for this purpose. One storage vendor (NetApp) uses a different pointer-based system that is closest to the redirect-on-write method, but some of the finer details are slightly different. This is why NetApp, the vendor that popularized the use of snapshots for data protection, could have so many snapshots without a performance impact.

Hold all writes

Finally, some vendors, such as VMware, perform snapshots in a *very* different way that you need to understand. With VMware snapshots, the filesystem driver holds all writes to the actual volume that the snapshot is from until the snapshot is released. Once the snapshot is released, VMware replays all the writes back to the source volume. I administered VMware for at least a year before I knew this, and was keeping snapshots around for weeks or months because I thought they were similar to the other snapshots. Then I deleted the snapshot and watched my disk drive go crazy. I honestly do not understand why this is the way VMware performs snapshots, but it is important to understand that they are very different and should not be kept around very long.

Pros and cons of snapshots

Snapshots are a great way to provide many versions of files and volumes while taking up very little space for the purpose, though if you have a large amount of churn on your volume, your snapshots can grow quickly as well. Depending on the system in question, they can even enable user-directed restores by simply letting them change a directory into a subdirectory (e.g., ~*snapshot*) containing all versions of all their files. Snapshots also make great sources for backups. VM snapshots are great for a quick snap before you upgrade some software or make configuration changes. If it fails, you can go right back to where you were. Another example is Windows VSS, which is a snapshot system that can create application-consistent images of databases running in Windows, and then allow you to take as long as you need to back up the snapshot. (See "What Is VSS?" on page 121.)

The main thing to understand about snapshots is that they rely on the source volume for most of their data. If the source volume is damaged, so is the snapshot. In other words, it does not conform to the 3-2-1 rule. Therefore, like replication, they are not a valid backup system by themselves.

Near-Continuous Data Protection (Near-CDP)

Two previous sections talked about replication and snapshots, both of which are very valuable components of data protection; however, neither of them qualifies as a valid backup system on their own because they do not satisfy the requirements of the 3-2-1 rule. Replication stores only one version of data, and snapshots rely on the original for most of their blocks.

The combination of snapshots and replication, however, is a wonderful data protection system referred to as near-continuous data protection (near-CDP). The most common way near-CDP manifests itself is by taking a snapshot of the primary volume you are protecting, and replicating it to another destination. Some systems do not perform the snapshot on the primary, but instead replicate the primary to a secondary and then take the snapshot there. The latter is a fine approach if you do not have data consistency concerns on the primary. For example, if you are backing up a database and need to put it in backup mode prior to taking a snapshot, that simply is not possible using the second approach. I therefore think the first approach of taking a snapshot and then replicating it is a much more universally applicable approach.

Whichever approach you take, you can conform to the 3-2-1 rule with this design by first replicating to an on-site system, which then replicates to an off-site system. This way, you have multiple physical copies of your backups, and one of them is off-site.

In "Hyper-converged infrastructure (HCI)" on page 125, I discussed the concept of HCI appliances, which are a complete computer, storage, and network system designed specifically for hypervisors. Some of them come with integrated data protection systems that are essentially near-CDP systems. The backup management system integrates with the hypervisor, which takes the appropriate pre-backup precautions, such as creating VSS snapshots in all VMs, and then takes a snapshot of any storage where VMs happen to reside. This is essentially a near-CDP backup system designed specifically for virtualization.

Whichever of these approaches you take, you now have multiple versions and multiple copies of those versions, and one of them can be off-site. It is possible to have a complete backup and recovery system using nothing other than near-CDP. Yes, you need management, control, and reporting for most people to consider this a valid backup system. I do not disagree with that, and not all systems that would qualify as near-CDP have those things.

Also considered by me to be near-CDP is any replication-based data protection (that can also go backward in time) that is not *completely* continuous. If you replicate every single change as it happens, even if you're asynchronous and can get a bit behind, you're CDP. If you're taking a mini-snapshot as often as every second and replicating the deltas found in those snapshots, you're near-CDP.

I actually coined the term near-CDP many years ago and not everyone likes it. Some have said that *continuous* is a binary condition; you are either continuous or you are not continuous. It's like so many other binary conditions, like full or empty. I hate it when I'm on a plane and they say we're very full. We're either full or we're not full. You cannot be more than full or less than empty. Oddly enough, I will accept nearly full or nearly empty—which is why I'm fine with the term *nearly continuous*.

The reality is that the time frames in which backups are typically taken fall on a very big spectrum. On one hand, we have continuous, which is, well, continuous. You replicate every single change as it happens. On the other hand, most backups run once a day. My argument for this term is that *near-CDP* is a lot closer to *continuous* than it is to *once a day*, since people tend to take near-CDP snapshots once an hour or even once a minute. So I stand by the term.

The near-CDP approach has its own pros and cons, but it does give you the best of so many things. You get the instant recovery features of replication and CDP, the local quick recovery options of snapshots, the storage savings that come from a block-level incremental approach that snapshots and replication use, and user-directed self-recovery of their own data. It works for block volumes and file volumes and, if done correctly, does not affect the performance of the system it is protecting. (See the comments in "Snapshots" on page 200 about the different ways snapshots are made and how that can affect performance.)

One argument against a completely near-CDP-based backup system is that it often places your entire data protection world in the hands of a single vendor. Near-CDP systems are typically based on a storage array or filer that provides both the primary system and secondary system. The concern is that a rolling bug could take out both your primary and all of your secondary systems, and all the snapshots with them.

This is a valid concern and, some would argue, a violation of the 3-2-1 rule if you do not address it. I have historically been a fan of making a tape copy at the end, but that is becoming increasingly difficult in today's world of cloud-based systems. What you might want to investigate is whether some other technology could be used at the very end to provide a backup that is both off-site and disconnected technologically from the primary. There are also third-party near-CDP products that wouldn't require everything to be from the same vendor. You could have your storage from one vendor and your data protection product from another vendor.

One other concern about near-CDP systems typically being provided by the same vendor is that this can make your overall storage system more expensive and prevent you from shopping around for different parts. Again, this is a very valid criticism that you will need to take into account when considering using such a system.

Finally, many near-CDP vendors do a poor job of application integration. You are left to your own devices and scripts to integrate the apps yourself. Again, this is not always the case, but it certainly is the norm in the near-CDP space.

Copy Data Management

A very similar approach to near-CDP is the concept of copy data management (CDM). They're actually very similar systems that are just designed with slightly different goals in mind. The idea of CDM is that copies of data are used for many purposes beyond backup, and a centralized system that can provide those copies for all such purposes should save money in storage and management. The way this works is typically a data split, where all writes to one system are also sent to a second system in an asynchronous fashion, essentially an asynchronous replication of the volume in question.

This secondary copy also maintains a log so that it can present the volume or filesystem in question at any point in time, just like a CDP system does. The difference here is that there is a lot of other technology on top of the system that is focused on delivering copies for various purposes while minimizing the amount of storage that those copies use. That could technically be done by a CDP system, but it's not its primary purpose.

If you take a look at the earlier descriptions of how CDP systems work, one maintains an active volume of the current point in time, and the other maintains all the blocks necessary to present a virtual volume at any particular point in time. The latter is how

CDM systems tend to work, since they are typically not advertising themselves as a high-performance target for disaster recovery. They seem more concerned with lowering storage costs and increasing the degree to which you use your copy data rather than accomplishing the single goal of a high-performance disaster recovery copy like a CDP system would do. (Like a CDP system, however, CDM systems can typically create another physical copy if you need it for long-term high-performance use.)

A full-function CDM system of course has its own pros and cons, and can provide all the typical services that a backup and recovery system would provide, in addition to providing copies of your data for test, development, and other purposes, without requiring each of these copies to be a separate physical copy. Many companies have used this model to do just that while also lowering their secondary storage costs.

One concern comes from the purpose that CDM is built for. CDM systems try to reduce the number of copies used for testing, development, and backup. However, their main development tends to focus on testing and development and not always on backup. This means they may not have the same level of functionality as systems built with backup as the focus.

Another concern that some have is similar to the concern about near-CDP systems based on one vendor. A CDM system can be very useful at a cost that is less than what all the various copies would cost you, but it does put all of your secondary storage data into one system, and some are concerned about that.

One other concern is that it's a *both feet in* kind of approach when, to garner the most benefit from the system, you have to convert many other systems and switch entirely to the CDM approach. Although the benefit probably will be less expensive than what you are currently doing, you have to stop using a number of systems for that actually to be true, and that's a lot for some people to bite off.

Other Software with Instant Recovery

There are a few products that don't quite fit into these other categories but also support the idea of instant recovery. They tend to be modern backup products that have figured out the importance of instant recovery and built it into their functionality. They range from products that built this into the core design to those that are added to it later. Depending on the product design, this may require anything from a minor to a major rewrite of existing code.

The functionality and capabilities of these various products are so varied that it's really impossible to discuss them in the abstract. I just thought it was important to say that you'll be seeing instant recovery features even in some very old products. In the end, it doesn't matter so much how they got there as what the product is and how it actually works. As with everything else in the data protection world, you should verify any vendor claims with your own testing.

Table 9-2 summarizes the various capabilities of the options covered in this section.

Table 9-2. Comparison of instant-recovery products

	Logical corruption recovery	Systems/ disk failure recovery	Recommended for backup/DR	RTA	RPA	Cost	Features similar to backup
Replication alone	No	Yes	No	0	0	High	No
Snapshots alone	Yes	No	No	Mins (If no hardware failure)	Mins (If no hardware failure)	Medium	Yes, except for hardware failure
CDP	Yes	Yes	Yes	0	0	Very high	Mostly
Near-CDP	Yes	Yes	Yes	Mins	Mins	Medium	Yes
CDM	Yes	Yes	Depends	Mins	Mins	Medium	Yes
Other	Yes	Yes	Depends	Mins	Mins	Low	It *is* backup

Please don't use replication or snapshots alone for backup or DR; replication alone can't recover from logical corruption (e.g., virus), and snapshots alone cannot recover from hardware failure.

If you're looking for instant recovery, your good choices are therefore CDP, near-CDP, CDM systems, and some of the other modern products that have added this functionality. You will get the tightest RPAs and RTAs with a full CDP product, but they are also very expensive. Near-CDP, CDM, and other products will all have different RTAs and RPAs and associated costs. Your job is to examine them and make your own decision.

Now that we've covered backup systems that support instant restore, I'd like to talk about a new idea, which is leveraging backups for more than just restores. It's a relatively new idea, but one that's taking hold.

Leveraging Backups for More

People in the data protection industry are increasingly interested in using their backup data for more than just backups. Backups are typically seen as a money pit from which you rarely get any benefit. Yes, backups and disaster recovery copies are incredibly valuable if you need them, but most people spend a significant portion of their time never doing actual restores. Therefore, some people in senior management might look at the dollar amount associated with data protection and wonder what they are getting out of their investment.

Some data protection people are starting to use the term *data management* to refer to the idea of using backup copies for more than just backups. What additional value can we get from the giant pile of data that is a historical look into your organization?

One answer to that tends to be modern data protection systems that now can provide both backup and archive functionality with a single copy. Those who read Chapter 3, where I drew a very thick line between backup and archive, might be led to think that I think these systems need to be separate. That is definitely not my point. My point is that if you have a system that is only capable of being a backup system (and that would probably be most backup systems on the planet), please do not use it as an archive system. Some backup systems can do both backup and archive, and I thoroughly applaud that effort.

Because most backups today are being stored on disk and, therefore, can be accessed in a random-access fashion, many backup systems have started to add the e-discovery functionality that is typically provided by an archive product. This would be a perfect example of getting much more use out of a copy that would otherwise go unused. If you can satisfy all your e-discovery requests with your backup system, more power to you. If you have a separate backup and archive system, perhaps now is the time to consider a more modern solution that does actually offer functionality to both areas.

Another area of functionality that backup systems are also starting to provide is ensuring compliance against various regulations. For example, you should not be storing personally identifiable information in certain places. You should not have an unencrypted Excel spreadsheet on your laptop that has Social Security numbers, for example. Modern backup systems are now being developed to read your data and determine whether the data that it's backing up complies with the regulations that you specify. You can configure your backup system to look for different patterns and notify the appropriate people of rules being violated. I remember 25 years ago working at a very large company where we discovered that an employee was using company servers to store some content that (if discovered) could have created a huge liability for the corporation. A modern data protection system could be told to look for such files, which should not be stored in locations other than specific ones specified by the administrator. Such a filter would have identified this person's compromising behavior.

Some backup systems are also scanning incoming backups to protect against ransomware. Backup systems have always been used to recover against things like ransomware attacks, but they haven't typically been used actually to identify that an attack has occurred. However, a backup system is actually at a perfect vantage point to detect that a ransomware attack has been perpetrated against one or more systems. Machine learning algorithms can notice patterns like a significant increase in the number of files included on an incremental backup. If the number of files that a given user has modified in a day suddenly goes from two to 5,000, that user most likely has been infected with ransomware. Stop their backups, notify their administrator, and assist in the ransomware mitigation process.

There are also backup systems that are starting to provide CDM functionality. They can be used to seed test/dev efforts by easily providing a snapshot that can be mounted read/write and spun up to provide that type of functionality. The key here is to ensure that the spun-up VM does not think it's the same host or is supposed to take over for the original application. That could be problematic. This, hopefully, can be easily handled by the backup application.

The newest area where data protection systems are being used for additional functionality is the idea of historical analysis for other reasons. A lot of machine learning and artificial intelligence work is being done on analyzing data to accomplish various organizational purposes, and some are starting to see that a completely disk-based backup system is a source of data to accomplish that purpose. The fact that many organizations store their backups in the cloud makes this even more interesting, because many of these analytical services are cloud-based and could just use your backups as a source of information without you having to do anything other than authorize and authenticate a particular process.

I think we are at the beginning of what will eventually become a very big industry: the reuse of backup and archive data for other purposes. As long as you are protecting the backup system from potential damage, I see nothing wrong with this idea. But that's a huge statement. We don't want to throw the baby out with the bathwater. I can be a bit of an old fogey sometimes and say things like, "Remember when cell phones were good at, you know, making phone calls? Now they stink at it." I'd hate to make a very reusable backup system that was actually bad at doing backups and restores.

Deciding on a Backup Method

The first thing to acknowledge when deciding on a backup method is that there is no perfect backup and recovery method. As you should be able to see in the previous descriptions, every backup and recovery method comes with its own pros and cons. The thing for you to do is simply decide which pros you're not willing to do without, and/or which cons you are not willing to live with. That should help to narrow down the list.

Does What You Have Meet Your Needs?

The grass is always greener on the other side of the fence. Everyone always looks at their current backup and recovery system and thinks that a different backup and recovery system would solve all their problems. Perhaps switching from tape to disk would do the trick. Perhaps moving from full and incremental backups to an incremental forever approach would solve the problems with your current system. Or perhaps everything would be better if you moved from a system that requires a restore to one of the systems that can do instant recovery.

You can almost always find a backup and recovery system that looks better than the one you currently have. But here's a really important question: Does the system you currently have meet your needs? Can you meet the RTOs and RPOs that your organization is asking for? Do the costs of the system fall within the budget that you have been given? What about the operational costs? How much time are you spending troubleshooting daily operational problems with the current system? Have you considered the cost of switching backup systems, which includes far more than the cost of simply replacing hardware, software, or services? There is also the cost of the training time and the risk that the new backup system might be needed for recovery while you still have your training wheels on.

If the answers to those questions are no, then my advice would be to seek an expert in the product that you are using to find out whether the problem is software, hardware, or wetware. I did a lot of backup consulting over the years and the problem with almost every backup system I worked on was not the software or hardware; it was the configuration (i.e., the wetware). The biggest issue was that people simply did not understand how tape drives worked and just kept buying more of them to make things better. I was the crazy person who told them that the backup system would actually go faster if they turned off some of the tape drives. So if you believe that your backup and recovery system is bad enough that it needs to be replaced, the cost is enough that I believe you should at least check with an expert to find out whether that's the case. The company providing the solution would be a likely place to go for this service; it might even offer it for free to keep you as a customer.

Advantages and Disadvantages of Different Approaches

I laid out the pros and cons of the various approaches in each of the preceding sections, so I'm just going to do a high-level review of them at this point. Backup solutions in the first part of the chapter (those that require a restore) will obviously not be able to meet the RTOs that the solutions in the second part of the chapter meet. It's really hard to compete with instant recovery. I do want to remind you, though, to make sure that an RTO of zero (or close to it) is actually what your requirement is. There's nothing wrong with having an eight-hour RTA if you have a 24-hour RTO. Just because you can find something faster doesn't necessarily mean you should, unless you can tie actual organizational benefit to that change.

As to RPO, many of the backup methods mentioned in this article can provide an RPA of one hour or less. That should be enough to meet the RPO requirements of all but the most stringent mission-critical systems. The traditional full and incremental systems, as well as the full-file incremental forever approach, probably will only be able to be run once a night, so the best RPA you can hope for is 24 hours.

Almost all these backup and recovery methods are virtualization-friendly and have a good way to back up and recover VMware and Hyper-V, but not all of them can back up other hypervisors, such as AHV or KVM. Those may require specialized solutions designed specifically for them.

As the world moves into the cloud, anyone buying a new backup and recovery solution at this point should be looking at one that sees the cloud in the way that you do. If you see the cloud as simply a place to put old backups or backups that you probably will not use (i.e., Iron Mountain), then backup and recovery solutions that can copy backups to the cloud should be your choice. If, however, you are starting to see the cloud as the future destination for new workloads and you see it as more than just a place to lift and shift VMs, you should probably look at systems designed for the cloud.

The first important thing would be whether they store their primary copy of backups in object storage rather than simply moving old backups there. If the backup solution requires you to store the primary copy of backups in block storage, you are guaranteed to spend at least four times what you would spend on object storage. (Object storage costs half what block storage costs, and object storage is typically replicated three times. Block storage is typically not replicated, so you would need two copies. Two copies at twice the price means four times the cost.) Object storage offers a lot of advantages for backup copies, and if you design your backup solution for how it works, it is a great place to store backups. Block storage can be faster at restoring a single large image, which is the way most backup systems store backups on disk. If that's the way your backup system stores backups in the cloud, there are real advantages to having that on block disk. However, if a backup system can leverage the way object storage works (and not store backups as one big blob), then restore performance from object can be even faster than that from disk. So if they are using object storage, make sure they're not doing it in a way that hurts your performance.

The next important thing would be whether the cloud version of a given solution has been designed to run in the cloud or it's just the same solution that would run in the datacenter. If it is the same product that you would run in the datacenter, chances are that its design is not made to take advantage of the economics of the cloud. For example, it will run your backup VMs 24 hours a day even if they are doing nothing. It will know nothing of containers or serverless functions that can accomplish quite a bit and save you a lot of money.

Complete Solution

Most backup and recovery systems today are sold as complete solutions. They might be an appliance that includes hardware and software, or they might be a backup-as-a-service offering that you simply use without having to manage the backup software. Quite often, the solution that you buy will end up determining the backup method that you used. So another piece of advice would be to have a list of the backup methods that are acceptable to you and that could meet your requirements, and then see which complete solutions offer those backup methods.

Takeaways

This chapter spelled out all the ways that products might create backups to foster good restores. They fall into two big categories: those that require a restore and those that support instant recovery. The important thing is at least to understand the pros and cons of all these approaches before you start evaluating products.

Understand the incredible range they offer from recovery point and recovery time perspectives. After you've followed the advice in Chapter 2 and ensured that you're designing a system based on real organizational requirements, look at products and services that support the backup methods in this chapter that come closest to your requirements.

One suggestion would be to look at backup products or services that support multiple methods covered in this chapter. That way, you can try them all out and select different methods for different workloads. Flexibility is king.

CHAPTER 10

Archive Software Methods

 This chapter is written by Dan Frith, aka @penguinpunk, an industry veteran from Down Under. Dan's a fan of my work, but not what I would call a fanboy. (He has enough *chutzpah* to tell me when he thinks I'm wrong. Must be an Australian thing.) He's got great field experience, so in addition to being a tech reviewer of the book, I asked him to write this chapter.

An archive is the one data protection system you probably need and most likely don't have. In Chapter 3, I defined an archive as a separate copy of data stored in a separate location, made to serve as a reference copy, and stored with enough metadata to find the data in question without knowing where it came from. Backup is, on the other hand, a secondary copy of data that you use to recover in the event that your primary copy of the data is affected in some way, whether from corruption, deletion, or some other misfortune.

You most likely have a backup system, but you just as likely do not have an archive system. Most people therefore have no idea what an actual archive system does or why you might want one. Let's explore that topic a bit.

A Deeper Dive into Archive

Another way I like to define *archive* is the *primary copy of your data that has secondary value* (i.e., is no longer primary data). Typically, archive data is no longer current, infrequently accessed, or simply no longer valued (as much) by the users who created it. Not every piece of data needs to be kept in a prominent place and displayed for all to see. Instead, less valuable data is normally *archived* to save space in primary storage systems, and usually serves as a historical reminder of something rather than a daily reference point.

project), the tools used to create the data (e.g., *CAD/CAM*), the users associated its creation, and the time frame in which it was created (e.g., Q2 2021). This metadata will be used later to retrieve this data. Please note that the servers the data is stored on are probably not part of the metadata; that's another big difference between backup and archive.

There are many reasons it might make sense for your particular organization to work with data for a period of time and then move it somewhere else for safekeeping. I used to consult for a customer in the construction industry. The company operated with a core group of staff across administration, engineering, and other construction activities. When the opportunity arose to bid on particular projects, such as bridges or office buildings, a team was assembled from a combination of internal staff and contractors to work on the bid in its various stages. If the bid was successful, the data associated with the project was maintained on production storage systems for the duration of the project. If, however, the bid was unsuccessful, the team was disbanded and the data was moved to an archival system and used as a reference for other projects. The reason the data wasn't kept on the production storage systems permanently was that a lot of data was associated with the creation of those bids and a number of projects that were being bid on. To keep the growth of the production storage system under control, it was decided that an archive storage system would be a more suitable location to store historical bid data.

I also worked at a satellite company, where all satellite designs were archived after they were built. Then the government that ordered the satellite five years ago might come back and say it wanted several more just like the ones it bought last time. We would look up the model of satellite it bought and then search for that model in the archive system. Poof! We had all the data on that model of satellite, from initial designs to final production instructions.

Real-Time Archive

When data is created or stored in the production storage environment, a real-time archive copies it to another location for archive purposes. This type of archive is normally used for compliance or auditing purposes.

When on-premises email systems were more common, journal email accounts were a popular example of real-time archives. As email entered the mail system, a copy of each message was placed in the journal mailbox, and the original was delivered to the intended recipient. The journal mailbox could be accessed by various auditors or managers to search for information in messages that needed to be used in legal cases or to provide information for freedom-of-information requests, for example.

This type of archive isn't normally accessed via a traditional email client but, rather, via a portal with a granular search capability. Note that a real-time archive doesn't alleviate the pressure on production storage systems (unless the product also had the features discussed in "HSM-Style Archive" on page 217), but it can improve an organization's ability to meet its compliance obligations.

The concept of real-time archive systems hasn't disappeared with the advent of SaaS-based email or other SaaS services. If anything, they have made them more mainstream. Microsoft 365 and Google Workspace both offer real-time archives of their products. Microsoft calls it Retention Policies, and Google Workspace calls it Google Archive. With the proper authorization and a few mouse clicks, you can tell these systems to store an archive copy of every version of every email and document created by or sent through the system. Microsoft 365 even supports a feature that would not allow any user, even an authorized admin, to delete this archive, protecting it from rogue admins, making it truly immutable. (See "Immutability" on page 55.)

Isn't That Backup?

Some say that Microsoft 365 retention policies and Google Workspace Archive do the same job as backup, and they can't be more wrong. This is covered in "Software-as-a-Service (SaaS)" on page 166, but I just want to reiterate it here.

It is important to understand that these are archives (i.e., not backups), so they do not store point-in-time images of your mailbox and are therefore incapable of restoring it to the way it looked yesterday, and these systems do not conform to the 3-2-1 rule. It also means that they are administered using the same tools that backup is supposed to protect you from.

This means they can do retrievals, but they're really lousy at restores. Just like it's really hard to do a retrieval (i.e., nearly impossible) from a backup product, it's also impossible to do a restore from an archive.

If you live in a country with labor laws that favor the worker, you may find the concept of an organization having access to every employee's email distasteful. Unfortunately, in a number of countries, agreements are in place that facilitate this kind of behavior. I prefer to think of these systems as effective tools to be used with e-discovery processes rather than as a way for managers to spy on workers.

HSM-Style Archive

One of the more popular archive systems is the HSM-style archive: one that uses hierarchical storage management (HSM) to manage data storage. As data ages, or is accessed less frequently, it becomes economical to move it to less expensive storage. If users aren't accessing the data on a daily basis, or the data has become dated but needs to be retained for compliance purposes, it makes sense for organizations to store this data on less expensive storage platforms. Depending on the volume of data, it might be appropriate to store this historical data on scale-out object-storage systems or dedicated, cloud-based cold storage systems offering retrieval times in hours and days rather than seconds. A number of solutions offer the ability to migrate archive data to tape to store off-site and offline. The thinking is that this approach offers some level of enhanced security by basically being unavailable unless absolutely required. Tape can also offer a more economical price per gigabyte than some storage systems. As mentioned in "Backup and Archive Myths" on page 77, tape is also really good at holding on to data for very long periods.

A very common implementation of this concept was to apply this concept of HSM to a real-time email archive system, which was very popular in the early part of this century. The mail servers of many organizations groaned under the increasing weight of users' bulging mailboxes as users discovered that HTML-formatted email messages and attachments came through in larger and larger sizes. Since all email was automatically archived, admins could specify that any emails older than n days and bigger than n megabytes would be moved to the archive and deleted from the primary system.

As organizations are increasingly looking to move their mail hosting requirements to third-party-as-a-service offerings, the focus has shifted to unstructured data being stored on networked file servers. Although industry analysts are quick to point out that such storage is becoming less expensive on a per gigabyte basis, it is also true that organizations need more and more of those gigabytes to store organizational data on. As such, any opportunity to reduce the spend on high-performance production storage is seen as a valuable thing.

HSM-style archives normally move data to different storage based on age or last accessed time. As data ages, it can be moved from its location on the filesystem into the archive system. It's expected that the data will leave behind some kind of pointer or stub in the source system to facilitate retrieval if the data is once again required. Some systems eschew the stub in favor of a robust search engine capability. Although this approach can increase compatibility across systems, it often falls foul of users not remembering what the data contained and only remembering where they think it was stored, making the search activity less effective.

Deciding on an Archive System

A number of factors go into deciding on an archive system, starting with the all-important question of whether you need one. If you do need an archive system, pick one that best meets your organization's needs. Let's walk through how you can determine this for your organization.

Do You Need One?

All kinds of data that are important to the ongoing operation of organizations are in use. Some of that data is created in-house, and some of it is imported from outside the organization. Deciding whether you need an archive system is not a simple question, and a number of factors need to be considered before committing one way or another.

First, what sort of data is in use in your organization? Is it primarily structured data, stored in databases and similar applications? Or is it unstructured data? Unstructured data tends to lend itself to archive systems more easily than structured data does. Do you have vast amounts of this data stored on large network volumes in myriad directories and subdirectories, owned by various departments and growing at a rapid rate? Is it user-generated data or machine-generated data? Some organizations rely heavily on logging and processing data from various industrial applications. This data can grow at a tremendous rate, depending on the features in use by the various logging and monitoring tools in the organization. Such data can be very important, but is rarely looked at by humans, which makes it a great candidate for archive.

Cloud service providers frequently store a tremendous amount of logging and monitoring data for months at a time. This is invariably referred to when there is a billing dispute with a customer or some requirement to conduct a root cause analysis after an unplanned outage. It could also be a legislative requirement in some countries that service providers need to retain customer access logs in the event that government bodies with an interest in such things request access to them.

In addition, what kind of retention requirements do you have for different datasets? In some environments I've worked in, it's a sad fact that the organization doesn't always have a good grip on exactly what the data retention requirements are or, worse, how to implement them in their specific situation. As a result, storage and data protection administrators are invariably advised that the organization would like to keep "everything forever, please." This works well for a short period, and then the storage system starts to fill up at an invariably faster rate than was forecast when it was first procured. Many meetings later, a decision is made to expand the system earlier than expected. This is invariably expensive and time consuming for the organization. Such retention requirements can really drive the need for an archive system and help justify the cost.

Even if you do have a handle on the retention requirements of the data your organization generates, where do you start when it comes to ensuring that the right data is stored in the right place to meet those retention requirements? I've seen many situations when one particular set of data has particular legislative requirements driving its protection and retention, while the organization is blissfully unaware that the bulk of the data related to that legislative requirement is actually sitting in various home directories or in a series of accidentally nested folders in a long-forgotten file share.

If you have data in your environment and are continuing to function, it's a good bet that your data storage requirements will continue to grow. If you're in the fortunate situation of generating data that is needed for only a short time, you can happily delete your old data without worrying too much about the need for an archive system. However, it's more likely that you've been advised that the organization would like to keep "everything, possibly forever," and you need to put it somewhere sensible.

Any project looking at implementing a potential archive system should use the same process I laid out in Chapter 2. Make sure to include legal and compliance as stakeholders in this project, because they both will have something to say about when you should delete data.

Requirements

If you're going to deploy an archive system, make sure to collect requirements before doing so. You need to think about how long this data will be kept and about any issues that might come with that. Let's dig a little deeper into some of these requirements. As already mentioned, make sure you follow the process outlined in Chapter 2.

Data format issues

An important consideration, when ascertaining what type of archive will work for your organization, is how you'll be storing and retrieving the data in the future. If it's thousands of plaintext log files, it's reasonable to expect that those files will be readable by some system when you need them. But what if the software is storing the data in some kind of proprietary application format? I have plenty of AbiWord files from my "Linux on the desktop" phase that don't look particularly pretty when I try to open them up with my current macOS word processing tools.

Office automation data is one thing, but what about the large amount of critical data stashed away in Microsoft Access databases in any number of environments? For the moment, there are still ways of getting the data out of that software and into another system, but not every bit of business software used in the world has the longevity that the Microsoft tools have enjoyed.

There are any number of proprietary small-business accounting and finance packages still in use the world over, whose developers have either retired or otherwise moved on. How will you retrieve the data from those systems in 50 years' time? In my many years of consulting, every organization I've worked with has had some kind of legacy server or application chugging away in the datacenter, serving information to some critical process via an application or workflow that has long been forgotten by its creator but that remains critical to the success of some process inside the organization. Should the organization have let the situation get to that point? Of course not. But the reality is that it happens more frequently than we'd all like to admit.

Storage media

The choice of the media the archive data will be stored on is also important. Do you have Iomega Jaz cartridges tucked away in a desk drawer but no Jaz drive to read them? Think of the number of digital data storage (DDS) tapes sitting in cupboards in organizations around the world, slowly rotting away, unreadable by modern tape machines. Got something important you'd like to read off a punch card? You'll have a rough time getting easy access to a reader. I have plenty of cassette tapes in storage with data created on a system in the '80s that is getting harder and harder to find. You don't want to store your historical copy of data on a system that itself doesn't have much longevity associated with it. If you don't have confidence that the storage system you're using to store your data on will be around in 50 years, you should ensure that you choose an archive system that can accommodate some amount of data sustainability while keeping the archive intact.

The crucial question is also why it is vital to consider an archive system that supports data portability. The appeal of software-based archive systems, for example, is that you can move the archive data from one hardware platform to another without needing to undertake an onerous and potentially risky migration activity. The downside of this approach is that some of the features traditionally associated with hardware-based archive platforms, such as encryption and data immutability, need to be built into the software and maintained on a regular basis. In an ideal scenario, a software archive solution will support data portability and protection and provide the user with the option of taking advantage of hardware platform features, such as encryption and data deduplication, if the features are available.

Other concerns

Depending on the data you're archiving, you also need to consider whether the data needs to be human-readable or simply understood by modern applications. If it's simply mapping data that might need to be fed back into a geographical information system to compare with current data, or analyzed for gaps, then it might be sufficient to export the raw data from the current system into an open format that can, hopefully, be read by software in the future.

If you need a human to access and make sense of the data, though, you might be in for a tougher time. Another approach might be to use virtualization tools to maintain aging systems and their associated data to access them long after they're no longer supported by their vendors. The software world changes at a rapid pace, and even though a number of the basic principles of look and feel might remain the same, anyone who's fired up a virtualized Windows operating environment from 1995 will see that things have changed significantly, and much of the data availability we take for granted now simply can't be understood by these systems.

Separate system or integrated?

There are two other key factors that will heavily influence your adoption of an archive system: storage sprawl and legislative compliance. If you pick the right system, you might even be able to accommodate both of those requirements. These aren't the only reasons that organizations choose to archive data, but they certainly play a large role in the decision-making process. As previously mentioned in this chapter, you also need to consider the type of data you must retain and how that data will be accessed in the future.

It's important to consider whether the archive system you deploy will be separate from your backup environment or whether it will be integrated with it. Ultimately, the safe storage and protection of archive data should be considered critical to a healthy data protection and retention system, but that doesn't mean that the archive system needs to be controlled from the backup system. Indeed, because the functions of the data types are different in many respects, it's not unreasonable to think that the systems for each could also be separate, as could the teams maintaining the systems. The backup team will invariably be involved in the operation of production data storage, whereas the team in charge of the archive system may well reside in the records management or compliance part of the organization, and could even be entirely separate from the technology function of the organization.

Another key consideration when choosing an archive system, particularly if you need to archive data for compliance reasons, is the ability of the system to maintain accurate metadata for the data that is archived. Every file/object/application record has some amount of metadata associated with it, including information such as the time the data was created, when it was last accessed, by whom, and so forth. It's important when archiving data that this metadata is maintained when the data is transferred to the archive. The metadata is normally an important tool used to provide context for the data. If it's a photo, for example, the metadata stored in the file provides information about where the photo was taken, the type of camera used, and so on. There may also be a requirement to ensure that the archive platform is immutable, that the data cannot be changed once it is stored on the archive platform. Why would it need to be immutable? If the data is used in a court case, for example, the court needs to be satisfied that the data has not been tampered with in any way and that it can be used as evidence. Unless the data is sitting somewhere in a vault or some kind of bunker in a mountain with no access to the outside world, there's also a chance that it will be vulnerable to nasty folks wearing hoodies and spreading their ransomware programs around. Immutability provides a level of security within the system that can help to avoid painful data loss events.

Another thing that needs to be taken into account is how the archive data will be accessed once it has been moved to the platform. This is particularly important when it comes to things such as compliance archive data. It's no use having terabytes of compliance records stored on an archive system if there's no way for the end user to search for particular information in that data. As I mentioned previously, if the data is stored in an application in a human-readable format, it's important for the archive system to continue to provide access to a functional application frontend. If, on the other hand, the archive data is simply swaths of text or images stored in files, then a robust search tool and sensible metadata tagging should provide sufficient access to the data.

Another consideration is how you will move the data from your production systems and applications into the archive system in the first place. The type of archive system you choose to deploy will influence whether the system should be integrated or separate from both your data protection and production storage environments. If you're using a real-time archive to audit incoming email, for instance, chances are you won't want the journal mailbox to reside too far from your primary email systems. If, however, you're using a batch mode system in which large chunks of data are archived off on a periodic basis, and no time limit governs when the data needs to get to its destination, then the system may not need to be heavily integrated with the production systems and applications.

I was once called in to help with an unfortunate situation where a backup server's filesystem had become corrupted. After many hours with the filesystem vendor, it was determined that the data on the filesystem was irretrievable. This wouldn't have been so bad if it was only the backup data that was stored on the system, or only production data (that could have been recovered from a backup set). Unfortunately, this particular system also hosted the organization's archive data on the same filesystem, and when it went bang, the archive data went with it. Of course, this wasn't entirely the fault of the archive solution vendor, because the end user should have taken some more precautions protecting the system. I do think, however, that it's a strong reminder that storing all data in one place is generally a bad idea. This is, of course, the whole point of the 3-2-1 rule introduced in Chapter 3, which applies to archives as much as it does to backups.

Takeaways

The activities that most organizations undertake to conduct their function don't always fit neatly into one category or another. Likewise, the applications and workloads that are used to support the function of those organizations invariably don't fit neatly in one specific category or another. As a result, the storage systems and associated infrastructure deployed to support those workloads, and the data they generate, are many and varied. It's for this reason that the archive system you choose to implement to support your organization should also be capable of supporting a diverse set of workloads and their particular needs. If it isn't, you may need to consider a combination of solutions to deliver the required outcome. After all, the ability to understand the requirements of a particular application or workload is critical to the successful delivery of solutions that support that application or workload. The choice of archive system should be no different.

It's important to remember that, regardless of the archive system you choose to deploy, the data stored in that system is very different from the data stored in your backup system on a regular basis. Your backup data can be used to re-create the data from a particular point in time on your production system if it goes bang, but your archive data is very much a historically important artifact that should be preserved and protected.

Archives are super important but can be a bit boring. They are, after all, a whole system built around data that is one step away from the trash can. Let's pick up the interest level, shall we? Let's go to the tip of the spear, so to speak. The next chapter is about disaster recovery, which I believe has become much more important since the advent of ransomware.

CHAPTER 11

Disaster Recovery Methods

Having a good backup and recovery system is important, and no one would argue with that. But for many years, the typical disaster recovery (DR) plan of most organizations consisted of a box of tapes at an off-site vaulting vendor. That never was an actual plan, as I'll cover in this chapter, but it's becoming less and less acceptable in IT circles to admit that is your idea of a DR plan. Having a solid DR plan that can recover your organization very quickly has become much more important recently, for reasons I cover in this chapter. Let's take a look at those reasons.

Disaster Recovery Becomes Paramount

DR has never been an *option* for most organizations; it's always been a *requirement*. But you'd never know it in many places. Data protection in general is rarely the first project that anyone talks about. Everyone knows the backup system is outdated and outclassed, but they also know that making the backup system better is rarely a competitive advantage. Data protection projects are often pushed further and further down the budget spreadsheet until they eventually pop off.

If data protection is last on the budget spreadsheet, disaster recovery is often the last line item under data protection. This has always been the case. Yes, we knew we had to have backups, and we knew that we should store some of them off-site. But push came to shove, and suddenly the DR plan is a box of tapes in somebody's trunk; we can't even afford an Iron Mountain account this year.

I cannot tell you the number of times I spoke to organizations who had no DR plan to speak of. Besides the issues with the budget, one common defense for not having a true DR system is that the likelihood of a disaster hitting any given organization is relatively small. They are obviously a little higher if you are in an area prone to natural disasters or a frequent target of terrorist attacks, but many organizations simply take a little too much comfort in the relatively good odds against their demise.

Excuses for Days

I've had many conversations over the years with organizations that did not have a DR plan other than "we send our tapes to Iron Mountain." When I would press them on this issue, I would get the craziest excuses. Here are just a few of my favorites:

- If our building blows up, I'll probably be dead and won't care.
- If our town is destroyed by a disaster, I'll be a lot more concerned about saving my family and my house and won't care about any DR plan.
- If we're destroyed by a terrorist attack, I won't have a job so I won't care.

If somebody working for me talked like that, I think I'd replace them on the spot.

But the "it probably won't happen to me" sentiment seems to have dwindled recently. Suddenly, everyone is trying to have a valid DR plan, and not just any DR plan. They want one with an RTO short enough that they can thumb their nose to ransomware attacks. Let's take a look at this relatively new threat to your data and how it's moved ransomware to the top of the priority list.

Ransomware Changed Everything

Ransomware appeared on the scene a few years ago, and since then it has become the primary reason organizations activate their disaster recovery plans. Not having a disaster recovery plan that works very quickly makes you a very attractive target for ransomware.

It's one thing to have your datacenter wiped off the map with a hurricane. You really have no choice but to physically rebuild everything and restore it. And no matter how much money you pay, you cannot change the fundamental laws of physics and the logistics of the hundreds of contractors required to accomplish this task. Sure, you could make it a *little* bit faster, but you cannot build an office building and datacenter in a matter of days. It's just not possible.

Contrast this with the choice that you are presented with as a ransomware victim, without a modern disaster recovery plan with a short RTA (i.e., recovery time actual, or the amount of time it will take you actually to recover from a disaster). Nothing has been physically destroyed, and no one will give you any sympathy that might come with a natural disaster. All they know is that all your data has been encrypted and you just need to unencrypt it. No big deal.

They expect you to be up and running very quickly, and you know that every day you are down costs your organization money. For businesses, it is most likely lost revenue while you're still paying your salaried employees. For a governmental entity, you are still paying all your employees while not accomplishing the purpose of your office. Once things come online again weeks later, you'll spend millions in overtime making up for lost time. No matter what type of organization you are protecting, being without your computing environment for weeks or months will be expensive.

The other big difference here is that unlike in a typical disaster, your organization will be presented with a very tantalizing option: paying the ransom. On one hand, you can wipe all your servers clean and restore them from scratch. This can take anywhere from many days to several weeks, depending on the efficiency of your backup and recovery system. On the other hand, you could pay the ransom and possibly be given a key to decrypt your data. Most organizations faced with this choice have chosen to pay the ransom, because they see it as the easy button that would ultimately cost the organization less money than not using it.

Please Do Not Pay the Ransom

I know I covered in Chapter 1 that paying the ransom is a bad idea, but I need to reiterate. *It's a really bad idea.* Paying the ransom makes ransomware look more attractive to those who spread it. Until everyone has a modern disaster recovery plan and can tell ransomware attackers to go pound sand, ransomware will continue to be a problem. I know that when a figurative gun is to your head, it's very hard to think altruistically. It's very easy to do a cost–benefit analysis and end up deciding to pay the ransom while not really thinking about the long-term damage that this does to the situation. So let's talk about the long-term damage to your organization.

One area of long-term damage is your organization telling everyone you're open to paying a ransom and not able to recover without it. Multiple organizations have been hit with ransomware more than once because of this issue. In addition, you will do long-term damage to your brand, because it shows that you don't properly protect customer data. There could even be fines from regulations like the GDPR, because it proves you did not comply with its data protection requirements.

Paying the ransom is no guarantee you will be able to recover your data. It is true that most organizations that pay ransoms do get their data back, but it's important to realize you're dealing with a criminal. They may take your money and disappear.

Hopefully, you are reading this before being hit with ransomware. If that is the case, this chapter is for you. Read it and take it to heart before you become a cautionary tale.

An Overview of Disaster Recovery

A DR plan is a process you enact when something makes a significant portion of your computing environment inoperable. This goes way beyond restoring one or two really important servers. When you enact or execute a disaster recovery plan, you are more than likely recovering an entire datacenter or even an entire computing environment that may span multiple datacenters and/or cloud environments. Let's first take a look at the different reasons you might need to use your DR plan.

When or where you might need to execute your DR plan will really depend on the type of resources you might be protecting. Historically, all DR plans focused on the datacenter, but things have changed quite a bit in that area. You now need to protect your datacenter, your IaaS/Paas resources, and the data stored in any SaaS apps your organization uses.

Datacenter

You might need to recover your entire datacenter if it was destroyed by fire, flood, or any natural disaster, as well as by things like terrorist actions. In recent years, we have also added ransomware attacks as a very common reason that organizations fire their DR plan in anger.

IaaS/PaaS

If your organization is using the public cloud, and you probably are, you also might need to recover from the loss of these resources as well. The cloud is not magic, and being in the cloud does not remove the chances of a disaster taking out your computing resources in the cloud. In fact, one can argue that it's more important to design for failure in the cloud. Where a typical datacenter DR plan is used *if* something goes horribly wrong, a DR plan for your cloud resources is more likely to be used *when* something goes wrong. Entire regions of cloud services occasionally go offline; you need a plan for that, and that plan would be called a DR plan. Cloud people use phrases like *anticipate failure* or *design for failure*.

SaaS

As mentioned in Chapter 8, it is very unlikely that any data recovery services are included in your favorite SaaS product. Yes, they use very highly available systems, and it's very unlikely that your SaaS product will be taken offline due to system availability or even a natural disaster or terrorist attack. What you will need protection from is ransomware attacks and other things that hackers would do to your data that is not handled by the data protection systems built into the SaaS vendor. Power users and system administrators can also do a significant amount of damage to your SaaS environment that might need to be dealt with by your DR plan for SaaS.

Now that we've looked at why you might want a DR plan, let's look into what might go into one.

Business Continuity Planning

Business continuity planning (BCP) is a very big process that ensures that the overall organization can continue after some major event such as a disaster. BCP encompasses a number of factors, one of which is DR. BCP includes all sorts of things outside the scope of IT, like facilities management and personnel management. This means that BCP might include things like replacing employees, at least temporarily. It might also include temporary offices and communication lines. This means by its very nature it's outside the scope of IT.

One example of business continuity plans being put into action is what happened while writing this book: COVID-19. Organizations around the world were trying to figure out how they could continue to function when their employees were forced to work from home due to the pandemic. Some organizations have done this better than others, and some organizations simply could not function remotely.

A great example of an organization that cannot function remotely would be a grocery store or restaurant. Employees cannot run a restaurant remotely. You could, for example, use employees to service remote customers, though. I think it's safe to say that COVID-19 put a number of organizations' BC plans to the test. You are hopefully reading this after the worst of COVID-19 is over, but perhaps you could use it as a lesson.

BCP is outside the scope of this book. I am focusing entirely on making sure that your data and systems can be quickly brought online after any kind of event, including a disaster. I will not be discussing business continuance issues other than that.

What Is in a DR Plan?

So you've decided to make a DR plan. Good for you. Let's take a look at what goes into one. Understanding the components of a DR plan is crucial to being able to design one that will actually be useful.

A DR plan assumes that you are starting from scratch. You will need to configure an entirely new environment and then restore your data and applications before you can resume normal operations. This means that the DR plan needs to take all of that into account. You need to have answers to all of the following:

Where will you get computing, storage, and network resources?
    In a typical datacenter environment, you will need to procure actual replacement hardware before you can start the restore process. Hopefully, you can do this in advance. In an IaaS/PaaS environment, you can easily script this problem away. If

your SaaS service is completely offline, however, you will probably not be able simply to make a new one appear. So your DR plan should address that.

How will you protect your replacement environment?

In a disaster, it becomes your production environment. One big thing people leave out of a DR plan is making sure that the temporary computing environment remains protected at the same level as the old one. How will you make sure the temporary environment is adequately protected? Can this be automated?

What are your recovery requirements?

Recovery point objective (RPO) and recovery time objective (RTO) must be agreed to in advance, and hopefully, you have designed a DR system whose recovery time actual (RTA) and recovery point actual (RPA) are up to the task. If not, those conversations need to happen now.

What are the recovery priorities and prerequisites?

Rarely can you recover everything at once, unless your DR system is fully automated. You should decide in advance what should be restored in what order.

What about people?

Who will execute the plan? What's the plan if that person (or those people) is unavailable? There should be something similar to a line of succession.

How good is the documentation?

Are the DR plan instructions (i.e., the DR runbook) sufficiently documented that a technical person unfamiliar with its operation would be able to execute it without assistance? Also included in the plan should be a review process to ensure that this documentation stays up to date.

How much of the DR runbook is automated?

Automation is the key to a good DR plan. The more things are automated, the more likely it is that you will be successful during a recovery. Not only will this make it easier for everyone, it will make it much easier if those most familiar with the DR plan are not available.

Has it been tested?

As has been said in other parts of the book, not testing your backups and DR systems is a recipe for disaster. The execution of a DR plan absolutely depends on regular testing, so you can learn what didn't work before you have to do it under the gun.

You Can Run, but You Can't Hide

A number of times, a lack of documentation caused me to lose personal time. I remember one vacation during which I spent two to three hours on the phone every day. I remember spending long nights in computer rooms because no one knew which button to press next. But none of those memories is as strong as the time when my first daughter was born. Right about now, you're probably saying, "Aaah, that's sweet." It's not what you think. Yes, she and my other daughter (and their two husbands and one granddaughter) have given me a whole other reason to get up every day, but that's not what this story's about.

The hospital in which my wife gave birth was about two blocks from my office building. I knew that. My coworkers knew that. (Anybody who looked out the window knew that!) The day my daughter was born, we lost a major filesystem. I knew it was on a backup volume, and I knew I was off duty. I left my beeper, which was normally welded to my side, at home. I did not call in to work. I knew the process was documented. The problem was that they weren't reading the documentation. "Call Curtis!" I was standing in my wife's hospital room, talking about our wonderful child, when the phone rang. Those guys tracked me down and called me in the hospital! They asked me to come in, but since I knew the system was documented well, the answer was "No! " (I think I actually hung the phone up without saying another word.) This is an example of the lengths to which someone will go to find you if you don't have proper documentation or if they have not been shown how to use it.

Before talking about any actual disaster recovery systems, I'd like to describe a few things that *aren't* a DR plan. If they're in your head as your DR plan, we need to remove them now, so we can start with a green field.

A Box of Tapes Isn't a DR Plan

Besides the fact that a box of *anything* isn't a DR plan, a box of tapes is particularly problematic. Tape never was particularly good at DR, but now it *really* isn't good.

As I mention in Chapter 12, I am not against tape. I think it makes a great long-term storage mechanism; however, the kind of single-threaded restores that happen during a disaster recovery process are at the top of the list of things tape doesn't do very well. In a large-scale disaster recovery, you need to restore dozens or hundreds of servers or VMs simultaneously, each of which will require a single-threaded restore, which may also be bottlenecked by the performance of the storage it is writing to. Not only will each of these restores require its own tape drive, but the tape drives will not be able to perform the restores very quickly.

If you are using tape in your backup and recovery system, you are almost assuredly using multiplexing to supply the tape drives with a backup stream fast enough to keep them happy. (See "Multiplexing" on page 191.) That multiplexed backup usually makes for a really lousy restore when you are restoring only one out of dozens of streams you interleaved together onto a tape to make that tape go fast enough to stream. Even if you address that issue, the requirement of every server needing its own tape drive during the execution of your DR plan makes its use really impractical. A box of tapes never really was a good idea for DR, and it's only gotten worse over time due to the speed mismatch problem discussed in "Tape Drives" on page 257.

A Replicated Dedupe Appliance Isn't Much Better

If your DR plan consists of making sure that your backups are replicated to a target deduplication system off-site and that's it, that is also not a DR plan. Sure, it's better than a box of tapes hidden inside an off-site vaulting vendor, but not much better.

The real problem here isn't the appliances; it's the restore itself. If your DR plan consists of you starting a full system restore from some kind of backup system *after* the disaster happens, it's probably not going to meet the kind of RTOs needed to ignore ransomware demands. Any kind of restore that has to be performed from scratch after the event will create an RTA that is unacceptable enough that your organization will be pressured to pay the ransom.

If you are somehow able to perform an instant recovery (as discussed in Chapter 9) with such an appliance, I'll concede that it's a possibility; however, I've never seen any target dedupe appliances do this at enough scale to satisfy most RTOs. The problem is the challenges associated with rehydrating the deduplicated data. There are significant performance challenges with that approach. It could work, but most likely will not. I stand by my opinion that the best way to have a successful DR is to pre-restore your data before the disaster happens.

It's All About the RTA

Imagine your *entire computing environment* being encrypted or destroyed, and then being forced to recover the entire thing. What is the actual amount of time it would take your organization to bring your entire computing environment back online after such an event? If your RTA for your entire computing environment is too long, you will get pressure to pay the ransom.

If you haven't agreed to an RTO and RPO for a major event such as this, now is the time. The key to surviving a ransomware attack is to decide now how long you are allowed to be down and how much data you're allowed to lose *before* you're attacked by ransomware. Then design your DR system so your RTA and RPA are under those values. As I said in the previous section, you most likely will not do that with a box of tapes or from backups sitting on a replicated storage array.

The only way you'll meet an RTO and RPO short enough to ignore ransomware is if the restore is already done before you need it. It's like the commercials for Dramamine motion sickness pills that said, "The time to take Dramamine is too late to take Dramamine." The time you need to start restoring your data is too late to start doing so; it needs to have been done already.

That's what this chapter will talk about. But before we talk about how to restore the data, we have to talk about how to re-create your computing environment. I'm going to use the generic term *recovery site* to refer to this replacement hardware, which will take the place of your primary computing environment, even though it will most likely not be a site, or even real hardware, per se.

Building a Recovery Site

A *recovery site* is the physical or virtual place that will take the place of your computing environment if the worst happens. If your datacenter burns to the ground, is flooded, or destroyed in a terrorist action, you'll need a recovery site to resume operations. Back in the day, a recovery site was always another physical datacenter that was hopefully a long way away from yours. Today it is more likely not physical and not owned by your organization. Today you've got three broad choices for a recovery site: roll your own, lease one from a service, or use the public cloud.

Roll Your Own DR Site

The idea of creating and maintaining your own DR center is the original DR plan. (It's the OG plan, as the kids say.[1]) You procure and maintain a completely separate datacenter (or datacenters) that have sufficient storage, compute, and networking capacity to take the place of your primary datacenters.

Maintaining your own recovery site is an incredibly expensive proposition, because it (at a minimum) doubles the cost of your computing environment. If the recovery datacenter is to take the place of your primary datacenter when a disaster or ransomware attack happens, it will cost roughly the same as the datacenter it is meant to replace. To that you will add the cost of actually executing whatever DR system you decide to use.

Some organizations try to reduce the cost by using outdated equipment for the recovery site. As they buy new equipment for their primary site, they move their older equipment to the recovery site. This reduces the cost, but the cost of moving equipment from one site to another is also expensive. In addition, you run the risk of the

---

1 My editor said I had to explain OG, so here goes. It means original gangster. It's a hip-hop term that means someone from the old school.

recovery site not having enough computing power or storage capacity to take the place of the primary site effectively. (It is old equipment, after all.)

Hardly anyone does this anymore, save the organizations who want to control everything about the process within their walls, and for whom money is no object. Neither of the more modern options offers the complete control of the recovery environment that this design offers.

Recovery-Site-as-a-Service

Instead of maintaining your own recovery hardware, you can pay a company to procure and maintain it for you. At first, this may sound expensive, but there are ways this option can actually save money, although those options come with their own cost.

The first way to use such a recovery service is to have it provide you dedicated equipment that is exclusively available to you in case of disaster. This will be more expensive than procuring and maintaining your own recovery site, because you will also be paying this organization to procure and maintain it for you. It will, however, put the recovery site in the hands of people who know how to maintain such a site and who are dedicated to making the site a success. This will not save you money, but it should significantly reduce the risk associated with maintaining a dedicated recovery site. (Self-maintained recovery sites have a history of becoming ignored and out of date.)

The more popular way that people use such recovery services is to pay a reduced fee for a certain level of equipment availability, with the understanding that this availability has limits. The organization contracts with you to provide a certain amount of equipment when a recovery is necessary. You are sharing this equipment with everyone else who uses the same service. This will therefore likely be less expensive than either maintaining your own equipment or having the DR service maintain dedicated equipment on your behalf. This model works fine as long as too many organizations don't need the equipment at once.

If too many organizations need this shared equipment at the same time, you would have the equivalent of a run on the bank. Shared equipment is probably a great way to respond to something like a ransomware attack, when only your organization might be affected. However, what happens during a natural disaster that takes out an entire geographical area? What provision does this organization have for providing equipment to several shared clients at the same time? What do you do if they are unable to provide equipment to you because of the shortage? These are all risks that you take by using shared equipment; therefore, these are questions that you must answer if you deploy this method.

The Public Cloud Was Born for DR

The public cloud is essentially the same model as the previous one (leasing shared equipment), but on steroids. It has so much excess capacity that you should never have a run on the bank, and the cost is almost nothing until you declare a disaster. This is why many organizations are looking at the public cloud for DR.

In a disaster, you need instant access to anywhere from a few dozen to perhaps thousands of servers or VMs as well as many terabytes (TBs) or petabytes (PBs) of storage and associated networking and security. You don't want to pay for it in advance, and you don't want to be subject to a run on the bank that might happen in a regional area when a natural disaster happens. You want to pay only for what you use when you use it, and you want to have an unlimited number of resources available at the push of a button.

This is literally what the cloud was made to do. A disaster recovery to you is simply a small burst in capacity to a typical hyperscaler. Even a disaster that takes out an entire geographical area would still be able to recover, because you can easily choose a different region for recovery. Simply pick one that is not subject to the same natural disasters that afflict your normal computing environment.

By using the public cloud, you can restore your systems far in advance of a disaster while paying only for the storage aspect of your configuration when you're not in a disaster situation. For example, suppose you have a 1 PB computing environment that consists of 1000 VMs. You will need to pay for the replicated and/or recovered copy of your 1 PB of data that will sit in the cloud in case of a disaster, but you will not need to pay for the 1000 VMs until you actually need them.

There are also economical ways that you can store recovery copies of your computing environment for less than it would typically cost to store that data in a typical data-center. For example, you can typically store what the cloud vendors call snapshots of your replicated data for half the price of storing that same data on primary storage in the cloud. (I discussed in Chapter 9 that I do not like that they call them snapshots, but they didn't ask me.) Although the snapshots do require a restore to be useful, this restore takes only a few minutes and can be done in parallel across all your VMs. Most such restores are done lazily in the background, whereas reads can begin against the volume that is not yet fully restored. If you don't want to use the volume with reduced performance, you can decide ahead of time to pre-stage the restored volume for faster restores. The former has performance ramifications, the latter, cost implications.

Once you've identified what type of recovery site you will use, you need to decide how (or if) you will pre-restore your computing environment to the recovery site so that it is ready to go in a disaster. The next section talks about those options.

Keeping the DR Site Up to Date

Whether you are providing the DR site yourself or using a service or the public cloud, you will need to make a decision about whether to pre-restore your systems in advance of a disaster. I've already made the case earlier in this chapter that I think most organizations should pre-restore their DR site, because it's the only way to meet modern RTO and RPO demands. But it is possible that your RTO is long enough that pre-restoring is not necessary.

Whether you pre-restore or not, there are a number of ways this can be done, including different kinds of recovery sites as well as different ways to get your backup data to those sites. Let's take a look at those options.

Cold, Hot, and Warm Sites

If you set up your recovery site in advance but wait until the disaster to start your restore, we call that a *cold site*. If you do pre-restore it, it's either a *warm site* or a *hot site*, depending on your RPA. Cold sites are much less expensive, but warm and hot sites offer much better recovery options.

A *cold site* is called that because the equipment is essentially powered off and ready for you to use it during a recovery, but no restore has been performed. In case of a disaster, you power on the physical or virtual machines and begin the restore. Most organizations prior to the advent of ransomware used a cold site for DR, if they had a DR plan at all. But most backup systems take far too long to restore this data, so many organizations have migrated to either a warm- or a hot-site configuration.

A *warm site* is a site that is kept *mostly* up to date with your organization's current dataset, but is also kept powered off until you need it. Depending on your requirements, it might be a few hours behind, or even a day or more. In a disaster, you may have one or two of the following options: accept the amount of lost data or use additional backups to bring the recovery site more up to date. For example, if you spin up your systems at the recovery site, and it is four hours behind your primary site, your organization will have lost up to four hours of data. If that's within your RPO, that may be perfectly acceptable. If, however, your RPO is one hour, and you're four hours behind, your DR system should have the ability to restore the last few hours of incremental backups to bring the recovery site to a point in time closer than the current time.

A *hot site* is fully powered on and ready to go, as well as synchronized to your primary dataset as much as possible. Obviously, this is the most expensive of the three options, but it also offers the shortest RTA and RPA: close to zero for both. You should be able to fail over to a hot site in a few seconds, and you should lose virtually no data. Such a site requires expensive software, hardware, and a synchronous network connection between your primary site and the recovery site.

Choosing Hot, Warm, or Cold

Choosing whether to do a hot, warm, or cold site really comes down to your requirements. If you have an RPO and RTO of zero, the only way you'll meet it is a hot site. However, very few organizations have an RPO and RPO that small. If you don't have an RPO and RTO of zero, a hot site is a waste of resources.

Most organizations' RTO and RPO are measured in hours, and it will simply come down to whether you can meet your requirements with a warm site or a cold site. This is a bit more complicated, because it will come down to the capabilities of the recovery site and those of the software or service updating the site for you.

In general, most organizations find that a warm site offers a nice balance of cost and speed. This is especially true if the DR software or service you use can perform the post-disaster incremental restore feature discussed earlier. This allows you to save bandwidth and keep the recovery site mostly up to date and then just update it a bit if and when a disaster happens. This may take an hour or two, but if that fits within your RTO and RPO, you save money and meet your requirements.

If, however, you have very slack RTO and RPO requirements, or a very small amount of mission-critical data, you might opt for a cold site. It is way less expensive than the other two options, and if it meets your requirements, it's the best option for you. If you've got a few terabytes of data and a one-week RTO and RPO, what do you need a hot or warm site for?

One important thing to understand is that to have a warm or hot site, you must have access to the equipment all the time. The recovery-site-as-a-service option mentioned earlier does not usually have that ability, so you will be forced either to run your own recovery site or use the public cloud.

We've covered the different requirements that you might have for updating your recovery site (e.g., cold, hot, or warm site). Now we need to talk about how you might make that happen.

Recovery Mechanisms

I mentioned that any modern disaster recovery plan will not depend on a box of tapes. This means that any modern disaster recovery system will rely on electronically copying the primary dataset to the recovery site by one of two methods: replication of the primary data or replication of backups. Each method has its advantages and disadvantages.

Primary data replication

Primary data replication immediately copies, or *replicates*, every change you make on the primary dataset to the recovery dataset. This can be done on the file or database level, but is usually done at the storage level because it is much simpler. I cover replication in more detail in Chapter 9, but the main thing to understand from a DR perspective is the difference between synchronous and asynchronous replication.

A synchronous replication system ensures that the data is replicated before it tells the original application the data has been written to disk, making sure every change is stored in both places. This makes the primary site and recovery site 100% in sync. Synchronous replication, and decent enough bandwidth and latency to support it, is required if you choose a hot site setup.

An asynchronous replication system first records the changes on the primary site and then updates the recovery site with those changes in the same order they were made in the primary site. However, because it is being done asynchronously, the recovery site is allowed to fall behind the primary site. Depending on the bandwidth, latency, and number of changes, it could fall very far behind. How far behind will determine your RPA.

If you want to use replication to update your recovery site, it can be accomplished by a variety of replication mechanisms, including replication based on the array, the host, or other storage system. Let's take a look at the ways you can accomplish primary data replication.

Primary data replication methods

Array-based replication occurs when one array replicates to another array. This is historically the most common form of primary data replication due to its simplicity and reliability.

Array-based replication provides a very easy and reliable way to make sure the data in the recovery site is exactly the same as the data in the primary site. It is also the most expensive replication method, because it typically requires the same vendor's hardware in both places. It may allow you to have different models with different performance and cost values on each side, but the choices are limited to the products available from the vendor you are using. In addition, because the storage hardware and replication software are provided by the same vendor, you can't do competitive price shopping. Even with these downsides, array replication is a very reliable way to ensure that the same data that is on premises is also off premises.

Host-based replication is the flexible counterpart to array-based replication; the replication is performed inside one or more hosts that are replicating their own data. There is a variety of ways by which one can replicate data from a primary host to a replication target in a recovery center. The first such products were software-based volume managers, and similar products have followed. More recently, there are products that replicate data from a virtualization perspective, meaning that they are aware of VMs and understand what data needs to be replicated for each VM.

Host-based replication is much more flexible than array-based replication because it doesn't care what storage you are using on either side; it is replicating the data, not the storage it resides on. This allows you to mix and match vendors on both sides to meet different performance and cost characteristics.

In between array-based and host-based replication is storage virtualization hardware. Hardware products sit between your servers and storage and virtualize the storage to the hosts. They are not typically provided by your disk array vendor or your host vendor (although sometimes they are) and allow you to replicate data between disparate storage systems. They can replicate from a Fibre Channel (FC) or SAS disk array to a SATA-based array or even to a cloud volume. Their performance and simplicity are similar to those found in array-based replication, but they also present the flexibility to mix and match storage vendors.

The one downside to this approach is that it's not likely to be supported by either your host or storage vendors. You will likely have to receive all support from the storage virtualization product. Depending on your feelings about such things, this could be a good or bad thing. It can result in finger-pointing if there are issues.

It's really hard to say which approach is better in any given circumstance. I think it's simply important to be aware of these different choices and the relative value that each brings to the table. You will have to choose based on your requirements for performance, simplicity, management, and cost.

Replication of backups

Compared to primary data replication, the replication of backups is relatively new, although it has now been around for around 20 years. It's really taken off in the past 10 years due to the preponderance of deduplication hardware and software in almost every backup environment.

Without deduplication, the amount of data that must be replicated is simply too much. Incremental backups are big, typically around 10% of the size of a full backup. And, of course, the occasional full backup is found in most backup software products. This means that the typical backup setup of a weekly full backup and daily incremental backups would need to replicate roughly 200% of the size of the datacenter every week (e.g., 100% + (10% X 7) = 190%). That would require an incredible amount of bandwidth.

By applying deduplication, both full and incremental backups are typically reduced to less than 1% of the size of a full. That means instead of needing enough bandwidth to replicate 200% of the size of the datacenter every week, you only need enough bandwidth to replicate 7% of the size of the datacenter or even less. That's a significant difference!

Yes, your mileage will vary with deduplication, and not every dataset dedupes to less than 1%. But properly designed deduplication should reduce the amount of data needing to be replicated to roughly the same size as would be replicated with primary data replication. In some cases, it may even reduce it to less than that. Consider what happens on patch Tuesday when every VM is the same batch of patches from the OS vendor. Once one of those VMs is back up, those patches will never be transferred again.

There is a problem, however, with replicating backups. Typically, this means that you are replicating something that needs to be *restored*. The primary data (e.g., VM or database) being replicated is typically put into some type of container (e.g., `tar`, `dump`, or proprietary backup format, not to be confused with a Docker container) that it must be pulled out of to be useful. If you are a Windows user, this is similar to putting a bunch of files into a zip file. That file must be unzipped for those files to be useful again. If you are a Unix or Linux user, this is similar to what happens when you use the `tar`, `cpio`, or `dump` commands. In all these examples, files are put inside another file and must be pulled out of that file to be used. In other words, backups must be restored to be useful, whereas replication creates a ready-to-use copy of the data that does not need to be restored.

Not all backup software puts its backups into a container such as tar. Some backup software products actually maintain their backups in a native state, meaning that data does not need to be extracted to be used. This is one of the ideas behind the concept of instant recovery, which was covered in Chapter 9.

But I am taking the position that for a modern disaster recovery system to protect you against ransomware, the recovery needs to have been done in advance. With primary data replication, the data is already in a format that can be used by servers or VMs that would use that data to boot during a recovery. This means that, unlike primary data replication, replicating backups will require a secondary process if this data is to be pre-restored prior to a disaster.

The way backup software products and services handle this issue is by regularly and automatically pre-restoring the VMs and servers in question prior to testing or declaring a disaster. The customer decides which VMs or servers need to be included in a disaster recovery and how often those servers need to be brought up to date in the recovery site. Typical backup software still backs up every night, and a typical setting would be to perform an incremental restore the next morning of the latest backup to the recovery image sitting in the recovery site, whatever that may be. Some software products can back up every hour or even every few minutes. The customer can then decide whether they want each of these backups immediately replicated to the recovery site or wish to do it less often.

Platform format issues

One challenge you will experience when designing a DR system is if you are still using computing platforms that are not Windows or Linux, such as Solaris, AIX, HP-UX, and of course mainframes and other proprietary systems. This hardware is typically not available in any cloud configuration, so this part of your computing environment will need some sort of physical recovery site. This is one of the many reasons these platforms have become less popular in recent years.

But if you are a fully virtualized environment using one of the popular virtualization vendors (e.g., VMware, Hyper-V, or KVM), there are a number of cloud-based options for you. The challenge you might experience, however, is the hypervisor itself. If you are replicating primary data or backups to your own recovery site, you can ensure that the server or virtualization platforms you're using on premises are the same as what you have in the recovery site. This makes server or VM-based replication very easy.

It's also easy if you use a cloud-based version of your favorite hypervisor. For example, there are cloud-based implementations of VMware, Hyper-V, and KVM. If a cloud implementation offers these hypervisors and the appropriate storage, networking, and security that you need, you can simply replicate your on-premises VMs directly into these hypervisors and everything will work just fine. As of this writing, a few companies are offering this choice. Organizations using a single hypervisor (e.g., VMware, Hyper-V), with no experience in any of the hyperscalers, are the type of organizations attracted to this option. Restoring their favorite hypervisor into a cloud version of the same hypervisor simplifies things and can offer quick RTAs and RPAs. There are downsides to this approach, though, which I'll discuss in the following section; it discusses another common option for DR in the cloud.

Another cloud DR method that has become common is to use your favorite hypervisor on premises, but use a hyperscaler in the cloud for DR. This has become popular for multiple reasons, including cost and availability of services. Recovering into a virtual datacenter in a typical hyperscaler is usually less expensive than recovering into a similarly sized environment running a traditional hypervisor. Hyperscalers have also offered virtual datacenters for a much longer period than the length of time cloud versions of traditional hypervisors have existed, so they (for now) offer much greater flexibility.

Recovering into a public cloud hyperscaler is typically less expensive for a variety of reasons. The first is that each VM simply costs less in a hyperscaler than it does in a cloud-based version of your favorite hypervisor. This might not make a big difference if you only have a few VMs, but if you have hundreds or thousands of them, it can add up to a lot. In addition, many more storage options are available in hyperscalers than are typically available with cloud versions of popular hypervisors. Many of these options are much less expensive than what is available in these other offerings.

For example, there are also some logistical challenges with some of the popular cloud-based versions of your hypervisor (e.g., VMware Cloud) that require a customer to make a choice between saving a lot of money or adding a few hours to your RTA as the virtual datacenter is being provisioned. As of this writing, it takes about two hours to provision a new VMware Cloud software-defined data center (SDDC), for example. Once it's provisioned, you are paying for it. If you don't want to pay for an SDDC that is just standing by for a DR, the only way to get around that is to provision once there's a disaster. But that means your minimum RTA is at least two hours. This is the case as of now, but that may eventually change.

Suffice it to say that many customers find the recovery options available in the bigger hyperscalers more desirable than the options they find with the other services. Therefore, they are looking for products that can recover their hypervisor (e.g., Hyper-V, KVM, or VMware) to a hyperscaler (e.g., AWS, Azure, GCP). Here's where you have your *real* challenge: Each popular virtualization platform has its own disk format, and each popular hypervisor has *its* own disk format. How do you recover a virtual disk from one format into a completely different format?

If the virtual disk formats of the two systems you are using are not compatible, they need to be made compatible to work during recovery. Your two choices to accomplish this are either *conversion* or *transformation*.

In conversion, you run the entire virtual machine image through some sort of conversion tool, such as the *AWS Import Tool*. This tool was originally designed to import VMs into AWS, which means it's very good at converting on-premises VM images into images that will run in AWS. The advantage of this approach is that it is time-tested and you are using a standard tool offered by the hyperscaler in question.

The disadvantage of the conversion process is that it takes a really long time. The first reason conversion takes so long is that it was never designed to be fast; it was designed to be thorough and reliable. People importing VMs into AWS—the original point of the tool—are usually not in a hurry.

The second reason conversion is not very fast is that the entire VM must run through the process. The bigger the VM, the longer the conversion takes. Tests I have conducted in the last year or so showed that a 100 GB VM took about four hours to convert. Turn that into a 1 TB VM and you are looking at well over 24 hours, possibly as many as 48. That's a significant hit to your RTA.

Transformation, on the other hand, is something done by the data protection vendor, which transforms the file in place and does not pipe the entire disk image through the process. It may put wrappers around the image, open up the image and insert drivers, and perform a variety of operations against the file to make the disk image compatible with the hyperscaler in question.

The advantages and disadvantages of this approach are exactly the opposite of the conversion approach. The advantage is that transformation can be relatively quick in comparison to conversion, taking only a few minutes per disk image. This is for two reasons, the first of which is that transformation was designed with speed in mind. Second, since you are not running the entire disk image through a pipe, the amount of time it takes to transform a disk image should be irrespective of the size of said image. You are not copying or moving any data; you are essentially performing surgery on data in place.

It is a proprietary approach that will be different for each backup vendor; it is not something that is provided by the hyperscaler, and certainly is not supported by the same. The support for this process will have to come from the disaster recovery product.

Choosing between these two methods

These two approaches drastically affect your RTA and RPA. Let's suppose you are considering two backup products that can both back up every hour, after which they can perform an incremental update of your recovery image in the cloud. Theoretically, this means you could support an RPA of 60 minutes, right? Not so fast. With one option, you will need to choose between a shorter RPA or a shorter RTA. Let me explain. Consider the backup and recovery schedule shown in Figure 11-1.

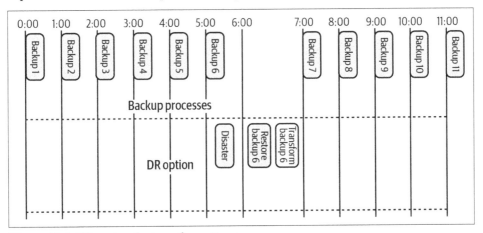

Figure 11 1. DR, using the transformation process

It shows an hourly backup that takes less than 30 minutes. It then shows a disaster happening at around 5:30. This product uses the transformation process that only takes 15 minutes (mins). That means your configuration would be up and running well before 7 p.m., after which you can resume backups. Your RTA looks to be about 30 mins, and your RPA is actually only a few minutes because you got lucky. The disaster happened just after you took a backup. (If the disaster happened during the 6 p.m. backup, for example, your RPA would be closer to one hour.)

Now consider the same configuration, but with a product that must convert the entire VM, a process that will take four hours or more. (As I said, my tests of the conversion of a 100 GB VM took about four hours. Many VMs are much bigger than that, so things can be much worse.)

In Figure 11-2, you'll see a similar configuration of hourly backups. You also see that after every backup, we start the four-hour conversion process to convert the latest backup to something that runs in the cloud. You'll see why this makes sense in a bit.

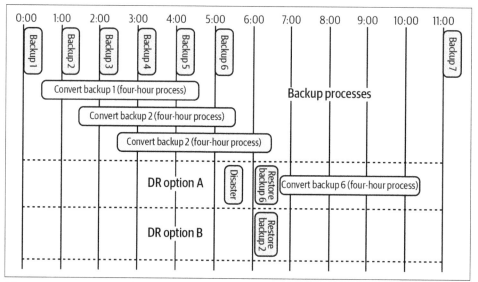

Figure 11-2. DR, using the conversion process

Again, a disaster happens at 5:30. Restore Option A restores Backup 6 and then converts it. If you choose this option, you will have an RPA of only minutes, because you're using a backup from just minutes before the disaster happened. Unfortunately, though, your RTA will be around 4.5 hours. If that meets your RTO, then great. If not, you will need to do something else.

If you want to have a much quicker RTA, you'll need to choose a backup that's already been converted. Since it takes four hours, the most recent backup that has finished converting is Backup 2, which finished converting just before the disaster. If you restore from Backup 2, you will have an RTA of mins, but an RPA of close to five hours, since Backup 2 happened at 1:00. This is what I meant by being forced to choose between a good RPA and a good RTA.

Now that we've talked about the various ways one can perform a disaster recovery, it's time to talk about the types of products that could support your DR plan. You will need to choose between buying a software product and managing it yourself or using some kind of service for DR. Let's take a look at that choice.

Software or Service

Once you've decided whether you want to create your own recovery site or use a service to provide one, decided whether you want a cold, warm, or hot site, and decided whether you want to do this via replication or backup software, you have one more decision to make. Do you buy and run the software yourself, or do you use a service to do it for you?

The decision here is very similar to the one that I discuss in Chapter 16 on commercial data protection software. There are advantages and disadvantages to owning and managing your own software, just as there are when using a SaaS solution. Let's review these again in the context of disaster recovery. (It will probably be helpful to review the longer discussion in "Data-Protection-as-a-Service (DPaaS)" on page 325 as well.)

Commercial DR Software

Procuring your own DR software means you will install it on your own servers that you manage. These could be physical or virtual machines that you actually own, or VMs that you are paying for from a cloud vendor.

The main advantage of this approach is control. You are entirely responsible for the servers upon which the software is running, and can control their security level in every way. You can ensure that all your favorite information security best practices are being executed on the servers, just as you do on every other server in your environment. You can know that they reside behind whatever firewall you are using, be it a typical datacenter firewall or one being provided in the cloud. You can know the user IDs of everyone who has access to the servers and can also control those who are given special access levels. These are not things you can do with a SaaS offering.

The main disadvantage of owning and installing your own software for DR is also about control. If you are installing and configuring the DR software on servers that you control, you are entirely responsible for their security. That means anything that goes wrong from a security perspective is your responsibility. You must maintain all the appropriate patches for the hardware itself, the operating system, any storage devices you might be using, and the DR software itself. Although this may not sound like a very big deal, I would like to point out that most of the successful ransomware attacks of the past two years have only been successful because the sysadmins in question did not install the appropriate security patches. Making the matter worse is the fact that many of those patches were over a year old, meaning they were given a year to install them and still had not done so.

The other disadvantage is cost. Just as will be discussed in Chapters 13 and 16 about commercial data protection software, buying and maintaining enough infrastructure to handle this requires purchasing excess equipment in advance, as well as the excess equipment to deal with various spikes in the load that will happen throughout the process. The tighter your RTO and RPO requirements are, the more costs can get out of control to manage this process. It's very easy to overbuy to make sure you always meet your requirements.

All of these advantages and disadvantages apply whether you purchase the software up front or through some type of subscription program. Many major software companies have gone to subscription-based pricing, where you pay a monthly or yearly subscription fee instead of one large purchase up front. This is simply a different way to pay for the software and doesn't ameliorate the other advantages and disadvantages.

If you do want to address the disadvantages of procuring and managing your own software, the only way to do that is to use SaaS. In the SaaS model, you simply use the software; you do not have to manage its infrastructure.

DR-as-a-Service

When you use a DR-as-a-service (DRaaS) product (i.e., a SaaS-based DR service), the most you typically have to do for DR is install an agent in the appropriate place. Everything else about the system is managed for you. In a true SaaS environment, you do not manage the infrastructure that makes the system happen. You should never be logging on as an administrator on any servers or storage, because that is entirely the responsibility of the SaaS vendor. If you are still logging in as the superuser on some servers somewhere, even if they are virtual machines in the cloud, you are not using a DRaaS product. You are most probably simply buying software through a subscription model.

If you are using a true DRaaS product, however, the advantages and disadvantages are basically exactly the opposite of those of owning or leasing your own DR software. You no longer have to worry about acquiring, provisioning, and managing the computing or storage infrastructure behind the service; all of that is provided by the service itself. The responsibility for maintaining the existence and security of all the DR resources is in the hands of the DRaaS provider. They are responsible for ensuring that there are enough resources to accomplish the task and that the resources are properly secured against attacks. Basically, all the things considered disadvantages when managing your own DR software are now advantages with a DRaaS solution.

You may still be responsible for managing the recovery site itself. In other words, you may still be responsible for managing the servers that will take over for your computing environment in a disaster. This is usually due to security concerns, because turning over the administration of those servers to someone else means they have unfettered access to unencrypted copies of your data.

There are only two ways around this problem: give them administrator access to these machines and let them manage them, or use the public cloud, where there are no VMs or unencrypted volumes to manage until a disaster actually happens. In a disaster, the unencrypted copies of your data and the VMs necessary to use that data are automatically created and/or restored during the failover process. This means there is no management issue for those resources until they are actually needed.

The main disadvantage of a DRaaS solution is loss of control. Many IT people feel they need to be the ones in charge of important things such as security, or they cannot be assured that things are being done correctly. This falls under the concept of, "If you want something done right, you do it yourself."

Another disadvantage to the DRaaS method is that it is typically delivered through cloud resources, and some people perceive the cloud as less secure than their own datacenter. In addition to the control concern previously mentioned, there is a general perception by some that the cloud is the wild wild West and that resources in the cloud have a higher percentage of being attacked.

Not everyone is as trusting in the cloud as yours truly, either. Some see the cloud as one giant security risk. My personal opinion is that I'll take the security of the typical cloud provider over the security of the typical datacenter any day. The things I've seen in typical datacenters only serve to remind me of why backup is so important.

After consulting at many dozens of organizations over the years, my opinion on this matter is that I would trust the security of the average cloud resource more than the security of the average datacenter that I have encountered in my many years in IT. I have no doubt the average computing environment in the average datacenter takes security seriously and is dedicated to ensuring that the organization is not attacked. However, with few exceptions, the IT department is not the purpose of the organization; the IT department *supports* the purpose of the organization.

Contrast this with a cloud offering where the IT department *is* the product. A cloud offering that is shown to be insecure is a cloud offering that will cease to exist relatively quickly. Strong security is table stakes in the cloud. That's why I would say that the average cloud vendor and, by extension the average SaaS vendor, is committed to the idea of security.

This is why I say that IT people are dedicated, but cloud personnel are committed. There's an old dad joke about the difference between these two terms. When it comes to breakfast, the chicken is dedicated. The pig is committed.

All-in-One or Best of Breed?

There was a time when backup software only did operational recoveries, and if you needed an RTO of anything less than days, you used replication. That meant that any organization serious about DR had both products. You certainly cannot be without day-to-day operational recovery, and if your organization believes it needs a strong DR system, you need that as well. There was also a time when you needed a separate backup product for your IaaS/PaaS apps and another one for your SaaS apps.

 It is important to understand that right now, there isn't really DR for SaaS apps, outside of whatever the SaaS provider does itself. All the SaaS backup tools rely on the app itself to be available. So the best you can do is be prepared to restore your data once the SaaS vendor has returned to normal.

Since each of these tools could do something the other tools couldn't, there was really nothing to do but buy multiple products. The main problem with that is that you had to learn and manage all of them, significantly increasing the complexity of managing data protection in a typical environment. You also had to *pay* for all the products, which is another reason many people didn't have all of them.

We live in the new world now, where there are several competing products that can perform day-to-day operational recoveries and disaster recovery for datacenters, IaaS/PaaS, and SaaS apps. This means that, once again, IT personnel responsible for operational recoveries and disaster recovery of datacenters, IaaS/PaaS, and SaaS apps find themselves with the age-old choice of procuring one product to do multiple activities or procuring a separate product for each activity.

From acquisition costs and training and management cost perspectives, it is certainly less expensive to purchase one product that can do two or three things than to purchase and manage two or three products, each of which only does one thing. This is also a universal truth that applies outside of IT as well. So which approach is better?

I always want to go back to requirements. Before you acquire any product, you should establish what your requirements are. If you have an RTO or RPO of zero, you're going to need a DR tool based on primary data replication. There are very few tools that can do that *and* do operational recovery. But if you find a replication-based tool that also meets your operational recovery needs, that sounds like a deal.

It's also possible that you might find a backup and recovery product that can also meet your DR needs for your datacenter, IaaS/PaaS apps, and SaaS apps. Such products cannot do an RTO and RPO of zero (as of this writing, anyway), but they can usually do one hour or less. If you find a backup product that can meet both needs, that also sounds like a deal.

If you found multiple products, whether backup software that also does DR or DR software that also does backups, you're definitely in luck. Having multiple competing products that can meet your needs is exactly where you want to be when you start talking about price.

The next thing you want to investigate is cost. Although it is usually true that one product that does two to three things is cheaper than two or three that can do one thing, that is not always the case. Remember, also, to include operational costs as well. If the acquisition cost is the same, managing and operating a single product will definitely be less expensive than two or three products. So if the acquisition cost is the same or close, my personal opinion would be that one product is better than two or three. If you have multiple competing products that meet your requirements, and one or two of them are significantly less expensive than the other, that should also help answer the question.

This really is no different than any other area of computing. I just thought it was important to mention that we have reached a point in technology when it is possible to get a single product to do operational recovery and disaster recovery for datacenters, IaaS/PaaS, and SaaS.

Choosing a Plan

It's important to start with your actual goal when choosing a plan. Your goal is to be able to bring your computing environment back online after some disaster that destroys it. That could be a natural disaster, a terrorist action, or some kind of ransomware or other malware.

Your goal is *not* to buy a replication product or a backup product that also does replication. Your goal is not to get to the cloud or to stay away from the cloud. Your goal is to be able to bring your organization back online if something happens to it. Try very hard to keep that goal in mind when trying to decide on a plan and vendors to execute that plan.

I like the analogy of an island. Your goal is to get a thousand cars a day onto and off the island. That's it. So you put out a bid for vendors to help you do that. You do not advertise that you are looking for someone to build you a bridge, or a tunnel, or a ferry. You advertise that you're looking for a vendor to help you get a thousand cars on and off the island every day. Let them tell you how they would accomplish that goal. One of them might actually have a transporter like you see in *Star Trek*. Specifying in the bid that you're looking for a bridge would cause you to miss out on a really nice tunnel, a less expensive ferry, or a really cool transporter device.

Before you ever talk to any vendors, make sure you know what your recovery requirements are for both operational recovery and disaster recovery. Tell them what those requirements are and let them tell you how they would solve those requirements. Examine their proposals on how well they meet the requirements and what the acquisition and day-to-day management cost will be for each proposal. Then make an organizational decision on which one is best for your environment.

Once you have agreed to DR requirements; decided on a design; procured the appropriate hardware, software, and/or services; and implemented everything, you need a DR *runbook*. The *runbook* is so named because it used to be the literal book that you would run the disaster recovery plan from. Nowadays, the DR runbook is more than likely maintained electronically.

This concept was already covered in Chapter 2, but here I'm going to do a deeper dive on what a runbook for DR should actually contain.

Creating a DR Runbook

Imagine the worst-case scenario has come to pass. Every piece of IT infrastructure has been destroyed in a disaster or encrypted by some ransomware program, and the people who understand the disaster recovery plan are no longer available. Maybe they won the lottery a few months ago. Maybe they got hit by a bus. Maybe they were caught up in whatever caused the disaster; who knows. The point is they are not available.

A DR runbook is designed so that an IT-savvy person should be able to follow it from start to finish and execute your disaster recovery plan. When trying to decide whether your runbook is good enough, that is the standard by which you should measure it.

Runbook Goals

Your DR plan is only as good as your runbook, and you should strive for a number of goals that will make it a good runbook to reach those goals. The following is a list of such goals. It's probably not an exhaustive list, but it's a pretty good one. One important thing to remember when reading this list is always to avoid alliterations.

Authoritative
Everyone should agree that there is one runbook. There should not be competing runbooks that say different things, and there should be no doubt about which version of the runbook you are using. An old version of your current runbook should not magically surface during a recovery, because that could be quite confusing.

Accurate

Nothing erodes confidence in a runbook more than being told to go to a certain server or directory, or click a certain button, only to find no such server, directory, or button. Running a disaster recovery is hard enough without incorrect information.

Accessible

The easiest way to make your runbook accessible these days is to put it online. Your electronic runbook should be available in multiple places, though, both on premises and in the cloud. They could easily be synchronized so that you are always using the most recent version. Just make sure you have thought through all the ways the runbook might need to be accessed in a disaster and prepare for them; depending on your infrastructure, this might include an actual printed runbook.

Absorbed

The runbook should be part of everyone's philosophy and mindset. To borrow a term from Douglas Adams's *Hitchhiker's Guide to the Galaxy*, everyone needs to grock it. This needs to come from the top down. Management buy-in can help make sure that everyone in IT grocks the DR runbook.

Active

The runbook should be continually updated and a part of your regular change control process. The change control process is the one you follow whenever you add a new server, VM, database, or cloud application, and part of that process should be adding that new item to the runbook. An alternative is something that automatically inventories everything and adds it to the runbook. Whatever the process you use to update the runbook, this process needs to be an active, living process that happens all the time.

Adaptable

Disaster recoveries never go as planned. Flexibility and backup plans for the backup plan need to be built into the plan. If things don't go right, there should be an alternate plan that enables you to adapt to the current situation. Do your best to build this kind of adaptability into the runbook.

Auditable

An outside entity should be able to look at your runbook and verify it. I used to work for a bank, and part of the job of the Office of the Comptroller of Currency (OCC) was to verify that we had a DR runbook and that it matched our current configuration. Failing that audit could have meant them telling us we couldn't be a bank anymore.

I'll admit it; I've pushed the definition of this word a little far to have a successful alliteration. What I'm saying is that a DR runbook that has not been tested should not be considered valid in any way. Without testing, it's just theory. There should be regular DR tests that use the runbook you designed and that use it as designed. That means that the tests should not be run by the DR or backup person; they should be run by an IT generalist. The more you test your disaster recovery like that, the better your runbook will be.

Overview

The DR runbook should start with an overview of your organization's DR process. This should start with an executive summary—an overview of the overview, if you will. You should be able to explain in just a few pages the overall process your organization will use in times of recovery.

The executive summary should be followed by a technical overview that goes into a lot more detail. This should have many pages and explain each of the technical pieces of the recovery, including names of products and services used, although this is just an overview. "Procedures" on page 254 will go into much more detail. This overview is simply something that a technical person can read before they read the rest of the runbook. It allows them to understand the high-level view before digging into the specifics. There should be a numbered list of each high-level step, and this list should be repeated in the Procedures section, except with details.

Here's a very brief example of what I'm talking about.

1. Access password database
2. Power on recovery site
3. Verify inventory
4. Locate list of apps and VMs to be recovered
5. Recover and verify each app
    a. Recover and verify each VM in app
    b. Verify application
6. Connect and verify network connections
7. Verify cross-app functionality
8. Notify stakeholders

Technology Inventory

Every single product that is used as part of the disaster recovery should be listed in the technology section, along with the contact information of each company providing said product. Also helpful will be where to locate contracts that might be necessary, including a summary of customer numbers, contract numbers, dates, and so on.

This section should also go into detail about what each product does as part of the overall DR plan, as well as any contractual agreements from each vendor. What service levels has each vendor agreed to? The following is a list of the kinds of things you should know:

- How quickly is your recovery-site-as-a-service vendor supposed to offer you hardware that you can use for recovery?
- How many servers is it contracted to provide you?
- How much storage is it contracted to provide you?
- How much bandwidth is it contracted for?
- For DRaaS vendors, have they agreed to any RTOs or RPOs?
- How quickly is an off-site vaulting vendor supposed to bring you your tapes? (I know I said not to use tapes; I also know that many of you probably will do so anyway.)
- If you are maintaining your own recovery site, what about your hardware and software vendors? Do they have any contractual obligations about how quickly they can get you new hardware and/or software?

The most important part of this section is the contact information. No disaster recovery goes exactly as planned, and you will need your vendors' help. Knowing who to call and what they are supposed to provide is crucial.

Contact Information

Speaking of knowing whom to call, you also need to know everyone inside your organization who might either participate in or facilitate the recovery process. This, of course, should include contact information for everyone in IT. You never know just who is going to be available after a major disaster. I would also suggest including every type of contact method that you have: mobile phone, home phone, work email, personal email, and anything else you can think of. When a disaster hits, time is of the essence, and having multiple ways to get in touch with your people will be helpful.

DR facilitators, otherwise known as senior management, are also really important. You should have the contact information for everyone in the chain of command all the way to the person at the top. If things are going poorly with the vendor, nothing helps like an angry call to it from a CEO, executive director, or senior government official. Again, I suggest you record as much contact information as you can get for all these people. I hope you will never need it. I'm suddenly reminded of a local bail bonds commercial: "Better to know me and not need me then to need me and not know me."

One suggestion is to keep this part of the runbook even in a lot of places. When the feces hits the rotary oscillator, being able to call the right people right away can be very helpful.

Procedures

This section is where the rubber meets the road. These are the pages to which the people who will actually execute the DR plan will turn when everything goes wrong. These instructions should be as detailed as possible and as accurate as possible. As I've already said in this chapter, these procedures need to be up to date. They should start with the same high-level list of instructions from the overview, and then flesh them out step by step.

The key here is to assume that the person running the procedure is familiar with IT, how to log in, and how to administer systems. What they are unfamiliar with are the details of this particular process. They should not be required to know server names, application names, usernames, and passwords. The inventory and password management systems will take care of that.

Everyone in IT should be trained with enough knowledge to be able to execute the DR plan if need be. You never know just who will be required to do what step, so cross-functional training like this is crucial. And this training can include the base level of knowledge to which the procedure is written.

I'll take the example given in the overview section down to another level. Keep in mind that this is just an example, and your runbook will be determined by your system. Perhaps you don't use a password database, for example. If all recovery systems have multiple administrator accounts that allow each person to maintain their own username and password, such a database might not be required.

1. Access password database—Log in to password database
2. Power on recovery site
   a. Log in to recovery site
   b. Power on each part of the recovery site
3. Verify inventory
   a. Log in to DR inventory system
   b. Check DR inventory against what you have
   c. Resolve inconsistencies

4. Locate list of apps and VMs to be recovered

    a. Consult DR inventory system

    b. Get list of apps

    c. Get list of VMs for each app

    d. Get priority list

5. Recover and verify each app

    a. Recover and verify each VM in app

        i. Identify VMs in app

        ii. Recover each VM

        iii. Verify all VMs in app are recovered

    b. Verify application

        i. Consult App inventory

        ii. Use procedure for each app to test it

6. Connect and verify network connections

    a. Log in to network management system

    b. Activate DR-specific VPNs

    c. Run network test to verify connectivity

7. Verify cross-app functionality

    a. Consult application inventory

    b. Identify any cross-app dependencies

    c. Test cross-app functionality

8. Notify stakeholders

    a. Consult application inventory for stakeholders

    b. Contact each stakeholder

    c. Contact senior management in your chain of command

Each of these steps would be followed by much more detailed information about which server or application to log in to to execute that step, and where to access the credentials to do so. It should also explain what the person executing the plan is expected to see on the screen as they are performing each step.

Exception Processing with Escalation

Nothing ever goes as planned. Things will come up that you did not plan for. Perhaps your DR plan is not as up to date as you'd like it to be. Perhaps the DR plan made assumptions that are now incorrect. Perhaps a system that was supposed to perform a particular task failed to do so. There should be an agreed-upon escalation procedure that you use in times such as this.

An escalation procedure should spell out things that might go wrong, and who should handle each type of thing. For example, if the network fails to initialize as designed, you should escalate that to the head network admin. If they are unavailable, you should escalate the problem to the director of IT. If they are unavailable, you should escalate to the CIO, and so on.

The point is that all of this should be decided in advance, so the person executing the DR plan does not have to know or figure out whom to call. They simply follow the procedures as outlined in the runbook.

Takeaways

Testing your backups is important; testing your DR plan is crucial. The more frequently you run a DR test, the more likely it is that your DR plan will be successful. As mentioned previously, pretend that everyone who knows what's going on in the DR plan is unavailable, and tell people who normally don't do such things to bring things back online. Experts in the process should be made available, but any time they have to answer a question, make a note. This is an indication the runbook isn't quite clear. If you test enough, and update your runbook and systems based on the results of that test, you will be much more comfortable when you must fire your DR system in anger.

The remaining chapters go into a little bit more of the meat. It's time to look at the actual types of products you could buy to make all this happen. We'll start with hardware, such as tape, disk, and cloud storage.

CHAPTER 12

Data Protection Targets

There are more data protection targets (i.e., devices to which you will send backups or archives) now than at any other time in the data protection industry. When I started as the "backup guy" at MBNA so many years ago, there was one choice: tape drives. The only question was which tape drive you would use, and since many server vendors shipped servers with pre-installed tape drives, even that wasn't a question most of the time. HP servers came with 4 mm DDS drives (2, 8, or 24 GB capacity), digital servers came with TK50s (94 MB!), and AT&T 3B2s came with QIC-80 tape drives that held 80 MB of data and were *not* quick. We also used 9-track tape drives for the mainframes. If you don't know what those are, they're the big reel-to-reel tape drives you see in every old computer movie.

Those tasked with backing up data today have so many other choices and decisions to make. These decisions often come with misinformation about the various choices. My hope in this chapter is to give you unbiased information about the choices before you, so that you can make an educated decision of your own.

Tape Drives

Tape drives are the oldest data protection device still in use in production environments today. Yes, there were punch cards and even paper tape, but magnetic tape drives were really the first device to catch on as a mechanism for backing up programs and data stored on servers. I remember backing up my TRS-80 to a cassette tape. Boy, that was a long time ago.

Tapes are less expensive than other options in almost every case, and yet, the bulk of the data protection industry no longer uses tape drives as its primary target for backups. Why is that? Let's take a look at what tape is good at and what tape is bad at.

What Tape Is Good At

Tape is better than disk in three areas: cost, reliably writing data, and long-term storage of that data. The latter two of these probably come as a surprise to most people, but they are a scientifically proven fact.

Cost

Tape is significantly less expensive than deduplicated disk, its closest competitor. An argument can be made that the total cost of ownership (TCO) of disk is actually less than tape, since it is much easier to use, as will be discussed in the next section. You can also make the argument that the functionality now provided by disk-based backup systems (e.g., replicating backups off-site) so surpasses what you can do with tape that cost is irrelevant. Setting all that aside, tape is still a very inexpensive medium.

One big reason tape is so inexpensive is that the recording medium (i.e., the actual tape) can be separated from the recording device (i.e., the tape drive). This is not possible with disk drives; therefore, every piece of media has to have a recording mechanism in it. The devices inside disk drives are also much more complicated than what you see in a tape drive. As a result, even a fully automated tape library that behaves very much like a large storage array is still usually less expensive than an equivalent disk array.

One area where tape really shines is in costs related to power consumption, because a tape sitting in a slot in a tape library consumes no power, and a tape drive not actively writing data (or a robot waiting to move tapes) consumes very little power. Compare this to the power consumed by a typical spinning disk drive, and the fact that all disks in a disk array are typically powered on all the time.

In a technique called massive array of idle disks (MAID), disks are powered off most of the time, but it is not in use very much anymore. It had some popularity prior to the advent of deduplication, but it turned out that the marriage of deduplication and MAID was a disastrous one. Deduplication requires all disks to work, and MAID wanted them mostly off.

The result is that every time I calculate power consumption for tape systems versus disk systems, tape systems win. The longer you are storing data, the more money you save in the power and cooling department. In fact, the difference between the cost of disk and tape is so stark that even if disk were free, it would still cost more than tape when you factor in power and cooling. One of the reasons for this is that multiple copies on tape cost the same (power and cooling-wise), but multiple copies on disk doubles power and cooling costs. Two copies of a backup on different disks will consume twice as much power as one copy. You could have 20 copies of a backup on tape, and it would consume no power—once it's created, of course.

Again, you can easily make an argument that the functionality provided by today's disk-based systems outweighs this cost difference, but tape is still less expensive than disk.

You buy the system once; you power it all day long every day. Power and cooling matter.

Reliably writing data

Tape drives write data more reliably than disk drives, and this difference is right on the box. The *uncorrected bit error rate* (UBER) of storage devices is a value published by every storage vendor for each of their storage devices, although it can be a bit hard to find. This value shows how often a drive writes a 1 when it was meant to write a 0 (or vice versa), and it cannot be repaired (corrected); tape is way better at writing 1s and 0s than disk is.

To ensure that a recording device reliably writes data, all modern recording devices do read-after-write checks. However, the error correcting code (ECC) and cyclical redundancy check (CRC) technologies used for this purpose are not block-for-block comparisons. The odds are the device writes the correct block most of the time, and the odds are the technologies to detect a failure detect failures most of the time. When you combine the odds of a write failure with the odds of a correction failure, the odds that you have both are actually quite low, but they are not zero.

A simplistic explanation of ECC and CRC is that the drive calculates a hash of the block before it writes, and then it writes the block. The drive then reads the block back and calculates the hash again from what it read back, and if the hashes match, all is good. However, since the CRC hash is so small (12^{16} bits), it is possible that the block doesn't match (because there was a write error), but the CRC does match (because the bad block and the good block generate the same small hash). The result is an uncorrected bit error. The rate of this happening is much higher than most people think, and it is worse for disk than it is for tape. The chance of a modern tape drive giving back incorrect data is extremely low; the drive may not be able to give the correct data (because the tape is damaged, for example), but it will NOT give you the wrong data. A disk will.

You can see from Table 12-1 that LTO-8 has an UBER of $1:10^{19}$, often expressed as 10^{-19}, and a SATA disk has a UBER of 10^{-14}. This will probably come as a surprise to many people, but that means that LTO-8 is five orders of magnitude—*10,000 times better*—at writing data than a SATA disk. That's the difference between 10 TB and 1,000 PB! You are 10,000 times more likely to have an unknown bad block on a SATA disk drive than you are on an LTO-8 tape of equivalent size!

Table 12-1. UBER rates of modern media

Media	UBER
Optical	$10^{-8} - 10^{-12}$ (typically, 10^{-10})
SATA Disk	10^{-14}
Enterprise Disk	10^{-15}
Enterprise SSD	10^{-16}
LTO-8	10^{-19}
IBM TS1160	10^{-20}

So 10^{-14} is one uncorrected bit error in roughly 12 TB, which is less than the world's largest SATA drives. That means at least one uncorrected bit error in every disk drive. Let that sink in a bit. Tape is *significantly* better at writing data than disk is. There really is no debate on this topic.

Long-term retention

Many readers will be surprised by this, but tape can reliably hold data for 30 years, but a powered-on disk can only do that for five years. If you are dubious of this claim, you should understand it is a well-published fact. Ask the right people, and that is the answer you will get. Let me explain.

All magnetic media degrades over time; it is only a question of how quickly it degrades. This degradation is colloquially referred to as *bit rot*, and it determines how long a file can safely be stored on a magnetic medium before it begins to degrade.

A formula determines the *energy barrier* of each magnetic medium, which is the energy required to cause a magnetic grain (the name for the thing on magnetic media that stores a single bit) to be *coerced* to its opposite state (i.e., turn a 1 into a 0, or vice versa). The formula is KuV/kT, where *Ku* is the anisotropy constant and *k* is the Boltzmann constant[1]. The relevant values in this discussion are *V*, which is the volume (i.e., size) of the magnetic grain, and *T*, which is the temperature of the medium in Kelvin. Larger values derived from this formula are better and mean that a given magnetic grain will be less likely to degrade over time.

The speed of bit rot is therefore determined by two factors: the size (i.e., volume) of the magnetic grain and the average temperature of the media. The bigger the magnetic grain, the better. The cooler the medium, the better. When compared to tape, disk has *much* smaller grains and much warmer media. Disk's smaller magnetic grains and constantly warm operating temperature mean that data degrades on it much faster than it does on tape.

---

1 This is a complicated formula, but it is not necessary to know the anisotropy or Boltzmann constants. What matters in this context are the variables *V* and *T*.

Those that study such things agree with the initial statement of this section: modern tape drives can reliably hold data without bit rot for 30 years, but such data can only be stored on disk for five years before it begins to degrade. Data stored on disk for long periods must therefore be refreshed by moving it around. But remember that every time you move it around, you are subject to disk's higher bit error rate. The summary is that tape is simply a much better medium for long-term storage of data.

When talking about storing data for 30 years on tape, some will automatically bring up the issues with drive availability. It is true that you must keep compatible tape drives around to be able to read media 10–30 years from now. All of the following related statements are also true.

- If you intend to keep data that long, part of your process will be to keep the appropriate tape drives around. Just like you have to maintain the database of what's on tape, maintaining the drives to read the tape is part of your job.

- It's not like you have to keep them powered on all the time, as you do with disk. Unplug all your old tape drives and put them somewhere safe. When you need them, chances are they will work just fine.

- Hand me a tape made in the past 30 years and give me a few days. I'll find you a tape drive that can read it. It's really not that hard. There's an entire industry around maintaining old tape drives.

- If you can't find a tape drive, there's a service somewhere that'll read it for you.

- Most people keeping data that long on tape will need to occasionally refresh the tapes. Not because it's necessary to keep the data safe, but because newer tapes are larger and faster which allows them to retire old tape drives and save money on storage. It costs about $4 per tape per year to store a tape in a commercial environment. If you are storing 10,000 400 GB tapes, that's $40,000 per year. If you copy the same dataset onto 334 12 TB tapes, you reduce your storage cost to $1,336 per year.

- This isn't even an option with disk, so why are we having this conversation?

Bit rot is one of the problems object storage addresses. If the underlying data changes due to bit rot, the UID, generated from a hash of the object, would change, and the failure would be detected and corrected. There are technologies to work around the long-term storage concerns about disk, but tape is still a more reliable mechanism underneath.

Some also make the argument that it is easier to regularly check the integrity of data stored in object storage, compared to doing so on tape. Some tape libraries can do regular integrity checks on tapes, but it is nowhere as easy as doing so on disk. So this issue should factor into any decision as well.

What Tape Is Bad At

Tape is bad at writing a typical incremental backup, which is a small amount of data written over a longer period. Since this sounds like a contradiction to the previous section (that said tape is better at writing data than disk), it requires a detailed explanation.

Tape drives work by passing a recording head across a recording medium (i.e., tape) in the same way a magnetic disk drive works. Pole changes in the recording head reposition magnetic bits on the recording medium, which stay in that position after the recording head passes, leaving either a "1" or a "0."

For the recording head to write data reliably to the recording medium, it must maintain a high signal-to-noise ratio, meaning a lot more signal (i.e., pole change in the recording head) than noise (i.e., electronic interference that might interfere with the signal). Low signal-to-noise ratio means bad data written to the device, and nobody wants that.

For reasons I would understand better if I had an electrical engineering degree, the key to maintaining a high signal-to-noise ratio is very quickly moving the recording head across the recording medium[2]. Disk drives accomplish this by spinning the recording medium at very high speeds, and tape drives accomplish it by pulling the tape at a high speed across the recording head.

The way this is accomplished with most tape drives (if not all tape drives that are currently shipping) is that the recording head is stationary and the tape is pulled across that head at a very high speed. (For those who remember audio cassettes, this is the same way they worked. The head was stationary and the tape was pulled across that head as the cassette spun around.) The use of a stationary head and quickly moving

---

2 I have spoken directly with the people who actually design tape drives. This is a fact and the core issue with tape drives over the past two decades: Tape drives cannot slow down and still reliably write data.

tape is referred to as the linear tape recording model, and it is what linear tape open (LTO) tape drives use, as well as the TS110x0 drives from IBM.

An LTO-8 tape passes across the recording head at speeds of about 20 feet per second, or 13 MPH (21 KPH). An LTO-8 tape drive running at full speed requires an incoming data stream of 750 MBs per second, and devices will soon be shipping that will need 1 GB per second. *The problem is that backups don't run at 750 MB/s.*

A 1 GB buffer in LTO-8 drives helps to deal with some fluctuations between the incoming data rate and the tape drive rate, but it can only handle minor fluctuations. (Do the math; it only holds enough data for one second at the tape drive transferring data at full speed.) When the speed of data coming into the tape drive is significantly slower than the speed of data being written to tape, the buffer will soon be empty, and the recording head will have nothing to write.

When this happens, the tape drive has two choices: waste miles of tape by writing nothing (which some are now doing) or periodically stopping and repositioning the tape to keep up with the lower speed. So the tape drive stops the tape, rewinds it, and starts pulling it across the recording head again at the same speed. This process is referred to as *repositioning* the medium, and it can take three to six seconds to happen. What about speed matching? We can slow the drive down to something like 70 MB/s; there are 14 steps to the speed ratcheting.

A tape drive that is constantly repositioning is said to be shoe shining, since it mimics the motion of a shoeshine person shining a shoe, moving a cloth back and forth.

Once the buffer is full again, the tape drive will begin writing data to tape until the buffer is empty again, after which another repositioning will occur. If this happens on a continual basis, the drive will actually spend more time repositioning than it does writing data, which causes the tape drive actually to appear slower than the incoming data stream.

I cannot tell you how many customers of mine over the years failed to understand this basic fact of how tape drives work. Send a 500 MB/s tape drive 500 MB/s and it's happy as a clam. Send it 250 and it's unhappy. Send it 50 and it's miserable. It becomes slower than 50, and then you blame the tape drive for being slow. Nothing tells that story better than the following sidebar, "You Don't Need More Tape Drives!"

You Don't Need More Tape Drives!

I was consulting at a large television station many years ago, and they were using 18 tape drives to back up a datacenter whose full backup was about 20 TB. They were backing up literally around the clock and still couldn't get their backups done. I remember looking at the numbers they gave me and knowing exactly what the problem was without ever actually looking at the system. I also knew that their proposed solution, two more tape drives, would actually make the problem worse!

I remember the cost of the tape drives was $35,000. I told them that I could make their backup system significantly better without any new tape drives, and I would charge them less than those two new tape drives were going to cost. Once they signed the contract, I went to work.

I started by immediately shutting off 12 of the 18 tape drives. I then turned on their backup software's *inline tape copy* feature so that every backup would go simultaneously to two drives, creating an original and a copy at the same time. (This technically means that I was actually only using the equivalent of three drives to do their production backups.) I also changed their backup selection system from selected filesystems to all local filesystems, because I suspected they were missing out on some data. Finally, I tweaked the multiplexing setting they were using to make sure enough backups were going to each drive to make it happy.

It turns out that their datacenter was actually 30 TB, not 20. (My guess that they were missing out on some data was correct; they were missing out on 10 TB of backups!) Their backup times went from 24 hours to 8, after which they had two copies of every backup. (Before I started, they weren't even getting one successful backup each night.) They were backing up 50% more, making twice as many copies, with one-third of the tapes we started with, all by simply designing the system so that it sent a stream of data to each tape drive that was similar to the rated speed of that tape drive. This is what matching the speed of the tape drive to the speed of the backup can do.

As explained in "Multiplexing" on page 191, it is true that multiplexing is usually a two-edged sword. It can improve the speed of backups, but typically at the expense of restore speed. But short of switching to disk as your initial source for backups, multiplexing is your friend for making your tape drives happy.

Modern tape drives have tried to address this issue as well as they can by using adaptive speed technology that attempts to minimize repositioning whenever possible by adapting the speed of the media to the speed of the incoming data stream. But the drive can only write so slow (due to the previously mentioned signal-to-noise ratio issue); eventually, repositioning will occur, and the effective performance of the drive will be reduced.

I return to my opening statement of this section: this is why tape drives are bad at writing incremental backups, which is the bulk of most backups. Incremental backups run at speeds that are barely registrable by a tape drive that wants to run at 750 MB per second. (Incremental backups are often only a few megabytes per second.) Your tape drive is not slow; your backup is slow. And since your tape drive is not capable of going that slow, it actually ends up going slower.

How Did This Happen?

This fundamental mismatch of technology is the result of the past three decades of tape drive design. Tape drives used to be slower than the backup; they used to be slower than the network. When I joined the IT industry, our network was 10 Mb, or roughly 1 MB per second. The tape drive I was using (Exabyte 8200 8mm drive) ran at 125 kB per second.

The industry asked for bigger tape drives, and the backup tape industry responded by storing the bits closer together on tape. If the bits are closer together, the tape drive gets bigger without having to add any additional tape to the cartridge. But if the bits are closer together, and the recording head has to go at the same speed, the tape drive also gets faster. So over the past two decades, tape drives have gotten faster and faster, and backups have stayed roughly the same speed. The result is a device that is fundamentally incompatible with the purpose for which it was originally created.

The backup software industry responded with multiplexing, which interleaves multiple backups to create a single, faster stream. However, this helps the backups, but it actually makes restores worse, because you have to read all the streams and throw away most of them to get the one stream you need. Multiplexing is covered in more detail in "Multiplexing" on page 191.

Another idea mentioned in Chapter 5 is disk caching, or backing up to disk and then copying to tape. This also made backups better because you didn't have to multiply your backups. It didn't help restores, though, since they still had the speed mismatch problem. No matter what we did in backups to make tapes happier, it really only kicked the can up the road a bit.

This is why so many people changed to disk as their primary backup target. It's not because disk is faster than tape; it's because disk can more easily match the speed of an incoming backup. Disk is a random-access device that can literally write as slow or as fast as you need it to write (up to its maximum write speed). It can also handle hundreds of simultaneous write or read requests while running each one at exactly the speed it needs. Disk is simply much more compatible with the way backups work than tape is, and this became even truer once we moved to an incremental forever backup methodology.

Tape Drive Technologies

Tape drives is one area where things have gotten quite simple. In most cases, you only have one or two tape drive types to work with if you want to use tape as a storage medium.

Before discussing tape drive technologies, it's important to understand the concept of *on-the-fly compression*. Modern tape drives manage to compress and uncompress data on the fly (in silicon) as it is going to or coming from the tape drive, more than doubling the effective speed and capacity of the drive. This is why all tape drives quote compressed and native (uncompressed) throughput and capacity numbers. (If tape-based encryption is turned on, they encrypt the data after it's compressed, because encrypted data does not compress.)

There are two main tape drives still in production today: LTO and TS11x0.

Linear Tape Open (LTO)

Linear Tape Open (LTO) drives are the predominant tape drive in use today. Their manufacturing specs are governed by the LTO Consortium, which as of this writing includes HP, Quantum, and IBM. The current generation is LTO-8 and is capable of writing at speeds of up to 750 MB/s (compressed) and 300 MB/s native. It can hold 30 TB of compressed data or 12 TB of uncompressed data. It has a UBER of less than 10^{-19}. LTO-9 was expected in 2020 but will probably be delayed due to the COVID-19 pandemic. It's supposed to have a 60 TB cartridge (compressed) and a compressed throughput of 1.7 GB/s.

IBM TS11x0

The TS11x0 line is an even more reliable drive, which is used in some tape libraries. It has a UBER of 10^{-20}, one order of magnitude better than LTO. The TS1160 drives are slightly faster than LTO-8 at speeds of 900 MB/s compressed, with almost double the cartridge capacity at 20 TB native or 50 TB compressed.

There were other popular drives, such as the DDS drives and the StorageTek T10000 drives, but they both appear to be no longer shipping. This is a shame, because they were both very popular drives with unique use cases. Now let's look at how modern tape drives are used.

Linear Tape File System

One interesting feature of modern tape drives is that they can be mounted as a filesystem, just like a disk drive. This is referred to as the Linear Tape File System (LTFS). Once mounted in a standalone or robotic tape drive, what the user sees is a filesystem just like they would if they had mounted a disk drive. The difference, of course, is that it is not an actual random-access device, so its performance when moving from file to file is not very good.

But this provides a product-independent way to write data to tape for the long term. I personally think this is a great idea for long-term archive storage, and I think you should push any vendor archiving data to tape to support this feature. Most support it, even if they try to convince you that their format has more features. My personal opinion is that the freedom of movement that such a product-independent data format provides far outweighs the value of any features a proprietary format might bring to the table.

Robotic tape libraries

Very few organizations back up or archive to standalone tape drives. Almost everyone uses some type of automated device that uses dozens (or thousands) of slots of tape with a few (or many) tape drives. At this point, these large tape libraries are being sold primarily as destinations for archives being used for long-term storage.

One surprising fact about these large tape libraries (and one of the world's worst-kept secrets) is that some of the biggest customers of these behemoths are large public cloud companies. It is interesting that the companies driving the cutting edge of technology are also continuing to use the oldest storage device still in use. There must be some value to them after all. (That value, of course, is $/TB/sqft/watt.)

Now that we've looked at the OG backup target, it's time to look at a few upstarts, relatively speaking at least. Some may find themselves wondering about that other removable media: optical. Let's take a look at what's good—and not so good—about tape's cousin, optical drives.

Optical Media

Optical devices store data with a laser, which performs a phase change on the underlying storage medium. The only optical devices in production today are DVD and Blu-ray devices. (There was a type called magneto optical, but they seem to have disappeared.)

Blu-ray discs have a capacity of 25 GB, or 50 GB with a double-sided disc, and have a current write speed of up to 72 MB/s. Most devices in the field write far slower than that, though, because they are often connected as external drives on a USB connection, and they are limited by the speed of that bus. But the main reason these devices are so slow in general is that the process of performing a phase change on a physical medium is a very slow process. As you saw in Table 12-1, optical media also has a very low UBER, some as low as 10^{-8}, most at 10^{-10}. I cover UBER in more detail later in this chapter.

Due to the cost of the media and other factors, very few companies use optical media as a data protection device, although some use them as long-term storage devices for important information. For example, I have talked to some media companies that use them to make a long-term storage copy of movies, in addition to their LTO copies. Whether it's true remains to be seen, but their thought is that the Blu-ray disc will be easier to read in 50 years than an LTO tape. One thing leaning in that direction is that the most modern Blu-ray device can read the oldest CDs and DVDs, so it is much more backward compatible than the typical tape drive, which generally reads only one or two generations back.

The overall gist here is that none of the optical media formats I have seen over the years have ever really taken off. Even the ones that did well in certain industries seemed to fizzle out. There are a few manufacturers out there, but I never see them in the field. As discussed above, I think it's the combination of relatively small capacities with relatively slow transfer rates.

One competitor that didn't help optical media's lifespan was the advent of removable individual disk drives. Let's take a look at this idea next.

Individual Disk Drives

Disk drives are used in a variety of ways in modern data protection systems, but they are rarely used as individual disk drives, at least in large datacenters. That doesn't mean it doesn't happen.

The type of backup device that makes the least sense to have is a second disk drive that is not removable, and to use that as the target for backups. The reason this is rarely done is that it violates the 3-2-1 rule; the device to which you are backing up is literally right next to the device that you are sending backups to. Therefore, this is a really bad idea.

There are removable disk drives on the market that are specifically designed to help disks be easier to remove as well as more rugged for transport. These drives either plug into a special receptacle in a server or are made to go into a tape library and fit into the same form factor as tapes. There are a few of these types of units on the market, and they can be found by searching for portable disk drives.

There are also tape libraries that have integrated removable disk with their design. They have hardened disk packs (consisting of several RAID-protected disks) designed for transport, but then connect to their tape library and look like a tape. Backup and archive software can write to them just like a tape and then eject them like any other tape.

These drives are marketed to those who want the portability of tape but without the drawbacks mentioned in "What Tape Is Bad At" on page 262. I see nothing wrong with the use of these hardened units in certain circumstances. It's an interesting way to provide an actual gap while still using disk as your backup medium. The stand-alone units are best suited for smaller organizations that don't want to use a cloud

backup service but are too small to afford a replicated dedupe system. These stand-alone units allow such organizations to have an on-premises and off-premises copy (complying with the 3-2-1 rule) with a relatively simple (i.e., easy-to-understand) backup design.

What does concern me is when I see USB-connected portable disk drives, typically designed for personal use, being used for commercial data protection. People concerned about the data on their laptops often use these as a device to send their personal backups to. Although these devices may seem convenient, and I happen to own a few of them, I do not recommend them for the backup of an organization's important data.

The biggest reason I do not like these devices for large organizations is, once again, the 3-2-1 rule. Although the drive is external, and therefore it might seem that you are not violating the rule, you have to think about how the device is typically stored. It will almost always be stored with the computer that it is backing up, if for no other reason than convenience. That means if your laptop is stolen, your backup drive will probably be stolen with it. If your laptop catches fire, your backup drive will be sitting right next to it as it is engulfed in flames. It therefore does not typically comply with the 3-2-1 rule.

Having said that, if you can come up with a backup technology that uses these drives, but follows the 3-2-1 rule, I'm all for it. The only caveat would be that most of the failed disk drives I have seen in my career have been these portable units. Make sure you always have at least two of them with a copy of your backups on them.

I use these drives sparingly for moving data between devices. I am a Mac user and a fan of Time Machine, although it has its issues. I use it with my personal devices to transfer the OS and personal data from one device to another. I do not use it for day-to-day backup and recovery of those same devices for a long list of reasons. I think that a backup and recovery service is a much safer method for important intellectual property of an organization.

Most disk I see in the field, though, is not individual disk drives. Most disk I see is in some type of an array. The next section covers the use of a standard disk array (without deduplication) in a typical backup system.

Standard Disk Arrays

Before we start talking about the way most people use disks in their backup systems (which is a deduplicated disk system), we need to discuss the use of a *standard* RAID array that has no special backup and recovery features. It is simply an inexpensive disk array consisting of a bunch of disk drives pretending to be one big disk, and connecting to your backup server by iSCSI, FC, NFS, or SMB.

The advantages of using such systems (over the deduplicated versions most people use) is that they are significantly less expensive to purchase than target dedupe systems; however, deduplication is so important that the use of disk without it doesn't usually make a lot of sense. The two times when it would make sense are disk staging/caching and when your backup software provides the deduplication for you. There are large commercial backup products that advertise their own deduplication software, and they can work well with any disk array such as these.

If you are using such a backup system and already have access to all these features, use of a standard disk array makes perfect sense. However, if your backup software either doesn't have these features or the ones that they have are not as good as what would be provided in a purpose-built system, you should at least compare and contrast what you can get with a purpose-built system with what you can get with a standard disk array.

Similar to, and yet quite different from, a standard block-based disk array is an object-storage system. These also use an array of disks, but the way you write to them with your backup system is very different. Let's look at them next.

Object Storage

If you haven't already read the definition of object storage in Chapter 8, be sure to take a look at "Object storage in the cloud" on page 161. The following discussion assumes that you are familiar with object storage and what it brings to the table from a data integrity standpoint.

The reality is that object storage is probably the future of long-term storage of both backups and archives because of the data protection features built into its core functionality. Although there are many uses for object storage other than backups and archives, the idea of a storage system that is self-healing and self-replicating seems like it was designed with backups and archives in mind. Since all data stored in an object-storage system can automatically be replicated to multiple locations, it conforms to the 3-2-1 rule by default. As much as I complain about other systems and how they do not conform to this rule, storage that automatically replicates everything to multiple locations sounds amazing.

In addition to providing protection against disasters that might take out one or two locations, object storage also protects against magnetic degradation, which is also something you should be concerned about with long-term storage. As mentioned in "Object storage in the cloud" on page 161, any magnetic degradation would be noticed because it would change the unique ID of an object. (See the discussion of bit rot in "Long-term retention" on page 260.) An automated system could regularly recalculate the hash for each object and compare it to its original UID, and any differences caused by bit rot would be immediately noticed and be fixed by copying one of the other replicated copies.

Object storage is also a single protocol layer that can be used with multiple types of underlying storage systems. This means that it can be layered on top of disk, tape, and optical devices, allowing the customer in question to use whichever storage device makes most sense for them without changing the overall implementation. As long as the system in question can write to object storage, it really doesn't care how the underlying system stores its objects. It cares, of course, about things like access time, but that can be addressed in the capabilities of various implementations of object storage.

Object storage is currently seen in both private and public clouds, and the most well-known object-storage implementation is Amazon's simple storage service, or S3. S3 is both a service offered by Amazon and a protocol that anyone can use to provide a compatible storage service. Azure Blob and Google Cloud Storage both support S3 as a protocol, as do a number of products that support object storage in the datacenter.

This provides customers great flexibility because they do not need to change their code simply to change their storage provider; they only need to change the destination. Backups and archives will suddenly start going to the new system as long as it is compatible with the same protocol. They can also be easily moved from one provider to the next; the system only needs to keep track of which S3 implementation has which UIDs.

Other non-S3 object-storage systems are out there. I do not have any experience with them, but this does seem another area of technology where the S3 protocol has won the popularity war. It's similar to Kubernetes and Docker. They are not the only implementations of containers and orchestration systems, but they sure are the only ones you hear anything about.

Each major public cloud vendor that offers an S3-compatible object-storage service offers a variety of versions of it at different price points and levels of functionality. Most of them make the more expensive versions deliver data quicker and have higher resiliency rates, although this is not always the case. (An object-storage implementation with a higher resiliency rate should be more reliable, even in the face of disasters, attacks, or simple mismanagement.) A perfect example would be the Google Cloud Platform, which has the same access time and reliability for all versions of object storage. The difference is in the cost of retrieval. The less expensive versions cost next to nothing for them to hold on to the data, but you pay dearly if you ever retrieve it. Amazon and Azure have similar price differentiations, but they are not as stark as what you see in the Google Cloud Platform. Make sure to take a look at all of the options available to you, from private cloud to various public cloud vendors, when considering object storage as a destination for backups or archives.

Object-storage systems present a lot of options to data protection people, and I believe they may ultimately become the dominant backup target over time. Today, however, the most popular backup target is easily target deduplication appliances, which are covered in the next section.

Target Deduplication Appliances

As of this writing, the most popular destination for backups and recoveries are target deduplication appliances. As covered in "Deduplication" on page 90, deduplication is a process by which duplicate data in a series of backups or archives is identified and eliminated, increasing the effective capacity of a disk storage system.

A target deduplication system is one that performs this function in the appliance itself. You use the same backup software that you have always used, but instead of backing up to a tape library or a standard disk array, you send your backups to the target deduplication appliance, which is usually connected to the backup server by a NFS or SMB, or it could be pretending to be a tape drive or library of tape drives (i.e., a VTL). (More on that in a few paragraphs.) NFS and SMB systems would connect over Ethernet, and a VTL would connect over Fibre Channel or iSCSI.

The appliance examines the backups; it chops them up into chunks and runs a cryptographic hashing algorithm against each chunk, resulting in what the industry calls a *hash*. The hash is an alphanumeric sequence that should be unique to that chunk. The target deduplication system looks the hash up in its hash table. If the hash is already in its hash table, it has seen the hash before, so the new chunk is discarded as a duplicate. If it has never seen the hash before, the new chunk is stored and the hash table is updated.

These target deduplication systems come in two very different forms: VTLs and NAS filers. VTLs were more popular early on, but NAS-based appliances have clearly taken the lead at this point. Let's take a look at these two types of target dedupe appliances.

Virtual Tape Libraries

VTLs are basically a server pretending to be a tape library and storing the results on disk. VTLs were actually the first mainstream, purpose-built, disk-based backup target. When VTLs first came on the scene, the problem they were trying to solve was that many backup products weren't able to back up to disk. If they could back up to disk, the functionality or performance was significantly less than when they went to tape. So various vendors combined a Linux-based operating system and SATA disk drives, and the VTL was born.

You typically connect a VTL to a backup server with Fibre Channel, but sometimes by iSCSI. As far as the backup server is concerned, it is backing up to a tape library. In fact, most VTLs emulate certain models of tape libraries, down to the number of virtual slots and virtual tape drives those tape libraries support. Some backup programs (e.g., NDMP) that only knew how to back up to tape were very happy. You could get much better performance over Fibre Channel into a block device than you could over a network connection to a NAS array.

Although VTLs offered very fast performance and much easier integration with some backup products, they did come with some downsides. The biggest issue was that since they were mimicking a serial-access device (i.e., tape), they had to continue to behave that way even though they were actually random-access disk. This meant that if you had a backup or restore using a particular virtual tape, another process could not use it at the same time. This may seem like a minor inconvenience, but to some it was not so minor. Although deduplicating VTLs are still on the market, they are much less popular than they were only a few years ago.

NAS Appliances

Over time, all popular backup products figured out how to back up to a filesystem-based target, such as what is provided by a NAS filer. NAS-based target deduplication systems that could be mounted by NFS or SMB were much easier to share then a virtual tape library.

Some backup programs actually found it easier to back up to a filesystem target than to tape. A perfect example of this would be database dumps, as discussed in "Dump and Sweep" on page 148. Dump and sweep has always been a very popular way to back up databases, but DBAs used to have to rely on the backup system to transfer the database dump to the backup system. With a NAS-based target deduplication system, the database server could mount the target deduplication system directly. This allowed DBAs to back up directly to the same device that the backup software was writing to, cutting the backup system out of the equation altogether. That this backup could be automatically replicated off-site made it even better. This change was very popular with DBAs but not so popular to those of us who are used to running all the backups.

NAS-based target deduplication systems also introduced a new security concern. The fact that backups were accessible through a directory on the backup server (e.g., C:\BACKUPS) allowed these backups to be either accidentally or maliciously deleted or corrupted, such as what a ransomware product would do.

Those of us who are very concerned about the advent of ransomware in today's datacenters are also concerned about this backup system design. Locking down the security between the backup server and the target deduplication system doesn't solve the problem, either. The real problem is that the backups are accessible as a directory on the backup server. Combine this with the fact that many backup servers today are Windows-based backup servers, which are the target of most ransomware attacks, and you begin to understand the concern. If the backup server became infected, the backups could be encrypted along with the data they are backing up, essentially defeating the very purpose of the backup system.

Most major backup software products have worked around this issue by creating custom protocols that allow the backup software to communicate with the target deduplication system without showing up as a directory on the backup server. If you are currently using such a system, you should immediately investigate the options that your backup software product has to make the backup directory invisible. If your backup product has no such options, you really might want to look at other products.

As mentioned earlier in this section when I talked about DBAs using these devices for their own backups, one very interesting advantage of using a target deduplication system is that they can replicate backups. This is possible because they reduce every backup (including full backups) to the new-unique bits that backup contains. The first backup will be quite large, of course, and take time to replicate, but subsequent backups can be quite small, even if they are full backups. New bits stored in the dedupe system can be replicated to another target deduplication system so that your backups are stored off-site. This allows you to conform to the 3-2-1 rule without ever touching a tape! Some products also support replicating such backups to the cloud, which would accomplish the same thing.

Target deduplication disk arrays provided a valuable means of transitioning the world of backup from tape to disk. As backup technology has evolved, however, other targets have started becoming more popular. I've already covered on-premises object storage, and I think that will get more popular over time. But I think the real contender to the throne is our next target: public cloud storage. Backup is the killer app for the cloud, so I believe it will not be long before the majority of backups are stored there. Let's take a look at public cloud storage for data protection.

Public Cloud Storage

The public cloud offers two main types of storage that can be used to store backups: block storage (usually presented as a filesystem) and object storage. Which target is more popular depends on how the customer's backup product is using the cloud.

Cloud out

If a customer is running a backup product in the datacenter that is copying some or all of its backups to the cloud, it is almost always copying those backups to S3-compatible object storage. Many products using this model see the cloud as a replacement for the customer's off-site storage company (e.g., Iron Mountain). Object storage in the cloud is an inexpensive place where customers can easily copy backups so that they are stored off-site. Although this is not always the case, they usually do not see object storage as the first place they would want to store backups.

On-premises backup software in cloud VMs

Another way that many organizations are using the cloud for backup is to run the same backup software from their datacenter in a VM in the cloud. When that backup software was running in the datacenter, it expected a filesystem target, so that is what it will probably look for in the cloud. This means that it will probably want at least its most recent backups to be on a filesystem target, which will require a block device underneath.

Cloud native storage

Some backup products have designed (or redesigned) their products to support cloud storage properly. These products see object storage as providing all the features they need in a backup destination, including performance.

Now that you are aware of all the types of storage devices you might use with your backup system, it's time to pick one! Surprise! The one that's right for you might be the one you already have. Let's take a look at the kind of logic I use when picking a storage device.

Choosing and Using a Backup Target

It's time to talk about picking the right backup target for you, as well as making the most out of what you have. Or perhaps you might pick more than one product. There is no perfect backup device that works for everyone, so let's talk about how to make this decision for you.

First we'll talk about making sure you actually need a new backup target by making sure you are getting the most out of the one you have. Then we'll talk about the things you need to think about when picking a new backup target.

Optimize the Performance of What You Have

I made a career out of helping people performance-tune their backup systems. Often, the discussion would start out with a conversation about replacing a backup system, and it would often morph into simply redesigning what they already had. My experience has been that misconfiguration is the most common cause of backup failure. This is especially true when it comes to tape.

Performance-tuning tape

Tuning the performance of a tape drive is quite a difficult thing to do, but it starts with a basic understanding of how tape works. You need to talk to your tape vendor to find out your tape drive's minimal transfer speed.

As I mentioned, the problem with tape in most backup systems is that the backups run too slow for the tape, and you need to design the system in such a way that the backup speed and tape speed are as close as possible to each other. This starts with knowing how low the bar is, as in: Just how slow can this tape drive go and reliably write data? I am referring to this as the minimal transfer speed, and every model from every manufacturer has a different answer to that question.

Most modern tape drives do have some speed-matching capabilities. For example, whereas an LTO-8 tape drive does have a maximum speed of 750 MB per second, it can also go slower than that. Each manufacturer is different, though, so you need to find out from your manufacturer the slowest speed your tape drive can match. That speed should then be your throughput target for how fast you should try to make the incoming backups. Yes, I would love it if you could get closer to the *maximum* speed of the tape drive, but we need to walk before we can run.

The first thing to look at when performance-tuning the tape drive is the incoming bandwidth of the backup server. Read the next sidebar, "Two Tons of Fertilizer in a One-Ton Truck". If you have a tape drive whose minimum transfer speed is 500 MB/s, but the incoming bandwidth to that backup server is only 100 MB/s, you have a problem. You can't generate a 500 MB/s stream of data through a 100 MB/s pipe. I'd recommend 10 GB Ethernet as a minimum input speed to most backup servers at this point. Even that will probably only keep one LTO-8 tape drive happy.

Two Tons of Fertilizer in a One-Ton Truck

I remember countless times in my career when I had clients who didn't seem to understand basic math or physics, so it's hard to narrow them down to one or two stories. But one particularly egregious one does come to mind.

A customer had ten LTO-2 tape drives behind a single media server. Each of those tape drives is capable of 80 MB/s. I believe the minimum transfer rate was around 25 MB/s. That's 250 MB/s when you have 10 tape drives. They had all these tape drives behind one server with a *100 MB network connection*! (That would be about 12 MB/s). The network connection was not capable of supplying enough bandwidth for one tape drive, let alone 10 of them.

When you divide 12 MB/s among 10 tape drives, each of which wants at least 25 MB/s, you get a lot of shoeshining. The throughput of the entire system was about 5 MB/s, which really illustrates my point; 12 divided by 10 is 1.2. If you give 1.2 MB/s to a drive that wants 25, it will spend most of its time shoeshining and not writing data, resulting in an effective throughput of each drive that became .6 MB/s for a drive that can go 80 MB/s! Multiply that times 10 and you get 5 MB/s of throughput for the entire system. I told them to upgrade their network connection, and immediately shut off nine of the 10 tape drives. The aggregate throughput of the system doubled immediately. I made the system twice as fast by using 1/10th of the resources. It's amazing what happens when you understand how tape drives work.

My personal opinion is that the easiest way to performance-tune tape in a backup system is not to back up directly to that tape with typical backups. The easiest thing to do is put a disk cache in front of your tape system that holds at least one night's worth of backups that are then immediately transferred to tape. A better design would be to put a deduplicated disk array in front of your tape system. Your deduplicated disk would hold all your on-premises backups, and you would use tape only for an off-site copy.

If you cannot afford to put *any* disk in your backup system, you need to do your best to make sure that incoming backup streams are at least as fast as the tape's minimum speed. The only way to do this with incremental backups—and even with some full backups—is to use your backup system's multiplexing setting to multiplex enough backups together to generate a stream fast enough to keep the tape drive happy.

If you need to use multiplexing to make your tape drive happy, I would definitely shoot only for the tape's minimum speed, because the higher the multiplexing setting, the greater the impact it will have on restore speed. We do want the backups to work, but we also want our restores to work as well.

Performance-tuning RAID

It is a lot easier to performance-tune a RAID array than it is to performance-tune a tape drive. The main thing to think about here is the impact of different RAID levels on the incoming write performance. Realize that all parity-based RAID has a write penalty that will have an impact on this performance.

If you are only using it as a disk cache prior to tape, you might consider a simple striping configuration with no parity. This is a personal call on your part, but it will significantly increase the performance of the disk by getting rid of any write penalty from parity. Yes, it means you will not be able to survive the loss of even one disk drive. If that happened in the middle of backups, or in the middle of copying those backups to tape, you could lose some backups. If this incident happened at the same time as one of your backup clients losing data that needed to be restored, you could lose data for good. I will leave it up to you about whether this is a good idea; I'm just throwing it out as a suggestion for the severely budget-minded environments.

Performance-tuning target dedupe array

There is very little advice I can give you on how to performance-tune a deduplication disk array, because so much of what you would do would be based on the actual deduplication implementation of that vendor. Having said that, a few things come to mind.

Do not perform full backups just to get a better deduplication ratio. I have seen deduplication vendor system engineers tell their customers to do a full backup every day because it increases their deduplication ratio. I discussed in Chapter 5 why that is nonsense. But it's also important to understand that it affects your deduplication system from a performance standpoint. If you are performing a full backup more frequently than your backup system needs you to, you are spending a significant amount of time deduplicating a lot of data, most of which is redundant. The computing capacity, RAM, and I/O you are wasting could all be used for better things like replicating your backups to another location, copying them to tape for an off-site copy, or running the garbage collection process to make room for new backups.

Investigate various ways to get data to your target deduplication array. Perhaps NFS is faster than SMB, or vice versa. Perhaps the vendor offers an iSCSI connection that would be even faster. Some vendors also offer proprietary connection mechanisms that are more secure and potentially faster. Run exactly the same backup with all these mechanisms to see which one is actually faster. You might be surprised.

Select a More Appropriate Device

If you've already done your best to make your backup target perform better and have been unable to do so, it's time to pick a different target. Let's take a look at the logic you should use when doing so.

Pick your backup software or service first

If you've already picked your backup software or service, talk to them about what they think is the best performing target for backups for their product. They may support multiple systems, and any good SE will know which systems perform better with their software or service. Get a recommendation from them and test it out.

If you are considering purchasing a new backup system, make sure you make that decision prior to making the decision on a new backup target. It would be a shame, for example, if you bought the greatest target deduplication disk array ever to exist, only to be told by your new backup software vendor that you no longer need it, and you would have been better off simply buying a basic RAID array. Worse yet, what if you buy the latest and greatest tape drive, and the backup software you end up selecting doesn't support tape at all? This is why you should make sure you have selected your backup software or service prior to purchasing new target hardware.

Pick what works for you

It's really easy for me, sitting here in my ivory tower, to say everybody should use this type of product and definitely not use that type of product. I'm not you, and I do not have either your knowledge of your environment or the budget constraints that you deal with. I don't know the history that you may have had with particular types of products that might dissuade you from those products. Those are all perfectly valid reasons for picking something different than what I might pick for you.

This is why whenever I work with a client to help them pick a new system, I always find out these kinds of things first. If they're a company that simply hates the cloud, I'm clearly not going to recommend a cloud-based system. (I might try to find out exactly why they hate the cloud and see whether their reasons are misinformation. I might give it a shot, but if in the end they hate a given type of system, there is no point in me recommending it.) You need to pick what works for you and within your budget.

On-premises disk

Prior to the advent of cloud-based backup services, a backup system based entirely on disk running in your environment was the most popular configuration. This configuration works with either a source-based or target-based deduplication system and is based on the idea that your backups are all deduplicated and can easily be replicated to another location. This design is one of the simplest, in that it is easier to performance-tune and much easier to move backups off-site. Unlike any systems involving tape in any way, you do not need to use a human being to send your backups to another location. You can simply set up replications, and you have an on-premises backup and an off-premises copy, no humans required.

As I will discuss in Chapter 13, sizing such a system will be your biggest challenge. Such systems are purchased in large capital purchases, so you will need to take a significant amount of growth into account. You will also need to take into account the performance required for doing backups and restores at the same time on the same device, because that might occasionally be required. Finally, you will need to size it for your biggest backup night, even though that capacity will go wasted most of the time.

Another important thing to consider is that not all disk systems have the same performance, and you will need to test the performance of any system you buy before you buy it. Just as an example, I can think of one target deduplication system whose speed during reads was 10 times slower than its speed during writes. You really need to test these things in your environment with *your* data before making a final decision and purchase.

Remember to test common things that will happen in production, such as the loss of a disk and subsequent performance penalties before the disk is replaced. Look into the performance penalty that happens during *garbage collection*, which is the industry term for the process of deleting old backups. This process is much more complicated in deduplication systems and can have such an impact that you are often told not to do it during backups. Test also the performance of doing backups and restores at the same time. There will likely be a performance impact; just be aware of what it is. It's also possible that different vendors will respond better than others in the scenario.

If you are shopping for a target deduplication system, you also need to back up the same data to multiple systems and see what kind of deduplication ratio you get. Remember, you can only compare the deduplication ratio between different systems if you send them the same data. Make sure to send them production data; anything else is simply a waste of time. (One really good way to do that would be to connect it to your backup system and copy the same set of backups into each appliance.)

One other thing to think about when shopping for a target deduplication system is whether you plan to do instant recovery, as discussed in Chapter 9. If you plan to run production systems—even in a disaster—directly from your backups, you need to test the performance of your deduplication system in that configuration. There is perhaps no area where the performance difference between different vendors is greater. Remember to test not just one or two VMs running directly from your backups, but as many as you plan to run in a disaster situation. (Some systems will perform fine with one or two VMs, but the rubber meets the road at many VMs.)

Cloud disk

If you are running your backup system in the cloud, then your only choice is to use disk in the cloud. Having said that, there are two very different types of disk in the cloud: block and object. Different backup vendors use these different backup targets differently. This is especially true when it comes to object. It is incredibly simple for a backup system to support object storage; it's an entirely different matter to support it well and with high performance.

Block storage would include products like Amazon's Elastic Block Store, Azure Disk Storage, and Google Zonal Persistent Disk. Object storage products include Amazon S3, Azure Blob, and Google Cloud Storage. Most comments apply to these products. Block storage is typically at least twice the cost of object storage in the cloud, but don't just pick object storage because it's cheaper, because there can be serious ramifications.

Object storage is self-healing and automatically replicates itself to multiple locations, typically three. Block storage, on the other hand, is essentially a virtual disk sitting on a single RAID array in a single datacenter. A failure of any part of that storage system (e.g., compute, network, or storage) would result in a loss of data. This requires you to do something to replicate that backup to another location, which then doubles the cost if you are replicating it to block storage. (There are some block storage products in the cloud that replicate, but they are even more expensive.)

With object storage, three copies are built into the price. One cost concern with public cloud object storage, though, is request pricing. Block storage in the cloud comes with all the I/O you want. With object storage, you pay for each I/O operation, referred to as GETs and PUTs. This is often referred to as *request pricing*. Depending on how your backup system uses object storage, request pricing can add quite a bit to your bill.

One advantage of block storage at this point is that the way most backup software reads and writes data is more conducive to filesystem and block storage than it is to object storage. Backup software products tend to write very large files; each backup stream from each backed-up system represents a file in the filesystem. It might split that file into slightly smaller files, but this actually doesn't solve the real problem. The real problem is restores. It still reads that large file (or several slightly smaller files) as one big file during a restore, just as if it had written that file to a tape drive. This single-threaded restore process, which is quite common in backup software products, needs all the performance it can get, which means that you would want that file to be on file/block storage, not on object storage.

Object storage is built for a lot of things. Competing with a typical block device when reading a single large file is not one of them. Object storage does just fine performance-wise when you read and write many smaller files simultaneously, but that is not how most backup products write backups to disk. This is why, even if a backup product is running in a backup server in a VM in the cloud, it still might prefer to write to a filesystem target, at least for the current backup set. Most backup products that need the current backup set to be on a block device can easily migrate all the backups out to object storage and make room for new backups.

If, however, a backup product rewrites its disk backup mechanism to optimize its writes for object storage, the performance of both backups and restores can actually be increased. Instead of requesting a single file and reading it in a serial fashion just as if it were on a tape, an object storage–savvy product can simultaneously request thousands of individual pieces of files and get a restore speed much faster than you could get with any block device.

Therefore, the appropriate cloud backup target for you will be based on which backup product you are using and how it uses object storage. If the company has rewritten its code for object storage, then choose that. Object storage is more resilient and way less expensive than block storage. However, if your backup product recommends that its primary backups go on block, hopefully you now understand why. Follow the recommendation; otherwise, your restore speeds will probably not be to your liking.

All tape

Given the advancements in backup in the past 20 years, I would only recommend an all-tape backup configuration in the most budget-conscious environment. Even then, smaller environments can actually buy a small disk array for less than they can buy a decent tape automation system. If you have passed that point where a tape automation system costs less than any type of disk system, and you are extremely budget conscious, a tape system might make sense.

If the reason you are buying tape is budget, you're probably going to end up with LTO. There are other choices, but they are much more expensive. One good thing about LTO is that it is always read-compatible to two previous generations and write-compatible to the previous generation. This means that an LTO-8 tape drive can read a tape written in LTO-6 drive, and it can write a tape that can be read in LTO-7 drive. This is one thing to keep in mind when deciding on a new tape model.

All LTO tape drives of the same generation are compatible with each other, regardless of which vendor you select, so that shouldn't drive your choice. What I think you should focus on is how easy it would be to upgrade the tape system that you purchase. Do not make the mistake of buying a non-upgradable tape library that is already at full capacity. There are a number of modular designs on the market that allow you to start small and grow quite large. Spend a little bit more to get a tape library that can easily be upgraded by adding additional slots or drives. This will allow you to get the best bang for your buck in an all-tape environment.

Then please make sure you design your backup system so that you give your tapes enough bandwidth to be happy. Make sure to read "Performance-tuning tape" on page 275.

Hybrid

The most common backup configuration at this point is a hybrid of two or more of the preceding approaches. You might have a target deduplication system for some of your backups and tape for other backups. You might be using a cloud-based backup service to back up your remote sites, laptops, and mobile devices, while sticking with a more traditional backup software for your on-premises infrastructure. That means that you will have different backup media for each of them.

I wouldn't recommend designing a system from scratch this way; I'm simply acknowledging that this happens and that it's not the end of the world to have multiple backup types. The most common hybrid backup target configuration is to have some disk and some tape. You might use disk for your on-premises backups and tape for your off-site copy. It's far from ideal in most scenarios, because, as I discussed in Chapter 11, I simply don't think tape is up to the task when it comes to disaster recovery. But I also understand that you might not be able to get the budget for what you actually need.

Takeaways

The most important takeaway from this chapter is that your tape drives are not slow or unreliable. Your tape drives are actually *too fast*, and you need to design your backup system to take that into account. If you do so, you will find they get much more reliable as well. This means that the answer to performance problems in your tape system is almost never to buy more tape drives or to buy faster versions of the tape drives you already have. If you learn nothing else from this book, it should be that. If you still have tape in your backup system, learn your tape's minimum throughput number and design your backup system so that each drive gets that number. Trust me, your tape drives, your backups, and your tape vendor will thank you. Things will work much better.

Another important thing to understand is that all target deduplication systems are not the same. They slice the data up differently, they deduplicate differently, and they write that deduplicated data differently. These differences can have significant performance and cost differences. Learn the advantages and disadvantages of the different approaches (especially inline versus post-process) and think about how those affect the performance of your backups and, more important, the performance of your restores.

Now that I've covered all of the various types of backup hardware, it's time to talk about backup software. Before looking at the various choices available to you, it's important to understand the historical and current challenges that each backup system is trying to address. That's why the next chapter describes these challenges.

CHAPTER 13

Commercial Data Protection Challenges

Before describing the different kinds of data protection solutions in the next two chapters, I want to give you a brief history lesson and explain what life was like before we had commercial backup products. You young whippersnappers don't know how good you have it.

I'll follow this history lesson with a comprehensive overview of all the challenges found in today's backup and recovery systems. Think of this big list as the problem statement in a typical technology presentation. This list of everything wrong in backup and recovery will be followed with two chapters of all the different kinds of commercial backup and recovery systems you can buy to solve one or more of these problems. Each solution category will include advantages and challenges of that particular architecture, followed by my analysis of the current state of that particular category of the backup and recovery industry.

A Brief History of Backup

To understand how important commercial backup software is in the world of data protection, you have to look at how backups were before they came along. Commercial backup software products for Unix and Netware started to appear in the mid-1980s, but it was not the prominent industry we have today. It was not an assumption that a large commercial Unix environment would be running a commercial backup product or any kind of tape automation system.

I know this because I lived in that world. In 1993, I worked at a $35B bank that had several hundred Unix servers, and all the backups were driven by a few shell scripts and cron jobs. I was backing up AT&T System V, DEC Ultrix, HP-UX, Solaris, and AIX systems to local tape drives that were included as part of the server. (As hard as it is for modern folks to understand, every server came with an internal tape drive.) My

AT&T 3B2s, the first servers built to run Unix, had QIC-80 tape drives that held 80 MB and were *not* quick. My DECs had TK-70s, and my HP-UX servers all came with DDS drives. (For the old timers in the crowd, my first external tape drive was a nine-track tape drive, but those were connected to the mainframe.)

We ran commands like `dump`, `tar`, and `cpio` to back up to these tape drives. The next morning, we would collect dozens of backup tapes and then copy them so we could send them off-site. I actually had these really cool standalone devices with two tape drives (akin to a dual-cassette tape deck for those who remember those) that would create a byte-for-byte copy from one tape to another, but they did it one tape at a time —a very manual process. There was no centralized configuration, scheduling, monitoring, and reporting about whether the backups or copies worked; we had to log in to each server to figure that out.

I was using a shell script to do all this, which had one core flaw: It assumed a server could fit on a backup tape. That was a perfectly valid assumption for my first two years at the bank. Then we started buying HP servers with (wait for it) 4 to 5 GB of storage and a single 2 GB DDS drive to back it up to. I started hacking at the script and figured out how to handle that for a while, but the servers kept getting bigger and the tape drives were the same size.

I have a very vivid memory of the day I went to my boss, in frustration and terror. I had to admit defeat and say that my scripting skills weren't good enough to deal with this problem. She said, "Aren't there commercial backup products?" I remember thinking, "Wait, I can spend money?" I did a lot of pre-Google research and discovered products like ARCServe, Alexandria, BudTool, and SM-Arch, out of which only ARCServe is still around today.

I wanted a backup tool that could just take the place of my script. I was going to continue using my local tape drives but have this software make the backup happen. Back then, ARCServe only supported backing up to a centralized server, so that was out. Alexandria looked way too complicated. (I remember one review saying it had won the award for the most GUI real estate. There were dozens of dialog boxes and options, and it just seemed too much.) BudTool looked interesting, but it considered each server with a tape drive a media server. So since we wanted to use our local tape drives, it was going to cost us $125,000 in 1995 dollars to buy this software. Then I found Minnetonka-based Software Mogul's SM-Arch, and it didn't care how many tape drives I had. I remember it was $16,000.

Suddenly my world got a lot better. But even then, all that tape swapping was quite problematic. And there was still the issue of servers being bigger than a tape. But the server that broke everything was the HP T-500 with 100 GB of storage! I remember going back to my boss and saying, "How exactly am I supposed to back up a 100 GB server with a 4 GB tape drive? Will you pay someone to swap tapes all night?" And that's the day we started looking for tape libraries. Our first tape libraries were

Spectralogic carousel units that came with 20, 40, or 60 slots, and one to four DDS tape drives. One really cool thing about these units was that you could buy a 20-slot unit and upgrade it yourself to a 40- or 60-slot unit. All you had to do was take the top off, turn a few screws, pop out the 20-slot carousel, put the new carousel in, and tighten the screws. The units specialized in what were called field-replaceable units (FRUs). This meant it was designed to have cheap people (like us) do their own upgrades and maintenance. I remember we had 16 of these units, so we had over 60 tape drives in production. I always kept a spare tape drive and power supply on hand, and the systems were designed to allow me to replace all those myself and then do a reverse swap to get the next one. I took a look at the current Spectra Logic offerings, and it has continued the FRU concept to this day.

These tape libraries changed my world again. Instead of having to run around to multiple locations to pick up individual tapes, you can create a centralized tape library (i.e., a room with tapes in it) that contains several tape libraries (i.e., tape automation systems). You can also have the backup system automatically create the tape copies, using the robotics of the tape library system. In some tape libraries, last night's backup tapes can even be collocated in a special drawer ready to be ejected in the morning.

Stories like this one were happening all over the world. The more complicated the distributed computing world got, the more important commercial backup software became to the average user. In the rest of this chapter, I'll continue the history lesson, but in a slightly different way. I'll look at how the computing environment changed over the years and how each advancement broke backup (again). I'll also explain other data protection challenges that continue to this day.

Challenges with Commercial Backup Solutions

Commercial backup software products did revolutionize data protection in many ways over the past 30 years. These products also come with a number of challenges that are important to understand when considering the different categories of data protection solutions discussed in the next chapter. It will help you judge the relative value each category has for your environment. All the product categories discussed in the next two chapters have addressed one or more of these challenges, sometimes by augmenting a current product and sometimes by replacing it altogether. Let's take a look at these challenges.

It's important to understand that this section is not intended as a replacement for a proper backup system design. This is merely an attempt to give you an overview of the kinds of discussions you should be having when designing a backup system, and to illustrate just how complex this process can be.

Size the Backup System

The first challenge of a typical backup system is that before you can purchase a backup solution, you must properly size it. Without some kind of system design, you will have no idea how much hardware, software, and tape or disk you will need to purchase.

The following discussion will center on building a typical on-premises backup system that will include a certain amount of software and hardware. A similar process would be necessary when designing such a system in the cloud, but this particular example will use an on-premises system for simplicity.

A typical backup sizing project starts with a few values: size of one full backup, daily change rate, RTO, RPO, on-site and off-site retention, and backup window. You will also need to decide what type of growth your data is expecting in the next three to five years. These values will determine how many backup servers you need, how many target devices (disk or tape), and what kind of bandwidth you will need.

The problem is that many organizations do not know the answer to one of the most crucial questions in this design when starting the process: the size of one full backup. I can't tell you the number of times I have asked this question of clients and had them respond with things like how much they backup in a week or a night (not the same at all). You must determine this number, which is not too hard to get out of most backup systems, assuming you only have one backup system to look at. The question is simple: If you were to perform one full backup of your entire datacenter, how big would that be?

You will also need to find out from the potential backup solution how often—if ever —full backups need to happen after the first one has been completed. Even if the additional full backups are synthetic ones, they must still be taken into the design of the system. (I cover the concept of synthetic backups in Chapter 4.)

The next thing to know is the daily change rate. (Sadly, many customers do not know this number either, so don't be surprised if you have to go digging.) The best value to use here is the size of a typical incremental backup in your current backup system. You will then need to know whether your current backup system is a full-file incremental product (i.e., backs up the entire file if any part of it has changed), or a block-level incremental product. You will then need to know which type of incremental backup system you are designing for. If you have to convert from one type to the other, this will be nothing more than a guess. But if the type of system you are designing for uses the same type of incremental backups as your current setup, then you have the value you need. In this example, we will be using a full-file incremental product on both sides.

Hopefully, your RTO and RPO values have been agreed to prior to designing the backup system, because it is impossible to design a backup system properly without knowing how quickly it needs to restore (RTO) and how much data you are allowed to lose (RPO). Sadly, however, this is another area where I have often been forced to design blindly based on assumptions that the design team agrees on. Please try not to do that. I cover RTO and RPO in detail in Chapter 4.

Retention is another value that should not be determined by those designing the backup system. Retention should be driven by organizational requirements, such as when your restores are typically performed from (e.g., within the previous 30 days), whether you have any regulatory requirements obligating you to preserve certain datasets for longer periods of time, and the degree to which you need to make sure certain datasets are definitely deleted within a certain period.

The only one of these values that the backup system admin should be able to help with is when restores typically happen, and this will almost always be within the previous few days, with a few exceptions that might go out a few months. But it is the regulatory and legal requirements that will usually determine whether backups need to be stored long term. Depending on the length of that term, you should be looking at archives, not backups, to meet that requirement. For more information on that topic, please read the section "What Is an Archive?" on page 47 and all of Chapter 10, for more information on that important topic.

It's also important to agree on when backups are allowed to run, also known as the backup window. This is an absolute requirement when designing a system that uses full-file incremental and full backups, because they will put a significant load on production systems while backups are running, especially during full backups. Products using a block-level incremental or a source-side deduplication approach tend to have a much lower impact on production systems during backup. With these systems, most environments will agree to a backup window of 24 hours per day.

With backup systems that create a large impact on their clients, the backup windows often have values such as from midnight to 6 a.m., or 6 p.m. to 6 a.m., with possibly more lenient hours during the weekend. It is common to allow backup systems to back up any time of the day between Friday evening and Monday morning. (Of course, this will depend entirely on how your organization does business and whether the weekend is less busy.)

As to what kind of growth your system can expect, this will simply be a scientific wild-ass guess (SWAG) that is typically something like 50% to 100% of data growth per year. This will be based on a number of factors that are based on your organization's plans for the upcoming years and how those plans are likely to include growth in the storage arena.

Once you have all these numbers, you can calculate the throughput and storage capacity requirements of your backup system.

Consider the numbers in Table 13-1, which describe an organization with a datacenter whose full backup would be 500 TB. Its full-file incremental backup daily change rate is 10%, or 50 TB. The organization has agreed to an RPO of 24 hours, which means it needs to get a successful backup every day. It has also agreed to a backup window that allows 10 hours a day during which it is allowed to back up.

The backup system requires periodic full backups, which the organization has decided to do once per month. My personal preference would be to spread those 500 TB out evenly across the month, which is 17.86 TB per day of full backups, assuming no single server is more than 17.86 TB.

To that 17.86 TB of daily full backups, the organization will add the 50 TB of daily incremental backups for a total of 67.86 TB of backup data per day. Your backup window is 10 hours, so that means you need a backup system capable of backing up just shy of 7 TB per hour on day one—no small feat. That requires a throughput of 1.88 GB per second.

Table 13-1. Calculating backup and restore speeds

TBs in DC	Change rate	Incremental/day (TBs)
500	10.00%	50
TB of fulls	**Month days**	**Fulls/day (TBs)**
500	28	17.86
TB each day	**Window hours**	**GB/second**
67.86	10	1.88
TBs to restore	**MB/s**	**Restore time**
10	750	3.70
10	37.5	74.07

If you are backing up to tape, you could do that with three LTO-8 tape drives, assuming you could stream them at their optimum rate of 750 MB/s. That, of course, is a ridiculous assumption, as you will see in "Performance-tuning tape" on page 275. A typical disk system would probably be able to handle that throughput.

This would, of course, require multiplexing all of your backups into three backup streams, which is far from an optimum setup. The multiplexing settings on your favorite backup might not even go that high. If they did, you would likely suffer severe restore performance issues.

Assuming you could address those issues, you will then need to take a look at your RTO value and determine whether you would be able to satisfy that RTO with the backup system as designed. When designing a pure backup system just for operational recoveries, and not a full-scale disaster recovery system, you need to make sure the system is at least capable of restoring the biggest system that you have within the RTO you've agreed to.

Continuing with the previous example, suppose the 500 TB datacenter has a single server that is 10 TB, and your agreed-upon RTO is four hours. That means your system should be able to restore at roughly 2.5 TB per hour, which is theoretically possible, given the tape drives we bought. However, the multiplexing settings you likely used to get there will probably create restore-speed problems.

Let's assume you bought the previously mentioned 3 LTO-8 tape drives and drove them at their maximum speed during backups. Restores tend to be, but are not always, single-threaded and will read from only one tape at a time, which means you get only one LTO-8 tape drive with its 750 MB/s of throughput. If you ran that LTO-8 tape drive at its maximum speed during the restore of 10 TBs, your restore would take around 3.7 hours, which is just within your RTO.

However, what would happen if you used a multiplexing setting of 20 to make sure that tape drives streamed during backups? Unless you used a backup software product that uses the mitigation approach (i.e., large chunk sizes) mentioned in "Multiplexing" on page 191, you'll get roughly 1/20th of the speed of the drive during a restore. It will read 750 MB/s of data and throw away 19 out of every 20 blocks. As you can see in the last row of Table 13-1, that would create an effective throughput for a single restore of 37.5 MB/s, which would make your actual restore time 74 hours. That is obviously nowhere near your RTO of four hours, so you'd need to rethink that. This is the core reason people have typically moved off tape as the initial target for backups.

This is why the restore capabilities of your system can drive the design more than the backup capabilities. It's much easier to back up 7 TB per hour from the entire datacenter than it is to restore 2.5 TB an hour from one backup system to one backup client. (Make sure to review "Multiplexing" on page 191 for the discussion of at least one vendor that has figured out how to address this concern.)

You will then need to work with an SME of the backup product in question to size the throughput of the system. To accomplish the throughput discussed in this example, you will likely need many media servers, each of which will have one or more disk or tape devices behind it. As mentioned in "Tape Drives" on page 257, you would most likely not design a system today that uses tape as the initial target for backups, but this section is meant to cover the challenges with many different backup systems. Suffice it to say that this would be the most complicated part of the design, and I will not be covering it in any more detail due to space limitations.

Each media server will have a maximum throughput that it can provide, and each disk or tape system will have a maximum throughput, and you may need to use a combination of both to achieve your design goals. You need to make sure you fully utilize each piece of the system's maximum capabilities to avoid wasting resources.

Once you determine how fast the system needs to be, you will need to determine how much capacity it needs to store, which starts with an agreed-upon retention period. For the purposes of this example, we will say that the retention period is 13 months for the full backups and 90 days for the incremental backups. In Table 13-2, you can see that 13 full backups of 500 TB means 6.5 PB of full backups. Ninety days of 50 TB daily incremental backups means 4.5 PB of incremental backups, for a total system capacity requirement of 11 PB. (If you are planning to use deduplication, this would be 11 TB of *effective* capacity; how much actual disk you need will vary, depending on how much dedupe you get.)

Table 13-2. Calculating backup system capacity

	TBs	Copies	PBs of capacity
Fulls	500	13	6.5
Incrementals	50	90	4.5
Total			11

All these numbers are what you need to calculate for the backup system capabilities (throughput and storage capacity) on *day one*. You also need to factor in a certain degree of growth that your organization asks you to estimate. Current growth estimates typically are close to 100% per year, which is 700% compounded over three years (100 + 100 + 200 + 400 = 700). Therefore, every one of the foregoing design numbers would need to be multiplied times seven if you are designing a system that would last for three years with 100% growth per year.

Maintain Backup Server OS

Once you have designed and implemented your backup system, you will most likely have a series of servers or virtual servers that are at its core. Those servers have operating systems that must be maintained, upgraded, and protected. Backup servers are the front door to an incredibly desirable asset: your backup data. Besides the obvious importance of this data to your organization, bad actors of all sorts would love to get access to this data and will see your backup servers as a great way to do that. If they can gain privileged access to an operating system account that then gives them privileged access to your backup software or hardware, they could do a lot of damage. (See the sidebar "This Is Why You Encrypt Backups" on page 51.)

This is why the operating system of your backup server must be the most up to date and secure server in your datacenter. Unfortunately, because backup systems are so often ignored in many other ways, this is yet another area where they do not receive the attention they deserve. But make no mistake: If you have one or more backup servers in your environment, you must properly maintain their operating system, all the appropriate patches, and all the usual security practices that go along with that.

Maintain Backup Software

Backup vendors are constantly adding functionality to their backup software. Perhaps they are supporting the backup of a new version of a particular operating system or application. Perhaps they are making it easier to copy backups from A to B. There are myriad areas of functionality that your backup software vendor may want to enhance when it comes out with a major release or even a minor feature update.

Your job, as the system administrator in charge of the backup system, is to do your best to keep up with these updates. Some of them are, of course, security updates, and those should be applied immediately. Other updates can be applied more strategically and therefore can be done when you have time for downtime.

In addition to upgrading the backup software on your backup server, you also have to upgrade the backup agents everywhere you installed them. Some backup systems can automate this; others leave it up to you to do manually.

There is nothing more terrifying than upgrading your backup system. The whole purpose of your backup system is to be there if everything else goes wrong. So what do you do when an upgrade to your backup system goes awry? This is far more complicated than an upgrade that simply doesn't work. What happens if you upgrade for a very important reason, but what if the new version that you upgrade to comes with a number of unintended features? If you want to hear just how bad that can get, read the following sidebar, "Working as Designed".

Working as Designed

When I think about upgrading a backup server, I think about the time I upgraded a very large customer's backup system to the latest major release of the leading backup software vendor at the time. We needed this new version for various reasons, so we upgraded to it in the fall of 1999. We then discovered dozens of unintended impacts the new version had on the backup system's ability to do its job.

Here's an example of what I mean. For various reasons, the customer didn't want to use the official Oracle agent and back up via RMAN. So I gave them my shell script that put Oracle into backup mode, and we were going to use the backup system's ability to run that script prior to the backup and another one to run it again at the end of the backup.

We were also using this backup software's feature to create a separate simultaneous backup job for each filesystem, to increase the performance of the backup. The problem was that each of these separate jobs would run my shell script and put Oracle into backup mode. Then the first job to finish would take Oracle out of backup mode. We contacted the vendor, and the response was, "working as designed."

I managed to write some very fancy shell scripts that figured out which job was first and which job was last and to run the scripts only on those jobs. It took me weeks of coding and lots of unsuccessful attempts before I finally got it right. I remember that by the time I was done with that particular customer, I had written 175 custom shell scripts to work around various "features" just like that one.

This experience was why in the fall of 1999, as we were all feverishly getting ready for Y2K, I was working 95 hours a week at this client. This client was 45 minutes from my house, and I was getting so little sleep that my employer got me a corporate apartment that was five minutes away so that I could get another hour of sleep per night and be closer to the client if my beeper went off.

One of my tech reviewers said this story underscores the importance of testing new versions of backup software. I couldn't agree more. I just remember we didn't have time for that. Y2K was coming, man!

Like I said: There is nothing more terrifying than upgrading your backup server software.

Manage Multiple Vendors

Prior to the advent of backup appliances and hyper-converged backup systems that I will talk about in Chapter 15, the typical backup system included at least four vendors: the backup server, the backup software, the tape or disk vendor, and the vaulting vendor. Four vendors might not sound like a lot, but it usually gets worse than that. It is extremely common for datacenters to have two to three backup products, each of which has different requirements for servers and storage.

You might think that in today's world, everybody has moved to disk-based backup, so they wouldn't have to deal with both disk and tape. It is true that all new backup systems are indeed sending their backups initially to disk. But because the cost of a replicated copy is so expensive, many people are still using legacy tape libraries, which is common in organizations that have long retention periods. This means that many environments are actually managing five to six vendors. One reason this often happens is due to mergers and acquisitions. The backup systems are low in the priority list for centralization and standardization.

The biggest problem with a multivendor environment is what happens when there is some sort of incompatibility between various systems. Nothing is worse than being in a situation in which your backup system isn't performing optimally, and each component in the system is trying to blame the other component in the system for the failure.

Separate System for DR

Most backup systems are rarely able to satisfy the RTOs their organizations have agreed to for recovering the entire datacenter. These RTOs are typically measured in a few hours, and the typical backup system simply isn't capable of satisfying an RTO that short.

What normally happens in this situation is that your organization purchases a second system to handle DR for mission-critical systems. This usually uses array-based replication from one expensive array to another very expensive array. This is a very effective way to accomplish DR, especially if you have the ability to go backward in time, such as what I discussed in "Continuous Data Protection (CDP)" on page 198 and "Near-Continuous Data Protection (Near-CDP)" on page 202. It's also a very expensive way to accomplish DR, especially when you consider that you already have a backup and recovery system.

I can hear you saying now, "You just said that the backup system wasn't capable of meeting the DR requirements. What are people supposed to do?" This is exactly why many organizations choose to have a separate system for DR. But it's also one of the challenges with most backup and recovery systems that cause people to examine more modern options that don't have this challenge. I'll be covering those systems in Chapter 15.

Separate System for E-Discovery

I spent a lot of time in Chapter 3 explaining the difference between backup and archive and then dedicated all of Chapter 10 to archive. Backups are for restoring systems after they've been damaged or corrupted. Archives are for satisfying e-discovery and compliance requests, and for lowering storage costs by moving unused data to lower-cost storage.

Most backup systems make lousy archive systems. If you need to restore a deleted file from a single directory from a single server that was present on a single date, your backup solution is your best friend. But if you need all the files that have the word *whatchamacallit* in them over the past three years, the typical backup system is simply unable to satisfy that request.

So if you get a lawsuit that believes files with the word *whatchamacallit* in them are the key to it winning the case, it will ask for those files, and it will cost your organization hundreds of thousands of dollars to prove that no such files exist. If you have an archive system, or a backup system capable of e-discovery, you could prove it right or wrong with a single query.

All it takes is a single large e-discovery request for your organization to realize that its backup system is incapable of satisfying it. You will spend hundreds of thousands of dollars satisfying the e-discovery request, and then there will be a large project to make sure it doesn't happen again. The most likely outcome is that you will create a separate system for e-discovery. This is because, although a handful of products support e-discovery from backups, most of them cannot. Depending on the type of lawsuits or government requests your organization tends to get, you will implement an email archive, a filesystem archive, or a database archive.

The cost of a separate e-discovery system will not be small, but it will still be smaller than what a large e-discovery request would cost you. That is why if your backup system is not capable of e-discovery—and most are not—you will most likely have a separate system for this purpose.

Tape-Related Challenges

If you're lucky enough to have a tapeless data protection system, you can ignore this section, or you can read it for historical purposes. The reality is, though, that at least half of the computing world is still using tape in some way in their backup systems. Therefore, it's important to discuss challenges that tape users will experience.

Tape drives are difficult to tune

You can't tune a tape drive, but you can tuna fish.

I've already covered that tape is still an integral component in many data protection systems, but tuning a backup system based entirely on tape is next to impossible. It is *somewhat* possible to design a system so that at least the full backup might go reasonably well to tape, and the tape drives might be reasonably happy and therefore not shoeshine all the time. It requires lots of work and constant performance monitoring, but it is somewhat possible if you really know what you're doing.

The problem is that full backups are a small portion of what you should be doing. Remember in the previous 500 TB example, 50 of the 66 TB of daily backups were incremental backups. Hopefully, your full backups are running once a month or less often than that. Hopefully, the bulk of what you're doing every day is incremental backups, but one of the challenges of that is that incremental backups are impossible to performance-tune.

Different backups take different amounts of time to transfer data. Different incremental backups take different amounts of time to walk the filesystem or database to figure out what needs to be included in the incremental backup. Different backup clients have different amounts of computing power or different levels of network conductivity. It is simply impossible to take all these variations into account when tuning your tape drive's performance for incremental backups. You can use multiplexing (covered in Chapter 9) to interleave several slower backups into one faster stream; however, when restoring, you usually have to read all those backups and throw most of them away. This is why it is said that multiplexing helps backups but usually hurts restores. (I do explain the exception in Chapter 9.)

I can think of many times throughout the years when I had the tape drives humming before I left. A few months later I would receive a phone call saying that things aren't running as well as they used to. I would go back on-site and take a look at things, and something had inevitably changed. The tape drive and backup settings were usually the same, but the incremental backups had changed enough that the tape drives were no longer performing like they should.

As discussed in "Disk Caching" on page 102, this problem is less likely to occur when you perform an initial backup to disk and are then simply copying those backups to tape. It is very similar to copying a full backup from disk to tape and it is being run on two devices specifically designed for the purpose. You can also schedule this process to occur at a time when nothing else is going on—typically during the day—which should allow each system to perform at its peak. This is why, although I am not a fan of tape as a source for disaster recoveries, one good thing is that environments choosing to do so at least don't have too much of a performance problem when they create their tape copy.

All these reasons are why performing backups directly to tape is no longer considered good backup system design. It's simply too hard to tune the performance of multiple tape drives and the hundreds of backups that will be sent to them.

Tapes can be lost

If you've moved to disk backup for your on-premises copy, but are still making tapes for the purposes of disaster recovery, you are most likely handing them to "a man in a van." Human beings make mistakes, and those tapes can get lost or stolen. A number of things can happen if and when that happens. On one hand, if the tapes have been encrypted, you really have only lost a copy of the data that no one else should be able to read.

 Tapes are a huge security risk if lost or stolen. Please encrypt any backup tapes that you make. The risk is too high otherwise.

If, however, the tapes are *not* encrypted, they can easily be read by a bad actor. Even if they do not have your organization's backup software product, every backup system of which I am aware has the ability to scan backup tapes back into the index if they have been deleted. That includes some products that advertise this isn't the case. So a black hat getting hold of an unencrypted backup tape is a bad day, indeed.

If your tapes are just lost and not necessarily stolen, the fact that you do not know where your tape is means that you are subject to a number of laws that require you to notify people that this has happened. The first US law of which I'm aware was California's SB 1386 back in 2005, which required organizations to disclose such a situation if it were to occur. The GDPR in the European Union, and the CCPA have similar provisions, as do many other laws around the world.

Manage an off-site vaulting vendor

If you are using a man in a van for your off-site tapes, this will be yet another vendor that you need to manage. Again, this is a process that will probably be ignored in many organizations, and it should not be. Back in the day, I remember managing our off-site vaulting vendor. In "Physical air gap" on page 52, I discussed the process we used to make sure tapes were always where we thought they were, and yet at least a few times a year a tape would go temporarily missing. The process would identify it and we would ultimately find it, but I always wondered what would have happened had I not been managing that process in the way we were.

The tip of the spear for an off-site vaulting vendor is the man in the van who, unfortunately, is a human. Humans make mistakes, sometimes purposefully and sometimes unintentionally. And sometimes, honestly, these people need to be fired. Read the following sidebar, "The *** You Just Say?", for a great story about this.

If your backup system uses off-site tape in any way, you will need an off-site vaulting vendor, and you will need to manage that relationship and the vaulting process. It is an unavoidable consequence of using tape.

The *** You Just Say?

Years ago, a client of mine received a box of tapes from their vaulting vendor, and when they looked inside, they found tapes that were not theirs. They called their representative to let him know, and he told them to read him the barcodes of the tapes in question. They did. His response was, "Yeah, I have no idea whose tapes those are. Go ahead and keep them."

The *** you just say?

Like I said, sometimes people just need to get fired.

Disk-Related Challenges

Although the use of disk as the primary target for backup and recovery systems has removed the challenges associated with tape, the use of disk has actually created new challenges in the backup space. It reminds me of the old adage, "In IT we never solve problems; we just move them."

Disk has no air gap

The best feature of tape besides cost is that it is easy to transport off-site and therefore create an air gap, as discussed in Chapter 3. Disk normally has no such ability, and that's a concern that must be addressed. (There are removable disk packs that can be used to create an air gap just like tape, but they are extremely rare in the wild.)

An air gap prevents a bad actor from deleting or encrypting your backups and then demanding a ransom (i.e., ransomware). Back in the day, a hacker had to break into your vaulting vendor physically to damage your off-site backup. Storing all your backups on a disk that is directly accessible via your backup system introduces a new risk to the backup system: encrypted or deleted backups. I discuss this concern in Chapter 12 when discussing target dedupe, as well as covering possible ways to mitigate this issue.

Customers using an entirely disk-based backup system need to address this concern, because it's a real security risk to the backups. Some are doing so by creating an occasional tape copy that goes off-site. Others copy backups to an immutable tier in the cloud, which cannot be accidentally or maliciously erased or corrupted even if you have the right credentials. SaaS services that do run in a completely separate infrastructure from the customer can also do this, because viruses or ransomware cannot directly attack it.

Bit rot

I discussed bit rot in Chapter 12; it is the slang term given to the degradation of the data stored on magnetic media over time. I also covered in Chapter 12 that disk has a much greater risk of bit rot over time than tape does. Those that study such things say that a block should not be stored on disk longer than five years, or it could suffer bit rot. This challenge also must be addressed if someone is storing backups that long on disk.

The only real solution to this is to have another layer that is occasionally tracking the integrity of the data. Backup software could provide such a layer, but it usually does not. The usual solution to this is to use object storage for any long-term storage requirements. Object storage by design should notice any magnetic degradation that happens on an object, and is equipped to fix it.

Large Up-Front Capital Purchases

There are now data protection methods that don't involve large capital purchases, but most backup systems require them. As mentioned in a previous section, you first start with a design that is made to last three to five years, usually because that is the depreciation schedule for the organization. You then put together one or more large capital purchases for this combination of hardware and software. You buy this giant piece of equipment, 75% of which will go completely unused for at least a year, and

50% of which will go unused for two years; yet you are buying all of that right now with capital funds.

This is the way IT systems are purchased, right? Yes, it is. But the many downsides of this process are also why so many organizations are switching to a SaaS model for as many systems as possible. It allows them to purchase these services via operating expenditures (i.e., opex) versus capital expenditures (i.e., capex).

Overprovisioning Is Required

In addition to buying more hardware than you need right now to plan for growth over the next two years, another thing you have to do is overprovision to plan for different things that might happen. You might have a big restore at some point, and you do not want the backup system to suffer because of the restore, and you do not want the restore to suffer because of the backups. Therefore, it is very common to design a backup system to have enough power to handle both a big backup load as well as a big restore load at the same time, even though that almost never happens.

If you are doing a series of full backups and incremental backups, you will most likely have days when you do more backups than on other days. That means you need to overprovision the system to meet the load for the bigger days, and over the rest of the week, that extra compute and throughput capacity will go unused.

Another thing about the way typical backup systems work is that in order to fit things within the backup window, you have to make the system much bigger than it would be if you could run backups throughout the day. If you are given an eight-hour backup window, for example, your backup system will need to be three times as big to meet the same backup load that could be done with a 24-hour window. Then, for 16 hours a day, this big beefy system you have goes completely unused.

Difficult to Scale

Typically, backup system components are scale-up components that can only go so fast or hold so much data. Even if you have a backup software system that supports a single backup server with multiple media servers, at some point that backup server runs out of compute capacity and is unable to process all the backups for the number of media servers that you need. The part that often breaks down is the backup index/catalog/database, because it is storing a record of every file and every deduplication chunk the backup system is making. If it cannot make those index/database updates fast enough, it affects the performance of the backup system negatively, and you end up having to buy another backup server and build an entirely separate system.

Many backup systems have multiple single points of scaling failure. They may be able to add additional capacity, but it might come with a downside, such as having to start over with a fresh index or not being able to share infrastructure.

Difficulty of Changing Backup Products

One of the problems that has existed since I joined the backup industry is that it is very difficult to change backup products. Each backup product has its own backup index format and backup format. One backup vendor cannot read another backup vendor's tapes. This is due both to the format issue and to many customers using encryption systems driven by the backup vendor. Even if a given vendor could read another backup vendor's backups, it wouldn't be able to decrypt them. The result is that many people are stuck with a given backup vendor because switching would be too difficult.

First I want to mention that this is on the list of why I don't like people keeping their backups for many years; it ties them to their backup system like this. If they just had 90 days' retention (or something like that), this problem would go away in 90 days. But when you retain your backups for 10 years, this becomes a real problem. The following is a list of the various options that can be used to deal with this ongoing issue.

Let Them Expire

The simplest method of dealing with this issue is simply to let your old backup expire. Keep running the old backup system in parallel with the new system; just don't send any new backups to it. This means, of course, you will need all new backup hardware (or a service), because the old hardware has to be dedicated to the old system.

This is an easy method if you only have 90 days of retention. If you are retaining backups for years, you'll run into a number of maintenance issues over the years. You'll have to upgrade server, disk, or tape hardware for a backup system that is technically no longer in use. It is less than an ideal situation, to say the least.

Use a Service

There are services that will take control of your backups and charge you a modest fee for keeping them safe. Then they charge you a very big fee if you ever have to restore or retrieve something. This is a much better option if you think you won't do many restores.

It puts the onus of maintaining infrastructure on the other company, and it allows it to apply economies of scale to the problem. For example, one big tape library could handle many clients. If you do this yourself, you will have to have your own dedicated tape library.

Restore and Backup

The idea that I see thrown around a lot but rarely used is the idea of restoring old backup data just so it can be backed up again. A lot of people suggest this idea, but it's logistically very difficult for a number of reasons.

One potential way this could happen, though, is if the backup system you are migrating off supports the concept of instant restore. If you can mount an image of VM and then back it up directly from the old backup system to the new backup system, I think that would be much less of a logistics nightmare. It will still be difficult and will take a long time, but it's a lot more manageable than a full restore followed by a full backup over and over.

Now let's take a look at the takeaways of this chapter.

Takeaways

It is my dream that in 10 to 20 years, someone will pick up this book, read this chapter, and laugh. They'll say, "Can you believe they used to have to worry about those things?" But the reality is that most backup and recovery systems today suffer from most, if not all, the challenges listed in this chapter. But we can still dream.

These challenges are significant. Sadly, many of them are so common that we don't even think about them anymore when thinking about our backup systems. But it's actually quite difficult to size, purchase, and maintain the typical backup system properly.

The good news is that all these challenges have been addressed to one degree or another by the products listed in the next two chapters. The bad news is some of the products I'll be talking about only address one or two of them. Let's take a look at commercial data protections next, starting with the traditional products that have been around 20 years or more.

CHAPTER 14

Traditional Data Protection Solutions

The data protection industry has evolved quite a bit in the past few decades. Each type of data protection solution discussed in this (and the following) chapter was designed to address what it saw as limitations and challenges of the solutions that preceded it in the market and/or challenges that were created by inflection points in the market (e.g., VMware, cloud).

The backup industry is a bit unique in that products we designed 10 or 20 years ago still have many happy customers. There have certainly been waves, starting with what I'm now calling traditional backup products that owned 100% of the market 20 years ago, followed by the virtualization-centric products gaining market share at their expense. Then there have been other waves of products, such as the hyper-converged and backup-as-a-service offerings, and those targeted at backing up IaaS/SaaS products. Whereas each wave also created its own following, many (if not most) of those who moved to those products have stayed with them. So the backup market today comprises a mix of products and services, some of which came out last year and some have been in the industry longer than I have.

I'll be explaining all these categories in the only way I know how: by telling you the story of how they got here. This story starts a long time ago with traditional backup products. They were developed because people like me were pulling out our hair trying to back up hundreds of Unix systems to individual standalone tape drives. Target deduplication systems entered the market when tape started to become problematic. The following is a summary of these various solutions and their respective advantages and challenges. This overview of traditional solutions will help you understand your product better and assure you that you are not alone with the challenges you have. In Chapter 16, I will discuss how to upgrade or replace your backup solution if the information you learn here gives you cause to do so. But before I start talking about the myriad products in the data protection space, I need to address the elephant in the room: I will not be naming any of them.

Not Naming Names

Just like in the rest of the book, I will not be using product names in the next few chapters when I talk about data protection products. Believe it or not, this is for your benefit as much as mine. What you get out of it is that I can be much blunter about the advantages and disadvantages by simply talking about potential pros and cons of a particular category. If I were to name names and be this blunt, I'd have to check and double-check every little statement I make about every vendor to protect you from misinformation and me from lawsuits. By speaking more generally, but directing my comments to product categories, I can be blunt, and you can do your own research on each product. This allows you to learn and think for yourself, with me as a guide. It should also help this book be a bit more timeless, because my concerns will still be valid 10 years from now. Hopefully, they'll all just be addressed by then. (Probably not.)

So what I'll be doing is discussing product categories instead of particular products. In each category are one or two products that everyone associates with that category, and I could make this a lot easier on both of us by naming that product. But I'm not going to do that for the reasons I mentioned in the previous paragraph, as well as my opinion that if I list one, I have to list them all, and there's no way I'll get them all. But this does make defining the categories a little bit harder. What I will do is use generalized rules to tell you the types of solutions I'm talking about in each section, starting with traditional backup solutions.

Traditional Backup Solutions

I discuss several categories in the next two chapters, including virtualization-centric, target dedupe, hyper-converged, and backup and DR-as-a-service solutions, and those are easier to define. Therefore, the easiest way to define *traditional* solutions is *not those solutions*.

If I were asked to define a traditional solution, I would say it has most likely been in the industry for more than 20 years and was most likely originally designed with tape at its center, although it has been adapted to use disk over the years. It also most likely performs a full backup followed by a series of incremental backups or differential backups, which are then followed by occasional full backups. If it requires an occasional full backup, even if that full backup can be synthesized, it is most likely a traditional backup solution. At least one popular traditional backup solution, though, was designed not to require occasional full backups for filesystem backups, so *not* having occasional full backups does not move you out of this category.

A traditional backup solution is typically purchased as a separate software-only offering that you install on a backup server of your choice. (Some of them are now available as an appliance, which I'm covering in "Traditional Backup Appliances" on page 334.) You will have a central backup server and, possibly, one or more media/storage servers managed by the central server, each of which is backing up to one or more storage devices. A smaller configuration might have a single central backup server that is also acting as the media/storage server.

When I started in the industry, we called these master servers and slave servers, but that terminology has largely been dropped in recent years, due to the negative historical connotations of those terms. What we used to call slave servers are now usually called media, storage, or device servers, and master servers may still go by the term *master* or may use a completely different term altogether for the central backup server.

Advantages of Traditional Backup

Traditional backup software allows centralized, scheduled backup from a variety of data sources, including all major Unix offerings, Windows, Linux, and MacOS as well as vSphere, Hyper-V, and AHV hypervisors. In fact, their breadth of coverage is easily their single biggest competitive advantage. They also support backing up all major (and some minor) database solutions, including Oracle, SQL Server, SAP, MySQL, and newer applications like Hadoop and MongoDB. They were also the first major companies to support Kubernetes backup.

Traditional backup solutions are the first commercial backup solutions to achieve what I would call the snowball effect. Many environments use these solutions due to how many platforms they cover, and they can cover so many platforms because of how many people are using the solution. This snowball has been building for the past 30 years. Although these solutions have lost a significant portion of the market share they had 10 or so years ago, they're not going away anytime soon.

Although many other solutions have taken aim at certain parts of their portfolio, no other solution category has even attempted their breadth of coverage. This means that many environments will continue to use traditional solutions as long as this kind of coverage breadth is a deciding factor—which is to say, for a while. Many of the newer solutions covered later in this chapter have gotten where they are by ignoring many smaller data sources and focusing only on low-hanging fruit: backup sources with vast market adoption (e.g., VMware, Windows, Linux, etc.). This simplifies their development and support model and allows them to spend all the R&D money on a longer list of features because they are supporting a shorter list of data sources. The side effect is that a lot of data sources have no choice other than traditional backup.

All leading traditional backup software solutions come with centralized monitoring and reporting functionality, although some of them leave a little to be desired. Actually, lack of good reporting is a common feature of many backup solutions, not just of traditional ones. In fact, it created a small industry of third-party backup reporting solutions, a few of which are still around.

What About Third-Party Reporting Tools?

Third-party reporting tools are not really a backup product, but they are used by a lot of people who use backup products. At one point, they were essential because many backup tools had horrible trend reporting. They could tell you what failed last night but not what has been regularly failing or whether the backup failure in question puts you out of compliance with your RPO.

When such tools are very helpful now is when you have more than one backup product. If you have two or three backup products, having a single product to report on all backups is actually quite nice to have. It'll normalize the data and tell you what's going on, including backup and restore success metrics, trend analysis, and capacity management.

If you happen to have more than one backup product, I highly recommend such a tool. If you have only one product, I still think they're a good idea. They're just harder to get budget for.

Traditional backup solutions also invented the idea of the backup agent that can interface with various pieces of the infrastructure for the purposes of backup. Prior to this, there was no such thing as a Unix or Windows backup agent or an Oracle or SQL Server agent. Everything was done with shell scripts and cron jobs and what we now call dump-and-sweep backup (explained in Chapter 7). Traditional backup software deserves credit for revolutionizing the industry when these solutions came out.

Challenges with Traditional Backup

Users of traditional backup systems experience every challenge discussed in Chapter 13. They can be difficult to size properly due to all the complex paths required to do so. Adding deduplication to the mix actually makes it harder. Once you decide on a product and design, you then need to maintain a backup server and its OS, along with the backup software. You will almost always be managing multiple vendors unless you have purchased a backup appliance from one of these vendors. This is probably why these appliances have become so popular among customers using traditional backup solutions.

You will most likely be required to have a separate system for DR and e-discovery, because traditional systems are rarely able to meet the kinds of DR requirements I talk about in Chapter 11 or the e-discovery requirements I talk about in Chapter 10. You may or may not be experiencing the problems associated with tape, including performance-tuning, lost tapes, and the management of a vaulting vendor. If you're not dealing with tape issues, you're dealing with the risks of storing backups on disk, including magnetic degradation of older backups and the fact that most disk systems have no air gap. These systems can be difficult to design and purchase, especially since they are always purchased via a big capital purchase.

Finally, once you have the system, it can only be scaled to a certain degree. At some point, the central backup server cannot handle processing all the index entries from all the backups. This requires you to create an entirely different backup system that will not share its data with the other system.

Analysis

Traditional backup solutions still hold the bulk of the data protection market share, so it would be a mistake to dismiss them as some do. The famous Mark Twain quote about the reports of his death being greatly exaggerated comes to mind. At the time of writing, every one of the Fortune 100—and most of the Fortune 500—is running one of these traditional backup solutions to some extent, and solutions in this category continue to win accolades from analyst firms.

The biggest reasons for you to choose one of these solutions are their time in market and breadth of coverage. Their customers benefit from decades of R&D and the reliability that usually comes with that. Most newer solutions covered in the next chapter do not have anywhere near the battle-tested longevity that traditional solutions offer. They also cover virtually every datacenter operating system, platform, and database, both new and old. They support backing up newer things like IaaS and PaaS offerings, Kubernetes and Docker, and Hadoop and MongoDB. They also still support backing up all the Unix variants, including at least one (HP-UX) that hasn't shipped a new version in 13 years! It is true that revenue growth for most leading traditional backup solutions has flattened or is decreasing, but this category still offers the only valid option for a significant portion of the market, so they're not going anywhere anytime soon.

These solutions also support every kind of imaginable backup, including target deduplication systems, every kind of tape library, and multiple cloud platforms. Unlike many of the newer solutions covered in later sections of this chapter, these solutions also still support the concept of bare-metal recovery on a variety of platforms.

These solutions have also adapted as the market changes. As smaller, scrappier solutions (that do not have to support their breadth of platforms) have added new features and chipped away at their market share, they have responded by adding similar features in their solutions. For example, some of these solutions have added source-side deduplication, although many (if not most) people using traditional backup software do tend to choose to back up to target deduplication appliances. They support VADP for VMware and VSS for Hyper-V, including the use of CBT for block-level incremental backups. Many also offer synthetic full backups, which help ameliorate the issues caused by the full backups they still tend to require.

In addition to copying off-site copies into object storage, some have added the ability to use cloud object storage as the primary storage for backups. (Most backup software of all types wants to store their primary copy of backups on file/block storage, not on object-based storage.) Another interesting option some of them have is the ability to replicate backups between central backup servers. Traditionally, each central backup server was a standalone thing that knew nothing of other backup servers. Being able to use deduplication to replicate backups between central backup servers allows multisite organizations to have on-site and off-site backups without involving a third-party vendor (e.g., cloud).

Although these solutions do offer quite a bit of functionality, it is also true that all the other backup solution categories (discussed in the next chapter) are aimed at addressing the previously mentioned challenges that are common to customers of traditional backup solutions. Traditional backup systems require a significant amount of design to size properly, after which you are left with backup servers and software that must be continually maintained in multiple vendor relationships that must be managed. Any stringent DR requirements usually create the need for a separate DR system, and the same is usually true of e-discovery. Even though most modern traditional systems (as oxymoronic as that sounds) are now backing up to deduplicated disk, many customers are still sending off-site backups to tape for cost reasons. This means they also have the issues of performance-tuning tape drives, concerns about lost tapes, and an off-site vaulting vendor to manage. Such systems are almost always included with a large capital purchase that must be overprovisioned to last multiple years and can be difficult to scale once initially designed and installed.

One question for customers of such solutions is what to do when part of your organization requires such solutions (e.g., traditional Unix servers), and other more modern parts of your infrastructure are drawn to more modern solutions or services. I harken back to the days when backups of virtualized servers were possible with traditional backups but were definitely better with solutions that were designed just for virtualization. My advice then was to stay with the traditional solution for everything—if you could still meet your recovery requirements. I advised people of the complexities of running multiple backup solutions and asked them to factor that into the equation. My answer today remains the same. Be sure to factor in the complexities of running multiple backup solutions if you're considering moving some of your traditional backups to a different solution. Some have told me that managing the newer solution is so much easier, that it ameliorates the issue of having to learn two solutions. As always, it's your call.

Target Deduplication Backup Appliances

A target deduplication backup appliance is an appliance consisting of a disk array sitting behind some type of frontend server (often called the *head*) running a specialized operating system, usually some variant of Linux. Like most appliances, the OS is usually hidden from you, and all administration is via a web-based interface. These appliances can present themselves as NFS/SMB servers, iSCSI targets, and VTLs, although most everyone connects to them via NFS/SMB. You configure your backup server to send its backups to these appliances that then deduplicate them and possibly replicate them to another appliance. Target dedupe appliances are covered in more detail in Chapter 12.

These solutions aren't technically a backup solution on their own, but I'm covering them in this chapter for two reasons. The first reason is that they are such a common part of many people's backup solution, even if it comes from multiple vendors. The second reason is that it is a complete backup solution for some people: DBAs. Many DBAs use them for their dump-and-sweep backups in a way that doesn't require a typical backup product. They dump the database to an NFS/SMB mount provided by the target dedupe appliance, which then replicates that dump off-site, using its integrated replication. The DBAs are happy and the backup people don't have to worry about database backups.

The addition of these appliances to the world of backup and recovery was an incredible gift to many organizations trying to address the challenges caused by tape drives that have gotten too fast for the task they were originally designed for. As mentioned in several other places in this book, the problem with tape drives when designing a modern data protection system is not that they are too slow; it's that they are too fast. Tape drives have two speeds: stop and very fast. Very few backups can keep up with the typical speed of modern tape drives, which now measure at over 1.7 GB per second. Therefore, something had to give.

Some organizations address the issues with tape by adopting the disk-caching approach discussed in "Tape-Related Challenges" on page 296. Disk caching is better than having no disk in the equation, but it is only a partial solution to this problem, since you are still dealing with tape for off-site. The key to success in most modern backup and recovery systems is to take tape out of the equation as much as possible. The only way to do that is to have enough disk to hold multiple generations of full and incremental backups on-site. This will allow you to restore any version of any file or database within the past 90 days to six months without having to reach for a tape.

The problem with this design, however, is that it requires a significant amount of disk. Using the example I provided in "Size the Backup System" on page 288, a 500 TB datacenter would need 6–11 PB of disk to hold six months to a year of backups. That's twenty times the size of the primary data!

That is where third-party target deduplication appliances stepped in to save the day. (An image of a certain flying rodent saying something like that comes to mind, but it's not actually here, for obvious reasons.) As discussed in more detail in "Target Deduplication Appliances" on page 272, these appliances crack open the backup format, slice the backup data into small chunks (the size of which depends on the solution), and run a cryptographic hashing algorithm that allows them to identify each chunk uniquely.

These appliances are very popular. Many (if not most) customers of traditional backup solutions will store the bulk of their backups on a third-party target deduplication appliance. (They are *third-party* in the sense that they are not supplied by the company supplying your backup and recovery software.) The following is a summary of the advantages and challenges of these popular appliances.

Advantages of Target Dedupe

The biggest advantage of the target dedupe approach is that the customer doesn't have to change very much in their backup system to use it. This means they don't have to throw away what they already purchased to add deduplication to their backup system.

The solutions discussed in the next chapter require you to switch out your entire backup system for their solution, at least for what you want that solution to back up. Many people will buy one of the other solutions discussed in this chapter to handle particular workloads, such as VMware, remote sites, or cloud workloads. To use those solutions for those workloads, you must stop using whatever you're currently using to back up those workloads. You can continue to use your current solution everywhere else. And that's one of the ways people end up with an average of two to three backup solutions.

In contrast, target dedupe appliances can easily be added to any existing backup and recovery system that can back up to external disk, which is usually less expensive than a complete replacement with a new system. They are also very versatile because you can connect them to a backup system by a variety of methods.

To use a target dedupe appliance, a customer only has to start sending their backups to a new device and manage the off-site copy process. Either they will copy to tape or replicate to another dedupe system. Although this is typically very easy to accomplish, a lot of tape-only environments don't copy their backup tapes and send their original tapes off-site. Such environments will need to add and manage a copy process that is entirely new to them.

Backups suddenly get more reliable when switching from tape to disk. This evolutionary (versus revolutionary) backup design change is what made these solutions so popular over the years. Buy one appliance and many of your tape problems go away.

Buy two and replicate, and *all* of your tape problems go away, including paying for a vaulting vendor.

Target deduplication arrays can find duplicate data across all kinds of backups, as well as backups that are from different servers and applications. It should also find duplicate files that are stored across multiple servers, and it should find duplicate blocks of data in different versions of files stored over time. There are a few caveats, starting with the fact that all backups that need to be deduplicated against each other must be sent to the same appliance. Even so, not all target dedupe appliances globally dedupe all data stored within an appliance.

The result of deduplication is a deduplication ratio that (when applied to a traditional backup and recovery environment) tends to be 10:1 or greater. This means that such a system would allow you to store six months' to a year's worth of backups of the previously mentioned example of a 500 TB datacenter (11 PB of backup data) in roughly 1 PB (or less) of physical disk. Your actual dedupe ratio will vary greatly, based on your data, your backup configuration, and the deduplication system.

For organizations that would like to get rid of tape completely, these systems also support replicating backups off-site to a second target deduplication appliance. As mentioned in "Target Deduplication Appliances" on page 272, this can be managed by the backup software or by the appliance, and both approaches have their advantages and disadvantages. Customers who have adopted this backup design can have on-site and off-site backups with no need for a man in a van, reducing the number of vendors they have to manage by two, and reducing complexity even more. These customers no longer have to worry about tuning their backup performance to match the speed of their tape drives properly. They also do not have to worry about managing the physical existence of tape and how it might get lost. And, finally, they do not need a contract with a vaulting vendor to transport and store their tapes.

Challenges with Target Dedupe

Deduplication appliances solved a lot of problems, but they actually created a few new ones. Three challenges are brought on by storing all backups on target deduplication appliances: sizing, pricing, and security. Let's take a look at each one.

The first challenge is that properly sizing these systems requires quite a bit of guessing. No vendor knows just how well your backups will deduplicate until it actually deduplicates your backups. There is no way around this. You can guess, the vendor can guess, a third-party consultant can guess all day long. Everybody's data and backup configurations are different; therefore, everybody's deduplication rates are different.

Another important thing to understand when sizing target dedupe systems is the following caveat: Their dedupe scope is limited to a single scale-up appliance, and sometimes the scope is even less than that. All of the popular target dedupe appliances are scale-up appliances that can only dedupe data within that appliance. These appliances normally come in a variety of sizes, each of which is a frontend appliance (i.e., *head*) behind which will be a certain amount of disk. More powerful heads can handle more disks and disk capacity behind them. If you buy a less expensive appliance based on a less-powerful head and then outgrow it, you have two choices: replace the head or buy another appliance altogether.

If you replace the head, you will be throwing away the first head you purchased and wasting money. If you buy a second appliance with its own disks, you will be starting over from a dedupe perspective. The dedupe systems in each appliance do not talk to each other, so you will need to split your backups between them to minimize waste. Most people opt for the second choice of buying another appliance, often buying many such appliances. As a result, their sizing may be a bit off, because it's usually based on a dedupe ratio that assumes that the dedupe system is globally comparing all backups. That won't happen if you buy more than one appliance; each appliance is a dedupe island.

In addition, underprovisioning can create an instant demand, which requires a rush purchase. These are never good for a variety of reasons, including the fact that (to borrow a phrase from George on Seinfeld) you "have no hand." First, you have no negotiation power with your vendor, because it knows you are desperate for the new hardware. Second, you don't have time to size things right, so you will probably over-buy so this doesn't happen again any time soon. The biggest risk is that you might be forced to delete some backups to make room, a position no backup person wants to be in.

What most people do to address this issue is overprovision from day one by buying a head much bigger than they need now, with less disk than it can eventually support. Then they add additional disk when they need it. They argue that they would typically be doing this anyway because the system needs to last three to five years. If they get it wrong, they either overbought or they will need to buy more hardware sooner. One way to get around this limitation is not to purchase the entire system until you have done some type of pilot program that gives you an idea of how all of your data will deduplicate. Each backup type will deduplicate differently, so make sure to back up all of the different types of data that you have in your datacenter and measure each of their deduplication rates separately. The backups of RDBMSs like Oracle and SQL Server are notoriously problematic and subject to various options that you can enable in the backup to change your dedupe rate drastically.

Target dedupe systems also have the air gap challenge mentioned in "Disk has no air gap" on page 299. If the target dedupe is directly connected to the backup server via NFS/SMB or VTL, a rogue admin or other bad actor could corrupt or delete all the backups stored thereon. This attack vector has been used by many ransomware

attackers to encrypt both the primary and secondary copies of a dataset. You can see this in the articles when they talk about how the backup was also affected.

The final challenge with target deduplication systems is that they are expensive. Whereas it may be easier to add target dedupe to an existing backup system than it is to buy an entirely new backup system, there is no question that the cost of the entire solution is usually more than another solution would be if you were in a greenfield (i.e., new) environment.

This cost is why many customers that store all their on-premises backups on a target deduplication system still copy those backups to tape and hand them to a man in a van. Some of them do this to provide an air gap that a replicated backup doesn't provide, and others do it because the cost of a copy on tape is still way less expensive than replicating their backups to another appliance and paying the dedupe tax a second time.

Analysis

Target dedupe systems were created to address the challenges associated with tape in a traditional backup environment. Target dedupe appliances provide a relatively affordable—compared to nondeduped disk—target device for backups that is much more suited for backups than the tape drives it is replacing. Even if your organization chooses to copy its off-site backups to tape and hand them to a man in a van, the main copy of your backups will be much easier to make and use. Backups and restores will work much better than if you're backing up directly to tape, and the number of times that you have to troubleshoot a backup because a tape drive malfunctioned are reduced to zero. (You may still have to troubleshoot your tape copies, but those should be much more reliable than sending backups directly to tape.) Deduplication also makes replication backups possible.

However, the evolutionary approach that makes target deduplication so popular did nothing to address the *nontape* challenges of a traditional data protection system. Target dedupe reduced complexity in one area, but did so by adding another solution and vendor, which increases complexity in another area. The resulting systems are much more expensive to buy and maintain than their tape-only predecessors.

Some would say that although target dedupe systems can be expensive, they are still less expensive than replacing your entire backup system. That is typically true. Just remember that by adding another solution and vendor to your backup system, you are increasing complexity, and that comes with a cost as well. Be sure to compare the overall TCO of your backup system when looking at major changes like this. You may find it's cheaper just to add on a target dedupe system, or you might find it's cheaper to start over with a fresh design. Only real-world numbers can answer that question for you.

Takeaways

Traditional backup systems are here to stay, despite the fact that they are pretty long in the tooth. They are still the only game in town when it comes to some legacy workloads, and they are also quite reliable due to decades of R&D. They've also not given up the market to newer players; they've continued to adapt as the market requirements changed. It's also a lot easier to find someone familiar with such products than it is to do the same for some of the newer players. It's unlikely, however, that these companies will be able to stem the tide that has moved away from them in the past two decades. There are simply too many good choices out there that have far fewer challenges and are less expensive to operate.

Target deduplication systems are also quite established and are not going away anytime soon. But like the traditional backup systems, many vendors have arisen to give them a run for their money. Most modern backup systems have their own integrated dedupe, so they have no need for a target dedupe appliance. This is why I see them as much more appropriate for traditional backup software customers, which is why I covered them in this chapter.

In the next chapter, we'll take a look at the new kids on the block. Some of these new kids have actually been out a while, but even those (the hypervisor-centric products) took a completely different approach to backup than these traditional products. That's why I included them in the modern data protection products chapter. Let's take a look at these modern products, shall we?

CHAPTER 15

Modern Data Protection Solutions

The previous chapter looked at traditional data protection solutions and the target deduplication systems that were designed primarily to address the tape challenges with those solutions. (The marketing slogan for one of those products was "Tape sucks. Move on," so I think that's a pretty fair assessment of why target dedupe products appeared on the market.)

One major change between the products in this chapter and those in the previous chapter is that all of these backup products were designed with disk at their center. Many of them are still disk only, and others are still disk-centric but with some support added for tape. But all these products were designed with disk as their primary (and often only) backup target.

In addition to being disk-centric, all these products were designed to address some shift in the marketplace. Things happened (and continue to happen) that kept breaking the backup process, and new products were introduced to fix that. Virtualization-centric backup solutions started to appear because the market perceived that existing solutions were not adequately addressing the challenges presented by server virtualization. Hyper-converged backup solutions addressed how segmented the data protection industry had gotten, with the typical backup configuration using solutions from four to five vendors. DPaaS offerings addressed the same need, but with a SaaS approach. Finally, in the past few years, we have also seen solutions specifically designed to back up the various IaaS, PaaS, and SaaS offerings that are starting to be so popular. Let's take a look at this new generation of data protection products.

Virtualization-Centric Solutions

Right around the same time that tape drives were starting to get too fast and target deduplication systems started coming to market, a little company called VMware started to make its mark. Within a few years, it became an incredibly popular way to virtualize the x86 architecture. It allowed organizations to share a single physical server among several virtual machines that would share that server's CPU, memory, and I/O resources.

One thing that VMware did not initially include in the design was a way to back up virtual machines easily. For the first several years of VMware's existence, the only way to back up a virtual machine was to pretend it was a physical machine. You installed a backup client on it and backed it up just like any other physical machine.

The problem with pretending that a VM is a physical machine is what happens when you do several backups at the same time, especially when some of those backups are full backups. You overburden the I/O system of the virtualization host, hurting the performance of both the backups and other VMs on that same virtualization host. Something had to be done.

VMware first tried something called VMware Consolidated Backup (VCB), and a lot of backup companies wasted a lot of R&D developing an API that VMware ultimately abandoned. (I used to call it Very Crappy Backup.) VMware then released the vSphere Storage APIs for Data Protection (VADP) that included changed-block tracking (CBT). This allowed backup software systems to back up virtual machines without having to install backup client software in each VM and enabled block-level incremental backups of VMs as well.

The only problem was that more than 10 years went by without any real fix that traditional backup solutions could use to address this problem. Between the failure of VCB and the uncertainty of the virtualization market in general, large backup companies didn't want to spend the R&D money to create a separate solution to solve the problem. This created a market demand for a new type of solution, and virtualization-centric backup solutions were born. They saw virtualization as the up-and-coming trend, and by solving the backup and recovery needs of that trend, they cemented themselves in the market.

These solutions took a disk-only, Windows-only backup approach, meaning the backup server software only ran on Windows and did not support tape. (Most have now added tape support, but they did not initially include it.) By focusing entirely on VMware and reducing their platform support to Windows, these solutions greatly simplified both their research and development requirements and the ease of the solution to use. The resulting solutions were usually very easy to use and catered specifically to the needs of the virtualization community, which eventually grew to include Hyper-V as well. As some of these vendors grow, they have also added support for other hypervisors (e.g., KVM and AHV), but their main solutions are still focused on VMware and Hyper-V, because those are table stakes.

Initially, these solutions were designed only for VMs, and it's hard for modern IT people to understand how much that simplified things. At the time, datacenters were full of Unix variants like Solaris, HP-UX, AIX, IRIX, DG-UX, and AIX, each of which ran on different physical architectures. Windows and Linux on x86 servers were growing in popularity but were nowhere near as popular as they are today. Since these vendors were only designing backup solutions for VMs, they didn't have to deal with all the complexities of all the other architectures and operating systems.

I've never been a fan of customers running two different backup solutions, so I didn't like it when customers started complicating their backup environments by replacing just their VMware backups with these new solutions. It meant they would be running one backup solution for their physical servers and a different one for their VMs. I remember telling customers that I preferred the limitations of treating the virtual machines as physical machines over the complexities of running two backup solutions. But companies releasing virtualization-centric backup software solutions felt differently. First, they felt that virtualization was the way of the future, and on that they were clearly right, which removes the "point solution" claim. (You're far from a point solution if you handle most of the datacenter.) Today's datacenters are almost completely virtualized, and virtualization laid the ground for what is currently happening in the cloud. Second, they felt that narrowing the focus would allow them to add more cutting-edge functionality than would otherwise be possible. History would show they were right on both counts.

It's also important to understand that although these solutions started with a Windows-only, disk-only approach, this is no longer true with most of these solutions. They added tape for long-term storage of backups, as customers complained that keeping all their backups on disk cost too much. (I would, of course, argue that you shouldn't be storing your backups so long that you need tape's long-term storage costs. Please read Chapter 3 to see my feelings on this subject.) Some customers also adopted the same design that is discussed in the previous chapter: on-premises backups on a target dedupe appliance and off-site backups on tape. The only way this was possible was if these solutions supported tape. Finally, some of these solutions now support Linux media servers, helping address the security concerns about Windows, which is discussed in more detail in "Challenges of Virtualization-Centric Backup" on page 318.

Advantages of Virtualization-Centric Solutions

Being based on Windows and disk makes the solutions easier for customers to understand. Tape libraries can be confusing and certainly much more difficult to configure. Putting your backups in C:\BACKUPS is a lot easier to grasp (although, as I mentioned in the previous chapter, there is a security risk of having your backups directly available in your filesystem). There is also no need for a huge manual that addresses all the Unix variants and the various command lines they come with. It is a typical Windows UI.

The disk-centric architecture also allows these solutions to store backups differently from more traditional backup solutions. They can store their backups in a way that allows more direct access to backup data, more akin to a copy or snapshot than to a typical backup. This design choice enabled a number of really important features. For example, it enables users to mount VMDK/VHD files as a filesystem to allow them to grab individual files for single-file recovery. (Without this, you would be forced to recover an entire VMDK just to restore one file.) It also allows similar features with Microsoft Exchange backups, so users can browse individual emails inside Exchange without having to restore the entire database before doing so. Both these features are very important to customers of these solutions.

The two biggest features they added to the world of backup, though, are instant recovery, which I covered in Chapter 9, and automated testing of backups. It's hard to overemphasize the impact these two features have had on the backup and recovery industry. The idea that you could instantly boot a VM from its backup and subsequently test that all of your VMs can be successfully booted—completely automatically—was a game changer. The first time I saw one of these vendors demonstrate a completely automated test recovery of dozens of VMs, I remember thinking that this idea was the coolest new feature I had seen in years. Many backup vendors to this day are still playing catch-up with these important features that were added years ago.

So many times over the years, I have joked about how no one cares if you can back up; they only care if you can restore. (I opened this book with that joke.) We used to talk about how nice it would be to test our backups by restoring them on a regular basis, but we usually never had the resources to do that. This was because we had to do a real restore, which required storage and compute resources that simply weren't available. This idea of instant recovery and automated regular testing of backups has changed the design of so many other backup solutions, and it was the virtualization-centric backup solutions that first brought this idea to the market.

Challenges of Virtualization-Centric Backup

Virtualization-centric backup solutions also introduced new challenges. Their customers have the same challenge as target dedupe appliances have with disk-based backups being accessible to bad actors. The simplicity mentioned in the previous section of storing your backups in C:\BACKUPS also makes it simpler for a hacker to damage them. This concern is exacerbated by the fact that most of these solutions are developed around the Microsoft Windows platform for the backup server. Windows is the number one target for bad actors, especially for ransomware. (Neither Linux nor MacOS are impervious, but they are not as big a target.) There are way too many stories of organizations whose primary systems and backup systems have been infected with ransomware.

Part of Windows' ease of use comes from the fact that everything is designed to use a GUI, which assumes you will be running it on a console. That console is usually in the datacenter and often isn't a real console. Many systems run in a headless mode or are connected to a KVM system that allows them to share a single monitor, keyboard, and mouse. Therefore, it's extremely common to enable the Remote Desktop Protocol (RDP) and for that to be the most common way for Windows system administrators to connect to the console of the machine and administer anything that is looking for a GUI. The problem with this is that RDP is an incredibly common attack vector for ransomware. This risk can be mitigated to a certain degree by following best practices for securing RDP, but many customers are either unaware of the issue or do not have the time to make such a change.

Some solutions in this category have responded to this vulnerability by supporting Linux media servers and by supporting the copying backups into immutable storage systems such as S3. The S3 *object lock* option is a good solution for the off-site copy, and the Linux media server helps make the on-premises copy more secure. The most important thing is that customers need to be aware of the risks and address them the best they can.

Analysis

Virtualization-centric backup solutions are a popular choice among virtualization-centric environments. The less likely you are to be running physical workloads and the various Unix variants that come with them, the more likely you are to prefer a virtualization-centric approach. The more Windows you run in your virtualization environment, the more likely it is that you will prefer these solutions.

The Windows-centric nature of these systems has become a much bigger security concern than it was when they first started to appear 15 years ago. This could explain why the revenue of these companies has followed a similar trajectory of traditional backup solutions. Their revenue growth has slowed in the past few years, and some have recently been acquired by private equity firms, just like what happened in the traditional space. My personal opinion is that the ransomware vulnerability of their Windows-centric post is at the heart of this trend. Only time will tell if they can regain some market share by enhancing their products.

Linux media servers and the use of immutable cloud storage help ameliorate most of these concerns, since together they move all backups off Windows-based storage. Some of the products also have a proprietary connection to storage that doesn't present the backup directory (e.g., C:\BACKUPS) to the operating system. That is another approach if you want to stay with Windows for your media server. However, the main backup server still runs on Windows, so it still may be attacked. At least the backups could be made safe from such attacks.

Unfortunately, the challenge of a Windows-based backup server is that addressing this issue head-on requires the vendor to point out the problem it has created. It's a bit reminiscent of how car manufacturers were initially against seatbelts because it meant they had to point out that people were being killed riding in cars. I do not think vendors providing these solutions have done enough to warn users that the default configuration (a Windows server with local storage and a `C:\BACKUPS` directory) should *never* be used, for security reasons. I believe it's because it goes against their ease-of-use message.

Reviewing the challenges with data protection discussed in Chapter 13, the biggest reason that these systems help is that most customers of these solutions are no longer using tape drives. This simplifies the design and reduces the number of solutions that must be used. Most customers are using a target deduplication system, however, which means that these solutions don't reduce the number of vendors that organizations have to deal with. The rest of the challenges mentioned in Chapter 13 also remain.

The number one reason you would choose these solutions is that you are a Windows-centric, virtualization-centric datacenter that is familiar with the security concerns such a world presents. You like that your backup system runs the same OS as the rest of your datacenter, and you can address the security issues that RDP and disk-based backups present. If this sounds like you, this is the solution category for you.

Hyper-Converged Backup Appliances

About eight years ago as of this writing, a few companies decided to try to address many of the challenges of traditional data protection with a completely new approach to an on-premises backup system: a scale-out storage system dedicated to secondary storage and/or backup. (Secondary storage is a bigger category, which includes solutions dedicated to data types that do not need high-speed primary storage. That's what secondary storage is for.) This new category is called hyper-converged backup appliances (HCBAs), and some systems in the category are dedicated to backup and recovery, whereas others try to service the needs of both backup and recovery as well as secondary storage. Much to the chagrin of the latter, I am really only focusing on the backup and recovery aspect of things here.

In case you're not familiar with the terms *scale up* and *scale out*, they are the two main ways of growing, or *scaling*, a computer system. A scale-up system starts with a single node and a certain amount of storage, and it grows by adding more disk behind that node. A scale-out system starts with a series of nodes, each with its own compute and storage, and all working together in a clustered configuration. Such a system scales by adding additional nodes, each of which adds more compute and storage to the configuration.

Prior to the creation of these systems, all backup systems were built with the scale-up approach. Even if they offered the ability to scale out with media servers, there was always a central backup server that was in charge of all the media servers. This central backup server was simultaneously a single point of failure and a limit to which a given backup system could scale. As mentioned in Chapter 13, a typical problem was the backup index. At some point, that index gets too big to keep up with the speed of all the backups that are happening in the various media servers, which requires you to get another central backup server and create an entirely new backup system. Finally, although some central backup servers can be put on a highly available (HA) cluster, that design was rarely used due to costs. HA also doesn't address the scalability issues associated with the index.

Hyper-converged backup appliances were employed to solve this with the scale-out approach. Borrowing techniques and technologies from other scale-out systems, the systems are built with a series of individual nodes that provide redundancy for backup data as well as scheduling, operations, and storage of the index of everything that is happening.

These solutions also offered the choice to adopt an appliance model versus a software-only model. Although not everyone took to the idea of physical appliances, what they did do was solve one of the biggest issues that so many people have with traditional backup systems: it gave them one number to call if something went wrong. (There does appear to be a demand for the simpler deployment model that appliances bring, which is why some traditional and virtualization-centric solutions have now come out with appliance versions of their product, as discussed in "Traditional Backup Appliances" on page 334.) Hyper-converged backup systems do not use third-party target dedupe; they use internal storage like other scaleout arrays. They do typically perform target dedupe, meaning they dedupe backup data once it arrives at their clustered array, but they do it themselves; they do not need a third-party appliance. They see these third-party appliances as another part of their competitors' solutions that don't scale very well.

Advantages of Hyper-Converged Backup Appliances

The scale-out design of hyper-converged backup appliances (HCBAs) is exactly what on-premises backup systems have needed for decades. I have always been a fan of scale-out designs. They offer so much more scalability without waste. Scale-up systems can only scale so far, and often you end up being limited by the power of the node you started with. You're forced to make an entirely separate system or throw away your old node and replace it with a new one. Scale-out systems are so easy to scale, and you never have to throw anything out unless it needs to be retired because a given node is too old. I've always wondered why backup systems are not more scalable, especially since they are supposed to hold 10 to 20 times more data than the datacenter. So I for one welcome the idea of applying scale-out concepts to backup design.

Although a scale-out design still requires an initial backup design, the fact that you can easily scale the system if you underprovision it significantly reduces the risk that the initial backup design can go horribly wrong. With almost every other backup system, your initial design being way off can cause lots of problems. You can easily missize your servers, RAID arrays, or target deduplication systems. That is one of the worst parts about the scale-up architecture of most backup systems. The scale-out design alleviates that concern.

As mentioned in the previous chapter, the biggest worry in scale-up systems' design is underprovisioning (i.e., making your initial configuration too small). If you fail to plan for growth, or underprovision your configuration, you may end up wasting money because you may be forced either to replace some of the hardware you bought or lower your effective dedupe rate by splitting backups across multiple appliances. Therefore, people tend to overprovision their backup environments massively so this doesn't happen. That method wastes money, too.

With the scale-out architecture of HCBAs, the danger of underprovisioning doesn't exist, so there's no need to overprovision to compensate. Design your system and buy what you think you need for the next year or so. If it turns out you underprovisioned, you just need to buy some more nodes and add them to the system; nothing is wasted.

These systems do offer some protection against ransomware, because they use a Linux-based architecture, unlike all virtualization-centric solutions and many of the traditional backup solutions. This offers them a major cybersecurity advantage over their nearest on-premises competitor.

Working Around the System

The only thing that might push you to overprovision anyway is if you have a very difficult capital purchasing process, and you'd rather not have to go back to the well every year. But that is a problem with your organization's processes, not with the design of the system. I remember back in the day how long it would take to buy anything that required a capital expense. It took months, even a year. And we were required to put in a capital expense for any single item that was over $1,000. I could buy $20,000 worth of tapes as an operational expense because each of them was under $1,000. But a $1,200 tape drive required a capital purchase.

Looking back on this, I am not proud of what I did, but I tell you this just so you know I understand your plight. We needed tape drives but had enough tapes for the

---

next six months or so. We got approval to buy the tape drives, but since it was a capital purchase, we knew it would be months before they arrived.

We found a reseller willing to sell us tape drives but put tapes on the invoice. When we got the money for the tape drives, he sold me tapes and put tape drives on the invoice. I now know just how wrong what we did was. But I do know the kinds of predicaments you can be put in for such things.

Instant recovery and automated testing of backups are also possible with HCBAs. They took that lead from the virtualization-centric solutions and made sure to include it in their design. As I mentioned earlier, this is starting to become table stakes for a lot of environments.

It is also the HCBAs that have popularized the idea of the reuse of backup data. You have historical copies of your environment dating back months or years; perhaps you should use them for some other purposes. For example, having all your backup in one place allows you to easily scan those backups for patterns, which can enumerate all kinds of information, like viruses, ransomware attacks, and data usage (e.g., file types and sizes). Like instant recovery and automated backup testing, the idea of the reuse of backup data has grown very popular.

These solutions also get credit for integrating a viable dedupe offering with their platform, versus requiring another solution to make it happen. Although traditional and virtualization-centric backup solutions usually now include dedupe in their solutions, for various reasons, many of their customers prefer to use third-party target dedupe appliances. This is not the case with HCBAs. Their integrated target dedupe scales well enough to meet their customers' needs.

Finally, these solutions offer the ability to copy some backups to object storage in the cloud. This is a good first step toward fully integrating with the cloud infrastructure.

Challenges with HCBAs

Although HCBAs scale up very well (due to their scale-out design), they don't scale down as well. This is because the HCBA solutions currently in this space decided to use target dedupe instead of source dedupe. This is not too big of a deal in the datacenter, where these systems work very well, but it doesn't scale *down* very well. If you have a remote site with a single server, you will need a local appliance to back up to If you plan to get any dedupe from that remote site. The solution from the HCBA vendors is to offer a virtual version of their appliance that you can run as a VM in your local site. The dedupe will be done there, and then any new data will be replicated to your off-premises system. This is nowhere near as flexible or manageable as a source dedupe solution that doesn't require a local appliance at all. Consider what you would do if the local system was a single laptop or desktop, not a virtualization host. Where would you install the virtual appliance?

Another challenge with HCBAs has to do with provisioning. Backups take a certain number of resources, and restores take another chunk. If you will reuse your backup data to do additional work on those backups, such as scanning it for viruses or ransomware, or looking for other trends that might help you, you will need to provision additional computing and/or I/O capacity to make that happen. This means that when such processes aren't running, you have an overprovisioned system.

Like other scale-out, hyper-converged systems (e.g., HCI), another concern with HCBAs is that you can't individually scale storage and compute. Every node comes with a certain amount of compute and storage; every time you buy a node, you get a little bit more of both, some of which you probably don't need. You will never perfectly match your compute and storage resources with an architecture like this, but that is the price you pay for the simplicity that this architecture provides.

Analysis

HCBAs have gone further than any other on-premises architecture in addressing the challenges of a traditional backup and recovery system, including addressing new challenges introduced by virtualization-centric solutions that run their backup servers on Windows. Using a Linux-based architecture addresses this risk and offers a slight cost reduction as well. Designing them is simpler than a modern traditional system (where you must independently design server, disk, and tape resources), and you usually only have to deal with one vendor. (Some customers have connected a tape to the backend of these systems for long-term retention purposes, so they will still experience the challenges of having to work with tape.)

Although these are on-premises backup servers that have an OS and application that must be maintained and upgraded, these solutions do tend to make this as easy as upgrading such things can be. The HCBA vendor typically provides a single image that you use to upgrade both the OS and the application, in a manner similar to the experience of upgrading firmware. So although it is still your responsibility to perform this upgrade, it's nowhere near as complicated as maintaining a typical backup server. These appliances have also been preconfigured with the most useful security settings.

Some of these systems have adopted the use of the cloud for disaster recovery and have added e-discovery capabilities to their system as well. These features address the challenges of needing a separate DR system and a separate e-discovery system in addition to your backup system.

HCBAs are still purchased using a typical large capital purchase order. In that sense, they are very much like a traditional IT system. However, as I already mentioned, overprovisioning just for growth is not required. It is quite easy to scale these systems by buying additional nodes for your existing configuration.

HCBAs tend to support backing up the most popular OSs, applications, and cloud services, so they do not have the breadth of coverage the traditional backup and recovery solutions do. Thus, for many environments, HCBAs offer the most advantages and the fewest disadvantages in the on-premises backup solution category.

Around the same time as HCBAs were being developed, another product category came to the fore: those that would attempt to solve the same challenges by offering backup-as-a-service (BaaS). These are very different products, and are the next category I will cover in this chapter.

Data-Protection-as-a-Service (DPaaS)

Data-protection-as-a-service (DPaaS) solutions are for those who would like to get out of the backup business altogether. Whereas HCBAs offer an easy-to-maintain on-premises backup system, DPaaS does not require the customer to buy, rent, or maintain any backup infrastructure. Many organizations have done this for other parts of the infrastructure, using SaaS versions of CRM, email, file sharing, collaboration, help desk ticketing, and hundreds of other types of solutions. The "SaaSification of IT" seems to be the current trend in computing, and some want to do the same with their backup and DR needs.

What Is Software-as-a-Service?

On one hand, defining SaaS is very easy. It's some kind of software provided only as a service. You use the software's functions without having to worry about how they are provided or provisioned. Distinguishing that from other things that may call themselves SaaS, however, is a bit more challenging. One way to look at it is what you don't need to do if you use a SaaS product.

A SaaS offering delivers an IT solution as a service, without requiring its typical customer to purchase, rent, provision, or manage the infrastructure upon which the service is running. Consider Salesforce Data Center (SFDC), which offers a CRM solution that you access via your web browser. There are servers, software, and storage behind that service, but *you never see them,* because the software is being delivered *as a service.* The same is true of other popular SaaS services, such as Microsoft 365, Google Workspace, GitHub, and Slack. Add all the users you want to these services, and all you need to worry about is paying the bill. The backend will automatically provision whatever it needs to provide the service to you.

Contrast this to Adobe Creative Suite, which some incorrectly call SaaS. It uses subscription pricing. You pay a monthly fee and you can download to your computer every solution Adobe has to offer. You can then install it and run it on your computer.

As of this writing, there is no web version of Photoshop. I'm not sure there ever will be, but I've been wrong before.

I thought about this when I heard the CEO of Oracle say it would be a 100% SaaS company in a few years. This is a company that still sells servers, disk, and tape, and a ton of Oracle licenses for servers. So unless they intend to stop selling all that and start offering Oracle only as a service on their servers or on the cloud, they will not be 100% SaaS. What I think he means to say is that it will go to a 100% subscription pricing model. That makes sense.

Before talking about DPaaS, let's continue examining what typical SaaS solutions have in common. The first thing, which the previous sidebar just discussed, is that you don't have to pay for or manage the infrastructure behind the solution; you just use the service. In addition, your pricing is based on usage, typically on how many users will actually use the solution in question.

Another important SaaS feature is that the company in question continually upgrades the software behind the service, and you do not need to worry about upgrading your Exchange server to get the latest version of Exchange Online—if you're using Microsoft 365. All you need to do is read the release notes of the latest version and familiarize yourself with the new features. (Some new features might require an update of client software used to access the service, such as Microsoft Outlook.) These systems typically offer unlimited scalability, limited only by your credit card, without you having to worry about any backend infrastructure changes that might be required to provide such scalability. If you decide tomorrow to add 100,000 new users to Microsoft 365, all you need is a credit card capable of paying that bill.

If you are purchasing a DPaaS offering, which could be BaaS or DRaaS or both, the experience should be the same as other SaaS solutions. Running your backup server in VMs in your AWS/Azure/GCP cloud account is not DPaaS. It is subscription pricing for your backup software. I like subscription pricing for backup software; it's just not SaaS.

To be considered BaaS/DPaaS/DRaaS, the solution in question should work as the previous paragraph describes other SaaS services. You should not have to buy, rent, or maintain backup servers; the service should just run and do what you need it to do. If your company acquires another company and you want to start backing them up to your DPaaS solution, you shouldn't have to do anything with the backend system to support that. You may have to call your account rep and upgrade your license, but the backend should automatically scale up and down without you having to do anything. The backend software should also repeatedly upgrade to the latest version without you having to do anything to make that happen. Your pricing will most likely be based on the number of users or terabytes you are backing up. Some vendors charge for the frontend terabytes (size of your datacenter), others charge backend terabytes (size of your backup data), others charge both, and others use per-VM pricing and eschew capacity pricing altogether.

As suggested in the previous paragraph, not all DPaaS solutions are built the same or work the same. One big differentiator is storage. Some require you to use their cloud storage, touting predictable security and cost models. They ensure that security best practices are continuously applied to your backups, and build the variable cost of cloud storage into a flat pricing structure. One concern of the all-in-one pricing model is that you cannot shop around for better pricing, short of completely switching DPaaS providers.

Some services do allow you to use your own storage and tout flexibility as their main advantage. It's possible to use your own on-premises storage, but if you are backing up cloud resources to your datacenter, you will get egress charges from your cloud vendor every time you do a backup. If you're backing up a datacenter, this would not be an issue. One concern with using your own cloud storage account would be unpredictable pricing, because you will pay for all storage operations, including all of the following:

Storage
> You are charged each month for the number of gigabytes in object storage.

API requests
> Every time you PUT an object in, GET one out, or LIST what's there, you will be charged.

Data retrieval
> If you decide to use cold storage, you will pay extra (per GB) to retrieve anything.

Data transfer
> Any time you transfer data from object storage to anywhere, you pay a per GB fee. This will happen during restores or when transferring data from object storage to cold storage. The slang term for this is *egress charges*.

Transfer acceleration
> You can ask that some data be pushed to edge locations for faster restores. If so, you pay per GB for that feature.

Data management features
> There are a number of other features you might use, such as inventory and scanning, that also incur charges.

It is quite possible that all of these may be less expensive than using the vendor's cloud storage, but it's also possible it could be much higher. The longer you decide to store your backups, the more important the cost differential between your own cloud storage and the vendor's cloud storage matters.

Using your own storage (or a cloud vendor's storage) with a DPaaS vendor goes against one of the core tenets of SaaS, which is that you're not supposed to have to manage any of the infrastructure behind the solution. It also means you're not reducing your data protection vendors to one. Some consider this a purist attitude, though, and prefer the flexibility and possible cost savings of using their own storage.

Advantages of DPaaS

The biggest advantage of DPaaS will be ease of use. If you look at the previous challenges mentioned in this chapter and the previous chapter, they are almost all about obtaining, purchasing, and maintaining the backend system behind your backup or DR system. Just like Exchange Online drastically simplifies the management of Exchange, DPaaS does the same thing for backup and DR.

Designing the backup system becomes much simpler, because your main design concern will be whether you have enough bandwidth to get the data to and from the backup service provider. The backend design, which is where most people spend most of their time in the design process, is handled for you automatically. Some of that might be being handled by human beings, but it is not your concern. This means you also do not need to maintain the OS or backup server software. You do not have to worry about any of the challenges associated with tape or disk that were mentioned in Chapter 13. You also do not need to manage multiple vendors, because there is only one, assuming you are using its storage.

When you consider the importance of protecting against ransomware, another big advantage of DPaaS is that all backup data is stored outside your datacenter in a completely separate account. If it is DPaaS (and not just backup software running in VMs in your cloud account), the data is stored in the vendor's cloud account, not yours (again, assuming you are using that storage). There should be no electronic path from your production servers to the backup data, so it should not be hackable or corruptible in that manner. The data will also be encrypted in transit and at rest. If you use your storage and the vendor's solution, the security of your backup data will be up to you.

Whether you need a separate system for DR or e-discovery will be based on the individual vendor in question. Simply being a DPaaS solution does not automatically mean the vendor addresses this particular concern. It does mean, however, that the problems associated with tape are completely out of the picture—no tape performance, lost tape, or off-site vaulting issues.

DPaaS solutions also do *not* tend to require large capital purchases. Instead, the money can come out of the opex budget. A typical customer does tend to pay for one or two years of service at a time, just as the customers of SFDC and Microsoft 365 do.

Challenges of DPaaS

Putting your backup needs in someone else's hands does introduce some new challenges. Some of these are the same challenges with any SaaS implementation, but some are particular to data protection.

One concern about DPaaS is the obfuscation of the design; you will never see the backend system or know much about how it is designed. You won't know whether the system is built to scale to your needs automatically, or how securely your data is being stored. The best thing to do to ameliorate this concern is ask a lot of questions and look for certifications.

Ask the provider how far the system is designed to scale. Might you reach thresholds and have to call someone so they can make backend changes? Or will the system automatically scale up to meet your needs? Does the system (and your costs) automatically scale down as well, if you decide to delete a lot of backups? How quickly will the cost reduction be reflected in your bill?

Ask about how your data is protected against site failures and bad actors. Whether they use a public or private cloud configuration, they must still design for failure and protect against hackers. Find out how they did that.

Another big group of questions is around deduplication. A lot of vendors make a lot of claims, but in the end, how many gigabytes you actually have to send and store is what counts. Many dedupe vendors say they have global dedupe, but they don't. Ask them what is compared to what; the answer may surprise you. Some backup services only compare a given client's backups to other backups from that same client. Others only compare backups against those that are sent to a particular appliance. Still others compare all backups to all backups, as long as they are backed up to the same service. Be sure to understand how their dedupe system works and then test. That's really the only way to know.

The amount of dedupe you actually get is especially important in DPaaS, because it will determine the amount of bandwidth you will need and how big your bill will get each month. Seemingly small differences can make a huge difference. The difference between a 90% reduction and a 95% reduction in backups is a doubling (or cutting in half) of the amount of bandwidth you need and the amount of data you will pay to store in the cloud.

The next challenge has to do with the first full backup. Do the math. If you have 500 TB of data and you are allowed to use all of your organization's 10 GB connection from 8 p.m. to 8 a.m., it will take you at least two weeks to back that data up across that 10 GB connection. You need a faster way to send that first backup, referred to as the *seed*, to the cloud. (This is especially true if you are currently unprotected.)

The usual way this is done is *sneakernet*. The provider ships an appliance to the customer in question. This can be anything from a portable disk drive to a physically hardened server designed for such a purpose. The customer sends the first backup to one or more such appliances and ships the appliances back to the service provider, who then uploads the backups into your account. You can easily seed multiple petabytes to the cloud in just a few days by using this method.

You also need to make sure you have enough bandwidth for each day's backups. Like with target deduplication appliances, you really won't know how much data your service will need to transfer to the cloud every day until you actually try it. You can use ballpark figures to know whether you're close, but in the end, the only way to know is actually to test it. Only then will you really know whether you have enough bandwidth for your daily change rate.

Assuming you have seeded the first big backup to the cloud, and your daily change rate is small enough that it fits within your available bandwidth and backup window, the remaining challenge you need to solve with DPaaS is how you are going to restore that data if you have to do a large restore. A direct-from-cloud restore might be fast enough for many scenarios, but at some point you may have a system that is too big to restore directly from the cloud in a reasonable amount of time. There are three ways service providers can solve this problem: a local cache, recovery to the cloud, and reverse seeding.

Some DPaaS providers offer the ability to back up to a local caching appliance that replicates its backups to the service. If this is done well, it should be functionally invisible to the customer. The customer chooses the backups that need a local cache, and sends those backups to this cache appliance, which may be a physical appliance or a virtual machine. Everything else should be completely managed by the backup service, because the backups sent to the local cache should automatically be sent to the cloud. One question to ask is whether the cache would cause backups or restores to fail if it is offline. (If it is truly a cache, the answer should be no.) Obviously, if it is offline and restores have to come from the cloud, they will take longer. However, if the caching appliance is online and has all recent backups, restores from those backups should come directly from the cache and be much faster as a result.

The next option, recovery to the cloud, was covered in more detail in Chapter 11. The gist of it is this: If backups are stored in the cloud (private or public), it should be quicker to restore one or more virtual machines in the cloud. It should also be possible to pre-restore certain VMs so that they can be restored instantly in the cloud. I feel this is the best of the three choices for large restores. If done right, the customer should be able to restore any mission-critical systems in the cloud, and restores of those systems may even be faster than restoring from a traditional data protection system that would happen to be on premises. The best part is that you do not pay for this infrastructure until you test it or declare a disaster. This is why many people think DR is the perfect workload for the public cloud.

Finally, there is reverse seeding, the worst of the three options for reasons I will explain in a moment. Having said that, it is the best option if you didn't plan ahead with either of the other two options. See whether your service provider supports the concept of reverse seeding, which is essentially the exact opposite of the seeding process discussed earlier. The service provider would restore the data in question to an appliance that is collocated with your backups, which should facilitate a much faster initial restore. The vendor would then ship the device to you, after which you could initiate a local restore very much like what you would have done if you prepared in advance with a local cache. This is not the best choice because it requires two restores and the physical shipment of the device in question. This means that your RTA will be measured in multiple days, whereas the RTA of the other two choices can range from minutes to hours. This means that, although you should check whether your service provider supports this concept, you should do everything you can to make sure that you never have to use it. It will be a very unhappy week for you if you do.

Analysis

DPaaS solutions are following the current trend in IT, which is to create SaaS versions of as many IT services as possible, especially infrastructure services. Very few people still maintain their own Exchange server; they use Microsoft 365 or Google Workspace. You get all the benefits of Exchange with no requirement to provision, buy, or manage the backend systems that make it work. Data protection, like email, is a crucial service that every organization must have, but it doesn't directly contribute to the bottom line. Even though everyone would agree that both services are important, the only time they come up in a budget discussion is when the question of cost arises.

Data protection is well suited as a service offering, because it's a task that is a lot more complex than many people think, and no one wants to be in charge of it. Even fewer people want to pay the salary of the person whose sole responsibility is the design and maintenance of the backup system. Therefore, outsourcing this critical task to a service provider that will make sure the backup system is always running makes perfect sense.

Besides all the typical advantages that come with SaaS, one of DPaaS's biggest advantages is the separation of your production and backup data. Having your backup data stored in a provider's account (i.e., not your datacenter or cloud account) protects it from some kind of rolling ransomware attack.

The one challenge that any potential DPaaS customer should be concerned with is how realistic it is for them to put their backup infrastructure on the other side of a WAN connection. The laws of physics dictate that this is not possible for every environment. If DPaaS sounds interesting, having a quick sizing conversation with a provider would let you know whether a longer conversation is worth having. There is no sense in wasting time if the math will never add up. Just as many environments turn just their virtualization backups over to a virtualization-centric vendor or a hyper-converged backup vendor, what some people turn over to DPaaS are backups that are harder than typical on-premises approaches but much easier with DPaaS. A few examples would be backups of remote sites, laptops, SaaS, and IaaS/PaaS.

If it looks like you have enough bandwidth for daily backups, you will also need to address the challenges of the first backup and any large restores. Different providers have different answers to these questions, and not all of these answers are the same.

In short, DPaaS will appeal most to those looking to get out of the backup business and those who are looking to protect their backups from ransomware attacks. As long as the customer's bandwidth is sufficient, and the provider has answers for the first backup and big-restore questions, DPaaS is another good choice for their data protection needs.

The next section discusses a data protection solution that is even more hands-off than a DPaaS offering: a fully managed data protection service provider that actually runs everything on your behalf. Let's take a look at them next.

Fully Managed Service Providers

The final category of commercial data protection solutions that I will cover in this chapter is *fully managed service providers* (MSPs). An MSP—specifically a fully managed MSP—is the next level of service-based data protection. I am aware that some organizations use the MSP term just to mean a reseller of other companies' services, and that it doesn't actually manage them for you. I just want to make it clear that in this section, I am referring only to those solutions when the company is actually managing the data protection system on your behalf. A comparison to DPaaS and other choices in the chapter might help you understand what I mean.

If you buy a traditional, virtualization-centric, target dedupe, or HCBA-based data protection solution, you are the one responsible for designing, buying, and managing the hardware, software, and operation of the backup system once it's in place. If you buy a DPaaS solution, the provider is responsible for the hardware and software, and you are responsible to configure it and monitor its operations. With a fully managed MSP, you tell it what you want the data protection system to do, and then the MSP configures and runs it to your specifications.

An MSP can have all sorts of software in the background. In fact, a single MSP might actually use multiple products to accomplish your goals. It might be using a DR-centric product (covered in Chapter 11) for your mission-critical systems, a DPaaS solution to back up your SaaS and cloud data, and one of the on-premises architectures to back up your datacenter. It packages all of that in one solution, charges you based on service levels and number of resources protected, and then runs all this software on your behalf.

Advantages of Using an MSP

The biggest advantage of using an MSP is that you potentially get to use best-of-breed solutions for each part of your environment, without having to learn, configure, and manage multiple products or services. You don't even need to learn one solution! You just tell your MSP what you want your solution to do, and it configures it to do just that. Easy peasy.

One universal truth that has existed since I joined the data protection industry in 1993 is that no one wants to be the backup person. The biggest advantage of using an MSP is that it completely removes the day-to-day operations from your organization. Please note that I did not say it removes the responsibility; that is still yours.

This is essentially a complete outsourcing of data protection to a third party. You don't have to worry about the design, its capacity, whether it is running or not running, or whether someone is closely watching it. You are literally paying someone to do all those things, and because it is a service provider, the people employed by the organization should be well-trained people who see backups as their main function. At an MSP, backups are not a collateral duty; they are the only duty.

Challenges of Using an MSP

Using a data protection MSP usually means that you are backing up over a wide-area network (WAN) connection, although that is not necessarily the case. But if you are backing up over a WAN connection, you have all the same challenges that DPaaS customers have: having enough bandwidth for each day's backups, achieving the first full backup, and achieving any large restores. I won't go into these challenges in any more detail, since I covered them in the previous section.

MSP customers actually have a bigger challenge than DPaaS customers regarding design obfuscation. If the MSP is putting together multiple products as a single product, the customer may know even less about the underlying architecture of the various solutions that may be providing their data protection service. In addition, the MSP may actually swap out portions of the infrastructure to reduce its costs or increase service levels. This is all part of trusting the MSP to do the right thing—while monitoring what it's doing to verify that.

This brings me back to one unique aspect of using an MSP for data protection. Some customers may enjoy the remote detachment that an MSP provides and begin to forget about backup. Remember that although you may outsource the operations, you cannot outsource the responsibility. If the MSP fails to do its job and subsequently is unable to restore your datacenter in a time of crisis, your MSP may lose its contract, but you will probably lose your job. This is especially true if it can be shown that you just let the MSP do whatever it wanted without monitoring and verifying the contracted service. Please do not get complacent if you use an MSP; it is just as full of human beings as your organization is.

Analysis

Using an MSP is the ultimate hands-off experience and is designed for organizations that really have no interest in even running a DPaaS-based backup system. If someone wants to run their backups, but doesn't want to manage the backend, they should pick a DPaaS solution. If they want their backups on premises, then they would pick a traditional, virtualization-centric, or HCBA solution.

If they want to have literally nothing to do with their backup system other than paying a bill, an MSP is the choice for them. The thing I like best about them is that you have a group of people that sees backups as their job. Very few organizations are big enough to pay someone to be responsible just for backups; it's always a collateral duty. Using an MSP gives smaller organizations their own admin who is dedicated to backups.

Notice I said "dedicated to backups," not "dedicated to your backups." One concern some have with the fully managed MSP model is wondering whether the person responsible for your backups will pay enough attention to your account, especially if you're a small one. This is among the reasons you must monitor what it is doing.

Now that we've looked at all the newer products and services to come on the market in the past 10 or so years, let's look at how the traditional data protection vendors responded to all these new products. We'll also see how some of these newer products respond to other products gaining market share, and to the popularity of the cloud in the market. Let's see how these products adapted to the changing data protection market.

Adapting to the Market

Many of the vendors providing the commercial solutions covered in this book do not like being pigeonholed and have done their best to adapt to the times. This section is therefore an explanation of how various solutions have evolved to remain current with the needs of the market.

Traditional Backup Appliances

The popularity of various backup appliances (especially HCBAs) has led traditional and virtualization-centric backup vendors to offer appliance versions of their solutions. Sometimes offered directly, and other times through partners, these appliances are aimed mostly at those more concerned about simplicity of design and ease of maintenance than they are about long-term scalability.

These appliances offer an easier way to buy a small to medium-sized backup solution all from one company. The systems are usually disk-based and only include tape if the customer adds it on themselves. It is very common to buy one of these systems to handle your day-to-day operational backup and recovery needs and then use a previously purchased tape library to manage the copies that would ultimately be taken off-site. Some customers also purchase multiple systems and use the backup software to replicate backups between them.

These backup systems reduce the number of vendors that a customer has to interface with, and remove the challenges of tape from most customers. Other than that, they have the same challenges as the previously discussed traditional and virtualization-centric backup solutions.

Subscription Pricing

Many customers who want to have an on-premises data protection solution are still concerned about the challenges of having to make a large capital purchase to get one. Many of the on-premises vendors have responded to this market demand by offering subscription pricing of their solutions. This may allow some customers to purchase at least the software part of their data protection system as an operating expenditure.

Subscription pricing for software is a win-win for everyone. It provides predictable costs for the customer and a predictable revenue stream for the vendor. It also allows you access to the latest version of the software offered by the vendor, although you do still have to upgrade your backup server to get it. (See "Maintain Backup Software" on page 293 for more information on that topic.)

The only thing to watch for is when vendors offering subscription pricing refer to it as SaaS. Although it is a common misconception that they are the same, SaaS requires completely removing both the hardware and software components and replacing them with a service. Subscription pricing simply changes the way you pay for your data protection software. See the sidebar "What Is Software-as-a-Service?" on page 325, earlier in this chapter.

Responding to the Cloud

Backup vendors have responded to the demand for cloud support in a variety of ways, including copying backups to the cloud, on-premises software in your VM, and on-premises (SaaS). The following is a brief summary of those options.

Copy backups to cloud storage

The first thing on-premises software vendors typically do is offer support for copying backups to the cloud, often called *cloud out*, *cloud copy*, or *cloud export*. The backup solution in question copies some or all of your backups to an object-storage service (e.g., S3) for various reasons. One reason is to comply with the 3-2-1 rule, where the cloud copy takes the place of tape and an off-site vaulting vendor. One question to ask is whether the vendor in question requires you to import the S3 copy back into its storage system (usually standard file/block storage) before it can be used for restores. If so, this option offers an inexpensive place to store backups off-site or to hold longer-term retention of some backups, but it does not support direct backup and restore.

On-premises software in the cloud

The next thing vendors are doing to be more cloud friendly is certify their software in the cloud. They usually specify a base configuration of the types of VMs and storage needed to run their software in a particular cloud provider. This is referred to in cloud circles as the lift-and-shift approach of moving an application to the cloud. You are essentially lifting a VM from your datacenter and shifting into the cloud. You are not refactoring your app for the cloud, which usually results in significant cost challenges in the cloud.

The advantage to this approach is the ability to continue using the backup software you are familiar with, without having to maintain actual backup hardware. For some, this will be enough of an advantage to overcome the challenges of the approach. One thing to understand is that moving your backup servers into VMs in the cloud doesn't address most of the challenges previously mentioned for each solution category, except that you will most likely be getting rid of tape and you will not have to worry about the backup hardware. But you will still have to manage the OS and application, provision the servers and storage, and manage vendors. And the lack of refactoring your backup app for the cloud can cost your organization a lot of money.

One big reason the lift-and-shift approach is more expensive is that the backup server(s) will be running 24×7. Paying for VMs to run 24×7 (when they're only used for a few hours per day) can really increase your bill. A backup system designed for the cloud would only use resources when backups are running, which would significantly reduce the compute side of the bill. If you have already used this approach to other traditional workloads in your datacenter, you have seen the cost of VMs first-hand.

Another cost challenge with moving into the cloud backup apps that were designed for the datacenter is the type of storage most backup software products use. Most backup software solutions still require the main backup repository to be on file-based storage or tape, meaning you can't usually use object storage as the main repository of your data. At best, such solutions usually see object storage as the place to store older backups. If you can find a solution that backs up and restores directly to and from object storage, it will reduce your storage costs by at least half. Unfortunately, most backup solutions on the market today do not do this.

An additional cost concern with backups, though, is restores. Any restores will be accompanied by a large egress charge. Finally, be sure to choose a backup solution that uses source dedupe, because you will want to deduplicate the data before sending it to the cloud. This will significantly reduce your bandwidth costs.

These cost issues are why the lift-and-shift approach is seen in cloud circles as a temporary solution—even outside the data protection world. Any long-term move to the cloud should be accompanied by refactoring that redesigns the app to take into account how the cloud works. A properly refactored app will give you all the benefits of the original app (and possibly more), while also reducing your costs. Unfortunately, none of the backup vendors using the lift-and-shift approach appear to be doing such refactoring.

Takeaways

The data protection space is alive and well. In the past 10 or so years, there have been four new product categories and dozens of new backup products in these categories. The world of disk-based and cloud-based backup is here, and many organizations have moved completely away from tape. At the very least, they've moved tape to archive only.

As I'll cover in the next chapter, this really comes down to what you prefer. Windows-centric, virtualization-centric shops will like the virtualization-centric products. People who prefer non-Windows backup systems, but still want an on-premises system, will prefer the scale-out approach of the HCBAs. Finally, some customers will want to get rid of the problem entirely by moving to a DPaaS or MSP service.

Some new companies and existing products from old companies are trying to jump on various bandwagons. Those who like the HCBA approach but don't want to get rid of the product they already know will be interested in the new backup appliances from the old guard. A lot of people will find subscription-based pricing an easier way to pay for their backup products, and a lot of vendors will call subscription pricing SaaS, though it's not. This is the way of things.

Finally, everything seems to be moving in the direction of the cloud. In a few years, almost everyone will be using the cloud in some way from a data protection perspective. And once again, in the cloud, you will continue to have options. Do you want to buy and run the software you already know, or do you want to move to a service that manages it for you?

If you've read these last three chapters and find yourself wanting to make a change, you came to the right place. The next and final chapter in this book will talk about either upgrading or replacing your data protection system. Let's take a look.

CHAPTER 16

Replacing or Upgrading Your Backup System

Congratulations! You've made it to the final chapter of what my daughter's friend calls the most boring book on the planet. (You and I know better, though, don't we!) We have covered a lot in around 350 pages, and a lot of it is a prerequisite to understanding the recommendations in this chapter.

It's very possible that you bought this book because you were convinced that your backup system needed replacing, so you jumped to this chapter to have me tell you which one to pick. Not so fast. If you did indeed skip right here, you really need to go back and understand everything else I put in this book before even considering upgrading or replacing your backup system. But just as a reminder, here's a quick summary of some of the important things you should know after having read this book:

Difference between backup and archive (Chapter 3)
> The idea that backup and archive are not even close to being the same is extremely important in designing your backup and archive systems. This is one of the top three things I'm constantly telling people, and it's crucial.

The 3-2-1 rule (Chapter 3)
> Three versions on two media, one of which is somewhere else. If your backup system doesn't conform to that, something has gone horribly wrong.

What to back up (Chapter 8)
> I never get any arguments about datacenters and IaaS vendors. But if you're not sure why (or if) you should back up your SaaS data, go read this important chapter.

Ways to back up (Chapter 9)

There are so many ways that backup products work. This isn't a list of products; it's a list of the various things those products can do. You need to understand all those options before embarking on this journey.

Disaster recovery (Chapter 11)

There are so many good DR choices now. Most of them are based on using the cloud in some way, but the combination of modern backup solutions and the cloud is a winning combo, to be sure.

Tape is not evil (Chapter 12)

Tape is not slow. Tape is not unreliable. It is faster, more reliable, and cheaper than disk. It's just a pain to work with in a backup system. Learn why that is the case before you throw the baby out with the bathwater.

Disk is not perfect (Chapter 12)

Disk helped make backups a lot easier, but it also introduced some new problems. You need to be aware of the air gap problem so you can decide how to address it.

Data protection challenges (Chapter 13)

I built a career out of repairing and upgrading backup systems. If there's one thing I know, it's the problems in this space. I spell them out, many of which I bet you haven't thought of before. You have to know the challenges before you can evaluate the solutions.

Traditional data protection solutions (Chapter 14)

Do you have one of these? Is it perhaps augmented with a target deduplication system? Does it need to be replaced? Understand the value these products bring to the table.

Modern data protection solutions (Chapter 15)

It's the title of the book, right? A lot of new products have come on the scene in the past 10 years or so. Some of them are amazing, but each of them comes with its own challenges. Know what those are before attempting to jump ship with whatever you're using now.

Now that you've gained all that knowledge, it's time to put it to work. You're thinking about either upgrading or replacing your backup system. Now what? Let's dive right into the deep end, shall we?

Which Solution Is Best for You?

There is no one perfect backup product. There are products that are a better fit to how you function, and products that aren't fit for your organization. In addition, what's right for you today might not be right for you tomorrow. You should constantly evaluate how you do data protection to make sure you're doing the best you can do with what is available.

 I did then what I knew how to do. Now that I know better, I do better.

—Maya Angelou

Each of the various product categories covered in Chapters 14 and 15 is right for someone. Of course, within those categories will be products that are better than others. I'll have to leave that part up to you, since I can't cover that level of detail in a book of this size.

I think answering the question about which product is best for you starts with understanding your unique requirements for data protection, which you can really only know if you followed the process outlined in the first part of Chapter 2. Make sure you know your organization's purpose, as well as the requirements (e.g., RTO and RPO) that your data protection system should meet before you attempt to design anything.

The next thing to understand is the *unique selling proposition (USP)* of each solution. This is a business term that refers to the unique reason you might want to purchase a particular solution. (In my following explanations, I'm also adding reasons they might *not* be good for particular environments.)

As different as these various categories are, and as different as the various solutions are within those categories, it's somewhat daunting to write about it at this level, but I thought it would be helpful. I'll include the main challenge of that category as well.

Traditional backup

These products are best for datacenters that have a mix of legacy workloads like traditional Unix, legacy database solutions, virtualization, and more modern workloads like IaaS and Kubernetes, and are looking for a one-size-fits-all backup solution. Traditional backup solutions are really the only solution that can back up most everything that has been developed in the past 30 years. Other categories might be better at certain workloads, or offer a lower TCO, but they also probably won't cover all your products in one solution. If you are new to such products, consider an appliance version to reduce your vendor complexity.

Target dedupe

Target deduplication arrays appeal to those who have an existing backup solution and are having difficulty backing up to tape or are unsatisfied with the deduplication system integrated into their backup solution. They provide the ability to have on-site and off-site backups via replication, without having to make significant changes to your existing backup infrastructure. Upgrading your existing backup system with a target dedupe appliance is less expensive than replacing it. It's also true that a new backup solution in a greenfield (i.e., new) environment that uses one vendor's backup solution and another vendor's dedupe solution is probably more expensive than using one of the solutions that does both.

Virtualization-centric

Virtualization products are perfect for Windows-centric or Windows-only environments because they have all chosen to design around Windows and disk. If you are a Windows-centric shop and are therefore familiar with how to ameliorate the security concerns of a Windows-centric architecture, this solution will appeal to you. Just make sure to configure your backups in such a way that the backup disks are not visible to the operating system of the backup server, to protect your backups from a ransomware attack.

HCBAs

If you are looking for an on-premises solution that addresses most of the data protection challenges mentioned in Chapter 13, HCBAs best meet that goal. Their scale-out appliance architecture makes them easier to design, maintain, and scale than other on-premises solutions, and some have support for legacy workloads as well. When designing such systems, remember that the capacity does not need to last three to five years like typical backup systems; you can add capacity over time. That will help minimize your initial capital purchase.

DPaaS

DPaaS solutions appeal to those who no longer wish to design, maintain, and scale an on-premises data protection solution. If you're looking to do with your backup system what you've already done with your email and CRM systems, where you get the benefits without any of the maintenance, take a look at DPaaS. Design obfuscation is the biggest concern here, because it can create an inconsistent experience and a bill that occasionally has large jumps in it. Make sure to learn as much about the solution before purchasing it, so you will know what to expect.

Fully managed MSP

Fully managed MSPs take the DPaaS model a step further and operate the service on your behalf. If the idea of a completely hands-off data protection system appeals to you, MSPs are the way to go. One concern here would be what happens if the vendor chooses to change the solution underneath your service, and how that is addressed in the service agreement. Make sure you understand the details of that, as well as how you will be charged over time for its services. You don't want any surprises.

Traditional appliances

If you like your current backup solution, but do not like the work required to design and configure the physical solution, there are independent software vendors (ISVs) and value-added resellers (VARs) that will create a package that allows you to stay with your favorite backup solution but make it a little easier to design and maintain. They solve the multivendor problem by giving you a single throat to choke; however, unlike the scale-out architecture of the HCBA systems, these appliances offer no greater scalability than the solution upon which they are based.

On-premises in the cloud

If you have received a cloud-first mandate, but do not want to switch data protection solutions to a cloud native solution, your only choice is to lift and shift your current backup solution into the cloud by migrating your on-premises backup servers into VMs in the cloud. The biggest concern with this idea is that your cloud bill is likely to be very high because these designs use VMs that run 24×7 and require the use of a lot of block storage, both of which are very expensive in the cloud.

No matter which type of solution you decide to pick, it's important to understand where your responsibilities end and the vendor's responsibilities start. (A perfect example of this is the common misunderstanding that SaaS products back up your data.) Let's take a look at what your responsibilities are in a data protection system.

Your Responsibilities

Another thing to think about when considering data protection solutions is which party is responsible for which tasks. There are a variety of tasks in the life cycle of a data protection system. You should know who is responsible for all these tasks. If you do not, these are questions you should be asking any current or prospective vendor.

Hardware

Someone must ultimately be responsible for designing the hardware (physical or virtual) that will comprise the data protection system. Who will be paying for that hardware, which includes either a large capital purchase of on-premises hardware, or negotiating a contract with a cloud vendor for virtual resources? Who will be responsible for upgrading the operating system on this hardware and ensuring that it is securely implemented? Whose job will it be to connect any storage systems, including regular disk arrays, target deduplication systems, or tape libraries? Finally, whose responsibility will it be to ensure that all hardware components are performing optimally?

Software

I'm including the operating system in the preceding hardware list entry, and focusing this section on the backup software itself. Someone must configure the backup software to recognize all of the virtual or physical hardware the backup system has been given. This task will also include maintaining the backup software system itself to the most recent version and ensuring that it is configured in a way that is secure as well. A prime example of this would be when disk-based backup systems started recommending (for security reasons) that their customers configure the backups so that the backup directory is not visible to the operating system. Whose job will it be to make those infrastructure changes?

Configuration

Once the backup hardware is physically installed and/or provisioned, and the backup system has been configured so that it understands what all its resources are, someone needs to configure the actual operations of the backup system. This includes installing any required agents on the backup sources, connecting the backup system to those sources, and creating backup jobs and schedules. This is a major job in the beginning of the implementation of a big backup system, and it is an ongoing job as additional backup sources are added to an organization's environment.

Monitoring

Someone needs to watch the backup system and make sure that it is actually doing what it is supposed to be doing. This can be accomplished in a number of ways, including connecting your backup system with your organization's operations management tool. On the low end, this might involve someone who looks at the backup interface once a day to ensure that last night's backups ran correctly. On the high end, it might involve automatically creating trouble tickets when backups fail. The question is, whose responsibility is it to monitor the backup system?

Operation

Even in the most automated backup system, there are ongoing tasks that must be done. In a tape environment, this might involve swapping tapes in and out and giving them to an off-site vaulting vendor. In an all-disk system, this might involve deleting old backups to make space or adding additional space as required. This task is something of a bridge between configuration and monitoring. If someone who is monitoring the backup system sees that something needs to be done, it is the operations person who will actually perform that task.

In almost all the data protection solutions mentioned in Chapters 14 and 15, someone in your IT department is responsible for all these tasks. Whether we are talking traditional, target dedupe, virtualization-centric, HCBAs, traditional appliances, or on-premises in the cloud solutions, your organization is responsible for accomplishing all those tasks.

With DPaaS, the hardware and software tasks are no longer your responsibility. Any backup infrastructure required to perform your backups is already designed and will simply appear when backups need to occur. No system management or storage management tasks are required of you. You are responsible, however, for configuring, operating, and monitoring the backup system. If you want to outsource even those tasks, that is where an MSP can step in.

However, no matter which organization is responsible for each task, one thing is always yours. The ultimate responsibility for data protection still rests on your shoulders. If the backup system fails, your organization is the one that will suffer and, therefore, possibly you or someone else might end up losing a job as a result. You can outsource design, maintenance, operations, and monitoring. You can never outsource responsibility. This is especially important to understand if you are using the MSP model, because it can engender complacency.

Now that you are aware of who does what in your backup system (or prospective one), it's time to take stock before you do anything else. You're most likely about to spend a lot of money. Let's take a moment to think about this before doing so.

Before You Do Anything

So many people jump immediately to purchasing new hardware, software, or services when things are not going right. I can think of so many times when this was the case. I have swapped out (and in) many of the major backup solutions that are available today. Although there were indeed (and still are) a few truly bad apples in the backup software universe, usually I was swapping in and out the same solutions! Before you do anything (translation: spend money) you really need to take a moment to take stock of what you're trying to accomplish and what you already have to accomplish that with.

This Is Your Backup System

Every vendor has something it wants to sell you. But you need to remember that in the end, it is your data and not the vendor's. It also may have the greatest backup system in the world, but it might not be great for you. Your requirements and your unique ways of doing things should drive which backup system is best for you.

That's one reason (among others) you won't see me saying in this book, "You should buy product X," or even, "Product category Y is the best way to go." Any statements I make like that will always be put in the context of your requirements and wants. For example, if you really want an on-premises backup system, then DPaaS is not for you.

If you're tired of maintaining a backup system and want someone else to do it, then DPaaS or MSPs are the only ways to do that. It's about your environment and what it needs. Let's take a look at some of the things that will drive your design, as well as some tasks you should do along the way.

Understand your requirements

I've already said that the way you configure your data protection systems should be driven by what your organization actually needs. Configuring your backup window, frequency, and retention should be determined by your organization's RTO, RPO, and legal retention requirements. Designing or configuring your backup system without a true understanding of the organization's actual needs is a waste of time.

For example, suppose your main frustration with the backup system is that backups fail every night. Therefore, you know that you could never meet an RPO of 24 hours. This offends you as a backup individual (as it would me), and you set out to fix this by replacing your backup system. You spend hundreds of thousands of dollars to replace your backup system so that you can meet an RPO of, say, 12 hours. Then you happen to run into an influential individual who tells you that your organization only creates new data once a week, so an RPO of one week is perfectly sufficient. That means you just wasted hundreds of thousands of dollars to meet a requirement you did not have. (This is not out of the question. I've had customers give me RTOs and RPOs measured in weeks before.)

Chapter 2 is dedicated to the concept of getting requirements out of the organization, properly documenting them, and turning them into a design. Take a look at that chapter for more information on this topic.

Understand what you already have

Someone at your organization needs to be an SME on your data protection solution(s). They should go to training, read all the documentation, and be your go-to person for all things data protection. This person will know how the backup system is designed and how it is supposed to perform, as well as what you need to do to get it to do that.

If you do not have an in-house SME, this is probably the first money you should spend. Pay for some professional services from the vendor(s) you are using to tell you how to configure your backup system properly for optimum performance and minimal data loss. In this initial step, try to avoid SME upselling you to a more expensive version of the solution to make it accomplish your task. That is not where you are in this process yet. You're just trying to understand what you have, how it works, and whether things have been optimally designed.

Understand what you don't like about your solution

This is usually the easy part for most organizations. Everybody knows what they don't like about the backup system. They remember the restores that failed. (I know I remember every failed restore I was responsible for!) They know about how the backups take too long or have too much of an impact on the performance of the systems they are backing up.

Did I Do That?

I think back to a SaaS vendor whose backup system I reconfigured. It had a database with an external object-storage system. The database held the actual customer data, and the object-storage system held scanned images related to the customer data. Because the two were so intertwined, you couldn't back up the database without backing up the ObjectStore at the same time; otherwise, you would get referential integrity issues between the two backups. The solution to this dilemma was to perform cold backups of the database, which of course shut down the SaaS solution using the database. Therefore, it was decided that this would only happen once every two weeks.

The other important thing to understand about this customer was that they got 90% of their business for the year within roughly a five-day time period. One day, the backup operations person was following his manual and shut down the database in the middle of the day—during the five-day period when they got the bulk of that year's business. This was national news, and the stock price of the organization lost 50% of its value the next day.

I remember my first meeting with this customer and how serious they were when they told me the story. They gave me the following direction, "We don't care how you do it; we just cannot have the backup requiring a shutdown of our primary application." Like I said, people have no problem telling you what's wrong with the backup system.

Consider TCO, Not Just Acquisition Cost

The common mistake made in any IT system is focusing only on the acquisition cost and not on the TCO. Backup systems are no exception to that challenge. You buy it once, but you use it for years. You basically have three choices when it comes to addressing challenges with your backup system: tweak the current system, upgrade it in some way, or replace it. Each of these has different types of TCO elements to consider.

Cost of tweaking the current system

The first challenge with tweaking the current system is that you will need someone to be an expert in how it works. The biggest difficulty with that is that typically no one wants to be the backup admin, which means that no one develops a level of proficiency in how the system works, making tweaking very difficult without the use of professional services. Once you do have someone who understands how the backup system works and how it is configured, the process of actually tweaking the backup system for better performance is a difficult one and is often likened to changing a tire on a vehicle that cannot pull off to the side of the road. It can be done, but you will probably need professional services and a significant amount of time and patience. When looking at tweaking the new system, the most common TCO aspect that most environments forget is the cost of all the time you spend constantly tweaking and maintaining the current system. These efforts may be worth it and pay for themselves, but just make sure to include them in your TCO calculations.

Cost of upgrading or enhancing the new system

The more common approach for problematic backup environments is to consider upgrading a portion of the system. The obvious step would be to upgrade your backup software to the most recent version and put it on more recent backup hardware, which could be new servers, new disk, or newer tape drives. This is another perfectly valid approach if done carefully. Make sure that you know which part of your backup system is the culprit. I can't tell you the number of times the customers told me that they knew that all they needed was more tape drives or faster tape drives, when they definitely needed neither.

So once again, choosing this path should probably involve professional services. It's probably best that the professional services come from either an independent source or from the backup software organization that isn't trying to sell you a new piece of hardware. The TCO elements that are often forgotten here are the long-term maintenance costs of the new system that you end up purchasing, especially if it is an additional type of hardware. For example, if you are currently a tape-only system and you're adding a deduplication system to the mix, the environment will get more complicated and therefore require more configuration, operation, and monitoring. Also be sure to include the ongoing maintenance costs of the actual system itself in your TCO calculations.

Cost of a new on-premises system

Very few environments are what we call greenfield environments, in which an entirely new datacenter meets an entirely new backup system. If you are purchasing a new on-premises data protection system, you should be comparing the TCO of doing that to the TCO of keeping what you have and enhancing it. In addition to the obvious large capital purchase of all this new hardware and/or software, remember to include in the calculations the costs of training someone on an entirely new backup system. If you are only replacing one portion of your backups, you will also be adding to the complexity of managing your backup system because your system administrators will need to understand and maintain both systems, which also adds to your TCO.

Cost of an on-premises system in the cloud

One trend happening over the past few years is for people to buy on-premises backup software, but run it in VMs in the cloud. The biggest TCO surprise that many people have with this configuration is that the cloud cost can be quite significant. Your backup server or VMs will run 24×7, and most backup solutions will require the primary copy of your backups to be on block storage. If you can configure the backup system in a way that minimizes the number of cloud resources it uses, it might help with the TCO. One really important thing to keep in mind is that if you are running the backup software in VMs in your cloud account, you will experience egress charges when you restore any of your data.

Cost of a SaaS or MSP system

Most SaaS or MSP solutions are not purchased with big capital purchases like the other backup systems and are instead purchased via opex dollars. Most such offerings have relatively predictable cost models and allow you to pay only for what you use, which is very different from purchasing a physical backup system in advance and using it over time. A few TCO elements are often overlooked, starting with the cost of bandwidth. You may be able to get by with your existing bandwidth if it is sufficient for the job, but if you're required to upgrade your bandwidth for your backup system, you should include its cost in your TCO model. Finally, since all such solutions are not created equal, not all of them have predictable pricing models. Try to get your vendor to explain and commit to just how your actual costs will increase over time.

Now that all the prerequisites are out of the way, it's time to consider actually purchasing something new. The final section of this book will help you with that. Let's look at the process of picking a new data protection solution.

Picking a Solution

You decided either to buy a new backup system or replace at least one portion of your backup system with an entirely new system. What should that process look like? In addition to following the procedure laid out in Chapter 2, the following is a high-level description of things you should consider as you purchase a new data protection system. Remember that you should identify your requirements and communicate what you believe them to be, back to those who gave them to you. Get sign-off on those requirements and then design a proposed solution based on the following advice.

Find Any Showstoppers

Purchasing a backup system can be a complicated process, and you will likely be presented with many options from many organizations. I want to mention the idea of identifying any *showstoppers:* the features of a backup solution you are unwilling to live without. I remember helping a big company select a storage solution whose showstopper was that the storage solution had to offer 90 days of user-browsable snapshots. That one requirement eliminated most storage solutions that were available at the time. Most storage arrays at the time used copy-on-write snapshots that simply did not allow you to store that many days of snapshots without significant performance degradation. It was a showstopper for this organization that reduced the number of vendors it needed to consider from a dozen down to three or four.

Identify your showstoppers. They may actually be in addition to the organizational requirements. For example, you might specify that a system must be manageable via a web page from any location without requiring a local management agent. You want to log in to a website, authenticate yourself, and begin managing the backup system. Again, such a requirement will narrow down the number of solutions that you will have to consider if you say that this requirement is a showstopper. (For the record, this would be a showstopper for me. I see no reason for me to need a local piece of software to manage my backup server.)

You should also identify a number of nice-to-have features. You might not use these to eliminate a solution, but you could rate solutions based on the number of nice-to-haves they offer. Consider two solutions that are equal in every other way and meet all your organizational requirements as well as any showstopper requirements you have, but one of them offers 10 of your nice-to-have features, whereas the other one offers only one. If it were me, I'd choose the former.

Making your solution selection about requirements, whether organizational requirements or usability requirements, helps make the process much more logical and professional. Without such a process, you often end up picking the one with the smoother-talking salesperson. A purchase of this magnitude should be made by Spock, not Kirk[1].

Prioritize Ease of Use

I cannot overemphasize the importance of ease of use. Try the solution without any documentation and see how easily you can figure out what to do. A UI is like a joke; if you have to explain it, it's not very good. Does it require significant training and ramp-up time to understand and properly configure? If all the solutions are that way, that's one thing. But if you have one solution that is significantly easier to use and

---

1 And if you don't get that reference, I really don't know what to say.

other solutions that are harder to use, I would suggest that you look strongly at the one that is easier to use.

The reason I feel so strongly about this is, once again, the concept of the revolving door of the backup admin—if you have one at all. If you have this backup system for many years, you will likely be training and retraining many people to use it over the years. Having a backup system that is easier to use minimizes how difficult it is to train the new person and makes it easier for them to maintain the system in the long run once they get the hang of it.

Prioritize Scalability

The next thing I think is really important in a backup system is scalability. How easy is it to add additional compute and/or storage capacity to the system without throwing away what you've already purchased? I really hate waste in every area of my life, but especially in really expensive IT systems. It's bad enough that some of these components cost hundreds of thousands of dollars, but throwing away something that costs that much simply because you outgrew its capabilities is something you should really try to avoid, and you can do so by picking a product that is easy to scale.

You should know—after reading Chapters 14, 15, and this chapter—that the data protection solutions that offer the greatest ease of scalability are HCBAs, DPaaS, and MSPs based on a cloud architecture. (Caveat: MSPs is a very broad category that sometimes includes systems that are not that scalable. Judge each system individually.) Each of them allows you to start relatively small and add incremental capacity over time.

To touch on the idea of TCO from earlier in this chapter, the way these two types of systems charge you can have a significant impact on your TCO. On-premises backup systems (e.g., HCBAs) require you to purchase your capacity in advance. If you think you'll need 100 TB this year, you buy 100 TB today and most of it will go unused for most of the year. (Actually, many people buy for three to five years at a time, but that is really not necessary with HCBAs due to their scale-out nature.) If that system ends up overprovisioned for whatever reason, you're still stuck with a 100 TB system.

DPaaS services tend to charge you only for what you use, when you use it, on a month-to-month basis. You still typically buy a certain amount of capacity in advance, based on an estimated usage for the year. But you would only be debited each month for the amount of storage you actually use. If you expect to be at 100 TB at the end of the year and are expecting a 100% annual growth rate, that translates into 40 TB in the first month, 45.6 TB in the second month and so on. In addition, if your actual capacity needs to be decreased, so would your bill. This is not possible with an on-premises architecture.

Prioritize Future Proofing

You need to look at the architecture of your potential backup system, as well as at the features it supports, and think about how forward-looking its architecture is and how the vendor offering it tends to design its solutions. Look at the up-and-coming technologies of the moment and see what your potential backup vendor is doing with them. At the time of writing, the up-and-coming interesting technology was Kubernetes and Docker, but by the time you read this, it may be something completely different. Talk to your prospective vendor about its support for these up-and-coming technologies. Ask the vendor about its history of when it came out with support for certain features. Was it slow or quick to adopt support for virtualization, the cloud, and Kubernetes? Its past track record can give you ideas about how it might handle the future as well.

Think also about your plans for the future of your computing environment. If you believe you will continue having a large on-premises infrastructure, then you should look at a backup system that is designed to support such an infrastructure. If you are thinking of moving everything to the cloud, then you should look at a cloud-friendly, cloud-centric design. Think about where your computing environment is likely to be in three to five years, and make your solution decisions based on that.

Takeaways

This final takeaways section won't summarize just this chapter; I'll be giving my big takeaways from the entire book. First, let me start by summarizing the most important points from this chapter.

You may or may not need a new backup product. You may need to upgrade or tweak the performance of your current product. It's important to understand how big of a risk it is to change your backup system. There is a learning curve, and that learning curve comes with risk. Make sure that you weigh the risk and cost of staying where you are against moving to a new backup system.

One way to do that is to reduce risk with the move. I discussed many times in the last few chapters how much cost, complexity, and risk comes from having multiple backup products. If you can move to a newer way of doing backup that reduces that number, it would go a long way toward reducing the risk of the move itself.

The only way I see you doing that is to move to one of the types of products discussed in Chapter 15 and do away with tape in your backup and DR systems. (I believe the best use for tape today is in your archive system.) There are exceptions to this, of course, but I'm just saying this as a general rule. I also know there is a cost to do that, but the whole idea of a backup system is risk reduction. One way to reduce risk is to reduce the number of types of products and vendors you are using. I think tape makes perfect sense for long-term archival storage, but no longer makes sense for backup or DR for most organizations.

There are simply too many good choices from the modern products discussed in this chapter to continue supporting tape as part of the backup system, especially when you consider the DR options that are only available on disk. Look at the modern data protection offerings mentioned in this chapter and pick the one that makes the most sense for your environment. I discussed multiple times in this chapter the types of products and services that would appeal to certain types of environments. Use that logic and pick a product or two and try them out. Remember when doing so to include the TCO of running it after the salesperson is gone. You buy the product once; you use it forever.

As to the rest of this book, how do I summarize 350 pages of data protection advice? I can't. But I'll give you a few things that come to mind.

If ever you get into the argument of "should we back this thing up?" just ask yourself two questions: Does the data have value to the organization, and is it already being backed up in a way that conforms to the 3-2-1 rule? Only your organization can answer the question about the value of a particular piece of data. If it has value, it should be backed up. The next question is whether it is already being backed up. Most of the time the answer is obvious; however, with SaaS products, it's not. Things may change in the years after this book is published, but right now I know of no major SaaS vendor that offers backup as part of the service. Just look at the service contract. It's either there or it's not. If it's not, then you need to back up that SaaS! If it is included in the service, make sure the vendor in question is placing some kind of air gap between its service and its backups.

Laptops are another weird one. I've pushed the idea of backing up laptops for years, and it's finally become mainstream. But some still seem to confuse file sync-and-share products (e.g., Dropbox, OneDrive) with backup. They're not, for a long list of reasons I go into in "File sync and share" on page 129.

You may or may not have the need for an archive system. But if you do, you've hopefully learned from Chapters 3 and 10 that this is very different from a backup system, and you've found something that actually behaves like an archive. And please, never use the phrase, "Archive a backup" when I'm around (or "Let's go golfing").

Finally, I have to talk about DR. The advent of ransomware combined with many products and services supporting cloud-based DR means you longer have any excuses, and it's time to get a backup system that supports a real DR plan. If you're living in the modern age and using virtualization for most of your workloads, this should be a no-brainer. There are multiple services and products that can make this happen at an affordable cost. Then we can all finally thumb our noses at ransomware.

I've wanted to write this book for over 10 years. I hope you enjoyed reading it as much as I enjoyed writing it. Either way, *Alea iacta est.*[2]

Back it up or give it up.

—Mr. Backup

"Files in a Backup"

A parody of "Time in a Bottle"
Original music and lyrics by Jim Croce
Parody lyrics by W. Curtis Preston

If I could save files in a backup,
The first thing that I'd like to do,
Is to save every file 'til eternity passes
So I could restore them for you.

If I could make files last forever,
If storage always stayed new,
I'd save every file like a treasure,
And then, again, I'd copy them for you.

But there never seems to be enough time,
To back up the files once you find them.
I've looked around enough to know,
That you're the one I want to make backups for.

If you'd like to see a music video of this song, you can do so here:

https://www.backupcentral.com/files-in-a-backup

Make sure to look for my cameo as the priest marrying the young couple.

---

2 These are the words that were spoken by Julius Caesar as he crossed Italy's Rubicon river with his army. It means "the die is cast."

Index

A

access control methods, 9-10
accidental loss of data, 3
accountability, in data protection plan, 21
administrators
    power to disrupt operations, 9
    role-based administration, 10
    separation of powers, 10
advisory/review boards, 22-23
air gaps, 51-55, 299
all tape, as target for data protection, 281
alternate media booting limitations, 10
appliance-level dedupe, 94
appliances, increased popularity of, 334
application-consistent backups, 121
archive, 37-57
    versus backup, 37-38, 81
    human access to data issue, 221
    metadata for, 48
    protecting, 50-57
    reference purpose, 48
    retrieve of, 49-50
    software methods, 213-224
    tape libraries for, 80
archive bit in Windows, 68
asynchronous deduplication, 97
asynchronous replication, 197
attribute, database, 144
authentication, multiperson, 11, 46
automatic inclusion, 85
AWS Aurora Serverless, 136
AWS Elastic Compute Cloud (EC2), 160
AWS Relational Database Service (RDS), 135, 165

Azure, 135

B

backup, 38-47, 81
    (see also recovery; targets for data protection)
    versus archive, 37, 81
    calculating frequency of, 71
    commercial challenges for, 285-302, 306
        backup product changes, 301-302
        in commercial backup solutions, 287-300
        and history of backup, 285-287
    container's ability to break, 180
    versus copy, 39
    database protection, 133-158
    full backup, traditional, 60
    incremental backup, traditional, 61-67
    item- versus image-level backups, 82-85
    maintaining software, 292-294
    metrics, 68-77
    modern solutions, 315-337
        adapting to the market, 334-337
        DPaaS, 325, 342
        HCBAs, 320-325
        MSPs, 332-334
        virtualization-centric, 316-320, 342
    myths about, 77-82
    protecting, 50-57
    reasons for, 1-18
        human disasters, 2-11
        mechanical or system failure, 12-14
        natural disasters, 14-18
    replacing or upgrading system, 339-353

restore process, 40-42
selection methods, 85-87
software methods, 189-211
   deciding on, 208-211
   leveraging with other features, 206-208
stored separately from original, 40
3-2-1 rule, 42-47, 152
traditional restore support, 190-195
traditional solutions, 303-314
   advantages, 305
   analysis of value, 307-308
   challenges, 306
   target deduplication backup, 309-313
backup database command, 152
backup replication, DR, 239-240
backup server, OS maintenance challenge, 292
backup set, deduplication scope, 94
backup window, computing capacity and usage, 74
bad code, 4-5
bare-metal backup and recovery, 108, 116
batch archive, traditional, 215
BCP (business continuity planning), 229
bind mount command, 182
bit rot, 162, 299
block storage in IaaS, 161
block storage vulnerability, 13
block-level backups
   image-level, 83
   incremental, 64, 193
business continuity planning (see BCP)

C

CAB (change advisory board), 22, 34
caching or staging
   disk caching, 102-103
   laptops as cache, 127
   NFS/SMB gateway, 177
California Consumer Privacy Act (see CCPA)
capacity metrics, 72-75
Cassandra, 78, 154
CBT (changed-block tracking), 84
CCPA (California Consumer Privacy Act), 25, 76
CDM (copy data management), 204-205
CDP (continuous data protection), 198-200
change advisory board (see CAB)
change review, 22
changed-block tracking (see CBT)

charge-back model discussion, 27
chunks, in deduplication, 93, 96
CI (converged infrastructure), 126
classification of data, 27
client-side deduplication (see source (source-side) deduplication)
cloud, 78
   (see also public cloud)
   best backup practices, 46, 78
   cloud in a box, 178
   compute capacity and usage, 74
   disk in cloud as backup target, 106-107, 280-281
   geographical location issue, 45
   hybrid cloud configurations, 177-179
   mechanical or system failure, 13
   on-premises backup in, 275, 336, 343, 349
   testing recoveries, 60
   throughput capacity and usage , 73
   unreliability as backup, 159
cloud gateway, 177-178
cloud in a box, 178
cloud native storage, 275
cloud out, 274
cloud sync, mobile devices, 131
cloud-level snapshot, database recovery, 157
codespaces.com, 46, 174-175
cold backup databases, 147
cold, hot, or warm recovery site choice, 236-237
collecting requirements, 23-25, 220-223
commercial challenges for data protection, 285-302
   backup product changes, 301-302
   in commercial backup solutions, 287-300
   and history of backup, 285-287
   in modern solutions, 318, 323, 329-331, 333
   in traditional solutions, 306, 311-313
compliance and governance, data protection requirements, 25
compression, in deduplication process, 94
compute capacity and usage, 74
console-only superuser login, 9
contact information, runbook, 253
container runtime environments (see Docker and Kubernetes)
continuous data protection (see CDP)
control file (Oracle), 145
convenience copies, 38, 40, 79

converged infrastructure (see CI)
copy data management (see CDM)
copy versus backup, 39
copy-on-write snapshots, 201
costs of replacement or upgrade, analyzing,
    347-349
crash-consistent backups, 121
CRM (customer relationship management),
    168
cryptographic hashing algorithm, in deduplica-
    tion, 93
cumulative incremental backup, 61
customer relationship management (see CRM)
cyclones, 16

D

D2C (direct-to-cloud), 106
D2D2C (disk-to-disk-to-cloud), 106
D2D2D (disk-to-disk-to-disk), 104-106
D2D2T (disk-to-disk-to-tape), 104
data creators, collecting requirements, 23
data file, database, 134, 144
data format issues, archive software, 220
data loss, establishing acceptable (see RPO)
data protection (see archive; backup; service
    levels)
data sources (see modern data sources; tradi-
    tional data sources)
data-protection-as-a-service (see DPaaS)
database replication, 198
databases, 133-158
    consistency models, 139-142
    delivery software, 133-136
    design models, 137-139
    Docker and Kubernetes (K8s), 183
    PaaS and serverless backup, 141, 150-155,
        165
    recovery, 155-157
    tag-based and folder-based inclusion, 87
    terminology, 142-146
    traditional backup, 146-150
datacenter
    as resource to protect from disaster, 228
    database model in, 140
    disk-based backup designs, 102
    Internet-based vulnerability of, 52
    loss of as center of backup, 115
Datastax, 154
DB2 database software, 153

dedupe index, 93
deduplication (dedupe), 90-102
    advantages, 90-93
    chunk size, importance of, 96
    D2D2T, 104
    file-level, 96
    hybrid, 100
    inline, 97-98, 111
    post-process, 97-98, 111
    ratio comparisons, avoiding, 95
    replicated dedupe appliance, 232
    scope, 94-95
    selecting a type, 101
    source, 64, 99-101, 106, 129, 194-195
    target, 96-100, 272-274, 277, 309-313, 342
design review, 22
design review board (see DRB)
desktops and laptops, backup options, 126-130
direct restore file-level recovery, 109
disaster recovery (see DR)
disk, using in backup system, 12, 102-114
    (see also deduplication)
    block-level incremental backup, 64
    cloud-based disk, 106-107, 280-281
    commercial backup solution challenges,
        298-299
    D2C, 106
    D2D2C, 106
    D2D2D, 104-106
    D2D2T, 104
    disk arrays, 269
    disk caching, 102-103
    incremental forever backups, 66
    individual disk drives, 268-269
    integrity-checking in firmware, 12
    recovery methods, 107-113
Docker and Kubernetes (K8s), 179-185
Docker commit command, 182
Docker Hub, 181
Docker image history command, 182
Docker inspect command, 184
Docker ps command, 184
Dockerfiles, 181
document templates, 21
documentation (see runbook)
Documents database design model, 138
DPaaS (data-protection-as-a-service), 325, 342
DR (disaster recovery), 225-256
    building the recovery site, 233-235

keeping up to date, 236-245
natural disasters, 14-18
plan development, 229-233, 249-256
ransomware, 226-227
recovery mechanisms, 237-245
resources to protect, 228-229
runbook, creating, 250-256
separate system for, 295
software or service choice, 245-249
DRaaS (DR-as-a-service), 246-247
DRB (design review board), 22, 28, 30
dump-and-sweep database backup, 148, 151, 152
DynamoDB database software, 136, 154

E

e-discovery, 48, 79, 170, 171, 295
earthquakes, 16
EBS (Elastic Block Storage), 160
EC2 (Elastic Compute Cloud), 160
edge computing, 185
electronic attacks, 5, 6
encryption, 50, 93
erasure coding array, 12
etcdctl snapshot save command, 182
etcdctl snapshot save db command, 182
eventual consistency database model, 139, 141, 157
exception processing with escalation, runbook, 256
executives, requirements for data protection, 24
expiration, allowing old backup, 301

F

file sync and share, 129
file-level backup and recovery
    combining with image-level backup, 84
    deduplication, 96
    from image-level backup, 84
    versus image-level backup, 83
    incremental backup, 128
    incremental forever, 192
    recovery from disk backup, 108-110, 113
filesystem versus object storage, 162-164
fires, 15
floods, 15
folder-based and tag-based inclusion, 86
forever incremental backups, 66, 75, 192, 193
    (see also source (source-side) deduplication)

four-eyes authentication, 11
full backup
    restore of data, 191
    synthetic, 65-66
    traditional, 60
full-file incremental backup, 61, 74
fully managed service providers (see MSPs)
future proofing consideration, 352

G

G-Suite (see Google Workspace)
GDPR (General Data Protection Regulations), 25, 76
GitHub, 172, 181
global-level dedupe, 94
Google Archive, 44, 48, 171
Google Workspace, 48, 127, 171
Graph database design model, 138

H

hash, 163, 164
hash table, 93
HCBAs (hyper-converged backup appliances), 97, 111, 320-325, 342
HCI (hyper-converged infrastructure), 125
hierarchical storage management (see HSM)
hold all writes snapshots, 201
host-level dedupe, 94
hot backup mode, databases, 147
hot, cold, or warm recovery site choice, 236-237
HSM (hierarchical storage management), 118, 217
human disasters, 2-11
    accidents, 3
    bad code, 4-5
    electronic attacks, 5, 6
    internal threats (employees), 8-11
    ransomware, 7
    terrorism, 6
hurricanes, 16
hybrid backup configuration, 97, 282
hybrid cloud configurations, 177-179
hybrid consistency database model, 139, 141
hybrid deduplication, 100
hybrid replication, 198
hyper-converged backup appliances (see HCBAs)
hyper-converged infrastructure (see HCI)

Hyper-V and VSS, 124, 166
hypervisors, specialized backups for, 64, 83,
    120, 122-126

I

IaaS (infrastructure-as-a-service), 45, 78,
    160-165, 228
IBM TS11x0 tape drive, 266
image copies, 40, 151, 161
image mount, restoring files with, 110
image-level backup and recovery, 83-85,
    107-108, 181
immediate consistency database model, 139,
    140
immutability, protecting backups and archives,
    55-57
immutable storage, 54
incremental backups, 61-67
    block-level incremental, 64, 193
    cumulative incremental, 61
    file-level, 128, 192
    image-level challenge, 83
    incremental forever, 66, 75, 192, 193
    incremental with levels, 62-64
    source-side deduplication, 64
    synthetic full backups, 65-66
    synthetic full by copying, 65
    traditional restore of data, 191
    typical incremental, 61
    virtual synthetic full backup, 66
index, database, 143
infrastructure-as-a-service (see IaaS)
initial seed backup in D2C, 106
inline versus post-process deduplication, 97-98,
    111
InnoDB tables, 153
instance, database, 143
instant recovery, 190, 196-206
    CDM, 204-205
    CDP, 198-200
    in disk backup, 103, 111-113
    near-CDP, 202-204
    product comparison, 205-206
    replication, 196-198
    snapshots, 200-202
integrated backup-as-a-service, 151-155
integrated versus separate archive, 222
internal threats (employees), 8-11
IoT (Internet of Things), 185-186

ISO image backup, 107
item-level backup, 82, 84

K

Key Value database design model, 138
KPMG, 175
Kubernetes (K8s) (see Docker and Kubernetes)
Kubernetes etcd, 182

L

laptops as a cache, 127
least privilege method of protection, 11
levels-based incremental backup, 62-64
license usage, capacity metrics, 72
logical hosts, 180
LTFS (linear tape file system), 266
LTO (Linear Tape Open) drives, 266

M

malware, 5, 7
master file, database, 145, 150
MDM (mobile device management), 131
mechanical or system failure, 12-14
media recovery, 156
metadata for archive, 48
metrics, 68-77
    capacity metrics, 72-75
    recovery metrics, 69-72
    and retention policies, 75
    success and failure of backup and recovery,
        75
    using, 76
Microsoft 365, 169-171
Microsoft 365 Retention Policies, 44, 48, 169
mobile device management (see MDM)
mobile devices, backup options, 130-132
modern data sources, 159-188
    Docker and Kubernetes (K8s), 179-185
    hybrid cloud configurations, 177-179
    IoT, 185-186
    making backup decisions, 186-188
    public cloud, 159-177
        as disaster recovery site, 235
        IaaS, 160-165
        PaaS, 165
        protecting data in, 172-177
        SaaS, 166-172
        serverless services, 166

targets for data protection, 274
modification time, file, 162
mongod command, 154
MongoDB database software, 78, 154
MSPs (fully managed service providers), 332-334, 342, 349
multicloud, NFS/SMB gateway, 178
multifactor authentication, 46
multiperson authentication, 11, 46
multiple vendor backup solution challenge, 294
multiplexing, in traditional restore of data, 191
MyISAM tables, 153
MySQL database software, 153
mysqldump command, 153

N
named accounts, 9
NAS (network-attached storage), 38, 117-119, 273-274
natural disasters, 14-18, 45
NDMP protocol, 118
near-CDP (near-continuous data protection), 189, 202-204
Neo4j database software, 155
neo4j-admin backup command, 155
Netflix, 160
network-attached storage (see NAS)
NFS/SMB protocols, 109, 117, 177-178
node-level recovery, database, 157
nodetool snapshot command, 154
NoSQL database models, 138
Nutanix, 126

O
object storage, 54, 72, 82, 96, 107, 161-165, 270-272
off-host logging, 9
on-premises backup
    in the cloud, 275, 336, 343, 349
    HCBAs, 320
    on disk, 279
operating system, backup server on different, 54
operational responsibility, 31
operations review, 22, 32
Oracle database software, 147, 152, 166
overprovisioning requirement, backup solution challenge, 300

P
PaaS (platform-as-a-service), 45
    myth of not needing backup, 78
    public cloud, 165
    resources to protect, 228
    and serverless database model, 141, 150-155
partition, database, 144
partitioned databases, 136
PDR (preliminary design review), 22
pg_dump command, 153
phishing schemes, 7
physical air gap, 52
physical servers, backup options, 116-119
physical sync, mobile devices, 131
platform format issues, DR, 241-243
platform-as-a-service (see PaaS)
point-in-time backups and restores, 134, 146, 156
portable hard-drive backup, 128
post-process versus inline deduplication, 97-98, 111
PostgreSQL database software, 153
power disruptions, 12
preliminary design review (see PDR)
primary data replication, DR, 237-239
privacy issue, 25, 76
project management, 23
proxy, using for NAS backup, 117
PRR (production readiness review), 22
public cloud, 159-177
    as disaster recovery site, 235
    IaaS, 160-165
    PaaS, 165
    protecting data in, 172-177
    SaaS, 166-172
    serverless services, 166
    targets for data protection, 274

R
RaaS (ransomware-as-a-service), 7
RACI (responsible, accountable, collaborator, informed), 31
RAID array
    failure possibility in, 12, 269
    myth of obviating need for backup, 77
    performance-tuning, 277
ransomware, 7, 46, 52, 127, 129, 226-227
ratio comparisons, avoiding in deduplication, 95

RDBMS (relational database management system), 136, 137
RDP (Remote Desktop Protocol), disabling, 53
RDS (Relational Database Service), 135, 165
real-time archive method, 216
recovery, 59
    (see also DR)
    database, 155-157
    in disk backup, 107-113
    file-level recovery, 108-110
    image recovery, 107-108, 113
    instant recovery, 103, 111-113, 196-206
    media recovery, 156
    metrics for, 69-72
    testing recoveries, 59, 71
Recovery Manager (see RMAN)
recovery point actual (see RPA)
recovery point objective (see RPO)
recovery time actual (see RTA)
recovery time objective (see RTO)
recovery-site-as-a-service, 234
redirect-on-write snapshots, 201
redundant storage systems, 12
referential integrity issues in databases, 140
rehydrating (reduplicating) backups, 98
relational database management system (see RDBMS)
Relational Database Service (see RDS)
Remote Desktop Protocol (see RDP)
replacing or upgrading the system, 339-353
    analyzing needs, 345-349
    DPaaS, 342
    ease of use consideration, 350
    finding showstoppers, 350
    future proofing, 352
    HCBAs, 342
    laptops, 128
    MSPs, 342, 349
    on-premises in the cloud, 343
    SaaS, 349
    scalability consideration, 351
    target deduplication, 342
    TCO consideration, 347-349
    traditional backup, 341, 343
    virtualization-centric products, 342
    your responsibilities in, 343-345
replicated dedupe as not enough, DR, 78, 232
replication
    asynchronous, 197

backup for DR, 239-240
database, 141, 198
hybrid, 198
instant recovery, 196-198
limitations of, 198
primary data, 237-239
snapshot for NAS backup, 119
synchronous, 196
requirements review, 22, 26
restore and backup option, 302
restore of data, 72, 190-195
    (see also recovery)
    block-level incremental forever, 193
    D2C consideration, 106
    versus e-discovery, 170
    file-level direct restore, 109
    file-level incremental forever, 192
    full and incremental backups, 191-193
    image recovery, 108
    and long-term backup retention, 79
    multiplexing, 191
    process, 40-42, 155
    versus retrieve, 49, 214
    SMB/NFS mount, 109
    source deduplication, 194-195
    and synthetic full backups, 65
    target versus source deduplication, 99
    and testing recoveries, 72
    time consideration, 187
retention and retention policies, 44, 48, 75, 79, 169, 260-261
retrieve versus restore, 40, 49, 214
review/advisory boards, 22-23
right to be forgotten, 76
RMAN (Recovery Manager), 152
robotic tape libraries, 267
rogue admin problem, 8
role-based administration, 10
rolling disaster, 51
rolling forward or backward from point in time, 135
root password restriction, 9
row, database, 144
RPA (recovery point actual), 29, 70
RPO (recovery point objective), 23, 24, 70
RTA (recovery time actual), 29, 70, 232
RTO (recovery time objective), 23, 69, 70
runbook, 22, 33, 250-256

S

SaaS (software-as-a-service), 325
  cost analysis, 349
  file-level data recovery, 110
  lack of real backup in, 167, 176
  myth of not needing backup, 79
  public cloud, 47, 166-172
  resources to protect, 228
Salesforce, 168-169, 175
SAS disk drives, 102
SATA disk drives, 89, 102
scalability consideration, replacing or upgrading, 351
Scale Computing, 126
scaling computer system, 320
scaling difficulties, backup solution challenge, 300
scope of deduplication, 94-95
scripting, and database backup methods, 149
Search Engine database design model, 138
search techniques for archives, 49
selective inclusion versus selective exclusion, 85-86
separate versus integrated archive, 222
separation of powers, 10
serverless services
  database backup, 136, 141, 150-155
  public cloud, 166
service as alternative to own products, 301
service levels, data protection, 19-35
  building the framework, 20-23
  collecting requirements, 23
  designing and building the system, 28-31
  documenting the system, 31-34
  implementing the system, 33
  purpose of organization, 20
service-level agreements (see SLAs)
sharding, database tablespace, 145, 156
shared-nothing architecture, 140
shell access, disabling or deleting, 9
sinkholes, 17
site-level dedupe, 94
sizing the backup system, 178, 288-292
Slack, 172
SLAs (service-level agreements), 26
SMB/NFS protocols, 109, 117, 177
SMEs (subject matter experts), in building data protection service, 23-25
snap and sweep, database backup, 147, 151

snapshots, 38, 39, 83, 119, 124, 200-202
  (see also VSS)
soliciting requirements, 25
solid-state media, 12, 103
source (source-side) deduplication, 64, 99-101, 106, 129, 194-195
sparse index, database, 143
split replica database backup, 147
SQL, 138
SQL Server database software, 152
SSD disk drives, 103
staging (see caching or staging)
storage
  capacity and usage, 72
  importance in disk backup, 111
  length of time for backups, 79
  media consideration for archive, 221
  persistent volumes for containers, 182
streaming to backup product, databases, 149
strong consistency database model, 139
subscription pricing, 335
synchronous replication, 196
synthetic full backups, 65-66
synthetic full by copying, 65
system failure, 13

T

table, database, 143
table-based recovery, database, 156
tablespace, database, 144
tag-based and folder-based inclusion, 86
tape drives, 257-267
  air gap handling of, 52, 55
  all tape as target for data protection, 281
  as not enough for DR, 231
  backup solution challenge, 102, 296-298
  cost advantage, 258
  D2D2T, 104
  incremental backup issue, 262-263
  long-term retention capability, 260-261
  loss of, 297
  myth of being obsolete, 80-82
  performance-tuning, 275-277
  with target deduplication, 97
  technologies of, 265-267
  throughput capacity and usage , 73
  writing-data reliability, 259-260
target deduplication, 96-100, 272-274, 277, 309-313, 342

targets for data protection, 257-283, 269
    (see also specific targets by name)
    cloud native storage, 275
    cloud out, 274
    disk arrays, 269
    individual disk drives, 268-269
    and object storage, 270-272
    optical media, 267
    optimizing performance, 275-278
    selecting a more appropriate device,
        278-282
    tape drives, 257-267
    target deduplication appliances, 272-274
TCO (total cost of ownership), 347-349
technology inventory, runbook, 253
terrorism, 6
testing backups, integrated backup-as-a-service,
    151
testing recoveries, 59, 71
theftware, 7
3-2-1 rule, 5, 6, 14, 42-47, 152, 165, 175
throughput capacity and usage, 73
Time Series database design model, 138
tornadoes, 17
total cost of ownership (see TCO)
traditional backup
    appliances for, 343
    best use of, 341
    databases, 146-150
    full backup, 60
    incremental backup, 61-67
    restore support, 190-195
    solutions, 303-314
traditional batch archive, 215
traditional data sources, 115-132
    desktops and laptops, 126-130
    mobile devices, 130-132
    physical servers, 116-119
    virtual servers, 119-126
transaction log, database, 145, 149
transaction, database, 145
truncating of transaction log, database, 150
typhoons, 16

typical incremental backup, 61

U

up-front capital purchases, backup solution
    challenge, 299
upgrading the system (see replacing or upgrad-
    ing the system)
user error, 3-5
USP (unique selling proposition), 341-343

V

VADP (vSphere Storage APIs for Data Protec-
    tion), 122-123
vaulting vendor, managing off-site, 298
versioning of files, NFS/SMB gateway, 177
virtual air gaps, 53-55
virtual servers, backup options, 119-126
virtual snapshots, 38, 39, 83
virtual synthetic full backup, 66
virtual tape library (see VTL)
virtualization-centric solutions, 316-320, 342
VM-level backups, 84, 84, 86, 111, 120, 160,
    180, 275
VMware Cloud, 166
vSphere Storage APIs for Data Protection (see
    VADP)
VSS (Volume Shadow Copy Service), 85,
    121-124, 148, 153
VSS writer, 121
VTL (virtual tape library), 118, 272

W

warm, hot, or cold recovery site choice,
    236-237
Wide Column database design model, 138
workload usage, capacity metrics, 72
WORM feature, 165, 178

Y

YAML files, 181

About the Author

W. Curtis Preston, also known as "Mr. Backup," is the author of four O'Reilly books and the founder/webmaster of *backupcentral.com*, a site dedicated to backup and recovery for over 20 years. He is also the host of the independent *Restore It All* podcast. He is currently the Chief Technical Evangelist at Druva, Inc., a data-protection-as-a-service company.

Colophon

The animal on the cover of *Modern Data Protection* is a seven-banded armadillo (*Dasypus septemcinctus*), an animal native to the South American countries Bolivia, Brazil, Argentina, and Paraguay. These animals have a protective carapace made of two stiff plates, connected in the middle of the body by six to seven flexible bands (which give it its name). The armor is made up of scutes: overlapping scales made of bone and covered with keratin.

Seven-banded armadillos are hairless and brown-black in color. Despite having short legs, they can move very quickly. A flattened snout and long claws help the armadillo forage for insects, which make up the majority of its diet. All armadillo species have poor vision, but a very keen sense of smell. They all also dig dens in the ground and do not cohabitate with other adults. When reproducing, seven-banded armadillo females give birth to genetically identical offspring.

In 2014, scientists created a "bio-inspired" protective glass material based on the hard scales of armadillos and similarly armored animals, which was 70% more puncture-resistant than a solid sheet of glass (*https://oreil.ly/LvnBO*).

Many of the animals on O'Reilly covers are endangered; all of them are important to the world.

The cover illustration is by Karen Montgomery, based on a black and white engraving from *Beeton's Dictionary*. The cover fonts are Gilroy Semibold and Guardian Sans. The text font is Adobe Minion Pro; the heading font is Adobe Myriad Condensed; and the code font is Dalton Maag's Ubuntu Mono.